# Memory and Cognition

**WALTER KINTSCH**

University of Colorado

ROBERT E. KRIEGER PUBLISHING COMPANY
MALABAR, FLORIDA
1982

Original Edition    1977
Reprint Edition    1982

Printed and Published by
**ROBERT E. KRIEGER PUBLISHING COMPANY, INC.**
**KRIEGER DRIVE**
**MALABAR, FLORIDA 32950**

## Library of Congress Cataloging in Publication Data

Kintsch, Walter, 1932-
    Memory and cognition.

    Reprint. Originally published: New York:
Wiley, c1977.
    Bibliography: p.
    Includes index.
    1. Memory.  2. Cognition.  I. Title.
[BF371.K475  1982]        153.1         81-18648
ISBN 0-89874-403-2                 AACR2

# preface

Cognitive psychology has flourished in recent years; experimentalists have used their methods to investigate more complex, more important, more interesting problems than ever before. In all areas of cognitive psychology, from perception to memory to thinking, important developments have taken place. This book presents an account of these developments and relates them to their roots in the earlier investigations of learning, memory, and concept formation. It emphasizes memory and thinking, and especially the use of language, rather than perception, but with this restriction it presents a fairly comprehensive picture of the research in cognitive psychology. Students or professionals who desire an introduction to this body of research should be able to find it here.

This book is the second edition of *Learning, Memory, and Conceptual Processes*, which was published in 1970. About two-thirds to three-fourths of the text is new, and the emphasis has shifted from "learning" to "cognition." A change in title seemed appropriate to mark this shift. In addition to the differences in the subject matter covered in the two editions (and the updating of information done for this edition), another important change has been made. Without abandoning the aspiration to write a reliable and fairly sophisticated introduction to the psychological research in the area, the present book is far less complicated and detailed than the first edition. It was written to better serve the needs of undergraduate students.

One of the consequences of the phenomenal growth of cognitive psychology is that there is more material than can be covered in a standard one-semester course. Rather than deleting important topics, I have written a book that is comprehensive, letting the instructor decide which parts of this book he wants to discuss in his course. Thus, this text provides a certain flexibility, and instructors can select chapters to emphasize various subareas, depending on their interests and requirements. A number of combinations of about five chapters from this text could be proposed for a one-semester course—and the material not covered is available to the interested student.

I am indebted to many people who helped me in preparing this text, including some users of the first edition whose comments have guided this revision. In addition, I am grateful to Gregory A. Kimble, who reviewed Chapters 1 and 2, and Peter G. Polson, who reviewed Chapters 3 and 7. George Mandler made helpful suggestions on all of the chapters. My main debt is, however, to Eileen Kintsch without whose editorial assistance this book could not have been written. Finally, of course, I acknowledge my debt to the authors of the works I have described in these pages: I hope I have done so fairly and accurately and have given credit whenever it was due.

Walter Kintsch

*Boulder, Colorado*

# contents

# the paradigms of verbal learning

Until about 15 years ago, the study of human cognitive processes was, for the most part, known as "verbal learning" research. It was characterized by a more or less explicit behavioristic orientation. Researchers were reluctant to try to infer what was going on in the human mind and they preferred to talk about how a task affects performance, instead of the psychological processes that might be involved in performing that task. Conditioning principles derived from the animal laboratories of that period provided the theoretical framework for this research. The intellectual climate is different today. We have learned from behaviorism how to do methodologically sound experiments, and we reject untestable speculations just as the behaviorists did. But our theorizing has become liberated; no one is afraid of the mind anymore. Data are of interest to today's experimental psychologists primarily because of the insights that they permit into the functioning of the human mind. We have come to realize that the attempt to understand human cognitive processes with a few conditioning principles and the patient accumulation of evidence concerning various "task variables" in three or four standardized experimental paradigms cannot be successful. A much broader theoretical outlook and a more sophisticated experimental approach will be needed. Nevertheless, the roots of modern research on cognitive processes stick deep in the verbal learning tradition. Anyone who wants to understand the current work must take the time to familiarize himself with that tradition.

A few basic experimental paradigms are frequently employed in the study of verbal learning. Of course, numerous variations of these paradigms exist, and entirely new experimental designs are occasionally encountered. New designs and variants of old ones will be discussed whenever the occasion arises, but the classical procedures as well as the standard learning materials of verbal learning studies will be described first.

In the classical verbal learning experiment each subject learns a *list* of *items*. (For illustration see Table 1.1.) Each *trial* usually involves a *study* phase and a *test* phase. Presentation rates are usually between 1

TABLE 1.1.    **Paired-Associate Learning. (Each row is exposed for a brief period of time in the window of a memory drum. One presentation of this eight-item list constitutes a trial. The items are adjective-number pairs.)**

| Anticipation Method | | Study-Test Method | |
|---|---|---|---|
| OVERT-? | (test) | OVERT-7 | |
| OVERT-7 | (study) | RURAL-6 | |
| RURAL-? | | CRINGING-2 | |
| RURAL-6 | | RHYTHMIC-8 | |
| CRINGING-? | | SORRY-1 | Study Phase |
| CRINGING-2 | | STRIDENT-5 | |
| RHYTHMIC-? | | FLABBY-3 | |
| RHYTHMIC-8 | | UGLY-4 | |
| SORRY-? | | OVERT-? | |
| SORRY-1 | | RURAL-? | |
| STRIDENT-? | | CRINGING-? | Test Phase |
| STRIDENT-5 | | RHYTHMIC-? | |
| FLABBY-? | | SORRY-? | |
| FLABBY-3 | | STRIDENT-? | |
| UGLY-? | | FLABBY-? | |
| UGLY-4 | | UGLY-? | |

and 4 seconds per item, but in some experiments the rate of presentation may be treated as an experimental variable, and in others the subject may be permitted to pace himself. Learning trials are continued either for a predetermined number of trials or until the subject reaches some performance criterion, such as a trial on which all responses are correct. Various performance measures are used. For instance, two frequently used statistics are the total number of errors made by a subject in learning a list, and the number of trials required to reach criterion.

## 1.1    PAIRED-ASSOCIATE LEARNING

A widely used procedure in verbal learning is *paired-associate learning*. In paired-associate learning the subject learns a list of stimulus-response pairs, a process similar to learning the vocabulary of a foreign language. A sample list is shown in Table 1.1. The first word serves as the stimulus for the recall of the second member of the pair, which is traditionally called the response word. There is an obvious parallel here between the conditioned stimulus and the conditioned response in classical conditioning: the subject learns to perform the conditioned response whenever the conditioned stimulus is presented; in paired-associate learning the subject learns to respond with the response member of an item-pair whenever the stimulus member is presented. There is some question whether this parallel is more than superficial, but this problem will be deferred until later. Several sub-problems of paired-associate learning may be distinguished. For example, an experimenter may study *stimulus discrimination* learning by varying the similarity of the stimulus terms in a list while keeping the response terms constant. A very useful distinction is the one often made between *response learning* and *associative learning*. In a paired-associate task the subject must learn two quite different things: he must learn what the responses are, and then he must learn to associate each stimulus term with the proper response term. The experimenter may manipulate the difficulty of one of these subtasks while keeping the other constant. For example, if an experimenter employs unfamiliar meaningless letter combinations as responses, response learning will be difficult. The problem is one of *response integration* in this case. When familiar words are the response terms, response integration represents no problem since the responses, being familiar words, are already available. However, some response learning will still be required, because the subject must learn which of the many possible words are actually used in the experiment. Response learning may be eliminated completely by informing the subject beforehand which response terms are used in the experiment. This is easiest if a well-defined set of response terms is used, such as the numerals from 1 to 10. In the extreme case, when only two responses are used, such as 1 and 2, such paired-associate tasks resemble classification learning except that the assignment of stimuli to response classes is entirely arbitrary.

Two major testing procedures are used. In the *anticipation* method an opportunity to study an item is given after each test; a trial thus consists of the sequential presentation of all items of a list for test and immediate study. In the *study-test* presentation method, on each trial all items are first shown one at a time for study and then presented again for testing. Both the anticipation method and the method of blocked presentations are used in paired-associate learning, with the anticipation method being favored by most investigators. List length is usually between 10 and 15 item-pairs. New random orders of presentation are used on each trial. It is interesting to note that when the order of presentation is the same on all trials, paired-associate learning is relatively little affected. If anything, constant order performance is slightly better than varied serial order, but the effect is small and unreliable. This observation indicates that the serial position of an item pair in a list is not an important learning cue for the subject in paired-associate learning.

A procedural variation in paired-associate learning consists in presenting a list in parts. Each part is learned separately, and finally all parts are combined and the whole list is learned. However, learning a list by parts is no easier than starting out with the whole list: each part is quickly learned, but when the parts are combined they must be learned over again. The main difficulty in learning a list of paired associates lies in learning to master the interference among the list members, and learning an item pair outside the list context is therefore of little help. Overall, there are only minor differences in efficiency between whole and part learning (Postman & Goggin, 1966).

Paired-associate learning is also remarkably insensitive to how one divides up the total learning time. It makes little difference whether one studies a list for 10 trials and spends 2 seconds on each item, or for five trials spending 4 seconds on each item. The total learning time is the same in both cases, and that, more than how this time is divided up, determines the level of performance reached. On the basis of such observations Bugelski (1962) formulated the total-time hypothesis, which says that only the total learning time but not the duration of the individual learning events are important. The total-time hypothesis is only roughly true, and many exceptions have been noted in the literature, but it provides a useful first approximation.

A point of controversy in the literature has been the question whether backward associations are as strong as forward associations. If a subject learns to associate a stimulus item $S$ with a response item $R$, is the association $R \rightarrow S$ just as strong as the association $S \rightarrow R$? Offhand, the answer appears to be "no," because it is easy to show that after $S$-$R$ learning subjects are much more likely to give $R$ as a response to $S$ than $S$ as a response to $R$. However, it has been argued that this asymmetry merely reflects the lower degree of learning of the $S$-terms in the typical paired-associate task and that all associations are symmetric (Asch & Ebenholtz, 1962); only if response terms are made to be as available as stimulus terms can the essential symmetry of associations be detected. This claim was proved wrong by Wollen (1968), who demonstrated convincingly that associations are directional even when all experimental confoundings are avoided and response and stimulus terms are equally available. The association between *A* and *B* may be quite different from that between *B* and *A*.

## .1    MATERIALS

Learning items are usually words, numerals, line drawings, or arbitrary letter combinations. In most experiments standardized materials are being used. With words as learning material experimenters attempt to equate them on the basis of number of syllables, or grammatical classes, with some apparent bias in favor of adjectives and nouns. Extensive tables published by Thorndike and Lorge (1944) and Kučera and Francis (1967) permit the selection of words according to frequency of usage in English. Thorndike and Lorge tabulated the frequency of occurrence of English words based upon a wide range of written materials. The number of occurrences of each word per million words was counted; words occurring more than 100 times per million were classified as AA words; words with a frequency between 50 and 100 per million were classified as A words; actual frequency counts were given for words occurring less than 50 times per million.

Letter combinations that do not form English words are also used as learning materials, usually in the form of consonant-vowel-consonant (CVC) combinations (the "nonsense syllable"), or as consonant trigrams. Nonsense syllables were originally introduced by Ebbinghaus (1885), who needed a pool of learning items that was sufficiently large (this was very important as Ebbinghaus was his own subject in his experiments), and which was at the same time simple enough and supposedly homogeneous with respect to learning difficulty. Ebbinghaus objected to the use of words in verbal learning experiments because he had noted that some words were very much easier to remember than others, depending upon their meaning and familiarity. Later investigators, however, observed that the use of nonsense syllables provided only an incomplete solution to this problem. Some nonsense syllables are more nonsensical than others and Glaze (1928) and others actually measured the differences in meaningfulness among nonsense syllables. Glaze introduced the construct "association value" of a CVC, which he operationally defined as the percentage of subjects who could provide a response on a brief association test, given the CVC: subjects were asked to respond with the first word that occurred to them. Glaze scaled 2000 CVCs this way COL and WIS are examples of syllables for which all of Glaze's subjects reported an association, while GOQ and XUW are syllables which did not mean anything to his informants. Glaze's data are based upon only 15 subjects, but have proved to be very useful. A number of later investigators have repeated Glaze's procedures, refined them, and explored several interesting variations. A notable example is Noble's index of meaningfulness (Noble, 1952). Noble asked subjects to give as many free associations as they could within one minute in response to disyllabic words, including both ordinary English words and artificial words. The mean frequency of associations in response to each item was taken as an index of meaningfulness, $m$. Thus GOJEY received an $m$-value of .99, FEMUR 2.09, and KITCHEN 9.61, for example. In other studies subjects simply rated the number of associations or ideas that they felt each stimulus item provided. Thus, scales of association value are now available for all CVC combinations (Archer, 1960).

The excessive use of nonsense syllables in verbal learning experiments has been criticized for a number of reasons. It is now well known that nonsense syllables are not a homogeneous set of items. On the contrary, variations in meaningfulness among nonsense syllables are greater than among words. In addition, most nonsense syllables do not have a unique pronunciation in English, and the number and kind of associations a CVC produces depend on the way it is pronounced. To avoid this problem CVCs are almost always spelled in psychological experiments. Spelling, however, introduces new problems. The spelled CVC is no longer a unitary response, but a collection of letters. Thereby problems of response integration are introduced that often are quite incidental to the main concern of a study. Furthermore, in the typical learning experiment employing CVCs learning is slow and subjects become bored quickly.

## 1.1.2    MEANINGFULNESS

The rate of learning in verbal learning experiments is in part determined by the characteristics of the learning material. Psychologists have studied extensively what happens when different groups of subjects are given lists to learn that differ in the nature of the learning material. With nonsense syllables, the meaningfulness of the syllables is an important factor. With words, the frequency of occurrence in the natural language is related to learning speed. A somewhat different problem concerns the interrelationship of the items within a list. No matter what the items are, the similarity among them is an important factor in learning. Some representative experiments that illustrate the nature of these effects will be described in this section.

There is little controversy about the effects of meaningfulness on verbal learning: meaningfulness facilitates verbal learning. The exact nature of this effect depends somewhat on the way in which meaningfulness is measured, as well as on the learning task under consideration, but the overall facilitative effect of meaningfulness has been demonstrated in many experiments. One of the first of these was a study by McGeoch (1930). McGeoch used a free-recall procedure with six groups of subjects. Each group learned a list of nonsense syllables selected from Glaze's (1928) scale such that the association value of syllables within each list was the same but varied over the whole range from 0 to 100% between groups. The number of items recalled was a positive function of the association value of the items. This result has been replicated frequently and extended to other learning procedures such as paired-associate learning. In paired-associate learning the effects of meaningfulness of items in the stimulus and response positions can be distinguished. For instance, Cieutat, Stockwell, and Noble (1958) selected items of high and low meaningfulness, both for the stimulus position and the response position. Four different lists of item-pairs were constructed in this way. A separate group of subjects learned each list. This factorial design permits one to study the effects of meaningfulness of stimulus items separately from the effects of meaningfulness of the response items. Figure 1.1 shows the results of this study. Meaningfulness was found to have an effect in both positions, but the effects of response meaningfulness were considerably larger than the effects of stimulus meaningfulness. The results of this experiment have also been replicated by later investigators.

## 1.3   FREQUENCY

Although psychologists are almost unanimous about the effects of meaningfulness on verbal learning, some controversy exists about the frequency variable. In a free-recall experiment by Hall (1954) the Thorndike-Lorge frequency count was found to be an effective variable in recall. Four lists of 20 words each were constructed from words occurring once per million, 10 times per million, 30 times per million, and more than 50 times per million, respectively. After three presentations, more words were recalled from the lists made up of the more

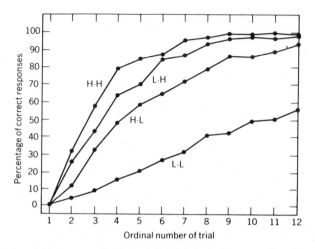

FIGURE 1.1   **Acquisition curves for lists of 10 paired associates as a function of practice. The four S-R combinations of low (L) and high (H) meaningfulness (*m*) represent the parameter. Each curve contains 20 Ss. (after Cieutat, Stockwell, and Noble, 1958)**

frequent words, although the effect was not very large: recall of the least frequent words was about 80% of the recall for the most frequent words. Similar results were obtained by several other experimenters, but a large-scale study of the frequency effect failed to yield positive results (Underwood and Schulz, 1960). These authors found that the learning of a list of trigrams was not related to trigram frequency. Instead, they proposed that trigram pronounceability was critical for learning speed. Others (Johnson, 1962; Terwilliger, 1962) have argued against the way in which Underwood and Schulz measured trigram frequency. They did this by breaking down the natural word unit into successive overlapping letter triplets, and counting the frequency with which these triplets were obtained. Thus, the word "triplet," for instance, would be counted 5 times: TRI, RIP, IPL, PLE, and LET. Such a procedure places undue stress on written language. Frequency of use presumably refers to the frequency of the spoken word (But note that even the Thorndike-Lorge count is based on written text!). Since there is no unambiguous relationship between letter triplets and the phonemes of the English language, the failure to obtain a relationship between frequency defined in this manner and learning is hardly critical. Some experiments have supported this position, especially an instructive study by Gibson, Bishop, Schiff, and Smith (1964). They showed that items that were both frequently used and meaningful are easiest to remember, irrespective of pronounceability. Three lists of trigrams were devised which contained the same letters rearranged as anagrams. In the first list meaningful trigrams such as AFL and TWA were used. These were rearranged so as to make them more pronounceable (FAL, TAW) for the second list. A third arrangement was used as a control with both meaningfulness and pronounceability absent (LFA, WTA). Retention, measured by both free recall and recognition, was best for the meaningful items and second best for the pronounceable items. Parenthetically, we might note the results of a perceptual recognition task that the authors also tried out with the same material. When items were flashed on a screen for a very brief period of time by means of a tachistoscope, recognition thresholds were lowest for the pronounceable items, followed by the meaningful items. This reversal illustrates that in order to understand the effects of an experimental variable, one must never lose sight of the actual task that the subject is asked to perform.

## 1.4   IMAGERY

When words are used as stimulus material the ease with which they arouse mental images is highly correlated with the ease of learning (Paivio, 1971). The image-evoking value ($I$) of a word is determined by methods similar to those used to determine its meaningfulness. Typically subjects are given a mimeographed booklet that contains the test words. The subjects are then asked to rate the words on the ease or speed with which they arouse an image from "very easy—image aroused immediately" to "very difficult—image aroused after long delay or not at all." Note that the $I$-values determined with this procedure are just as objective as meaningfulness values.

Learning materials vary widely in their image-evoking value from abstract nouns to concrete nouns to pictures and objects. As the concreteness of a learning item increases it becomes easier to learn. Interestingly enough, if the $I$-values of both the stimulus and response terms are controlled in paired-associate learning, variations in the $I$-value of the stimulus terms have a much more powerful effect on learning rate than variations of the $I$-value of the response terms. Paivio argues that the stimulus member of a pair serves as a "conceptual peg" to which the response is connected during learning, and from which it can be retrieved on test trials. The more concrete a stimulus item is, i.e., the more likely it is to arouse an image, the better it will serve this function. A concrete stimulus readily elicits the compound image that was formed during learning and from which the response component may be retrieved. Note that the greater effect of imagery on the stimulus side rather than on the response side in paired-associate learning is exactly the opposite of the effects of meaningfulness. It has been shown above that stimulus meaningfulness plays a minor role compared to response meaningfulness.

The image-arousing potential of a word (*l*) and its meaningfulness (*m*) are, of course, highly correlated. However, the suspicion that *l* is effective only because items that easily arouse an image are also meaningful proves unfounded. On the contrary, Paivio reports that if one varies *l* independently of *m*, its effects on learning are undiminished; if, on the other hand, *m* is varied but *l* is kept constant, the effects of *m* upon learning are reduced to zero. Thus it seems that concreteness is a more basic variable in learning than the traditional meaningfulness.

## 1.1.5    INTRALIST SIMILARITY

Intralist similarity may be defined in several ways. When the experimenter uses nonsense syllables as learning material, the number of letters that are common to the syllables is taken as an index of intralist similarity. When words are employed, the criterion is usually similarity in their meaning. Letter-overlap is referred to as formal similarity; similarity in meaning as associative similarity.

The similarity among the items of a list has complex effects in paired-associate learning, depending on the locus of similarity. If one increases the similarity among the stimulus terms of a paired-associate list, stimulus discrimination becomes more difficult and confusions among the stimuli slow the learning process. However, when the response members of a list are made more similar, the greater confusability is balanced by an opposing effect: similar terms are easier to recall. In general, therefore, similarity among items hinders paired-associate learning, but at the same time there is a facilitative effect of response similarity that may partly or completely override the negative effects of similarity.

The classic study of intralist similarity in paired-associate learning was performed by Gibson in 1942. Gibson had subjects learn a 12-item list that consisted of simple figures paired with nonsense syllables. For different lists the difficulty of stimulus discrimination was varied systematically by making the figures that served as stimulus items more similar to each other. Intralist similarity hindered learning. A number of later studies were concerned with the locus of the similarity effect in paired-associate learning (e.g., Underwood, 1953).

When similarity is increased in both stimulus and response pairs the difficulty of learning also increases. Increasing only stimulus similarity has the same effect, but increases in the similarity of the response members has complex effects on learning. High similarity may help rather than hinder paired-associate learning in some respects. Note the relevance here of the distinction between response learning and the associative phase of paired-associate learning. At first, the subject simply has to learn what the response alternatives are; later, his task becomes one of hooking up or associating each stimulus item with its corresponding response. Underwood, Runquist, and Schulz (1959) have shown that high similarity among the members of the response set actually facilitates the response learning phase, even if the overall effect of similarity is negative. Two lists of paired-associates were used with CVCs as stimuli for both lists. The responses were similar adjectives for one list and dissimilar adjectives for the other. Control subjects were given 16 paired-associate trials with both lists. In another experimental condition of interest, separate groups of subjects received from 1 to 13 regular paired-associate trials and were then stopped and asked to recall as many as possible of the adjectives that served as responses. Although performance was better for the low-similarity list throughout the 15 trials of the experiment, subjects could recall more of the responses from the high-similarity list, at least for the first few trials of the experiment.

This brief review of paired-associate learning can do no more than provide the reader with some of the basic concepts and findings in this area. It certainly cannot do justice to a literature that consists of literally hundreds of studies. Some of these studies are discussed later in this book; most of them are of no concern here because they are merely elaborations on the general theme of the work just reviewed: that paired-associate learning can be viewed as a quite simple psychological process, consisting of a stimulus discrimination phase plus an associative learning phase, in which the responses become conditioned to the stimuli. We show later that this is an impoverished view of human cognitive functioning and how the modern research on learning overcomes these limitations, but first we must look at the other verbal learning paradigms and the kind of information that they have provided.

## SERIAL LEARNING

In *serial learning* each item serves both as a stimulus and as a response. Items are presented always in the same order and the sub-

TABLE 1.2.   **Serial Learning. (Each item appears in the window of a memory drum for a short time during which the subject must anticipate the next item. The same presentation order is used on each trial.)**

\*

OVERT
RURAL
CRINGING
RHYTHMIC
SORRY
STRIDENT
FLABBY
UGLY

\*

ject learns to anticipate the next item of the list in response to each item. A special signal serves as a stimulus for the recall of the first item of the list.

The same task variables discussed above in the context of paired-associate learning (meaningfulness, frequency, similarity) have also been studied in serial learning. Generally, they have the same effects in serial learning as in paired-associate learning. The problem, however, that has aroused the greatest interest in serial learning concerns the nature of the functional stimulus in serial learning. In paired-associate learning there is a clearly defined stimulus term, but in serial learning each item doubles both as a response term for the preceding item and as a stimulus term for the following item. But what precisely is the "real" stimulus in a serial learning task?

## 1.2.1    THE PROBLEM OF THE FUNCTIONAL STIMULUS

The conditioning view of learning predisposes the investigator to search for the stimuli to which each response is conditioned and which elicit it, as in paired-associate learning. In serial learning each item, quite obviously, serves as the nominal stimulus for the recall of the subsequent item in the list; but does it really function as the stimulus, or is the actual, functional stimulus something else? Rather than a single item, is the real stimulus perhaps all the preceding items or even the serial position of an item in a list? A great deal of work and ingenuity has gone into answering that question, with the result being confusion more than enlightenment. It is, nevertheless, instructive to trace the history of this work, because it sheds some light on the problems inherent in the conditioning view of learning, and the reasons why so many contemporary psychologists have turned away from this view.

The father of verbal learning, Hermann Ebbinghaus, asserted that serial learning consisted in the formation of associative bonds between each word and its immediately succeeding neighbor. Furthermore, associative bonds are also formed beyond intervening items to every item in a list, with the strength of these bonds decreasing the greater the distance between items (Ebbinghaus, 1885). Today, Ebbinghaus' view is called the chaining hypothesis of serial learning. It, together with the rest of Ebbinghaus' ideas, dominated theorizing about serial learning until the early 1960s, when an opposing hypothesis, first formulated by Woodworth (1938), was championed by Asch and others, setting off the present controversy (for a detailed and informative review, see Bewley, 1972). Woodworth had argued that serial learning involves organizing a list into a whole by associating each item with its serial position. This serial position hypothesis assumed, therefore, that an item's position rather than its predecessor was the functional stimulus in serial learning.

A number of experimental designs have been used in trying to decide this issue. For instance, one can have subjects first learn a paired-associate list of the form A-B, C-D, E-F, and then have them learn the serial list ABCDEF in which the ordering of the pairs has been retained. Or, one can have subjects first learn a serial list and then a paired-associate list in which the already established associations are used, which should, according to the chaining hypothesis, facilitate learning. On the other hand, there are designs in which subjects first learn associations between a position and an item, without forming interitem associations, and are then transferred to learning serial lists. According to the serial position hypothesis, such pretraining should facilitate serial learning. The results of these studies show quite clearly that both the chaining and serial position hypotheses, as well as several combinations of the two, are correct—at least in the sense that there are experimental results supporting each one. This outcome is somewhat disconcerting; it is possible to criticize many of these experiments for methodological reasons (Bewley, 1972), but the general conclusion remains that transfer studies do not discriminate among the alternative hypotheses. Furthermore, it is hard to interpret these studies, no matter what their outcome; if a subject utilizes in the transfer task serial information acquired during pretraining this does not imply that the subject had learned a chain of associations. He may have learned the first list in any conceivable manner and is now simply using what he has learned in the transfer task. Similarly, the fact that subjects have available serial position information does not imply that serial position was the functional stimulus during the learning phase; such information could be identified even if subjects had, in fact, learned a chain of associations. Thus, transfer designs do not permit logically valid conclusions about the nature of the stimulus in serial learning.

Single-list designs, however, which were also used to determine the functional stimulus in serial learning, proved to be no more illuminating. It could be shown by varying the starting position of a serial list from trial to trial that serial positions are important. On the other hand, other experiments showed that interitem associations were important, e.g., in lists that contained associatively related words. Investigators began to suspect that the question about the nature of the functional stimulus was wrong; obviously it was not going to have a simple yes-or-no answer. Battig and Young (1968) gave their subjects two serial lists to learn which were related in different ways. They found evidence that neither the item-item associations nor the position-item associations were crucial for performance, but that subjects learned the rule that related the two lists and made use of it. More and more it seemed that there simply was no functional stimulus in serial learning; instead, subjects learned serial lists using various strategies, which might involve interitem associations, serial positions, or any other kind of cue, such as the rules in the Battig and Young study. A probe technique developed by Posnansky, Battig, and Voss (1972) demonstrates this point quite clearly. Posnansky et al. had their subjects learn a 15-item serial list. On each trial subjects studied the items of the list as they appeared on a memory drum, and immediately after the last item they attempted to recall the whole list in the correct order. After the recall probes all items that were recalled correctly for the first time on that trial were given a probe test. Either a diagrammatic representation of the item's serial position, or, alternatively, its preceding item in the list was shown as a recall cue. The effectiveness of the two probe types provided an index of the extent to which subjects used either serial position or preceding items as recall cues. It could be shown quite clearly that both cues were used by subjects, with position cues being predominant at the ends of the list. In the center section of the list, quite frequently, neither type of cue worked, indicating that these items were coded in a more complex way.

What all this means is that there is really no answer to the question, "What is the functional stimulus in serial learning?" Serial learning is not some fixed process subject to inflexible rules, the "laws of learning." Instead, subjects have options, they can use one strategy or another, depending on what they think they ought to do, instructions, and various features of the task. We should not look at serial learning as a process of conditioning, where a (possibly obscure) functional stimulus becomes gradually associated with its response, but we should inquire how the subject encodes the list items, what the process of storing these items in memory is like, and what factors influence his learning strategies. In other words, we should concern ourselves with the subject's information processing, asking entirely different kinds of questions in our experiments than those inspired by conditioning analogies of learning.

## 2    THE SERIAL POSITION EFFECT

One of the most striking findings in the area of serial learning is the constancy of the serial position effect. Suppose subjects are learning a serial list to some criterion; note for each item the number of errors made in learning the list; a plot of these errors against the serial position of each item is called a serial position curve. Depending on the nature of the list and on the experimental conditions, serial position curves may look quite different. For instance in Figure 1.2 the mean number of errors for two 14-item lists are shown. In one case the items were nonsense syllables, in the other familiar names. Obviously, the names were much easier to learn than the nonsense syllables. However, the serial position effect is remarkably alike in both instances. McCrary and Hunter (1953), from whose work these examples are taken, replotted the data of Figure 1.2 in terms of the percentage of the total errors made at each serial position. The resulting serial position curves are essentially identical (Figure 1.3), and, furthermore, typical for many other serial position curves that have been obtained under different experimental conditions. In all cases slightly bow-shaped, asymmetric serial position curves are observed as long as percentage of errors is plotted along the ordinate and as long as the anticipation method is used rather than recall.

The reasons for this remarkable constancy of serial position curves are quite general ones, and have little to do with serial learning per se.

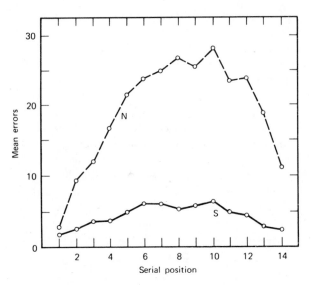

FIGURE 1.2  **Serial position for a list of names (N) and nonsense syllables (S). (after McCrary and Hunter, 1953)**

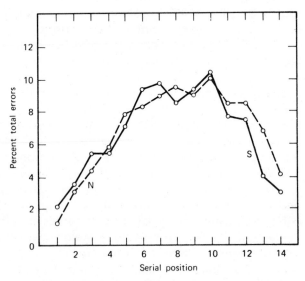

FIGURE 1.3  **The data of Figure 1.2 replotted in terms of percentage of total errors. (after McCrary and Hunter, 1953)**

Murdock (1960) has pointed out that the typical serial position curves are found whenever subjects must discriminate items that are ordered along a dimension, whether temporal or sensory. Serial position curves for tones varying in intensity, lines of varying length, different shades of colors, weights, areas of geometric figures all have the same bow-shaped, asymmetric form exemplified by Figure 1.3. Indeed, when items vary along semantic dimensions, e.g., *beautiful-pretty-fair-homely-ugly*, as in a study by Pollio (1966), similar serial position effects are also obtained. Murdock (1960) hypothesizes that differences in the distinctiveness of the stimuli give rise to this ubiquitous serial position effect. He believes  that the end points of an ordered sequence, no matter what this order is, are more distinct than the center portions of the sequence, and the subject's tendency to select one end of an ordered series as the "beginning," and start processing from that point can account for the observed asymmetry of the serial position curve.

The serial position effect, therefore, appears to be the result of the subjects' strategies in dealing with ordered sequences. Specifically, subjects appear to start learning an ordered sequence at the beginning, next learn its end, and then work toward the center from these anchor points. Thus, Jensen (1962) showed that subjects learned a 10-unit list in the following order:1,2,10,3,9,4,8,5,7,6—which results in the typical serial position effect.

## FREE RECALL

In a typical *free-recall* experiment subjects are given a list of items and are later asked to recall as many as possible. Usually from 10 to 40 items are presented, one at a time. Recall may be oral or in writing. Subjects are instructed to recall as many words as they can, without regard to the order in which the items have been presented. The recall periods vary from 30 seconds to 2 minutes. Order of presentation is randomized from trial to trial.

Free-recall data show typical serial position effects, as illustrated in Figure 1.4. This figure is based on data from a free-recall experiment by Murdock (1962) in which list length and rate of presentation were varied. Each curve shows a strong recency effect, such that the last item of the list is recalled almost perfectly, with recall decreasing rapidly over the last five items of the list, where it reaches a plateau that is constant throughout the center section of the list. In addition, there is a primacy effect extending over the first four items of the list,

TABLE 1.3.   **Free Recall. (Each item appears for a short period of time in the window of a memory drum. After all items have been shown the subject is asked to recall as many of the words as he can. Different presentation orders are used on each trial.)**

       \*

OVERT
RURAL
CRINGING
RHYTHMIC
SORRY
STRIDENT
FLABBY
UGLY
      \*

    recall

which is not quite as pronounced as the recency effect. Several features of these data are important. First of all, the recency effect is quite constant and appears to be independent of either list length or rate of presentation. On the other hand, the flat center portion of each curve clearly depends on both of these variables: the longer the list, the lower the recall probability becomes for items in the middle

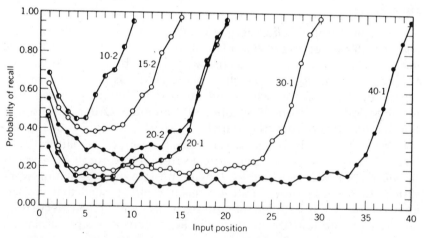

FIGURE 1.4   **Serial position curves for six different groups with lists of unrelated words varying in presentation time and list length. (after Murdock, 1962)**

of the list (varying from about .12 for the 40-item list to .45 for the 10-item list); secondly, a 2-second rate of presentation per item increases the recall probability for items in the center of the list over that obtained with a 1-second presentation rate, as is shown by a comparison of the two 20-item lists. As these data show, it is extremely important in trying to understand the effects of various task variables on free recall to determine the locus of these effects, i.e., whether the central portion of the serial position curve is involved, or the primacy or recency position.

Of the task variables that have been studied in free-recall experiments, the most significant one is intralist similarity, or redundancy. It is interesting because its effects are reversed from what one finds in paired-associate or serial learning: intralist similarity facilitates free recall, while its effects are negative in other learning situations.

## 1    INTRALIST SIMILARITY AND REDUNDANCY

Several experiments have demonstrated the facilitative effect of intra-list similarity in free-recall learning. In one of these experiments (Miller, 1958) similarity was manipulated not by controlling the amount of letter-overlap in CVCs but by imposing constraints on the learning material in the form of generating rules. Miller employed the mechanism shown in Figure 1.5 to generate his similar stimulus lists. This mechanism is a finite state system that generates strings of letters (S, N, X, and G) of length 2 or more. An admissible string of letters is any sequence obtained by starting in State 0 and ending upon reaching State 0'. The system has three states, represented by the circles

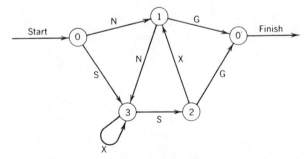

FIGURE 1.5    **Diagram of the finite state generator of the redundant strings in Miller's experiment. An admissible string is any sequence of letters generated by starting in State 0 and ending on the first arrival at State 0'. (after Miller, 1958)**

numbered 1, 2, 3. The permissible transitions are shown by arrows. Whenever a transition occurs the system generates as its output the letter shown next to the arrow. The reader can easily check the working of this mechanism by tracing out a possible path in Figure 1.5, writing down the appropriate letter as each transition is made. One way of listing the total set of well-formed strings generated by this system that clearly shows the similarities that obtain within this set is achieved by using parentheses to denote optional symbols. All well-formed strings are variations of the following four basic strings: NG, NNSG, SSG, and SSXG. Embedded within these basic strings are optional loops: N(N(X)SX)G, N(N(X)SX)NSG, S((X)(SXN))SG, and S((X)(SXN))SXG. Of the 22 strings of length 7 or less Miller selected 9 as items for his similar list. A low similarity list was constructed by generating strings at random from the four letters S, X, N, and G, with the constraint that the list should have the same number of strings of each length as did the high similarity list. Because of the way in which the two lists were constructed, Miller speaks of a redundant list and a random list, rather than high and low similarity. Part of the results of Miller's free-recall experiment are shown in Figure 1.6. It is obvious that the redundant list (high similarity) was much easier to learn than the random list. Subjects who noticed the similarity among the redundant strings had much less to remember than the subjects who had to memorize the random strings. Once one knows the rules for the generation of redundant strings, the pattern of each item becomes highly predictable; hence each item contains less information than a randomly generated item. Letter sequences in random items are

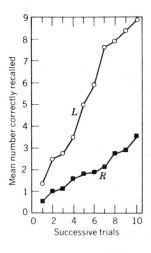

FIGURE 1.6  **Mean number correct as a function of the trial number.** *L* **indicates a redundant list and** *R* **indicates a random list. (after Miller, 1958)**

unpredictable, that is, each letter must be memorized separately. Similarity in the Miller experiment is obviously confounded with information content. The higher similarity becomes, the less information is to be remembered.

Garner (1962) has pointed out a very important implication of experiments like the Miller (1958) experiment. What determines the difficulty with which an item will be learned is not so much a function of the characteristics of that individual item but rather of the internal structure inherent in the total set of items to be learned. In free-recall learning the task of the subject is to learn which subset of items out of the total set of all possible items make up the learning list. Garner hypothesized that the ease of free-recall learning is not a question of the characteristics of the individual items but of the structure of the subset that is to be learned and its relationship to the total set of potential stimuli. In a series of experiments by Garner and his coworkers evidence for this position has been obtained. In the first of these studies Whitman and Garner (1962) constructed an item pool of 81 figures by using three levels of values, each of four variables. The variables and their levels were shape (square, triangle, and circle), lines (0, 1, or 2) spaces (right, left, or none), and dots (above, below, or none). Three subsets of 9 figures each were selected from the set of potential stimuli so that each level of each variable occurred equally often, but with different correlations between variable pairs. The three sets are shown in Figure 1.7. Set A has no correlation between variable pairs (all variables are orthogonal); for set B one pair of variables is perfectly correlated, while the others are orthogonal, (shape and space covary: all squares have a space on the left, all triangles have a space on the right, and circles have no space); the maximum possible constraint is achieved in set C, where three variables are correlated and only the dot-variable is orthogonal. Separate groups of subjects learned each list with a typical free-recall procedure, after having been familiarized with the way in which the stimuli in this experiment were constructed. The median number of learning trials to criterion for the three subsets of stimuli were 19 for list A, 12 for list B, and 2 for list C, respectively. Thus, the list with the greatest intralist similarity was by far the easiest to recall. Note that three of the items in lists B and C are identical. In spite of this one-third overlap in items, learning rates for the two lists were widely different. In fact, when the proportion of correct responses for the items common to both lists B and C is plotted as in Figure 1.8, the learning curves for these items are almost identical with the learning curves for the subsets within which they were contained and appear to be unrelated to each other.

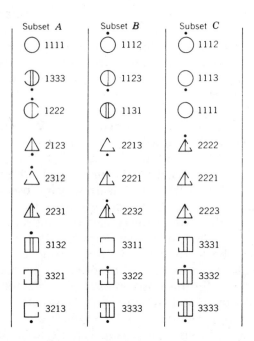

FIGURE 1.7 **The three subsets of the stimuli used by Whitman and Garner. The number to the right of each figure provides the coded values for the four variables, in the order: shape, space, line, and dot. (after Whitman and Garner, 1962)**

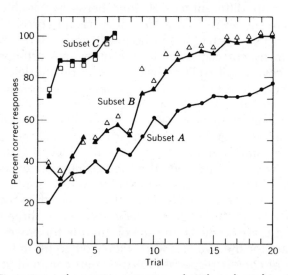

FIGURE 1.8 **Percentages of correct responses as a function of number of trials for the various subsets of figures. The open points are data from just those three figures in subsets B and C which were identical. (after Whitman and Garner, 1962)**

The conclusions of Miller (1958) and Whitman and Garner (1962) were supported by the results of an experiment (Horowitz, 1961) in which a more conventional definition of similarity was employed—the extent to which trigrams in a list share the same letters. Horowitz constructed a low and a high similarity list by using 12 or 4 letters, respectively, to construct his trigrams. In one condition subjects were given standard free-recall instructions. Subjects recalled more from the high similarity list than from the low similarity list, at least on the first learning trials. What makes this study particularly interesting is that Horowitz also included a second experimental condition in which subjects were given an ordering task. On each test trial, subjects were given cards with the test items printed on them and were asked to put them into the correct order. Needless to say, items were presented in the same order on all trials in this condition. Contrary to the results with the free-recall procedure, but in agreement with serial learning studies, the high similarity list was more difficult to learn. Obviously the effects of intralist similarity depend on the task given the subject. A larger parent population may be constructed from 12 letters than from 4 letters and hence the low similarity list is selected from a larger set of potential stimuli. Horowitz's free-recall results are exactly what one would expect if amount of information is a critical variable in learning: there is more information in the low similarity list and hence there is more to learn. Horowitz's ordering task, on the other hand, primarily involves discrimination between items. As Garner (1962) has shown, discrimination performance is optimal if each stimulus dimension provides as many discriminations as possible, and does not duplicate information provided by another variable—which is more nearly the case in the low similarity list than in the high similarity list.

Instead of studying the learning of artificially constrained item lists, the effects of the natural structure of language upon free recall may be investigated. The speaker of English generates well-formed sentences just as the finite state mechanism of Miller (Figure 1.5) generates well-formed letter strings. The rules according to which a speaker generates his sentences are the syntactic and semantic rules of the English language, and these are, of course, greatly more complicated than the transition rules in Figure 1.5. However, one can approximate a natural language by means of finite state generators and one can distinguish between degrees of approximations depending on the complexity of the generating mechanism (Shannon, 1948). Basically this is achieved by using actual word frequency statistics extending over word sequences of various lengths. A zero-order approximation is obtained by selecting words at random from a dictionary. Thus, one word is as likely to appear as any other, and there are no sequential dependencies among words. For a first-order approximation words are again drawn at random, but with probabilities proportional to actual word frequencies in English. Still there are no sequential dependencies among the words that make up a string, but the more frequent words are more likely to be used. For second-order approximations, word-pair probabilities of actual English are used. Thus, knowing a single word, one can guess to some extent what kind of word would follow it: for instance, after ARE, one could expect GIRLS, or LEARNED, or COLD, but not IS, or PERAMBU-LATE. A third-order approximation is based on the actual frequencies of word triplets, and in general, a $k$-th order of approximation takes into account the distributional statistics of $k$-tuplets of words. A finite state mechanism generating a $k$-th order approximation to English has as many states as there are different English word sequences of length $(k - 1)$. For each state there exists a probability distribution over the set of all English words that determines the likelihood that a word will follow this particular string of $(k - 1)$ words. Every word in the English language has a certain probability of occurrence after a particular string of $(k - 1)$ words. For instance, after the string of length 2, FAMILY WAS, such words as LARGE or MY have a relatively high probability of occur-ring as the third word, while DARK, IS and CAME are unlikely in this position. The following two illustrations are taken from Miller and Selfridge (1950) and show word triplets and word quintuplets with fre-quencies representative of English:

1.    Third-order approximation: FAMILY WAS LARGE DARK ANIMAL CAME ROARING DOWN THE MIDDLE OF MY FRIENDS LOVE BOOKS PASSIONATELY EVERY KISS IS FINE
2.    Fifth-order approximation: ROAD IN THE COUNTRY WAS INSANE ESPECIALLY IN DREARY ROOMS WHERE THEY HAVE SOME BOOKS TO BUY FOR STUDYING GREEK.

It is important to understand the purpose of these statistical constructions. They are not presented here as a theory of language; more precisely, it is not maintained that a speaker of English generates sentences in the same way as the devices described above. This issue will be more fully discussed in Chapter 6, but at this point one can state that the rules of language are not finite state devices. Such devices are much too clumsy, even for relatively short strings; the number of different sequences that must be considered is extremely large; and, for each of these sequences, one would have to know the probability with which every word of the English language follows it. However, statistical approximations provide a very useful way of generating learning materials for psychological experiments in which some of the short-range relationships of the natural language are preserved, without encountering the full complexity of natural language material.

In practice, a technique taken from an old children's game may be employed to obtain a *k*-th order approximation quite readily. Speakers of the language know, by definition, what a well-formed word sequence is like. Suppose a speaker is presented with THE MIDDLE, is asked to guess the next word of the sentence, and responds with OF. Now the first word of the string may be deleted and the remainder is presented to another subject with the same instruction. This subject's response to MIDDLE OF may be MY. This procedure can be repeated any number of times, thus generating a third order approximation like the one presented above.

Miller and Selfridge (1950) obtained passages of 10, 20, 30, or 50 words for each order of approximation from 0 to 7, as well as English text. These lists were read to their subjects one at a time. Subjects were instructed to write down as many words as they could remember, preferably in the correct order, although order was not used as a criterion for scoring. The results are shown in Figure 1.9. As in the experiments on artificial constraint, free recall was better with the more highly constrained lists. The absence of an improvement

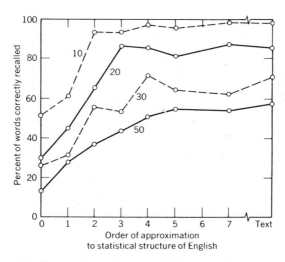

FIGURE 1.9  **Percentage of words correctly recalled as a function of order of approximation to the statistical structure of English for lists of 10, 20, 30, and 50 words. (after Miller and Selfridge, 1950)**

after about the fourth-order approximation led the authors to conclude that the short-range, familiar relationships between words
facilitate learning and that meaningfulness per se is less critical. Later
investigators have shown this conclusion to be erroneous (Marks and
Jack, 1952; Coleman, 1963). When order is used as a criterion in scoring and when prose and approximations are matched in syllabic
length and word frequency, recall continues to be improved as the
order of approximation increases, and text is recalled significantly better than the highest order of approximation studied. In fact, the
greatest improvement in recall seems to occur between the highest
order of approximation and text. This finding is, of course, in
agreement with the statement made earlier that finite state devices
(and the approximations generated by them) are insufficient as
models of natural language. There is obviously something about
natural language that facilitates recall above and beyond mere statistical redundancy.

A number of conclusions may be drawn from this review of experiments concerned with the effects of intralist similarity and redundancy. First, the importance of the total set of learning items must be
stressed. Verbal learning is not a question of the acquisition of single
items, but of sets of items. Whether an item is easy or hard to learn
depends mostly on the structure of the list (or sentence) in which it is
embedded. This effect was most noticeable in free-recall experiments:
the better structured the learning material is, the easier it is to recall it.
However, the interrelationships of the items of a list are equally
important in paired-associate learning: if the response set is coherent
and highly available, response learning is facilitated; if the stimulus
items are very similar to each other, stimulus discrimination is more
difficult.

Secondly, a confounding of the two experimental variables, similarity and redundancy, is apparent. The two are obviously related, but
it would be interesting to see whether similarity, defined either as letter overlap or semantic similarity, can be manipulated separately from
the sequential constraints within a list. It is possible that the facilitative
effect of intralist similarity on recall is entirely due to the confounding
of similarity and redundancy that is present in all of the experiments
described above. To appreciate the nature of this confounding, note
that if only highly similar items are used to make up a list, there are in
general fewer items to choose from than when all kinds of items are
selected as list members. Hence, high-similarity lists are more
redundant in a statistical sense.

Finally, it appears that an understanding of the effects of variables such as the ones discussed in this section can only come after a better understanding of the learning process itself has been achieved. The effects of task variables such as similarity and redundancy obviously depend on the learning task. There is no such thing as verbal learning, only paired-associate learning, free recall, or other such procedures. A much more detailed analysis of what the subject actually does while he learns a list of items is indicated.

## RECOGNITION

In a *recognition* experiment items are presented as in free-recall experiments, but different testing procedures are employed. Basically, there are three types of recognition tests; all three involve the use of *distractor* items. The distractor items are selected from the same set as the learning items, and new distractor items are used on each trial in multitrial recognition experiments. In a single-item test, learning items and distractor items are presented one at a time in random order, and the subject responds with either "old" or "new" to each item. In a variation of this procedure, the subject is given a printed list of all learning and distractor items in random order and is asked to check

TABLE 1.4.   **Recognition Learning. (Items are presented as in Table 1.3. After the study phase, subjects are given a test sheet and are asked to circle the items they were shown before.)**

```
        *
OVERT
RURAL
CRINGING
RHYTHMIC
SORRY
STRIDENT
FLABBY
UGLY
        *
```

| Test sheet: | | | |
|---|---|---|---|
| SORRY | NAIVE | SUBLIME | RHYTHMIC |
| TINY | RURAL | BLATANT | STRIDENT |
| HOSTILE | FLABBY | OVERT | CANDID |
| CRINGING | POLITE | UGLY | GOLDEN |

those items that have been presented before. In a *multiple-choice* test each learning item is combined with several distractor items and the subject is asked to pick out the old item from each set of alternatives.

We shall be concerned here solely with item recognition, as distinguished from class recognition. In item recognition, or individual recognition, study and distractor items belong to the same set of homogeneous items. In class recognition the study and distractor items come from different sets. It is obvious that if the study items are words and three-place numbers are used as distractors on the recognition test, the subject will perform on a completely different basis than if both the study items and the distractors are three-place numbers. In more subtle cases it might be less obvious that the subject is either wholly or in part responding on the basis of class recognition. For instance, if all the words used as study items are associatively related (say they are associates of HOSPITAL), and unrelated words are used as distractors, class recognition and item recognition would be inextricably confounded. Class recognition may present quite different problems from item recognition; it may be more related to concept identification and will not be discussed here further.

In all recognition tests the similarity between the learning items and the distractor items is a very powerful variable. Underwood and Freund (1968a) have shown that if subjects are given a multiple-choice recognition test consisting of the correct word, a high associate of the correct word, a formally similar word, and a neutral word, the high-associate words provide the major source of errors. Similarly, Anisfeld and Knapp (1968) have demonstrated that in a yes-no recognition task in which subjects were shown words that had been presented before, words that were common associates or synonyms of preceding words, and neutral control words, subjects made more false-recognition responses to common associates and synonyms than to control words.

In recognition tests it is often possible to recognize an item correctly on the basis of some remembered detail; in recall, on the other hand, memory for an isolated detail is usually less helpful. The nature of the learning material determines how important part-recognition will be. If the learning material is poorly integrated, for instance if consonant trigrams are to be studied, part-recognition may be quite effective, depending upon the confusability of the distractor items used in the experiment.

The most striking characteristic of experiments on recognition is the high level of performance that subjects achieve. In paired-associate experiments subjects need several trials before they master lists of only 10 or 12 pairs. In recognition experiments subjects can recognize almost perfectly several hundreds of items after only one presentation under suitable conditions. An experiment by Shepard (1967) is instructive in this respect. Shepard selected 300 frequent and 300 infrequent words from the Thorndike-Lorge count (Thorndike and Lorge, 1944). Of these 540 were shown to subjects as study items. The remaining 60 words together with a random subset of 60 of the words previously selected were used as test items. An old word and a new word were shown together and the subject had to indicate which member of the pair he believed to be the old word. Subjects identified correctly 88% of the words, on the average. Since the test items were randomly selected from 540 study items, one must suppose that subjects had retained about 475 words after a single exposure.

In passing, a curious phenomenon concerning the recognition of frequent and infrequent words should also be noted. Half of Shepard's words occurred frequently (CHILD, OFFICE) and the other half occurred very infrequently in the Thorndike-Lorge count (JULEP, WATTLED). The infrequent words were recognized better than the frequent words. This is an interesting finding, because when subjects have to recall a word, rather than merely to recognize it, they perform better with frequent words (see the discussion on page 10). Later we shall comment more explicitly upon this difference between recall and recognition.

Shepard reported two more experiments that resulted in even higher retention scores. The procedure in these experiments was similar to the one just described. In the first experiment subjects were shown an inspection series of 612 sentences. The recognition score was 89%. Two cooperative subjects who agreed to undertake the boring task of studying 1224 sentences performed about as well as the subjects given the standard inspection series (88% correct). In a final experiment the stimulus material consisted of colored pictures that were selected for high individual saliency and low confusability. Again an inspection series of 612 items was used. Retention tests in the usual manner were given immediately after inspection, and in addition a second test (constructed with different test pairs) was given either 2 hours, 3 days, 1 week, or 4 months after the first session. Percent correct recognitions on the immediate test was 97%. Scores on the delayed tests were 100%, 92%, 87%, and 58% for the four conditions described above. Thus, even after a delay of 7 days recognition was extremely good. After 4 months, on the other hand, the mean percent correct was not significantly different from chance.

The basis for this remarkable ability of subjects to recognize stimuli seems to depend on the use of distractor items that are dissimilar to the study items and therefore not easily confused. However, highly confusable letter and digit combinations tend to be the standard materials in recognition studies. Although not at all suitable for studying the upper limits of recognition performance, such materials are more convenient for studying the effects of other experimental variables in the laboratory.

Performance on recognition tests is highly sensitive to changes in context. If a subject is to recognize an item as one that he had experienced as a member of some list before, it is very important that the item appear in the same context on the test trial as on the study trial. In an experiment by Light and Carter-Sobell (1970), for instance, homographs were used as study items, but they were presented in a different context on the study and on the test trial, such as *soda cracker* on the study trial and *safe cracker* on the test trial. This change in context greatly reduced recognition performance. Subjects who had encoded a test item as *soda cracker*—a little thing to eat, just could not remember that they had seen *cracker* before when it was presented as *safe cracker*—some kind of specialized crook. Context effects are not restricted, however, to meaning changes such as those involved in the Light and Carter-Sobell experiment. They have also been observed in several experiments in which the basic meaning of a word was retained but contextually modified. For instance, if the to be remembered word is *green,* it may be presented once in the context *green cheese* and the other time in the context *green grass.* In this case the meaning of *green* remains the same, but the way the word *green* is encoded by the subject depends, nevertheless, on the context. If it is encoded as *green cheese,* recognition of *green* is significantly reduced when the test item is *green grass.* This effect has been demonstrated in several experiments, with a study by Thomson (1972) being representative. Thomson varied context by either adding a context word to a single item at the time of test or by deleting a context word that had been employed on the study trial. In four different experiments test items with a context change were recognized correctly 14% less often than test items that appeared in the same context on both study and test trials. The only time when Thomson did not obtain context effects was when the input list comprised only single, unrelated words (that is, in the standard experimental situation). Thus, context effects in recognition can be very strong in properly arranged experimental situations, but they appear to be effectively neutralized in the standard experimental situation.

Several procedural variations must be distinguished among recognition experiments. Some experiments use a list-learning procedure. A list of study items is presented to the subjects, usually one by one, either visually or auditorily. It is then followed by a test. For a yes-no recognition test the study items plus a number of distractor items, which were selected from the same item pool as the study item but which have not been shown before, are presented in random order and the subject is asked to tell whether each item is old or new. For a multiple-choice test each study item is paired with one or several distractor items, and the subject is asked to select the old item. The Shepard (1967) experiment just discussed used a list-learning procedure, together with a two-alternative multiple-choice test, except that only a subset of the study items was tested. In experiments on recognition learning several study and test trials may be given with the same list of items. To avoid learning distractor items, new distractor items are introduced at each test trial.

In the steady-state procedure study and test trials are combined and items are introduced and dropped continuously. The experimenter presents items one at a time from a pool of homogeneous items. Some items are repeated and the subject's task is to judge whether an item has been shown before or not. Shepard and Teghtsoonian (1961) have introduced this procedure. An adaptation to study forced-choice recognition memory under steady-state conditions has been described by Shepard and Chang (1963). In their experiment items were always presented in pairs after the first few trials. One item of each pair was an old item (i.e., it had been presented as a member of an earlier pair) and the other member was a new item. The subject's task was twofold: first he had to judge which item was the old item and then he had to memorize the newly presented item for a later test trial.

The experiment of Shepard and Teghtsoonian (1961) provided some of the basic data concerning short-term recognition memory. Items were randomly selected from the set of all 3-digit numbers and were presented exactly twice per session. All items were printed on 3 × 5 inch cards. The subject was given a large deck of cards (200 in most conditions) and was asked to go through the deck at his own rate, noting on a record sheet for each item whether or not he had seen the number on an earlier card of the deck. No feedback as to the correctness of the response was provided. The experimental variable of principal interest was the lag between the first and second presentation of an item. The experimental results in terms of the probability of an "old" response to an old item as a function of the number of intervening presentations during the retention interval are shown in Figure 1.10. Even for the longest delays the probability of a correct

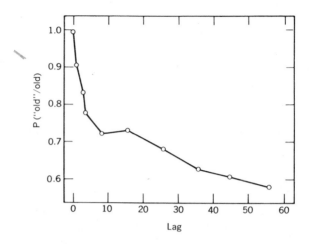

FIGURE 1.10 **The probability of an "old" response to old items as a function of the number of intervening presentations since the last presentation of a stimulus.** (after Shepard and Teghtsoonian, 1961)

recognition is well above the probability of a false recognition. The last point in Figure 1.10 for a lag of 50 to 60 was still about .57, while the probability that a new number was classified as old averaged only .22. A completely steady state was not achieved, though. In this, as in all later experiments using the same procedure, the false recognition rate was not constant but increased throughout the experimental session. However, after the first 40 cards the increase was very small.

## 1.4.1 DECISION PROCESSES IN RECOGNITION

A subject can easily identify all old items correctly, simply by saying "old" whenever a stimulus is presented. Or he can be sure of never making a false recognition if he responds "new" all the time. Usually a subject chooses a bias somewhere between these two extremes. A subject may increase his hit rate by responding "old" on a proportion g of all trials on which he does not recognize the stimulus as such. Such a guessing strategy will, of course, indiscriminately increase the hit rate and the false recognition rate.

Models with such a guessing mechanism are called high-threshold models. The assumptions that high-threshold models make are briefly these. There exists a state (or several states) in which recognition of an item that has been presented before is perfect. Let the probability that an item is in this state be $p_s$. If an item is not in this state, and hence is not truly recognized, the subject can still guess that it is an old item with probability $g$. For new items there is a corresponding probability $p_n$ of identifying the new item as new. If the new item is not recognized as such, a false identification will occur on a proportion $g$ of trials, because the subject is assumed to guess "old" with probability $g$ whenever he can not identify an item. If we let $P(\text{"old"}/\text{old item})$ and $P(\text{"old"}/\text{new item})$ be observed proportions in a recognition experiment, the assumptions of the high-threshold theory may be expressed more formally as follows:

(1a)            $P(\text{"old"}/\text{old item}) = p_s + g\,(1 - p_s)$
(1b)            $P(\text{"old"}/\text{new item}) = g\,(1 - p_n)$

Egan (1958) has discussed two special cases of Eq. (1) that have been implicit in much work on recognition memory. In the first case, we assume that $p_n = 0$, in spite of the fact that this assumption is somewhat counterintuitive (it implies that subjects can never recognize new items as such). Solving for $P(\text{"old"}/\text{new item})$ in Eq. (1b) and substituting into Eq. (1a) we have

(2)        $P(\text{"old"}/\text{old item}) = p_s + (1 - p_s)\, P\,(\text{"old"}/\text{new item})$

Equation (2) says that the two observable variables, $P(\text{"old"}/\text{old item})$ and $P(\text{"old"}/\text{new item})$, are linearly related. The line passes through the points $(0, p_s)$ and $(1,1)$: for $P(\text{"old"}/\text{new item}) = 0$, $P(\text{"old"}/\text{old item})$ becomes $p_s$, and for $P(\text{"old"}/\text{new item}) = 1$, $P(\text{"old"}/\text{old item})$ becomes 1. The function relating $P(\text{"old"}/\text{old item})$ and $P(\text{"old"}/\text{new item})$ is called the memory operating characteristic in analogy to psychophysical terminology, or isomemory function because all points on this function have the same memory strength $p_s$ and differ only in the subject's guessing strategy. A family of curves for different memory strengths are shown in Figure 1.11a. If $p_s = 0$, all the subject can do is guess and his performance will fall on the main diagonal. If $p_s = 1$, the operating characteristic will be the upper boundary in Figure 1.11a. Three intermediate conditions are also shown.

A more realistic threshold model would assume that subjects can sometimes recognize the new stimuli as new, i.e., $p_n \neq 0$. Suppose we let $p_n = p_s$. In this case we obtain

(3)            $P(\text{"old"}/\text{old item}) = p_s + P(\text{"old"}/\text{new item})$

by combining Eqs. (1a) and (1b). The true recognition probabilities can be estimated from Eq. (3) as

$$P_s = P(\text{"old"}/\text{old item}) - P(\text{"old"}/\text{new item})$$

which is the traditional correction for guessing (Woodworth, 1938).

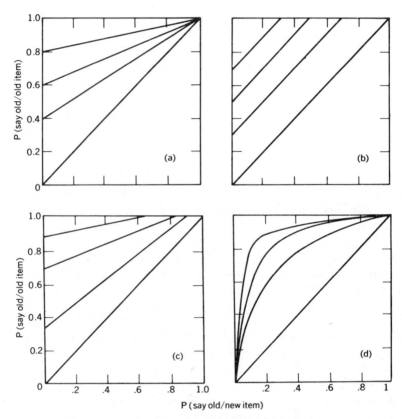

FIGURE 1.11    **Memory operating characteristics according to four models.**

The operating characteristics implied by Eq. (3) are shown in Figure 1.11b for several values of $p$ .

It might seem more appropriate to consider a third case intermediate between Case I and Case II, where $p_n$ is larger than zero, but not as large as $p_s$. As Egan (1958) has shown, the operating characteristic for such a case is still a straight line, but with an intermediate slope as in Figure 1.11c.

Curved operating characteristics are obtained from assumptions similar to those of the theory of signal detectability. Suppose that subjects can evaluate each item in a recognition task on a scale of familiarity. Because of stimulus generalization effects items that have never been presented before do not all have the same familiarity value but are characterized by a distribution of familiarity values $f(s)$. The familiarity values of items that have been shown once before are distributed according to another probability distribution $g(s)$, but are on the average higher than the familiarity values of new items. Figure 1.12 illustrates the familiarity distributions of old and new items. Note that in general there will be some overlap between the two distributions. Suppose that the subject's recognition response is completely dependent on the familiarity value of the item being tested. If the value is high enough, the subject will respond "old"; if the value is low, the subject will respond "new." If the two distributions overlap, perfect responding is impossible. The best decision rule for the subject to follow is to fix a cutoff point $c$ so that misses and false recognitions are balanced at some acceptable level, given the constraints of the situation. The area to the right of $c$ under the curve $g(s)$ gives the probability of a hit; the area to the right of $c$ under $f(s)$ gives the probability of a false recognition, which is associated with the cut-off point $c$. Bias changes in this model imply a curved operating characteristic as shown in Figure 1.11d: as a very strict criterion (a $c$-value in the extreme right in Figure 1.12) is progressively relaxed, large increases in the hit rate occur first, accompanied by only minor increases in the false recognition rate; as the criterion assumes lower and lower values, the gains in the hit rate become smaller and are paid for with disproportionately large increases in the false recognition rate.

Before we can turn to experimental results an alternative method of constructing operating characteristics must be mentioned. Most operating characteristics in psychophysical tasks have been obtained by inducing the subject to assume different criteria through variations in instructions, payoffs, or the frequency of signal trials. Typically, a whole experimental session is run under one experimental condition, and the data from this session provide one point on the operating characteristic. A much more efficient method of data collection based upon confidence judgments has been suggested by Egan, Schulman, and Greenberg (1959) and Pollack and Decker (1958). An adaptation of the latter method is generally used in studies of recognition memory.

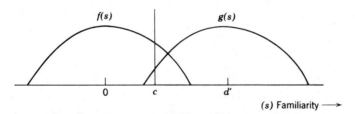

FIGURE 1.12    **Familiarity distributions of new items ($f(s)$) and old items ($g(s)$).**

The method relies on the assumption that subjects can assume multiple criteria on a single trial. Instead of merely asking the subject for a binary recognition response, the subject also gives a confidence judgment. With confidence judgments on a 4-point scale, we have effectively 8 different response categories, ranging from "certainly a new item" to "certainly an old item." The frequency of each response category is recorded separately for old and new items, as shown in Table 1.5. Normally the data provide only one point on the operating characteristic: the proportion of "old" responses given a new item, and the proportion of "old" responses given an old item is plotted. This corresponds to the cutoff between New-1 and Old-1. In our example the estimated hit rate corresponding to this cutoff point is $Pr("old"/old item) = 200/300 = .67$ and the estimated false recognition rate is $Pr("old"/new item) = 110/300 = .37$. Now suppose we repeat our calculation, but place the cutoff between Old-1 and Old-2. In effect we are saying that if the subject had used a stricter criterion he would have called "new" those items that he did call "old" but was least confident about. In this case we obtain as a second point on the operating characteristic $Pr("old"/old item) = 160/300 = .53$ and $Pr("old"/new item) = 80/300 = .27$. A similar argument can be made for the placement of the criterion between any of the other categories, and in this manner one can generate seven points from one set of data. It has been shown that operating characteristics based on con-

TABLE 1.5. **Hypothetical Data to Illustrate the Construction of Operating Characteristics from Confidence Judgments: Response Frequencies for Eight Response Categories from New-4 ("Certainly a New Item") to Old-4 ("Certainly an Old Item") for Both New and Old Items.**

| Old Items | | | | | Response | | | | |
|---|---|---|---|---|---|---|---|---|---|
| | | New | | | | | Old | | |
| | 4 | 3 | 2 | 1 | | 1 | 2 | 3 | 4 |
| Observed frequency: | 10 | 20 | 30 | 40 | | 40 | 50 | 50 | 60 | (300) |

| New Items | | | | | Response | | | | |
|---|---|---|---|---|---|---|---|---|---|
| | | New | | | | | Old | | |
| | 4 | 3 | 2 | 1 | | 1 | 2 | 3 | 4 |
| Observed frequency: | 80 | 40 | 40 | 30 | | 30 | 30 | 30 | 20 | (300) |

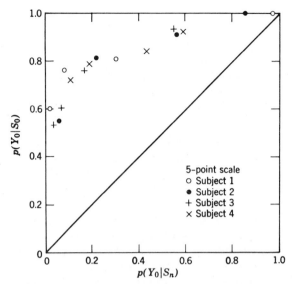

FIGURE 1.13   **Operating characteristics for four subjects (the upper middle quarter of 16 subjects). A list of 100 old words was presented once and then a 200-word recognition test was administered. (after Egan, 1958)**

fidence ratings give comparable results to more conventional procedures. However, the two are not equivalent for all purposes. At this time, work on memory has almost exclusively relied upon confidence ratings.

An example of an empirical memory operating characteristic is shown in Figure 1.13. This figure is taken from Egan (1958). Egan's subjects studied a list of 100 words and were then tested for recognition with a list containing the 100 study words plus 100 distractor items. Subjects used a 7-point rating scale, where a 1 meant "certainly old," a 4 meant "pure guess," and a 7 stood for "certainly new." The results shown in Figure 1.13 are data from 4 subjects in Egan's first experiments. Egan grouped his 16 subjects in groups of 4 according to their performance; the data shown here are for the upper middle quarter. The other subjects produced comparable operating characteristics, with the faster learners tending more toward the upper left in Figure 1.13, and the slower learners regressing toward the main diagonal. It is certainly clear that the memory operating characteristics in Figure 1.13 are not straight lines. Instead they look rather like the operating characteristics derived from signal detection theory. In fact, Murdock (1965b) reported some memory operating characteristics that could be well fitted by assuming that the familiarity distributions of old and new items are normal with equal variance and differ only in that the distribution of old items is $d'$ units (measured in terms of the common standard deviation) higher. The data of Egan (1958), Murdock (1965b), and others to be discussed below clearly exclude all models that require straight-line operating characteristics, and hence all high-threshold theories of recognition memory. The conventional correction for guessing is therefore contraindicated by this analysis.

The measure $d'$, the mean familiarity difference of the old and new items, is an unbiased indicator of memory strength. The placement of the criterion $c$ is influenced by factors only partially under the control of the experimenter. Parks (1966) has studied the question where subjects set their criterion. He hypothesized that subjects match their response probability to the proportion of repeated items in the experiment. In other words, subjects choose a criterion in such a way that the overall probability of saying old is directly proportional to the probability that a test item is actually old. Parks analyzed several sets of recognition data and found them to be in good agreement with this matching hypothesis.

One of the most powerful variables in recognition experiments is the nature of the recognition test. The proportion of correct responses in a yes-no recognition test are not directly comparable to that in a multiple-choice test. If a multiple-choice test is given, the probability of a correct response is inversely proportional to the number of distractor items (e.g., Postman, 1950). The traditional correction for guessing does not remove differences between testing conditions with different numbers of alternatives. However, we already know that this correction is based on some false premises, and it is still possible that differences between testing conditions could be predictable from more adequate theories of recognition performance if conditions of acquisition are controlled. For instance, the signal detection model permits the strength of memory to be estimated independently of testing conditions in terms of $d'$ and specifies rules that govern a subject's performance in various recognition tests.

A relevant experiment has been reported by Kintsch (1968a). He observed 4 subjects for 11 sessions each. Each session comprised 30 trials. A trial consisted of the presentation of five meaningless letter combinations, a delay of 20 seconds filled with a subtraction task, and a test. Five types of test trials were used: one of the study items was presented and the subject was asked to respond with either "old" or "new"; an item not shown before was presented and again the response was either "old" or "new"; or one of the study items was shown together with 1, 3, or 7 distractor items that had never before been presented and the subject had to select the old item. During the study period the subject did not know which testing condition was to be used on that trial. Subjects gave confidence judgments with their responses.

Figure 1.14 presents the most interesting results of this study. The data are shown separately for each subject, as well as a group average. Also given are 95% confidence intervals around the data points. Note that large differences were obtained when a single item was presented for test, depending on whether this item was new or old. Three subjects had a bias for saying "new," while the other subject responded with the opposite bias. For all subjects the probability of a correct response decreased as the number of alternatives on the multiple-choice test increased. The predictions labeled TSD for the multiple-choice performance were obtained in the following way. A memory operating characteristic was constructed for each subject on the basis of his performance in the yes-no condition. From this operating characteristic $d'$ was estimated by standard methods. This estimate of $d'$ was then used to predict subject's behavior under the multiple choice conditions. For this purpose it was assumed that in a $k$-alternative forced choice task the subject selects that alternative which has the highest familiarity value. Mathematically this means that the probability of a correct response is given by the probability that the correct item has a higher familiarity value than any of the $(k-1)$ distractor items. Tables prepared by Elliott (1964) make such computations very easy. Except for one subject, the predictions obtained in this way agreed with the data quite well.

In spite of the successful predictions in Figure 1.14, one should be wary of accepting the analogy to signal detection theory as a satisfactory theory of recognition performance. Other models of choice behavior describe the multiple-choice data in Figure 1.14 almost as well. There is, for instance, the cross-out rule, suggested by Murdock (1963b) and Bower (1967). This rule assumes that a subject crosses out all alternatives that he thinks are wrong and chooses randomly among the remaining alternatives. Another decision rule that may be used is the Bradley-Terry-Luce choice theorem (Bradley and Terry, 1952; Luce, 1959). Suppose that old items have response strength $s(o)$, and that new items have response strength $s(n)$. Then, by the choice theorem, the probability of a correct response in a $k$-alternative recognition test is

$$P(C) = \frac{s(o)}{s(o) + (k-1)\, s(n)}$$

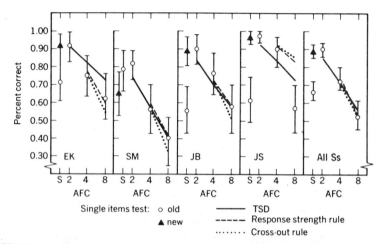

FIGURE 1.14   **Proportions of correct responses under the five experimental conditions (single item tests with old and new items, and 2, 4, and 8 alternative forced choices) with 95% confidence intervals and theoretical predictions.** (after Kintsch, 1968a)

Predictions from both the cross-out rule and the choice theorem are also shown in Figure 1.14. In both cases the data from the two-alternative forced-choice condition were used to estimate the model parameter. It is quite obvious that all three sets of predictions are about equally good and that we are in no position at this time to decide in favor of one or the other choice model. However, the successful prediction of recognition performance in multiple-choice tests has surely reinforced the general position taken throughout this section that memory and decision processes in recognition must be clearly distinguished.

## 1.5    VERBAL DISCRIMINATION LEARNING

In *verbal discrimination learning* the subject is given a set of items (usually two) and must learn to select one of the items which has been arbitrarily designated as correct by the experimenter. For example, item pairs printed one above the other are shown for about 2 seconds, during which time the subject must make his response; the correct item is then shown alone for study. List length is comparable to that used in paired-associate experiments.

Of all the verbal learning paradigms, discrimination learning appears to be the simplest one. That, at least, is the conclusion that must be drawn from the astonishing success of a very simple explanation of verbal discrimination learning, the frequency theory of Ekstrand, Wallace, and Underwood (1966). The frequency theory proposes an extremely simple learning mechanism. Basically, each time an item is processed a frequency unit accrues to it, and the subject responds on the basis of a count of these frequency units, choosing as the right one that member of a pair which has more frequency units. Ekstrand et al. distinguish four types of item processing, each leading to an increase in frequency: when an item is perceived during the study phase of a trial, when it is pronounced in the anticipation phase, when it is rehearsed following the experimental feedback, and when it is rehearsed because some other associated item in the list elicits it. In brief, any kind of processing—reading, pronunciation, rehearsal, or an implicit associative response—adds a frequency increment to an item, and the frequency count is the only thing that determines performance. This is a very simple theory, and experimental predictions are readily generated from it. Ekstrand et al. tested two of these. First, consider what happens when the same item is used twice in a list. If it is used as a Right item both times, the additional

TABLE 1.6.   **Verbal Discrimination Learning. (Each row is exposed for a short period of time during which the subject chooses one item of the pair. A study-test procedure may also be used. Different orders are used on each trial, as well as different left-right positions for the members of each word pair.)**

| | | |
|---|---|---|
| OVERT | CANDID | (test) |
| OVERT | | (study) |
| RURAL | NAIVE | |
| RURAL | | |
| TINY | CRINGING | |
| CRINGING | | |
| RHYTHMIC | HOSTILE | |
| RHYTHMIC | | |
| POLITE | SORRY | |
| SORRY | | |
| GOLDEN | STRIDENT | |
| STRIDENT | | |
| FLABBY | BLATANT | |
| FLABBY | | |
| SUBLIME | UGLY | |
| UGLY | | |

frequency units accruing to it should help performance, but if it is used both times as a Wrong item, the same processes should produce interference, because now a Wrong item gains extra frequency units and therefore is more likely to be selected as the correct one. If an item is used once as a Right item and once as a Wrong item, on the other hand, interference should be maximized and learning most difficult. All of these predictions were confirmed by Ekstrand et al. In addition, Ekstrand et al. also investigated the influence that a strong associate of a list item has on verbal discrimination learning. Clearly, if the associate tends to elicit a Right item, performance should be increased, but if it elicits a Wrong item, the additional frequency units accruing to that item will produce interference. Again, this prediction was verified experimentally. Another prediction that follows from the theory concerns the role of overt pronunciation of items: if Right items are pronounced overtly, they should receive an extra frequency unit (in comparison with a control group that reads all items silently), and pronunciation should help learning. The opposite effect is predicted, however, when Wrong items are pronounced. Both effects have been demonstrated experimentally (e.g., Underwood and Freund, 1968b). Similarly, if Right items acquire some frequency units before the beginning of a verbal discrimination experiment (e.g., by using these items first in a free-recall task), performance should be facilitated, while the opposite should be the case if Wrong items are allowed prior frequency units. Again, Underwood and Freund (1968b) have shown that this is actually the case.

So many correct predictions from such a simple theory are most gratifying, but there are indications that the theory is too simple, after all. For instance, it is not clear how frequency theory can explain the learning of a list in which each item is used exactly twice, once as a Right item and once as a Wrong item. In this case each item will have the same number of frequency units, and a discrimination cannot be based on these, but must include reference to the context in which the items appear. Some additional conceptual apparatus is needed for frequency theory in order to handle this situation. Similarly, Rowe and Paivio (1971) have shown that verbal discrimination learning is greatly facilitated by instructions to form an image of the correct member of each pair. Image formation appears to be another type of processing that must be considered a potential contributor of frequency units. Thus, frequency theory needs to be extended to account for phenomena that are at present outside its domain, and, even more importantly, it should be made more specific so that it can make quantitative predictions rather than merely qualitative ones. Nevertheless, it is no exaggeration to say that today almost all work in verbal discrimination learning is dominated by this theory, whether it is pro or con.

## ,6     TRANSFER

In the previous section experimental variables that affect the learning of a single list were discussed, such as the nature of the learning material and the similarity of the items within a list. In the present section some studies will be described that show how the learning of one list affects the learning of another list, as well as the experimental variables that enter into this relationship. If a person is interested in the effects of learning one list on the learning of a second list, the problem is one of *transfer of training*: if learning one list helps learning a second list, transfer is *positive*; if learning one list interferes with learning another, transfer is *negative*. Alternatively, one may inquire how learning a second list affects the *retention* of the first list. Two kinds of transfer must be distinguished: *specific transfer* is obtained if it can be shown that some particular aspect of one list causes the effects on the second list (for instance, high similarity between lists); *nonspecific transfer* is the result of more general factors, such as warm-up effects, fatigue, or learning-to-learn.

Two experimental designs are used to study how the learning of one list influences what happens with another list. Müller and Pilzecker (1900) studied the *retroactive* interference effects of learning a second list on retention of a first list by comparing an experimental group that learns two lists, A and B, in succession and is then tested for recall of list A with a control group that only learns list A and rests while the experimental subjects learn the second list. In the study of *proactive* effects the first list serves as the transfer-producing list, and learning (or retention) of the second list becomes the dependent variable of interest. The two designs may be outlined as follows:

|  | Retroactive Paradigm: | | |
|---|---|---|---|
| Experimental Group: | Learn List A | Learn List B | Recall List A |
| Control Group: | Learn List A | Rest | Recall List A |
|  | Proactive Paradigm: | | |
| Experimental Group: | Learn List A | Learn List B | Recall List B |
| Control Group: | Rest | Learn List B | Recall List B |

## ,.1     SPECIFIC TRANSFER

Note that in these experimental paradigms specific and nonspecific transfer effects are confounded. If learning two lists A and B is compared with learning only one list, sources of nonspecific transfer and the specific transfer from *A* to *B* are confounded. If one is interested in how the relationship between *A* and *B* affects learning, a more appropriate control group would be one where subjects learn two lists, first an unrelated list *X* and then *B*. In this case, the nonspecific transfer over tasks is controlled, and any differences between learning *A-B* and *X-B* may be attributed to the specific effects of *A* on *B*.

It is customary to express transfer effects by a percentage score. Suppose *E* is the total number of correct responses in the experimental group and *C* is the total number correct in the control group. Then a measure of transfer is obtained by calculating

$$100 \times \frac{(E - C)}{C}$$

The sign of this measure indicates whether transfer is positive or negative. Percentage scores are usually calculated, rather than the simple difference score $(E - C)$, to facilitate comparison of transfer effects between different experiments in which the overall scores, and hence their differences, may vary over a wide range.

The experimental paradigm best suited to the study of transfer effects is paired-associate learning. In paired-associate learning an explicit distinction is made between stimuli and responses, and hence the nature of transfer effects may be explored more fully by studying various relationships between the stimulus and response terms of the two lists. In Table 1.7 the most basic transfer designs are shown, employing the customary notation. A capital letter refers to either a stimulus or a response set, depending on its position: $A = (a_1, a_2, \ldots, a_k)$, where $a_i$ is the *i*th item in list *A*. Different sets of items are denoted by different letters. Thus in Transfer Paradigm I, a different set of items is used for the stimulus and response terms of the two lists. In the second paradigm, new response terms are used in the

TABLE 1.7. **Basic Transfer Designs**

| | List 1 | List 2 | Description |
|---|---|---|---|
| I | *A-B* | *C-D* | *Basic control list* |
| II | *A-B* | *A-C* | *Different responses to the same stimuli* |
| III | *A-B* | *C-B* | *Same responses with new stimuli* |
| IV | *A-B* | *A-B$_r$* | *Stimuli and responses are re-paired* |

second list, but the stimuli of the first list are repeated. In the third paradigm response terms are retained but combined with new stimuli, and in the last paradigm both the stimulus and response terms of the first list are retained in the second list, but they are repaired. These basic transfer paradigms can be varied in many ways by manipulating the relationship among the various terms. For example, suppose the second list in Paradigm II does not repeat exactly the same stimulus terms, but uses related, though not identical terms; for instance, if A is a set of nonsense syllables, a related set A' may be obtained by changing the vowel of each syllable, leaving the consonants intact; if A is a set of nouns, a related set A' may be constructed by replacing each term in A by its synonym, and so forth. Different degrees of similarity between lists may be investigated in this way.

It is clear that the maximum amount of positive transfer is produced if both the stimulus and response terms of the two lists are identical; in this case subjects receive simply two learning trials with the same list. The conditions that produce maximal negative transfer, or inhibition, are not intuitively obvious. Early experiments were ambiguous. In some experiments moderate degrees of similarity resulted in maximum inhibition. In others retroactive inhibition increased proportionately to increases in similarity. In a very influential paper, summarizing the evidence available at that time, Osgood (1949) argued that interference effects depended on the locus of the similarity between two paired-associate lists. According to Osgood's analysis, opposite effects will be observed, depending on the relation between the response terms of two lists, when the similarity between the stimulus terms of two paired-associate lists is increased from neutral to identical. If the responses are identical, increasing stimulus similarity will result in increasing facilitation, but if the response terms are unrelated or antagonistic, inhibition will be produced. The relationship between similarity and retroaction which Osgood hypothesizes is shown in Figure 1.15, the transfer and retroaction surface.

In Figure 1.15 stimulus similarity is represented by the width of the figure; it ranges from functional identity to neutrality. Response similarity ranges through identity, similarity, neutrality, opposition, and antagonism, as represented by the length of the figure. Identity is the point of maximum similarity in both dimensions, i.e., the upper left-hand corner. The direction and degree of transfer and retroaction effects are shown by the vertical dimension. The median plane represents a zero effect; whenver the surface rises above, facilitative effects are expected; whenever it falls below, interference relations exist. For unrelated stimuli Osgood's transfer surface always implies

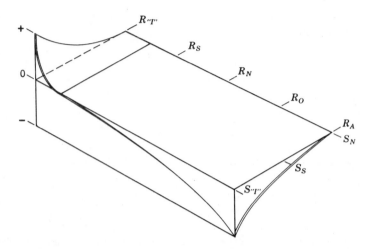

FIGURE 1.15   The transfer and retroaction surface: medial plane represents effects of zero magnitude; response relations distributed along length of solid, and stimulus relations along its width. (after Osgood, 1949)

zero effects; maximum interference is found when the same stimulus is paired with an antagonistic response; maximum facilitation occurs if the same stimulus response pair is repeated. Between these points Osgood drew a smooth, unbroken surface that represents the transfer effects for other stimulus and response relationships.

Osgood himself tested several points on the transfer and retroaction surface. He used two-consonant combinations as stimuli and adjectives as responses. Stimuli were identical for both the original list and the intervening list, but the response terms were varied in meaning. In the intervening lists, responses were either identical, similar, neutral, or opposite adjectives. Recall of the original list was best when the intervening list was identical, next best when similar responses were used; and worst for the neutral and opposite response conditions. No significant differences between the latter two groups were obtained, however.

A study by Bugelski and Cadwallader (1956) was designed as a more extensive test of Osgood's retroaction surface. Both the response and the stimulus similarity of the intervening list were varied in a 4 × 4 factorial design. Osgood's adjectives were used as response terms, and the nonsense figures of Gibson (1942) served as stimuli. Stimulus similarity was varied in four steps: identical, similar, less similar, and neutral. For identical stimulus terms, manipulation of response similarity produced effects on recall of the original list that are exactly opposite to Osgood's results: an intervening list with responses opposite in meaning to the first list responses produced less interference than either similar or neutral responses, which did not differ from each other. On the other hand, the effects of stimulus variability were in agreement with Osgood's hypothesis: as the stimuli became less similar to the original list, all effects decreased in magnitude. No significant differences among groups were obtained when the intervening stimuli were not at all related to the original list.

Both Osgood's and Bugelski and Cadwallader's studies used a retroaction design. A systematic investigation of the transfer surface using a proactive interference design was reported by Dallett (1962). With material similar to the two studies above, Dallett investigated the recall of a common paired-associate list as a function of different first list learning. The most striking result of Dallett's study is his failure to obtain interference effects at all. The only statistically significant effect obtained was a facilitation of second list recall when the first list had identical responses and similar stimuli.

Wimer (1964) made another attempt to explore similarity effects in a proactive inhibition design. Two hundred and fifty subjects were assigned to 25 groups according to a 5 × 5 factorial design. Adjectives served both as stimuli and responses and were categorized into five degrees of similarity: identical, similar, unrelated, opposed, and antonymous. For instance, for the adjective "tense" the five similarity classes were tense, hard, basic, soft, and relaxed. Each group of subjects learned a different first list and then a common second list. The dependent variable in this experiment was trials to learn the second list. After an adjustment for performance differences in first list learning, only one group showed a statistically significant effect: positive transfer was obtained when both stimuli and responses were identical with the first list. In particular, there was no evidence for inhibitory effects of meaningfully dissimilar material at all. If anything, antonyms tended to facilitate learning.

It is obvious that Osgood's transfer surface does not describe the data correctly. At this point it is worthwhile to consider how the transfer surface was derived in the first place. It was not based on extensive theoretical notions; instead, it was a low-level empirical generalization, a simple and meaningful description of the data on transfer available to Osgood in 1949. Only two factors, the similarity between the stimulus and response terms of the two lists seemed necessary in order to account for the results of transfer experiments. The failure of subsequent research to conform to Osgood's generalization could be due to several factors. For one, other experimental variables, which Osgood did not account for, may be important in transfer. Secondly, it may be that Osgood's measurment of similarity was inappropriate. There is reason to believe that both these factors need to be considered. Several comments have already been made about similarity. The basic problem appears to be that the relevant similarity dimension does not go from same to neutral to opposite, but that opposite falls somewhere between the same and neutral points of the scale. Instead of similarity, the axes of the transfer surface could be relabeled as "relatedness" and thus would range from "same" to "unrelated." By definition, opposition implies some degree of relatedness. Thus, if one would place the data points from opposition relationships somewhere near "similar" on the transfer surface, some of the results of Bugelski and Cadwallader (1956) and Wimer (1964) could be accommodated within Osgood's framework.

Among the experimental variables that have been shown to be important in transfer studies, in addition to those considered by Osgood, are degree of learning, response meaningfulness, stimulus meaningfulness, and stability of the experimental environment.

Degree of learning of both the first and the second list significantly influences transfer of training. McGeoch (1929) studied the effects of this variable with a retroactive inhibition design. He varied degree of first list learning in five steps: subjects learned a nine-syllable list for either 6, 11, 16, 21, or 26 trials. All subjects were then given an interference list for 11 trials, and finally relearned the original list. Retroactive inhibition was found to decrease with greater amounts of first list learning. In a complementary study Melton and Irwin (1940) kept first list learning the same for all subjects but varied the amount of learning of the intervening list from 5 to 40 trials. They found that retroactive inhibition increased when more second list trials were given, at least up to a point. When the intervening list was learned very well (40 trials), retroactive inhibition of the first list actually decreased again.

Degree of learning affects proactive inhibition in a similar way, as an extensive study of Postman and Riley (1959) has shown. Postman and Riley's subjects learned serial CVC lists for either 5, 10, 20, or 40 trials of original learning. Then a second list was learned, again for either 5, 10, 20, or 40 trials. After a 20-minute rest, subjects relearned the second list. The more trials subjects were given on the original list, the more proactive inhibition was produced, at least up to a point. This result agrees with the retroactive inhibition studies just mentioned: as interfering responses increase in strength, retention decreases. When second list learning was varied, a more complex relationship was found: with very low and very high degrees of second list learning, proactive inhibition was found, but not with 10 or 20 learning trials. The significance of this result is unclear. It might mean that at very high degrees of learning, factors other than interference among associations become important. Note, for instance, the reduction in interference which occurs when the interfering list is very well learned: if strength of association alone were the determining factor, this result would be quite inexplicable. Possibly high levels of learning result in a structure of the learning material which prevents it from interfering with other associations, as Mandler (1962) has argued.

Response meaningfulness, measured in any of the variety of ways that were discussed earlier, is another factor that must be considered in transfer studies. In general, increasing amounts of meaningfulness of the responses of the first list impede second list performance. An illustrative experiment is one by Merikle and Battig (1963). Merikle and Battig studied transfer in an A-B, A-D paradigm for three conditions of meaningfulness of the first list responses (B). Consonant trigrams were used as low-meaningful material, nonsense syllables as medium-meaningful material, and words as high-meaningful material. Although strong negative transfer was obtained with the high-meaningful material, none was observed with low-meaningful material, with the nonsense syllables providing intermediate results.

Stimulus meaningfulness also has important effects on transfer of training. Negative transfer is increased when highly meaningful stimuli are used, but little or no transfer occurs when low-meaningful stimuli are used. A relevant experiment was reported by Martin (1968). Martin used six-item, paired-associate lists, with either high-meaningful nonsense syllables or low-meaningful syllables as stimuli and the digits 1 to 6 as responses. Transfer was studied in an A-B, A-B$_r$ paradigm relative to an A-B, C-B control group. Learning to re-pair the old stimuli and the old responses was very difficult for the group that had the high-meaningful syllables as stimuli, but not for the group that had the low-meaningful stimuli.

When the similarity of learning conditions in general was varied experimentally, stable results were obtained, in agreement with the proposition that anything that helps to differentiate the general conditions of learning of the original list and of the interfering list reduces interference. Postman and Postman (1948) report a study in which four groups of subjects learned two paired-associate lists by the method of anticipation and were tested for recall of the first list after a 15-minute rest interval. Lists were made up either of compatible word pairs (*doctor-heal*) or incompatible word pairs (*war-peaceful*). For Group I both lists consisted of compatible word pairs, and for Group II only incompatible pairs were used. For Groups III and IV the original list and the interference list were not both of the same kind. The results showed better retention for the latter two groups. Bilodeau and Schlosberg (1951) demonstrated a similar effect. They had three groups of subjects learn a paired-associate list in a messy storeroom. Then one group learned a second list in the same storeroom, a second group was taken to a cardroom which was quite different in appearance for second list learning, and a control group did long division in the storeroom. This last group retained the first list best, but of more interest here is the fact that the subjects who learned the second list in a different environment showed less interference effects than the subjects who learned both lists in the same environment.

Many other studies could be described in this context. However, a continued accumulation of experimental results would only confuse the reader. Enough has been said to identify the principal experimental variables of interest. In order to understand how learning one list affects the learning of another list the following variables have been shown to be important: the similarity between the stimulus terms of the two lists; the similarity between the response terms of the lists; the meaningfulness of both the stimuli and the responses of the first list; and the degree of learning of the lists. All of these factors interact with each other, so that empirical relationships become quite complex. However, there is no need to abandon the effort to account for these complexities in some reasonably simple way. For instance, Martin (1965, 1968) has shown how some of the newer findings can be combined with the classical results of Osgood in quite a satisfactory manner. However, Martin's approach was theoretical rather than inductive, and will be discussed later. In fact, we shall return repeatedly in later chapters to aspects and portions of the rich mass of empirical results that have been described above. All theories of learning have something to say about transfer processes, and in discussing a particular theoretical problem it is often necessary to reconsider some of the empirical results that were mentioned here, thus permitting us to explore their meaning in a wider context.

## 1.6.2    NONSPECIFIC TRANSFER

Suppose a subject learns two unrelated lists in a verbal learning experiment. Frequently, he will find the second list easier to learn than the first, though this is not necessarily the case. If the lists are very long and very boring, he may be fatigued or lose his motivation to learn, and therefore perform more poorly on the second list. However, in general, subjects tend to get better as they gain more experience with learning lists in the laboratory. Two sources of nonspecific transfer have been identified: first there is a simple *warm-up* effect and secondly subjects learn how to learn. *Learning-to-learn* is an extremely important phenomenon. If subjects are given many lists to learn there may be continued improvement due to learning-to-learn, which poses some methodological problems in transfer experiments. As has been noted above, control groups in transfer experiments must be given experience with learning as many lists as experimental groups, otherwise there will be serious discrepancies between control and experimental subjects in their general learning facility.

Learning-to-learn has been studied in many experiments. An illustrative study is one by Postman and Schwartz (1964). These authors showed that the learning-to-learn effect is quite specific, and is maximized if the learning experience is with the same task and the same material as the criterion task. They trained subjects either with trigrams or adjectives, and with either a serial or a paired-associate task. Adjectives were used for the criterion task, which was paired-associate learning for half of the subjects and serial learning for the other half. Relative to a control group that learned only one adjective list, all experimental groups showed improvement. The biggest improvement occurred when the pretraining task and the criterion task were the same. Similarily, subjects pretrained on adjectives did better than subjects pretrained on trigrams on the criterion task, which, as will be remembered, involved adjectives. From this study, and others not reported here, one may conclude that subjects learn techniques of learning that, at least in part, are quite specific to the task and the learning material at hand.

## FORGETTING

This chapter has focused primarily on studies of learning, but one cannot understand learning without also asking questions about its counterpart, forgetting. Actually, the experimental study of forgetting processes has a long history: Ebbinghaus performed the classic experiments on this topic in 1885. Thus, these studies stand at the very beginning of the experimental psychology of learning and memory. Ebbinghaus estimated memory losses by means of a savings procedure. He learned a list of nonsense syllables, waited a certain number of hours, minutes, or days, and then relearned the list. The time that relearning took was compared with the original learning time, and the savings calculated in percent were used as estimates of retention. Figure 1.16 shows the forgetting curve that resulted from Ebbinghaus' pioneering work. The curve is negatively accelerated: most forgetting occurs during the first few hours after learning; after that the rate of forgetting decreases greatly.

At the time of this investigation, Ebbinghaus (who served as his one and only subject) was about 40 years old. Each day he learned 8 lists of 13 nonsense syllables to a criterion of two successive correct trials. Whenever he was conscious of an uncertainty or hesitation, a trial was not accepted as correct. The total time needed to learn the 8 lists was then compared with the relearning time after retention intervals ranging from 20 minutes to 31 days. During the course of the experiment, Ebbinghaus learned and relearned more than 1200 different lists. Ebbinghaus was a very careful worker and having noted that learning time depended on the time of the day (he was 12% slower around 7 p.m. than at 10 a.m.), he adjusted his results for diurnal variations. For instance, with an 8-hour retention interval, original learning and relearning necessarily had to be conducted at different times of the day.

Mathematically, Ebbinghaus' forgetting curve can be closely approximated by an exponential function

(4)                                    $$Y = ab^{-t}$$

where Y is a measure of the amount retained, a and b are constants,

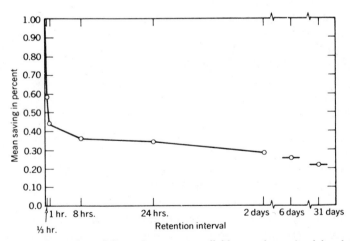

FIGURE 1.16  **Retention of lists of nonsense syllables as determined by the savings method. (after Ebbinghaus, 1885)**

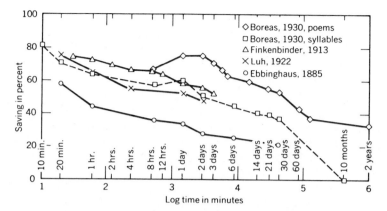

FIGURE 1.17  **Retention curves plotted on a logarithmic abscissa. The materials were nonsense syllable lists except for the uppermost curve. (after Woodworth and Schlosberg, 1961)**

and $t$ is the retention time. Taking logarithms of Eq. (4), we obtain

(5)  $$\log Y = \log a - t(\log b) = a_0 - a_1 t$$

such that $\log a = a_0$ and $\log b = a_1$. Equation (5) implies that amount retained in memory is linearly related to the logarithm of retention time. Hence, if plotted on semilogarithmic paper, the retention function should be a straight line. The slope of the line is determined by the constant $a_1$, while $a_0$ is the $Y$-intercept of the line. Figure 1.17 shows a plot of Ebbinghaus' data in semilogarithmic form. It is obvious that a straight line provides a fairly good description of the data points. In addition, the results of a number of other investigators are shown in Figure 1.17. With the exception of the uppermost curve, all other curves are based on memory for lists of nonsense syllables using the savings method. Ebbinghaus' original results are amply confirmed by these data. Straight lines can be fitted to all curves. The fact that these curves show somewhat better retention throughout seems to be the only difference between Ebbinghaus' data, based on one subject learning many different lists, and the other sets of data shown here, which give averages for groups of subjects learning a single list. The curve showing retention for poetry is the only one where memory does not decrease monotonically. However, these results are questionable since the experimenter did not exclude the possibility of voluntary or involuntary rehearsal during the interval between learning and retention test, as Woodworth and Schlosberg (1961) point out, from whom this figure has been taken.

Various other retention tests have provided similar results. Although estimates of the amount retained depend greatly on the exact testing procedure employed, the exponential shape of the forgetting curve seems to be quite independent of these factors. Thus, recognition tests tend to give much higher estimates of amount retained than recall tests. However, in both cases the typical negatively accelerated forgetting curve has been obtained. An interesting consequence of this shape of the forgetting curve is known under the name of "Jost's law" (Jost, 1897). When two associations are of equal strength but of different ages, the older one will lose strength more slowly with the further passage of time. If strength of an association is identified with the ordinate of Figure 1.16 and 1.17, the law follows, since a relatively old association will have reached a flatter part of the forgetting curve, while the newer association is still at a point of the curve where considerable forgetting occurs.

Many early experimenters believed disuse to be the primary cause of forgetting. However, what the subject does during the retention interval was soon shown to be a crucial factor in forgetting. Jenkins and Dallenbach (1924) demonstrated that if the subject sleeps during the retention interval forgetting is markedly reduced relative to a waking control group. In their study subjects learned a list of 10 CVCs and were tested for recall after 1, 2, 4, and 8 hours of ordinary waking activity or sleeping. For all retention intervals recall was much better after sleep. The effect was quite strong: for example, after 8 hours sleep about six syllables could be recalled, while after the same time spent awake only about one syllable was recalled. This and related findings prompted McGeoch to attack the view that disuse is a major factor in forgetting (McGeoch, 1932). He maintained that time per se has no effect, but that the events that occur in time are important. Iron does not rust because of the passage of time, but because of certain chemical reactions that take place in time; similarly, forgetting is not a passive decay process, but is determined by the environmental events occurring during the retention interval. New activity during the retention interval interferes with what has been learned before, thus producing forgetting. Memory would be perfect if the retention interval were completely devoid of activity.

The interference theory of forgetting, to be discussed in Chapter 2, originated from observations such as those reported above. Thus, this theory is a direct outgrowth of the work of Ebbinghaus and his followers. A characteristic of all this work is that it is concerned with rather long retention times. Forgetting is tested hours or even days after learning. Only recently have psychologists begun to study systematically much shorter retention periods. To their surprise, large amounts of forgetting were found over very brief time intervals—seconds, rather than the hours and days of Ebbinghaus. Furthermore, this forgetting is orderly and lawful. In fact, the shape of short-term forgetting functions is exponential, just like the long-term forgetting curves of Figure 1.17. Such data suggest taking another look at the learning process and trying to specify the role of short-term forgetting in learning.

Behavior changes in a learning experiment represent a balance between the processes of acquisition and forgetting. Immediately after presentation of a paired-associate item the probability of a correct response is close to unity, if certain precautions have been taken to insure adequate perception of the stimulus. Since in almost all verbal learning experiments perceptual conditions are very favorable, the question arises why learning is usually so slow, since directly after each item presentation items are always "learned." Similarly, if only one item were used in a paired-associate experiment it would practically always be learned in one trial; only with longer lists do subjects need many learning trials.

Such observations suggest that forgetting between presentation of an item and its test is an important factor in learning. Acquisition processes and memory interact to cause the trial-to-trial changes that are investigated in most verbal learning experiments. Acquisition (learning proper) depends on variables operating at the time of item presentation, or prior to it. Forgetting depends on conditions during the retention interval. One way to describe the performance changes during a learning experiment would be to say that items become more resistant to forgetting as learning proceeds. This does not mean that learning is nothing but increased resistance to intertrial forgetting, as there are other factors (e.g., stimulus encoding, subjective organization) that play an equally significant role in verbal learning.

The interaction between memory and acquisition processes in verbal learning has long been recognized (McGeoch, 1942), but has been regarded as little more than a truism. Only recently, stimulated by the findings of experiments on short-term memory, has its profound significance been appreciated.

Murdock (1963a) demonstrated the close relation between short-term memory experiments and paired-associate learning. In a short-term memory experiment, which also can be regarded as the first trial of a regular paired-associate study, subjects were presented with lists of common word pairs. After the presentation of each list, retention was tested by presenting the first member of each pair alone. The results are shown in Figure 1.18 for lists two to five pairs long. Strong forgetting effects are apparent: probability of recall is a decreasing function of the number of subsequent pairs in the list. The last item in each list, for which little opportunity for forgetting existed, was almost always "learned." The less than perfect performance for the last item might have been caused, at least partially, by Murdock's procedure, because in some instances recall tests of other items intervened between the presentation of the last item of a list and its test. In any case, subsequent list pairs clearly lead to much forgetting, although the effect seems to level off with about three intervening pairs in this experiment. Thus Figure 1.18 suggests two performance components: a short-term memory factor that is especially prominent when the retention interval is brief, and a second factor that accounts for the performance with longer retention intervals. This second factor seems to be independent of the number of subsequent list pairs, but is influenced by list length.

Tulving (1964) has also argued that some of the phenomena of learning and memory may be identical. He developed a method for the analysis of free-recall data which permits tracing the course of forgetting throughout a multitrial experiment. Instead of merely plotting the average number of correct responses or the number of incorrect responses per trial, Tulving distinguishes four (nonindependent)

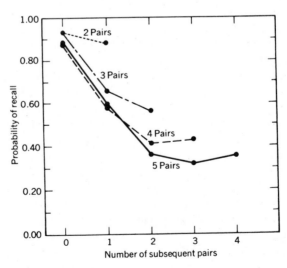

FIGURE 1.18    **Probability of recall for lists of 2–5 pairs. (after Murdock, 1963a)**

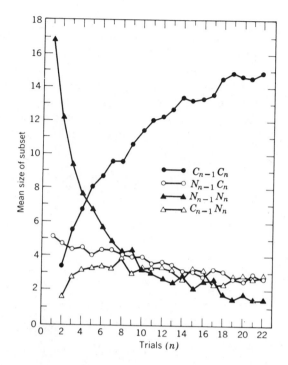

FIGURE 1.19  **Four different components of performance derived from trial-to-trial analysis of recall data. (after Tulving, 1964)**

categories of responses on each trial: recall of an item that was also recalled on the previous trial $(C_{n-1}C_n)$, recall of an item that was not recalled on the previous trial $(N_{n-1}C_n)$, nonrecall of an item that was recalled on the previous trial $(C_{n-1}N_n)$, and nonrecall on two successive trials $(N_{n-1}N_n)$. Data from an experiment in which subjects learned to recall a 22-word list are shown in Figure 1.19. The usual mean learning curve is the sum of two of the components from Figure 1.19, intertrial retention $(C_{n-1}C_n)$ plus intratrial retention $(N_{n-1}C_n)$. Of these, only the former shows an increase as a function of learning trials. Intratrial retention actually decreases. However, Tulving argues that this decrease is an experimental artifact caused by the fixed list length used in his experiment, and that without this restraint intratrial retention does not change over trials. The increase in intertrial retention was found to be correlated with a tendency of the subject to group the words in the recall list into higher order subjective units.

These results suggest two subprocesses of learning: intratrial forgetting or short-term memory processes and more long-term changes which have something to do with the subject's organization of the learning material. Chapters 4 and 5, respectively, will be devoted to the investigation of these processes. But first we shall turn our attention in Chapter II to learning theory; that is, to attempts to understand the kind of experimental data that were discussed in the present chapter, without necessarily giving explicit consideration to memory processes.

# 2
# learning theories

In the field of human learning, there are two comprehensive
theoretical systems that are important today: the interference theory
of forgetting, which goes back to the 1930s, and the stimulus sampling
theory of Estes from the 1950s. Neither of them now dominates the
field (as interference theory had done until about 1960), and neither is
universally accepted. In fact, neither is even a solid, unified system;
both are more like broad viewpoints within which specific problems
can be worked out. But both of these systems are still useful today,
apart from their historical significance. Interference mechanisms play
a crucial role in our conception of forgetting, and stimulus sampling
processes have aroused new interest in connection with the present
emphasis on encoding processes in memory. What is happening is
that modern cognitive, information processing approaches are beginning to absorb the learning theories of the past. We shall pay special
attention in later chapters to current developments within these
systems and the intertwining of learning theory and information
processing approaches, but first the two systems themselves must be
introduced, and a few comments need to be made about the neglect
of conditioning theories based on animal research in learning in this
book.

## CONDITIONING AND REINFORCEMENT IN HUMAN LEARNING

Historically, the psychology of learning has had two immediate roots. One is Ebbinghaus' book *On Memory* in 1885. Ebbinghaus is truly the "father of verbal learning." He introduced the nonsense syllable, the favorite stimulus material in verbal learning research for generations; he initiated the continuing concern with serial learning; and, finally, he gave verbal learning its theoretical base in associationism. There is no need to describe Ebbinghaus' contributions in more detail, because throughout this book we shall be dealing with work that grew out of this tradition, or we shall be struggling to relate developments from other sources to that tradition.

The second source from which most of the research on learning derives is Pavlov's work on conditioning (Pavlov, 1927; 1928). Like Ebbinghaus, Pavlov provided a whole subarea of psychology with its basic experimental methods and theoretical constructs. Much of animal learning can be regarded as a continuation and extension of Pavlov's work. The experimental paradigm that Pavlov introduced is today called *classical conditioning:* a stimulus that naturally elicits a certain response (as food elicits salivation) is paired with a neutral stimulus (e.g., a tone) which, through repeated pairings, comes to elicit the same response as the original stimulus, or a response very similar to it. The first stimulus-response pair is called the *unconditioned stimulus* (UCS) and the *unconditioned response* (UCR); the originally neutral stimulus is called the *conditioned stimulus* (CS); the CS evokes the *conditioned response,* or CR. A CS-UCS pairing constitutes a *reinforcement.* If reinforcement is withheld, i.e., if the CS is repeatedly presented alone, the CS loses its power to evoke the CR. This process is called *extinction.* If a stimulus that is similar to the CS, but not identical, is presented instead of the CS, the CR may still be evoked, but to a lesser degree and with a lesser probability; this is an instance of *generalization.* If two stimuli are presented to the organism, one of which is always followed by the UCS and one of which is never followed by the UCS, the CR will occur when the reinforced stimulus is presented, but not when the nonreinforced stimulus is presented; the organism is said to have acquired a *discrimination* as a result of such training. Conditioning, extinction, generalization, and discrimination were all first studied by Pavlov.

A second kind of conditioning must be distinguished from Pavlovian or classical conditioning. In this case there is no unconditioned stimulus present that can be used by the experimenter to elicit the to be learned response. Instead, the experimenter must wait for a spontaneous occurrence of that response, or some rudimentary version of it. Once the desired response has been emitted, the experimenter can reinforce it by presenting a reinforcing stimulus. The reinforcement increases the likelihood that the response will be repeated. The prototype for this kind of conditioning is given by a hungry rat learning to press a bar that delivers a food pellet as reinforcement. The main difference between classical conditioning and this kind of *instrumental* conditioning is operational: in the former case the experimenter can evoke the response that is to be conditioned through presentation of the UCS, while in instrumental conditioning this degree of control is not available. Otherwise, conditioning, extinction, generalization, and discrimination apply identically to both types of learning. Whether classical and instrumental, or *operant* conditioning, as it is frequently called, really represent two different types of learning is another question. The strongest evidence in favor of distinguishing two different types of learning is that some responses (e.g., visceral responses) can be conditioned classically, but not instrumentally, though this claim has been disputed.

Whatever their position regarding the two types of learning, learning theorists in the past have been primarily concerned with the concept of *reinforcement* (Tolman, 1932; Guthrie, 1935; Skinner, 1938; Hull, 1943; Premack, 1965). Different investigators agree quite well what a reinforcement is at the empirical level, but formal definitions and explanations depend on the theoretical position of the experimenter. The "law of effect," as it was first formulated by Thorndike in 1931, maintains that a response is strengthened if it is followed by satisfying consequences and weakened if it is followed by dissatisfying consequences. The law of effect has since undergone numerous revisions: For Hull, drive reduction was central to the problem of reinforcement; Skinner emphasized the reinforcing properties of stimuli; Premack has argued that the more frequent responses reinforce less frequent ones. We need not be concerned with the theoretical controversies that surround the law of effect. Common to all notions of reinforcement is the idea that reinforcement has a direct and automatic strengthening effect on a response. And many learning studies have been concerned with behavior changes occurring as a consequence of reinforcement. However, reinforcement seems to be primarily a matter of motivation, rather than learning, and for that reason studies concerned with reinforcement are not directly relevant to the psychology of human learning.

To make clear what is at issue here, let us compare in detail the experimental procedures of verbal learning and animal conditioning.

Their similarity is best illustrated by comparing the classical conditioning paradigm with paired-associate learning. In paired-associate learning an item (say, a word) is connected with an arbitrary response (say, a digit). The stimulus is presented first and the subject is given an opportunity to anticipate the response item. This is followed by a joint presentation of the stimulus-response pair, which serves as a reinforcement for the subject's response. The parallel between paired-associate learning and classical conditioning is obvious: in both cases a previously neutral stimulus comes to evoke a new response as a consequence of repeated CS-UCS pairings. However, this parallelism is based on superficial features of the two experimental paradigms and is quite misleading. A reinforcement in paired-associate learning, as defined above, does not directly strengthen the stimulus-response connection according to the law of effect. Rather, it serves as an occasion for the subject to acquire information about the association that is to be learned, and thereby determines the subject's future behavior. This viewpoint is, of course, entirely in disagreement with Thorndike (1931), as well as with many explicit and implicit beliefs long held by researchers in verbal learning. However, the evidence supporting it is quite convincing. In reviewing this problem Estes (1967) has concluded that the evidence upon which Thorndike had based his law of effect was not convincing. Thorndike himself was quite aware that there were alternative interpretations of reinforcement in terms of providing information about the environment. He called it the "representational" or "ideational" theory, but rejected it for a number of reasons. The strongest of these was based on an experimental demonstration of the greater effectiveness of saying "right" after a response than saying "wrong." Estes showed, however, that Thorndike's data were not conclusive and that therefore his reasons for rejecting the informational interpretation of reinforcement were insufficient.

Estes furthermore argued that the law of effect is actually wrong and that reinforcement in human learning does not consist in an automatic strengthening effect of rewards (or a complementary effect of punishment). The argument is based on a comparison of the effects of amount of reinforcement and delay of reinforcement in human learning and in conditioning studies. Numerous studies have shown that magnitude of reward is positively related to learning rate in animal experiments and that as the delay of reward increases (beyond a certain point) learning is inhibited. These are some of the best established findings in animal learning (e.g., Kimble, 1961). Yet, these variables have no comparable effects in human learning experiments.

In order to understand the latter, one must analyze each experiment in terms of the manner in which the subjects treat the relevant information, rather than in terms of an automatic strengthening effect of increases in the amount of reward, or automatic inhibitory effects of delay.

Arguments like those above have convinced most investigators in the field of human learning that the concept of reinforcement is not a very useful theoretical construct, at least in the way Thorndike originally proposed it. Indeed, some go so far as to question the evidence for conditioning in adult humans altogether (e.g., Brewer, 1974). Therefore, we shall not give any further consideration to reinforcement theories or to the bulk of the work on animal learning. Nevertheless, out of this conditioning viewpoint have developed some of the most influential current theories of human learning. These theories started out as conditioning theories—in the spirit of their times—but have developed more and more into cognitive, information processing theories as the field of human learning developed during the last decades. Today, they provide the classical interpretations of human learning which we need to study, if for no other reason, as a backdrop for the more current work. The first case in point is stimulus sampling theory.

## 2.2    STIMULUS SAMPLING THEORY

Stimulus sampling theory (Estes, 1950; Neimark and Estes, 1967) is a supertheory in the sense that it specifies a set of basic terms and procedures that are to be applied to specific problems. It is really a collection of miniature models, just as the other comprehensive learning theories are today, except that it is formulated mathematically so that it can be stated more precisely than other approaches.

On a continuum from strict behaviorism to information processing models stimulus-sampling theory falls somewhere in between. Its basic terms are stimulus, response, and reinforcement, and thus it is an S-R theory. On the other hand, it contains some features of information processing models. It is not necessary in stimulus-sampling theory that responses be directly determined by S-R connections, but S-R connections may be treated as "information" upon which the subject may base his response. Thus stimulus-sampling theory may be well suited to form a bridge between the divergent approaches that characterize the field of learning today—especially because it is stated in precise mathematical language, making it possible to separate the really substantial issues from those that merely reflect the semantic difficulties of translating one theoretical language into another.

The basic assumptions of the theory are quite simple. Consider what the subject is doing in a learning experiment. On each trial he perceives a certain experimental situation, and on the basis of what he perceives he makes his response. The response is followed by some sort of feedback from the experimenter, which may change the way in which the subject will perceive the experimental situation on further trials. For instance, the feedback may inform the subject that for the stimulus item presented on that trial his response was incorrect, and therefore the subject will try something else when that item comes up again, if he can still remember it. This common sense description of an experiment is readily translated into the terminology of stimulus sampling theory. The experimental situation as the subject perceives it, that is, primarily the learning item that appears on a particular trial but also other aspects of the environment, is represented in the theory by a set of stimuli $\{S\}$. Let us suppose there are $N$ stimulus elements in this set. It is not necessary to be specific about precisely what corresponds to these $N$ elements in the experiment; we merely, by assumption, postulate that the experimental situation is to be represented by $N$ (hypothetical) stimulus elements. The subject perceives some of these elements on each learning trial; in theoretical terms, we say that the subject samples a subset of the $N$ elements. We have to be specific, however, and state precisely how elements are sampled. Therefore, let us assume that each element of $S$ may be sampled with a certain probability $\theta$, independently of what happens to other elements. Thus the sampling of elements is like picking balls out of an urn, with a fixed probability. On each trial there will be some variation in the number of elements sampled, but on the average this number will be $\theta N$. Furthermore, a different subset of elements will be sampled on each trial.

We now have our subject at the point where he has perceived the experimental situation on a trial, that is he has sampled a subset of stimulus elements. On the basis of these elements he now must make a response. Suppose that there is a correct response and a class of incorrect responses and that each element in the set $S$ is connected to exactly one of these responses. We can then state the following response rule for our subject: his probability of selecting a particular response should be the same as the proportion of elements in the sample that are connected to that response.

After the subject made his response the experimenter identifies which response was the correct one on that trial. The effect of this feedback is to connect all stimulus items that were sampled on that trial to the correct response. In common sense terms, this means that the subject learns which response is the correct one, given the particular perceptual situation occurring on that trial. We want to leave open the possibility that the experimenter's feedback might be ineffective (e.g., the subject pays no attention on that trial, or forgets before the next trial), and so we introduce another parameter $c$, the probability that a sampled element actually becomes connected with the correct response after the experimenter's feedback on a trial.

An illustrative example of this process is diagrammed in Figure 2.1. Suppose $S$ contains 15 elements, 5 of which are connected to the correct response (call it $R_1$) on trial $n$, and 10 are connected to incorrect responses ($R_2$). Further suppose that the sampling probability equals .2 for each element, i.e., $\theta = .2$. The possible outcomes of the sampling process are then that either 0, 1, 2, . . . , 15 elements may be sampled on a trial, with the probability of each outcome given simply by the binomial distribution. In Figure 2.1 we have shown the case where 3 stimulus elements have been sampled, which occurs with probability

(1)      $P(3 \text{ elements from } 15; \theta = .2) = \binom{15}{3} .2^3 .8^{12} = .2501$

In our example we have assumed that of the 3 elements sampled 2 are connected to the correct response and 1 to the incorrect response. Given the composition of the stimulus set $S$, this is not the most likely event, but it may happen, and we can easily calculate its probability as

(2)    $P(\text{sampling 2 correct, 1 incorrect out of 3}) = \dfrac{\binom{5}{2}\binom{10}{1}}{\binom{15}{3}} = .2198$

Given this sample, the subject's response probability is easily calculated as $P(\text{correct}) = \frac{2}{3}$, $P(\text{incorrect}) = \frac{1}{3}$. The experimenter's information that $R_1$ was correct on that trial then changes the one stimulus element in the sample that was connected to $R_2$ to $R_1$ with probability $c$. In Figure 2.1 we have assumed that $c = 1$, so that at the end of trial $n$ the composition of $S$ has changed as shown: now 6 of the stimulus elements are connected to $R_1$, and hence the overall likelihood of that response increases somewhat on the next trial.

The description of stimulus-sampling theory just given is merely an illustration. There are many possible variations on this scheme of sampling-plus-connection, each one leading to a slightly different

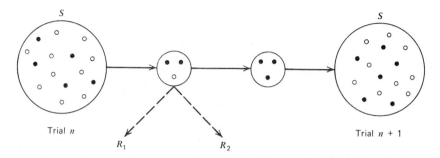

FIGURE 2.1   An illustration of stimulus sampling theory. The stimulus set $S$ contains 15 elements, 5 (filled circles) connected to $R_1$, 10 (open circles) to $R_2$. It is assumed that $R_1$ was called correct by the experimenter on trial $n$.

model with features adaptable to various experimental requirements. It is, for instance, possible to change the assumption made above that each element of the stimulus set $S$ is sampled with equal probability, and postulate that on each trial the subject draws a random sample of a fixed size $s$; in this way calculations such as Eq. (1) to determine sample size are no longer required. Or, one can make special assumptions about $N$, the number of elements in the stimulus set. The most interesting ones are to assume the extremes, $N \to \infty$, and $N = 1$. If $N$ is allowed to approach infinity, the theory becomes formally equivalent to the linear model of Bush and Mosteller (1956; Estes and Suppes, 1959), where learning is viewed as the gradual strengthening of a stimulus-response connection. If, on the other hand, the assumption is made that the whole stimulus situation can be represented by one single stimulus element—Estes calls it a stimulus pattern—then learning becomes an all-or-none process, depending on whether this single stimulus pattern is or is not connected to the correct response. This is not the place to describe the various versions of stimulus sampling theory and their uses in detail. Excellent technical discussions are available to the serious student (e.g., Atkinson and Estes, 1963). Instead, we shall take a closer look at the question suggested above, whether learning should be regarded as continuous and incremental, or all-or-none, and then describe a few applications of the theory that illustrate both its strengths and weaknesses.

## LEARNING: DISCRETE STATES OR CONTINUOUS INCREMENTS?

Traditionally, learning has been regarded as a process of gradual improvement. Stimulus-sampling theory, however, makes one wonder whether traditional wisdom is indeed correct in this case. Furthermore, the theory also provides the necessary techniques to investigate the problem. It will turn out that the question as stated here is a bad one, in the sense that it is impossible to decide experimentally whether learning is discrete or incremental, because for every discrete learning model one can always generate a continuous counterpart, and vice versa. Nevertheless, this question without an ultimate answer has fundamentally changed our whole view of the learning process, and it has immeasurably enriched the analytic procedures used in the study of learning.

Clearly, anyone who wants to observe all-or-none learning must look only at very simple learning processes. If we consider paired-associate learning it is surely necessary that the task be strictly one of learning to associate stimulus and response item, and that other subtasks frequently found in paired-associate experiments, such as response learning or stimulus discrmination, must be avoided. We shall see later on how models that assume discrete learning states can be extended to more complex, multiprocess learning tasks, but let us first of all consider the issue in its simplest terms.

The discussion to follow will be much clearer if the reader who is not familiar with the general approach described here takes a few minutes to look at some sample paired-associate data, the way they are coded, and the kind of summary statistics that are calculated from them.

The results from a paired-associate learning experiment are shown for one subject in Table 2.1. In this experiment subjects learned a 10-item list by the method of anticipation. The nonsense syllables that served as stimuli are shown in the table. Only two response alternatives were used ($A$ and $B$). During a 3-second anticipation interval the stimulus syllable was shown on a memory drum and the subject responded with either $A$ or $B$. The subject was instructed to guess if necessary. The stimulus-response pair was presented jointly for 2 seconds. The items were presented in a new random order on every trial. The intertrial interval was 30 seconds. Learning continued until a criterion of two successive correct trials was reached. The subject's responses were recorded only as correct (0) or incorrect (1).

The second part of Table 2.1 shows a number of typical data statistics that may be used to evaluate the adequacy of a theory. Most of these are frequency distributions of one sort or other; for example, in Table 2.1(a) the distribution of the number of errors per item is shown. For each item, either 0, 1, 2, . . . errors occur. Table 2.1(a) is simply a count of the number of items in the data for which exactly 0, 1, 2, . . . errors occurred. Thus, in the sample data shown here, on exactly two items (LAM-*A* and PEB-*B*) the subject made one error. It is often convenient to summarize the information contained in a frequency distribution such as Table 2.1(a). The most important summary

TABLE 2.1.   **The Performance Record of One Subject Learning a 10-Item Paired Associate List to a Criterion of Two Successive Correct Trials and Some Common Statistical Analyses of the Data. Correct Responses are Denoted by 0 and Errors by 1.**

| Items | 1 | 2 | 3 | 4 | 5 | 6 | 7 | 8 | 9 | 10 | 11 | 12 | Total Errors |
|---|---|---|---|---|---|---|---|---|---|---|---|---|---|
| MUC-*A* | 0 | 0 | 0 | 0 | 0 | 0 | 0 | 0 | 0 | 0 | 0 | 0 | 0 |
| WAV-*B* | 1 | 0 | 1 | 1 | 1 | 0 | 0 | 0 | 0 | 0 | 0 | 0 | 4 |
| CID-*B* | 0 | 1 | 1 | 0 | 0 | 0 | 1 | 0 | 1 | 0 | 0 | 0 | 4 |
| LAM-*A* | 1 | 0 | 0 | 0 | 0 | 0 | 0 | 0 | 0 | 0 | 0 | 0 | 1 |
| KOL-*A* | 0 | 1 | 0 | 1 | 0 | 1 | 1 | 0 | 0 | 0 | 0 | 0 | 4 |
| DOR-*B* | 0 | 0 | 0 | 0 | 0 | 0 | 0 | 0 | 0 | 0 | 0 | 0 | 0 |
| NAZ-*B* | 1 | 0 | 1 | 0 | 0 | 0 | 0 | 0 | 0 | 0 | 0 | 0 | 2 |
| PEB-*B* | 0 | 1 | 0 | 0 | 0 | 0 | 0 | 0 | 0 | 0 | 0 | 0 | 1 |
| HIG-*A* | 0 | 0 | 0 | 0 | 0 | 0 | 0 | 0 | 0 | 0 | 0 | 0 | 0 |
| VEL-*A* | 1 | 1 | 0 | 0 | 0 | 0 | 0 | 0 | 0 | 0 | 0 | 0 | 2 |
| Total errors | 4 | 4 | 3 | 2 | 1 | 1 | 2 | 0 | 1 | 0 | 0 | 0 | 18 |
| Proportion of errors | .4 | .4 | .3 | .2 | .1 | .1 | .2 | 0 | .1 | 0 | 0 | 0 | |

(a)   *Distribution of number of errors per item.*

| Number of errors per item: $k$ | Frequency: $f(k)$ | Proportion: $p(k)$ |
|---|---|---|
| 0 | 3 | .3 |
| 1 | 2 | .2 |
| 2 | 2 | .2 |
| 3 | 0 | 0 |
| 4 | 3 | .3 |
| | 10 | 1.0 |

Mean number of errors per item: $M(k) = \dfrac{\sum k\, f(k)}{\sum f(k)} = \dfrac{18}{10} = 1.8$

Standard deviation: $s(k) = \dfrac{\sum (k - M(k))^2 f(k)}{\sum f(k)} = 1.7$

TABLE 2.1 **(Continued)**

**(b)** *Distribution of the number of errors before the first success.*

| Number of errors before the first success: $j$ | Frequency: $f(j)$ | Proportion: $p(j)$ |
|---|---|---|
| 0 | 6 | .6 |
| 1 | 3 | .3 |
| 2 | 1 | .1 |
| | 10 | 1.0 |

Mean number of trials before the first success: $M(j) = .5$
Standard deviation: $s(j) = .7$

**(c)** *Distribution of trial of last error.*

| Trial of last error: $n$ | Frequency: $f(n)$ | Proportion: $p(n)$ |
|---|---|---|
| 0 | 3 | .3 |
| 1 | 1 | .1 |
| 2 | 2 | .2 |
| 3 | 1 | .1 |
| 4 | 0 | 0 |
| 5 | 1 | .1 |
| 6 | 0 | 0 |
| 7 | 1 | .1 |
| 8 | 0 | 0 |
| 9 | 1 | .1 |
| | 10 | 1.0 |

Mean trial of last error: $M(n) = 2.9$
Standard deviation: $s(n) = 3.1$

**(d)** *Distribution of error runs of length i.*

| Error runs of length $i$ | Frequency | Number of runs per item |
|---|---|---|
| 1 | 9 | .9 |
| 2 | 3 | .3 |
| 3 | 1 | .1 |
| | 13 | |

Total number of runs per item: $R = 1.3$

statistics are the mean, or average, and the standard deviation of the frequency distribution. Calculational formulas for both statistics are shown in the table. The interpretation of the other parts of Table 2.1 is generally obvious, but readers who are not familiar with the methods of data analysis described here should make sure that they understand how each statistic has been calculated from the sample data. The examples shown here, of course, are not exhaustive; for instance, we could find the distribution of the number of errors between the first and second successes, or any other pair, or we could look at some sequential statistics, like the number of times an error is followed by an error $k$ trials later, without regard to intervening responses, which is the so-called autocorrelation of errors $k$ trials apart. Some other sequential statistics that play an important role in evaluating the goodness of fit of a model will be introduced below.

A model built upon the assumption that learning is an incremental process is called the *linear model*. The alternative assumption that learning is a discrete process may be embodied in a *two-state Markov* model. Both models will be described here and differential testable implications will be derived.

In the simple linear model (Bush and Mosteller, 1955) learning is viewed as a continuous process. On each trial $n$ the probability of the correct response $(q_n)$ changes. It starts from some guessing level $g_1$ at the beginning of the experiment and increases to an asymptote of 1. Since in the paired-associate learning experiments to be discussed here reinforcement occurs on every trial (i.e, the stimulus-response pair is shown to the subject on every trial), every trial has the same effect, i.e., the same operator can be applied to the response probability on every trial. As the name of the model implies, this operator is linear: the response probability on trial $n$ is related to the response probability on the next trial by a linear equation. Because of the restriction that the same operator be applied on all trials the model is called the single-operator linear model. The formal statement of the model is very brief:

**Definitions.**    For a single subject and item there exists a probability $q_n$ that the subject will give a correct response on trial $n$. The presentation of the stimulus-response pair constitutes a reinforcement. The response probability on the first trial is $q_1$.

**Learning Axiom:**    When a reinforcement occurs on trial $n$

(3)                         $$q_{n+1} = q_n + (1 - q_n)\,\theta$$

The linear model generates a sequence of response probabilities $q_1$, $q_2, q_3, \ldots, q_n, \ldots$ that increase continuously. Errors become more and more rare as learning proceeds, but there is no state in which errors are impossible. As a sample derivation, the mean number of errors per trial, i.e., the mean learning curve, will be derived from Eq. (3). Let $p_n$ denote the probability of an error on trial $n$; since the probability of an error and of a success on a trial must sum to 1, we have $p_n = 1 - q_n$. Multiplying Eq. (3) by $(-1)$ and adding 1 to each side we obtain

$$1 - q_{n+1} = 1 - q_n (1 - q_n) \theta$$

Substituting $p$ for $1 - q_n$

(4) $$p_{n+1} = p_n(1 - \theta)$$

The mean learning curve can now be obtained by induction; start with $p_1$ and apply Eq. (4) repeatedly to compute successive $p$-terms and see what pattern emerges:

$$p_2 = p_1 (1 - \theta)$$
$$p_3 = p_2 (1 - \theta) = p_1 (1 - \theta)^2$$
$$p_4 = p_3 (1 - \theta) = p_1 (1 - \theta)^3$$

$$\begin{array}{cc} \cdot & \cdot \\ \cdot & \cdot \\ \cdot & \cdot \end{array}$$

(5) $$p_n = p_1 (1 - \theta)^{n-1}$$

The correctness of this conjecture can be verified by resubstitution into Eq. (4). Many other statistics could be derived for this model, but this one example will do for the moment.

The assumption that learning is all-or-none naturally leads to a two-state Markov model (Bower, 1961). Basically, the model assumes that an item can be in either one of two states: it is learned or it is not learned. On each learning trial there is a certain probability $c$ that the item becomes learned, i.e., it leaves the initial state and enters the learning state. There is no provision for forgetting in this simple model (nor is there in the previous model); once an item is in the learning state, it remains there. If an item is in the learning state, a correct response occurs; if an item is in the initial state, a correct response occurs with probability $(1 - p)$ and an error occurs with probability $p$. The learning rate $c$ and the probability of an error in the initial state $p$ do not change over trials.

The axioms of the model may be stated formally as follows:

1.  **State Axiom.** On each trial an item is either in the initial state I or in the learning state L.
2.  **Learning Axioms.** On trial 1 all items are in state I. Whenever a stimulus-response pair is presented jointly, the item may become connected to that response with probability $c$, i.e., it enters the learning state L. L is an absorbing state, that is, an item remains in L once it enters it.
3.  **Response Axioms.** If an item is in state L the correct response is always made; if it is in state I, errors occur with probability $p$ and successes with probability $(1 - p)$.
4.  **Constancy Axiom.** $p$ and $c$ are independent of the trial number $n$.

It is convenient to express these axioms in the form of a *transition matrix*. The rows of this matrix correspond to states L and I on trial $n$, the columns to the same states on trial $(n + 1)$; entries show the probability of a transition from the row state to the column state on any trial:

$$(6) \qquad \begin{array}{cc} & \begin{array}{ccc} L & I & P\text{ (error)} \end{array} \\ \begin{array}{c} L \\ I \end{array} & \begin{bmatrix} 1 & 0 \\ c & 1-c \end{bmatrix} \begin{bmatrix} 0 \\ p \end{bmatrix} \end{array}$$

A *starting vector* $[0,1]$ provides the information that items start with probability 1 in state I. Equation (6) is to be read as follows: the first row says that if an item is in L, it will always remain in L; the probability of an error on that trial is 0; if an item is in I, it will go to L with probability $c$ and stay in I with probability $(1 - c)$; the probability of an error in I is $p$.

This model is called a Markov model because, in general, processes are called Markovian if they have discrete states and transition probabilities between these states that depend only on the state in which the process is at the moment.

In order to derive the predicted mean learning curve from this model, note that an error can occur on trial $n$ only if the item is still in state I on that trial. The probability that an item does not leave state I on a trial is $(1 - c)$, the probability that it is not learned on that trial. Hence the probability that an item is still in State I after $(n - 1)$ trials is $(1 - c)$ taken $(n - 1)$ times, or $(1 - c)^{n-1}$. If an item is in I, an error occurs with probability $p$. Hence the mean learning curve is given by

$$(7) \qquad P(\text{error on trial } n) = p(1 - c)^{n-1}$$

Equation (7) is identical with Eq. (5), the mean learning curve for the linear model. This simply means that as far as the distinction between incremental and all-or-none processes is concerned, mean learning curves are worthless. They do not differentiate between alternatives.

The models are clearly distinct with respect to behavior on trials before the last error. According to the two-state Markov model, errors occur only in the initial state I; hence at least up to and including the trial of the last error an item must have been in state I. (It is impossible that an item may have left I and later returned: once state I has been left, return is impossible according to the model.) The important point now is that in state I the probability of an error is constant and does not depend on the trial number. Thus, the all-or-none model predicts no improvement in response probability up to the trial of the last error. This prediction is called the *stationarity* prediction. According to the linear model, performance on trials before the last error is not stationary, since response probability rises continuously on every trial, and there is nothing special about the last error in any particular response sequence.

How can one test the stationarity prediction? The most obvious procedure would be to look at each item sequence separately and to determine whether response probability on trials before the last error is indeed a constant or not. However, in paired-associate learning typically only a few errors are made for each item; therefore not enough data are available from a single item to provide a serious test of the stationarity hypothesis. Thus, we depend on proper averaging responses from many items but omitting the last error and all later responses, as shown in Table 2.2(a). If precriterion performance is stationary, no incremental trend should be present in data thus averaged. Alternatively, one can use the trial of the last error as a reference point to construct a backward learning curve, as shown in Table 2.2(b). The portion of the curve to the right of the last error is of course entirely an artifact of the averaging method employed, but stationarity may be examined on the trials before the last error. Suppes and Ginsberg (1963) have pointed to a possible source of confounding in this way of plotting learning curves. In a plot such as the one shown in Table 2.2(a) the number of data points upon which successive points are based decreases as more and more items are learned and are therefore omitted from the calculations. The last points of the curve are based on those items that were learned last, i.e., the hardest items. It is conceivable that the later portions of the curve are depressed because they are based on the most difficult items, and that therefore any incremental trends in the data are masked by this effect.

The backward leaning curve is similarly confounded with item difficulty. Suppes and Ginsberg (1963) have suggested the construction of Vincent curves to avoid this confounding. In a Vincent curve each learning sequence contributes equally to each point of the curve irrespective of the length of the sequence. For instance, short sequences such as those obtained in paired-associate experiments may be divided into halves, and the number of errors and successes in each half may be counted and averaged over all sequences. Thus, each sequence contributes equally to both points of the Vincent curve. If sequences of sufficient length are available, they may be partitioned into 3, 4, or even 10 equal parts to yield Vincent curves of 3, 4, or 10 points, respectively. A chi-square test can be employed to test the hypothesis that the proportion of errors is the same for all points of the curve. The sample data of Table 2.1 are Vincentized into halves in Part (c) of Table 2.2.

In an experiment by Kintsch (1965) 32 subjects (college students) learned a list of 10 paired-associate items to a criterion of 2 errorless trials. Stimuli were high association value nonsense syllables, and the numbers 1 and 2 served as responses. The anticipation procedure was used. The average number of errors per item for all items and for only those items for which the last error had not yet occurred are shown in Figure 2.2. It does not show the regular decrease of the mean learning

TABLE 2.2.  **An Analysis of the Trials before the Last Error for the Data of Table 2.1.**

(a)  *Performance on trials before the last error.*

| Items | 1 | 2 | 3 | 4 | 5 | 6 | 7 | 8 | 9 | 10 | 11 | 12 |
|---|---|---|---|---|---|---|---|---|---|---|---|---|
| 1 | | | | | | | | | | | | |
| 2 | 1 | 0 | 1 | 1 | | | | | | | | |
| 3 | 0 | 1 | 1 | 0 | 0 | 0 | 1 | 0 | | | | |
| 4 | | | | | | | | | | | | |
| 5 | 0 | 1 | 0 | 1 | 0 | 1 | | | | | | |
| 6 | | | | | | | | | | | | |
| 7 | 1 | 0 | | | | | | | | | | |
| 8 | 0 | | | | | | | | | | | |
| 9 | | | | | | | | | | | | |
| 10 | 1 | | | | | | | | | | | |
| Frequency of errors | 3 | 2 | 2 | 2 | 0 | 1 | 1 | 0 | | | | |
| Total frequency | 6 | 4 | 3 | 3 | 2 | 2 | 1 | 1 | | | | |
| Proportion of errors | .50 | .50 | .66 | .66 | .00 | .50 | 1.00 | .00 | | | | |

TABLE 2.2  **(Continued)**

(b)  *The backward learning curve. Trials before the last error.*

| Items | -9 | -8 | -7 | -6 | -5 | -4 | -3 | -2 | -1 | Last Error |
|---|---|---|---|---|---|---|---|---|---|---|
| 1 | | | | | | | | | | |
| 2 | | | | | | 1 | 0 | 1 | 1 | 1 |
| 3 | | 0 | 1 | 1 | 0 | 0 | 0 | 1 | 0 | 1 |
| 4 | | | | | | | | | | |
| 5 | | | | 0 | 1 | 0 | 1 | 0 | 1 | 1 |
| 6 | | | | | | | | | | |
| 7 | | | | | | | | 1 | 0 | 1 |
| 8 | | | | | | | | | 0 | 1 |
| 9 | | | | | | | | | | |
| 10 | | | | | | | | | 1 | 1 |
| Frequency of errors | 0 | 1 | 1 | 1 | 1 | 1 | 3 | 3 | | |
| Total frequency | 1 | 1 | 2 | 2 | 3 | 3 | 4 | 6 | | |
| Proportion of errors | .00 | 1.00 | .50 | .50 | .33 | .33 | .75 | .50 | | |

(c)  *The Vincent curve.*

| Items | First Half | | | | Second Half | | | |
|---|---|---|---|---|---|---|---|---|
| 2 | | 1 | 0 | | | 1 | 1 | |
| 3 | 0 | 1 | 1 | 0 | 0 | 0 | 1 | 0 |
| 5 | | 0 | 1 | 0 | | 1 | 0 | 1 |
| 7 | | 1 | | | | 0 | | |
| Frequency of errors | | 5 | | | | 5 | | |
| Total frequency | | 10 | | | | 10 | | |
| Proportion of errors | | .50 | | | | .50 | | |

curve but fluctuates around a line somewhat below ½. The deviations from this line are not statistically significant ($x^2 = 4.68$, 5 *df*, $p > .30$). When the responses before the last error were divided into equal halves, values of .50 and .47 were obtained for the first and second half of the trials, respectively. With a chi-square of .53 for 1 *df*, these values are not significantly different from each other. The conclusion is therefore justified that in this experiment learning was not an incremental process, but occurred in an all-or-none manner.

A number of experiments in the literature support this conclusion since the all-or-none model was first applied to paired-associate learning by Bower (1961, 1962). However, stationarity is observed only when the experiment is of the particularly simple type described here, that is, the stimuli are easily discriminable and, most importantly, there are only two response alternatives and the subject is told what they are.

Another prediction of the all-or-none model that may be easily examined also concerns performance on the trials before the last error. On those trials, an item is in the initial state I, and, according to the assumptions of the model, correct responses in this state occur with probability $(1 - p)$, whereas errors are made with probability $p$. Responses on successive trials are assumed to be independent, just as if they were determined by tosses of a biased coin which comes up "correct" with probability $(1 - p)$. More specifically, the conditional probability of a correct response on any trial $n$ given an error on the previous trial $(n - 1)$ should be equal to the conditional probability of a correct response on trial $n$ given a correct response on trial $(n - 1)$. Table 2.3 illustrates these calculations for the sample data provided earlier, the two desired statistics being 6/8 and 2/8, respectively. In the experiment mentioned above we obtain $P(0_{n+1} \mid 1_n) = .50$ and $P(0_{n+1} \mid 0_n) = .61$, where 0's and 1's denote correct responses and errors respectively. A statistical test shows that these two values are significantly different. Precriterion responses are therefore not independent, but successes tend to follow successes. This failure of the

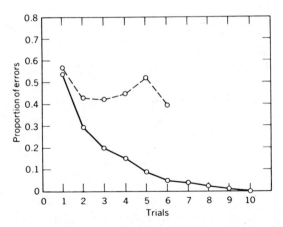

FIGURE 2.2  **Proportion of errors on all trials (solid line) and proportion of errors on trials before the last error (dashed line).**

TABLE 2.3 **Frequency of Successes and Errors after Successes and Errors on the Previous Trials for Trials up to the Last Error**

|         |   | Trial $n + 1$ | |   |
|---------|---|:---:|:---:|:---:|
|         |   | 0 | 1 |   |
| Trial $n$ | 0 | 2 | 6 | 8 |
|         | 1 | 6 | 2 | 8 |
|         |   | 8 | 8 | 16 |

model need not deter us from further analysis. It is hardly likely that a model as simple as the present one can give a completely satisfactory account of paired-associate learning, but before one can make the model more realistic it is necessary to determine how far its simplest version can be pushed and exactly where it breaks down.

Bower (1961) has derived many quantitative predictions from the simple all-or-none model for statistics such as the mean learning curve, the total number of errors per item, and others discussed above. Using only elementary probability theory, it is quite easy to derive theoretical expressions for all of the statistics calculated in Table 2.1 in terms of the parameters $c$ and $p$. (For details see Atkinson, Bower, and Crothers, 1965; Greeno, 1968; or Restle and Greeno, 1970). Values for these parameters can then be estimated. In experiments where there are two responses, $p$ obviously should equal ½. Various estimates of $c$ are possible, but in any case part of the data must be used to determine what the value of $c$ is in a particular experiment. A convenient procedure is to estimate $c$ by equating the theoretical expression for the expected number of errors per item in the experiment with the number of errors actually observed and solving for $c$. The required theoretical expression can easily be calculated. Eq. (7) gives the probability, of an error on trial $n$; if one sums (7) from $n = 1$ to $n \rightarrow \infty$, an expression for the total number of errors in the experiment can be obtained:

$$(8) \qquad E(\text{errors per item}) = \sum_{n=1}^{\infty} P(\text{error on trial } n)$$

$$= \sum_{n=1}^{\infty} p(1 - c)^{n-1} = \frac{p}{c}$$

Note that the summation above is taken over all values of $n$, while in any actual experiment only a finite number of trials can be given. However, once an item enters the learning state L no more errors occur and we assume that our learning criterion is sufficiently strict so that when a subject reaches criterion all items are in L. In the Kintsch (1965) experiment already mentioned, 1.39 errors were made per item on the average, hence

$$1.39 = \frac{p}{c} = \frac{.5}{c}$$

and

$$\hat{c} = .35.$$

By using these estimates of $p$ and $c$ in the expressions derived by Bower (1961), one can calculate numerous precise theoretical predictions and compare them with the experimentally obtained statistics. Several investigators have demonstrated that these predictions fit the data extremely well. One can safely claim that if the data are stable enough (that is, based on a sufficient number of observations), and the task is the simple kind of paired-associate learning described, the data and predictions will fall right on top of each other, and summary statistics such as means and variances will be predicted with spectacular accuracy (spectacular for psychology, that is). The problem is that none of this proves that the one-element pattern model is true, and that learning is, indeed, discrete.

Restle (1965) has shown that it is possible to construct several types of incremental models that are formally equivalent to the all-or-none model, and hence provide equally good fits to the data. For instance, Restle described an all-or-none Hullian model with gradual learning. It is a relatively complex model, but by no means an implausible one, in that traditional Hullian assumptions about learning are employed, with a response threshold providing the crucial mechanism that allows Restle to accommodate all-or-none type phenomena. Thus, no matter how often one demonstrates experimentally that the response probability on trials before the last error is stationary, there is no way to prove thereby that learning is discrete. All one can say is that the all-or-none model provides the simplest and most elegant theoretical account of the data (e.g., there is no need to introduce a threshold concept), but whether someone wants to describe learning as discrete or incremental becomes a matter of preference and taste, because what one model can do, the other can too.

If this outcome appears disappointing, one must not forget the highly positive side effects of this inquiry into all-or-none learning.

First of all, the unquestioned acceptance of the incremental viewpoint is forever dead today, and our conception of learning processes has become much more sophisticated. Secondly, the Markov methods, which were developed here, have proven to be very useful in later work, so much so that today almost all formal work on learning employs Markovian models, i.e., the discreteness assumption, rather than the mathematically cumbersome continuous models. An additional reason for the preference of most investigators for Markov models is the ease with which such models can be extended from the one-stage model discussed above to various kinds of multistage models.

Multistage Markov models will be our concern in several later chapters. Here, I shall merely discuss some early examples of this approach, in which different subprocesses of paired-associate learning were explored.

Kintsch (1963) was concerned with the distinction between an associative stage and a response learning stage in paired-associate learning suggested by Underwood and Schulz (1960). Since the data discussed above indicate that the associative stage of learning may be described as all-or-none, it appears possible that a two-stage process of which each stage is an all-or-none step could account for the total learning process. Kintsch has developed such a model and shown that it fits the data quite well. His experimental data came from an eight-item paired-associate list with nonsense syllables as stimuli and two-place numbers as responses. Some response learning was thus required, because subjects had to learn which numbers served as responses in the experiment. As expected, the all-or-none model could not describe the data adequately. For instance, performance before the last error was not stationary. A two-stage model, on the other hand, did quite well. In this model items are thought to be in an initial state at the beginning of the experiment where neither responses nor associations are known. Therefore, the probability of a correct response is zero as long as an item remains in the initial state. The intermediate state is a partial learning state in which the response is available but not yet hooked up to the correct stimulus item. Correct responses occur with some probability $(1 - p)$ in this state, and errors occur with probability $p$. The third state of the model is a learning state in which responses are always correct. Transitions between states occur with fixed probabilities and are independent of the trial numbers. Thus a three state, two-stage Markov model is obtained and predictions for various learning statistics may be derived in the same manner as for the two-state model. Note, for instance, that although performance before the last error is no longer stationary, stationarity should hold for performance in the intermediate state. A test of this prediction is obtained by computing Vincentized learning curves for the data between the subject's first correct response on a particular item and his last error on that item.

However, more interesting than a mere demonstration of the goodness of fit of the model was a successful application of the two-stage model to an experimental design introduced by Rock (1957). Rock had devised an ingenious experimental procedure for demonstrating all-or-none processes in paired-associate learning. He argued that if learning is all-or-none, replacing an item with a new one whenever an error occurs should not interfere with learning at all, and in fact he found that a paired-associate list was learned with such a substitution procedure just as easily as a control list in which the same items were presented on all trials. Although Rock's findings were replicated a number of times, his conclusions came under much attack (e.g., Postman, 1963). It could be argued that list difficulty was a source of confounding in this experimental design. Subjects tend to make errors on the most difficult items, which were then replaced with new items. On the average, new items will be easier to learn than the ones discarded and therefore subjects in the substitution group end up learning an easier list than subjects in the control group. A proper control subject would learn a list composed of the same items which were finally learned by a subject in the substitution group. Using such a control, it was shown that the substitution procedure actually did retard learning. This finding could be very serious for the concept of all-or-none learning, except for the fact that in the critical studies learning tasks involving both response learning and association were used. The all-or-none model is therefore not applicable, but the two-stage model correctly predicts the slower learning with the substitution procedure. Whenever an error occurs for an item that is already in the intermediate state, this item will be replaced by a new item, and hence a loss occurs. However, a mathematical model is not limited to such qualitative predictions. It is a simple task to rewrite the model taking into account the procedural change brought about by the substitution method and to derive exact quantitative predictions for the course of learning with this procedure. This can be done without estimating any of the model parameters from the data of the experimental group, because one should be able to transfer the parameter estimates obtained from control subjects learning the same kind of material with a regular paired-associate procedure. This was done in two experiments by Kintsch (1963). In both cases the retardation of learning with the substitution procedure could be predicted accurately from the two-stage model.

Although we have been talking about response learning and association stages, no direct experimental evidence exists that would permit an unambiguous identification of the two stages of the model in this manner. All that has been shown is that a two-stage model describes paired-associate learning better than a one-stage model when response learning is involved, and that, in addition, it can account for the results obtained with Rock's substitution procedure. It seems plausible, of course, to identify the two stages of the model as response learning and association, but such an interpretation would be strengthened if the two stages could be separated experimentally. This has not yet been done in the present case (though note Section 2.3.6), but Polson, Restle, and Polson (1965) have reported a related experimental application of a two-stage model where such a separation was successfully achieved. In their experiment response learning was avoided by using a response set familiar to the subject, but a stimulus discrimination stage was added to the association phase of the experiment.

Polson, Restle, and Polson (1965) used a mixed list design. Sixteen simple line drawings served as stimulus material. Eight stimuli were unique and the others consisted of four confusable pairs, such as two slightly different diamonds, two Chinese characters with one small change, etc. Five common words were randomly assigned to these stimuli as responses with the restriction that twin items never received the same response. All subjects were familiarized with the five response words before the beginning of the experiment proper. Items were presented in random order for as many trials as necessary to reach a criterion of two successive correct trials.

Unique and confusable items were analyzed separately. Learning of the unique items was quite well described by the simple all-or-none model, except for a slight improvement in performance on trials before the last error, as is typically obtained with more than two response alternatives. The analysis of the confusable items was based on a distinction between two kinds of errors. Since twin items never had the same response, confusion errors within stimulus pairs could be scored separately from nonconfusion errors. The nonconfusion errors represent failures of association. When a confusion error is made, the subject obviously has established an association between a stimulus pair and a response, but cannot yet discriminate between the two similar stimuli of the pair.

According to the two-stage model, since nonconfusion errors are made in the associative phase of learning, they should not be different from the errors made in the case of the unique items. Therefore it should be possible to predict the nonconfusion errors from the simple all-or-none model, using the parameter estimates obtained from the unique items. Indeed, Polson et al. have shown that such predictions fitted the data very well. As for the confusion errors, the authors could show by an analysis of the total number of confusion errors per item that they too were generated by an all-or-none process. On the other hand, when performance on the confusable items was analyzed without distinguishing between different kinds of errors, the all-or-none model was clearly inappropriate; a two-stage model was necessary in this case.

Before concluding this section, we should not resist the temptation to sneak another look at the dead issue: whether learning is "really" discrete or incremental. Obviously we shall not find an answer by the kind of analyses that have been performed, but are there other data that might provide one? Two kinds of evidence, both in favor of the all-or-none conception of learning, appear to be relevant. First, the changes in response latencies that occur during paired-associate learning correlate quite strikingly with the state changes postulated by the all-or-none model. Millward (1964) has plotted response latencies in a simple paired-associate experiment in the manner of a backward learning curve. He obtained the average latency for the trial of the last error, for items 1, 2, . . . trials before the last error, as well as for items 1, 2, . . . trials after the last error. He found that on trials before the last error the latency was large and did not change much, but that after the last error, response latencies decreased rapidly to an asymptotic value. This finding has been replicated in a number of other studies. In addition, it has been observed that the maximum response latency occurs at the trial of the last error (Suppes, Groen, and Schlag-Rey, 1966, summarized several sets of relevant data). These findings clearly support the assumption of two distinct states. Latencies are high initially and stay high as long as the item is not learned. On the trial of the last error, which for many items is also the trial on which learning occurs, latencies increase sharply. Afterwards, latencies decrease and finally reach an asymptotic value. The gradual decline of latencies after the last error is no embarrassment to the all-or-none model. There exists no logical necessity why continuous and discrete processes should not both be considered simultaneously: it is not unreasonable to assume that when an item is in the learning state, as far as response probabilities are concerned, response latencies undergo a continuous decline. What is interesting, and what may be regarded as strong support for the all-or-none model, is that response probabilities and latencies change dramatically at the same point in the learning process—upon transition from an initial state to the learning state.

The galvanic skin response during paired-associate learning behaves in very much the same way (Kintsch, 1965). Whenever an alert subject is presented with a stimulus, he reacts to it with an orienting reflex (Pavlov, 1928). The orienting reflex is a nonspecific response, consisting of a number of components, one of which is the galvanic skin response (Sokolov, 1963). One characteristic of the orienting reflex is that it habituates rapidly when the same stimulus is presented repeatedly. Repeated presentation of a stimulus is, of course, essential to a learning experiment and a question arises concerning the course of habituation of the orienting reflex during learning. It is possible that habituation is not at all affected by learning instructions. On the other hand, it seems more likely that some relationship between the two psychological processes exists. If so, the all-or-none model tells us how to look for such a relationship. In the experiment of Kintsch (1965) subjects learned to associate 12 nonsense syllables with the responses 1 or 2. Whenever an item was presented the temporary change in the subject's resistance level (GSR) was measured. When the average GSR was computed as a function of learning trials no particularly interesting effects emerged. However, when items were arranged before averaging with the last error as a reference point in the manner of a backward learning curve, an interesting relationship between the habituation of the GSR and learning could be observed. On trials before the last error, subjects reacted with a rather large GSR to the presentation of an item, and there seemed to be some tendency for the GSR to increase during those trials that preceded the last error. After the last error, habituation set in and reactions declined in magnitude. These results parallel the latency data reported above. The postulated transition between learning states apparently represents an important reference point not only for response probabilities but also for other aspects of the total response of the subject, such as response latencies and the orienting reflex.

Neither of these two observations is enough to convince the skeptic that the learning process is really discrete—but observations such as these provide welcome justification to those investigators who are easily seduced by the elegance and ease of Markov models.

## PROBABILITY LEARNING

When stimulus sampling theory was first developed, one of the most important areas of application was probability learning. Probability learning was thought to be a simple enough learning situation, which would make an ideal testing ground for the theory. In a way it did, but in a somewhat negative way: no matter how the theory was formulated mathematically, with learning being discrete or continuous, the theory could not fully describe what went on in these experiments, as long as the view that performance was determined by a conditioning process was retained. Under certain conditions the theory describes what subjects are doing very well, but subjects are not restricted to that, they appear to have available an almost endless number of strategies to handle this experimental situation, and their behavior is much more flexible than any learning theory can account for. The conditioning approach to probability learning was one of the triumphs of the learning theories of the 1960s in terms of specificity, elegance, and, even, its partial success. At the same time, its ultimate failure was one of the main reasons why many psychologists today have abandoned the conditioning approach.

Consider a simple probability learning experiment, such as the one introduced by Humphreys (1939) and Grant, Hake, and Hornseth (1951). The task of the subject is to predict which one of two (or sometimes more) events will occur (e.g., whether a light will be turned on or not). After the appearance of a pilot light, which signals the start of each trial, the subject makes one of two possible prediction responses, usually a key press. Then the experimenter provides some feedback to the subject, that is, he turns a light on, or does not turn it on. The light serves as a reinforcement for the subject's response. In most experiments to be discussed here, the experimental events are not contingent upon the subject's responses. Before the experimental session the experimenter decides for each trial whether or not the light will be turned on, e.g., by flipping a coin. In this case the experimental events form a random sequence, with the probability of "light on" being .5. Estes and Straughan (1954) introduced a modification of this basic experimental paradigm that has been widely accepted: in order to make the symmetry between the two responses and the two events on each trial more explicit, they used two event lights, one corresponding to each response. This experimental arrangement is familiar to many students of psychology as the "Humphreys Board": two telegraph keys for the two response alternatives, a pilot light above each key for the two feedback events, and a pilot light in the middle of the board to indicate trials.

Some standard notation is needed at this point. Call the two response alternatives $A_1$ and $A_2$. Let $P(A_i)$ denote the proportion of $A_i$ responses during an experimental session, or during a block of trials, where $i = 1,2$. The two events are designated by $E_1$ and $E_2$. We shall only consider event sequences that are randomly generated and not contingent upon the subject's responses. Let $\pi$ be the probability of the event $E_1$. By the symmetry of the situation, $E_2$ must then occur with probability $1 - \pi$. The value of $\pi$ is the most important independent variable in probability learning experiments. Note that, as far as the subject is concerned, there is no "solution" to the experimental situation. The subject is asked to predict whether the $E_1$ or the $E_2$ light will come on, but what really happens has been determined by a random choice. The only thing a subject can do is to learn something about the relative frequencies of $E_1$ and $E_2$ (i.e., the $\pi$-value) and adjust his behavior accordingly.

The outcome of probability learning experiments that has excited most interest is the fact that subjects, in general, adjust their responses to the relative frequencies of the experimental events $E_1$ and $E_2$. Other features of the data are at least equally important, but we shall neglect them for the time being, until we have developed a theoretical framework within which they can be studied.

During the first few trials of a probability learning experiment subjects choose the two response alternatives equally often, but as training continues they start to predict the more frequent event more often, in fact the frequency of prediction $E_1$ matches the frequency of the occurrence of $E_1$. This probability matching is, of course, irrational: if subjects were concerned with maximizing their number of correct predictions over a block of trials, they would always choose the more frequent event. Instead, after some training $P(A_1) = \pi$, which is not a maximizing strategy. A numerical example will demonstrate this: suppose the experimenter presents $E_1$ on random 70% of the trials, i.e., $\pi = .7$. By always making response $A_1$, a subject can therefore be correct 70% of the time; if, however, a subject probability matches, $P(A_1)$ will be .7, and the expected number of correct trials will be 70% of the $A_1$ responses and 30% of the $A_2$ responses, i.e., $P(\text{correct}) = (.7)(.7) + (.3)(.3) = .58$, which is less than what a maximizing strategy can achieve. Of course, subjects do not always probability match. In some experiments subjects were found to maximize instead and in others subjects performed somewhere between these two: They overshot the matching value without going to the extreme of always predicting the same response. As Estes (1964) has concluded, experimental results are widely discrepant, but the data are not unsystematic. Estes notes that probability matching is found in experiments in which the subject is led to concentrate upon every trial. This is sometimes achieved by asking the subject to state his expectation on each trial (e.g., Estes and Straughan, 1954; Friedman, Burke, Cole, Estes, Keller, and Millward, 1964), or by simulating a psychophysical or problem-solving situation (e.g., Goodnow, 1955). Overshooting occurs when subjects are instructed to maximize successes over blocks of trials (Das, 1961) or when the random character of the event sequence is specially stressed (e.g., Edwards, 1961). Estes points out that these findings help to indicate the boundary conditions within which matching behavior is obtained.

Although deciding whether or not probability matching occurs appears to be a straightforward empirical problem, Estes (1964) notes that actually complex questions exist concerning the interpretation of probability matching data. Matching is supposedly a property of "asymptotic behavior," a stable performance level reached after an initial learning phase. In the early probability learning experiments, subjects appeared to reach a stable level after about 80 trials. This level was used as an estimate of asymptotic performance. It soon became apparent, however, that when the experiment was continued for many more trials (say for 300 trials, or up to 1200 trials) further changes occurred, i.e., performance was not "really asymptotic." But it is impossible to maintain that these further changes that occur with prolonged training are due to learning effects as conceptualized by the model. Learning is only one factor that determines behavior and one can hardly suppose that, if there is a stable performance level due to learning effects, it will be maintained forever. People get tired, lose interest in the experiment, or simply get bored and want to try something new. In fact, as Estes notes, the instructions given to the subjects often preclude stable performance for long periods of time: subjects are often urged to do their best, and thus the lack of improvement associated with stable performance level will be interpreted by the subject as a sign of failure, and this becomes a reason to vary his behavior. Thus asymptotes in a probability learning experiment are inherently unstable. Apparently the subject has several response systems available in this experimental situation, and he will choose among them depending on instructions and other experimental conditions. One mode of response, and it appears to be the dominant one, leads to the phenomenon of probability matching.

Stimulus sampling theory predicts that probability matching will occur. Suppose we have a stimulus set $S$ of elements, each of which is associated either with $A_1$ or $A_2$. Let $p(n)$ be the proportion of elements in $S$ that are connected to $A_1$. Assume that on each trial a proportion $s$ of the elements are sampled. Then, on the average, the probability of the response $A_1$ on trial $n$ will equal $p(n)$, the proportion of elements connected to that response and the probability of an $A_2$ response will be $(1 - p(n))$. The theory also assumes that all elements sampled on a trial become connected to the response that is reinforced on that trial. From these assumptions, it is easy to derive equations that describe the change in response probability from trial to trial. Consider first the case that on trial $n$ the event $E_1$ occurred, i.e., that $A_1$ was called correct. Then all elements in the sample on that trial become connected to $A_1$. On trial $n + 1$, the proportion of elements connected to $A_1$ consists, therefore, of two components: the fraction $s$ of newly connected elements, plus a fraction $(1 - s)$ of elements that had not been sampled and, therefore, did not change so that, as on the previous trial, $p(n)$ of them are connected to $A_1$. Hence we obtain for the case of event $E_1$ on trial $n$

(9) $$p(n + 1) = (1 - s)p(n) + s$$

If, on the other hand, event $E_2$ occurs on trial $n$, all the elements sampled will become connected to $A_2$, and the only elements still connected to $A_1$ will be those not sampled (with probability $(1 - s)$) and connected to $A_1$ on trial $n$, so that

(10) $$p(n + 1) = (1 - s)p(n)$$

The average change in the probability of the $A_1$ response from one trial to the next can be obtained by noting that increases will occur with probability $\pi$ (whenever $E_1$ is presented) and decreases will occur with probability $(1 - \pi)$ whenever $E_2$ is presented. Thus,

(11) $$p(n + 1) = \pi\{(1 - s)p(n) + s\} + (1 - \pi)\{(1 - s)p(n)\}$$

A solution of Eq. (11) consists of expressing $p(n)$ as a function of $\pi$, $s$ and the initial condition $p(1)$. By letting $n$ vary in this equation, the mean learning curve can be traced out. However, our main interest lies in asymptotic behavior, and it is not necessary to obtain an explicit solution of (11) in order to obtain asymptotic predictions. By definition, asymptotic performance is stable performance, i.e., there are no more changes in the mean response rates per trial: mathematically this means that $p(n) = p(n + 1) = p_\infty$. Thus,

$$p_\infty = \pi\{(1 - s)p_\infty + s\} + (1 - \pi)\{(1 - s)p_\infty\}$$

Rearranging terms we obtain

(12) $$p_\infty = \pi$$

Various other versions of stimulus sampling theory, e.g., the pattern model and the linear model discussed in the previous section, make the same asymptotic prediction, and, as we have already noted, this is also the usual outcome of probability learning experiments.

Mathematical models can, of course, predict many other features of probability learning data, in addition to mean asymptotic performance. Particularly interesting are the predictions concerning sequential statistics of the data. The theory predicts, like any other reinforcement theory, that on any trial a subject should be more likely to produce a response $A_i$, the more $E_i$ events have immediately preceded that trial, i.e., $P(A_{i,n}) \leq P(A_{i,n}/E_{i,n-1}) \leq P(A_{i,n}/E_{i,n-1}, E_{i,n-2}) \leq \ldots \leq P(A_{i,n}/E_{i,n-1} \ldots E_{i,n-j})$, etc. This follows because reinforcement theory assumes that reinforcement strengthens a response. In one of the early experiments on probability learning Jarvik (1951) noted that this was not true and that, in fact, subjects tend to behave in exactly the opposite way: the longer a run of any particular event, the more likely the subject is to predict the opposite event. This phenomenon has been called the "gambler's fallacy" and has been replicated in a number of later experiments. Such a finding is, of course, sharply critical of reinforcement theory. As mentioned above, reinforcement theory predicts positive recency curves (increases in response probability as a function of number of reincorcements), while negative recency curves are observed (subjects become less likely to predict an event after it has occurred several times in a row). To be more precise, most empirical recency curves are not strictly negative: they increase at first, pass through a maximum after one or two reinforcements and then decrease (see Estes, 1964 for a review of the relevant experiments). A completely satisfactory explanation for this finding is not available at the present time, but Estes (1964) argues that it might be merely an experimental artifact. The subjects in a probability learning experiment are not entirely naive with respect to the experimental procedure, but have some extraexperimental experience with gambling situations and the like. Habits from such extraexperimental situations will generalize to the experimental situation and may be responsible for the bow-shaped recency curves which have been observed. It is possible that people are not used to very long runs of the same event in a gambling situation, and hence, when such a run occurs, they tend to predict the opposite event because they feel it is time for a change. All this would mean is that people have a poor understanding of the concept of probability, because long runs do occur in a random sequence, although not very frequently. The term "gambler's fallacy" seems to imply that this kind of maladaptive behavior may be observed outside the laboratory. In the laboratory the "gambler's fallacy" should extinguish through lack of reinforcement, just as other extraexperimental habits extinguish, and should be replaced by the appropriate prediction behavior characterized by a positive recency effect. Estes' explanation implies that when training is extensive, or when practiced subjects are used in an experiment, the negative recency effect should disappear.

Such reasoning motivated the probability learning experiment of Friedman, Burke, Cole, Estes, Keller and Millward (1964). These authors studied the performance of well-practiced subjects in three experimental sessions, each consisting of 8 blocks of 48 prediction trials. The main interest in this study centered around the performance of subjects at the end of the third session. By that time, subjects had experienced over 1000 trials with the experimental procedure, and whatever the influence of preexperimental habits might be, this massive training must be expected to have extinguished such behavior tendencies. The outcome of this experiment was a triumph for stimulus sampling theory. First of all, subjects nicely matched their response probabilities to the outcome probabilities. An example is shown in Figure 2.3: at the beginning subjects were shifted from a reinforcement schedule with $\pi = .5$ to one with $\pi = .8$; at the very end of the session, the $\pi = .5$ schedule was reinstated. It is obvious that the

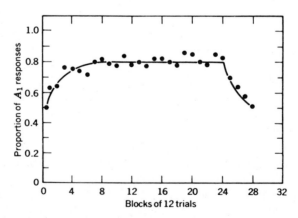

FIGURE 2.3   **Observed and theoretical proportions of $A_1$ responses per 12-trial blocks during $\pi = .8$ series and following $\pi = .5$ series. (after Friedman et al., 1964)**

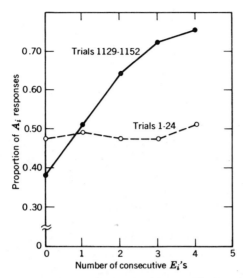

FIGURE 2.4    **Recency curves for initial and terminal** $\pi = .5$ **blocks. (after Friedman et al., 1964)**

subjects' performance adjusted quite readily to the schedule changes, and that probability matching was quite accurate in this case. The continuous lines are predictions from the model, and they are obviously just about as close to the data points as possible. Even more gratifying was the success of the sequential predictions, as shown in Figure 2.4. For the last block of trials, a pronounced positive recency effect was obtained, just as predicted by the theory. At the same time, note that at the beginning of the experiment subjects did not behave as predicted by the theory. Response probability did not increase as a function of the number of reinforcements, as is shown by the flat recency function in Figure 2.4. This is, of course, what Estes had argued: that the failure to observe positive recency was due to bad habits that subjects bring into the laboratory, but that sufficient training in the experimental situation will extinguish these habits, so that eventually subjects will come to respond to the experimental contingencies in just the way the theory claims they do.

As impressive as these successful predictions are, they remain isolated instances. There are too many other experiments where the crucial predictions of the theory (probability matching, positive recency effects) fail. If one looks at that literature, one gains the impression that subjects can do almost anything in these experiments.

The important factor seems to be how they interpret their task. They can, as they did in the Friedman et al. study and many others, behave like an organism being conditioned. But they can, and do, assume many other kinds of response strategies: they can maximize their gain by always choosing the more frequent response, they can regard the task as a problem-solving task, trying to find out the hidden rule that determines when a response will be correct (except, of course, that there is none in this task), or they can just take it easy and respond according to some simple scheme, e.g., alternating between the two responses, as rats do in a T-maze. It is not the case that subjects must respond in the way the theory assumes, if you just give them enough training. People are much more flexible than that, and they seem to have a great deal of control over their response strategies, selecting them at will (which simply means that we do not understand the factors that control this selection process). The experiment that shows this most convincingly is one by Friedman, Carterette, and Anderson (1968). They trained 10 cooperative subjects for 25 days, with 350 trials each day, on a random 50:50 noncontingent reinforcement schedule. Will a subject, after a few days, become like a machine that prints out responses as prescribed by conditioning principles? The answer was a clear no. These subjects did almost anything, responding occasionally in accordance with the theory, then in some other way, and then merely alternating responses. None of the theories the authors investigated were able to account completely for the observed sequential dependency data. The outcome should not be surprising: 25 days on a boring task, in which one cannot possibly succeed, should produce some peculiar behavior. Nevertheless, the demonstration shows that, whatever the laws of learning are, they are not some inflexible principles that strictly control behavior in the same way that a stone falls off a tower, and our theories must make room for alternative behavior strategies and for principles of choice among these strategies.

What, then, is the verdict as far as the application of stimulus sampling theory to probability learning is concerned? Clearly the theory has failed in that it is not a general theory for choice behavior, but applies only in certain limited situations. This failure is an instance of a more general phenomenon. The theory as applied here is a reinforcement theory, and what may be wrong may be the reinforcement assumptions of the theory. It just does not seem that reinforcement automatically strengthens associative bonds between stimuli and responses, thus leading to learning. The process appears to be much more complex and flexible, as we shall try to show in the remaining chapters of this book. Stimulus sampling theory, however, is not necessarily tied to reinforcement principles, and the notion of stimulus sampling can be quite useful in itself. One interesting application of stimulus sampling theory that definitely goes beyond the traditional conditioning framework will be described here in connection with probability learning experiments.

Suppose a subject can make one of two responses $A_1$ or $A_2$. On each trial the subject wins or loses 5 cents. Let $\pi_1$ be the probability of winning if the response $A_1$ is made, and $\pi_2$ the probability of a win given $A_2$. In general, $\pi_1 = \pi_2$. A theoretical treatment of this experimental paradigm within the framework of stimulus sampling theory has been provided by Estes (1962). Estes observed that the familiar probability learning experiment is embedded within this choice situation. He assumes that on each trial of the experiment the subject predicts the reinforcement for each response, and then, on the basis of his predictions, selects a response. The subject's predictions are governed by the same processes as in a conventional probability learning experiment. In particular, as we shall be concerned here only with asymptotic performance, the overall frequency with which a subject predicts reinforcement after responses $A_1$ and $A_2$ will come to match the actual reinforcement probabilities $\pi_1$ and $\pi_2$, respectively. Thus, the probability of predicting reinforcement for both responses will be $\pi_1.\pi_2$. In general, the probabilities that a subject will predict the four possible outcome combinations on trial $n$ (for large $n$) are:

| Prediction | Probability of prediction |
|------------|---------------------------|
| $A_1A_2$ | $\pi_1\pi_2$ |
| $A_1\bar{A}_2$ | $\pi_1(1 - \pi_2)$ |
| $\bar{A}_1A_2$ | $(1 - \pi_1)\pi_2$ |
| $\bar{A}_1\bar{A}_2$ | $(1 - \pi_1)(1 - \pi_2)$ |

where the bar over a response alternative denotes that the subject expects no reward for this response on this trial. If the subject expects either the second or the third of these outcome combinations, his decision rule is obvious: he will always choose $A_1$(or $A_2$ in case of the third outcome), since he prefers winning to losing 5 cents. On the other hand, if the subject predicts rewards for both or for neither of the two response alternatives, his decision rule is less obvious. One of the possibilities which Estes has explored is that in case of a tie the subject chooses a response with a probability equal to its current choice probability on all types of trials, i.e., $A_1$ is selected with probability $P(A_1)$ and $A_2$ is chosen with probability $P(A_2)$. With these assumptions, the asymptotic probability of an $A_1$ choice may be expressed recursively as

$$P(A_1) = \pi_1\pi_2 . P(A_1) + \pi_1(1 - \pi_2).1 + (1 - \pi_1)\pi_2.0 + (1 - \pi_1)(1 - \pi_2)P(A_1)$$

$$(13) \qquad\qquad = \frac{\pi_1(1 - \pi_2)}{\pi_1 + \pi_2 - 2\pi_1\pi_2}$$

Estes shows that Eq. (13) predicts asymptotic performance quite well for three groups of subjects in an experiment by Atkinson (1962). Atkinson's subjects were asked to press one of two response keys for 340 trials. When they were correct, they received 5 cents, when they were incorrect they were fined 5 cents. The three different reinforcement schedules used in this experiment to determine whether a response was correct or not are shown in Table 2.4 together with the observed choices on the last block of trials and the predictions calculated by Eq. (13). Note that the predictions are truly *a priori*, in that no part of the data had to be used for parameter estimation. Table 2.4 also summarizes the relevant features of an experiment by Siegel and Abelson (Siegel, 1961). In this experiment, as in the previous experiment, subjects could win or lose 5 cents on each trial; 20 subjects participated for 300 trials for each condition.

Observed and predicted values in Table 2.4 are quite close, thus lending some support to the notion that subjects scan the response alternatives on each trial, generate a prediction of the reward that will be received for each response, and then choose a response accordingly. The scanning model is further supported by some data reported by Lieberman (1962). In this experiment the amounts won and lost were not the same for both response alternatives as was the case in

TABLE 2.4. **Predicted and Observed Asymptotic $A_1$ Choice Proportions for Two Experiments with Response Contingent Reinforcement**

|  |  |  | $A_1$ choice | |
|  |  |  | Predicted | Observed |
| --- | --- | --- | --- | --- |
|  | $\pi_1$ | $\pi_2$ |  |  |
| Atkinson (1962): | .6 | .5 | .600 | .601 |
|  | .7 | .5 | .700 | .685 |
|  | .8 | .5 | .800 | .832 |
| Siegel (1961): | .75 | .25 | .900 | .929 |
|  | .70 | .30 | .846 | .850 |
|  | .65 | .35 | .775 | .753 |

the previously reported experiments. Lieberman played a game with his subjects in which both the experimenter and his subject held cards with a 1 or 2 on it and each placed one card face down on a table. After both had made their choices the two cards were turned up, revealing their choices and determining the outcome of the play according to the following deterministic payoff matrix:

|       | $E_1$ | $E_2$ |
|-------|-------|-------|
| $S_1$ | 3     | -1    |
| $S_2$ | -9    | 3     |

If $S_1E_1$ occurred the subject received 3 cents from the experimenter. If $S_1E_2$ occurred the experimenter received 1 cent from the subject, and so on. Subjects were given $2.50 at the start of the game and played for 300 trials. The experimenter's choices were all fixed in advance. For one group of 10 subjects the experimenter reinforced $S_1$ responses with probability .25 and $S_2$ responses with probability .75 (Group O). A second group of subjects was rewarded 50% of the time, no matter which response a subject made (Group N). Predictions for subjects' asymptotic choices may be derived from the scanning model by considering the four outcome possibilities on each trial and the probabilities of the subject's predicting each outcome:

| Outcome: (Gain for subject) | | Probability of prediction: |
|---|---|---|
| 3 | 3 | $\pi_1 \pi_2$ |
| 3 | -9 | $\pi_1(1 - \pi_2)$ |
| -1 | 3 | $(1 - \pi_1)\pi_2$ |
| -1 | -9 | $(1 - \pi_1)(1 - \pi_2)$ |

If the subject expects any one of the last three outcome combinations his decision rule is unambiguous, since he prefers winning to losing, or losing 1 cent to losing 9 cents. If the subject expects on any trial that both responses will be rewarded, we shall assume as before that he will choose response $S_1$ with the overall probability of that response. Hence, for asymptotic performance,

$$P(S_1) = \pi_1 \pi_2 P(S_1) + \pi_1(1 - \pi_2) + (1 - \pi_1)(1 - \pi_2)$$
$$= \frac{1 - \pi_2}{1 - \pi_1 \pi_2}$$

Substituting $\pi_1 = .25$ and $\pi_2 = .75$ (Group O), we obtain $P(S_1) = .31$, which is not too far off the observed asymptote of .38. For Group N the model predicts an asymptote of .67, which is identical with the observed proportion of $S_1$ choices over the last 50 trials of the experiment.

Before concluding this discussion a serious deficiency of the scanning model must be mentioned. As Estes has pointed out, the model is only concerned with a subject's preference for one of the two response alternatives but does not handle different absolute payoff values. As long as one outcome is preferred to the other, the model always makes the same predictions no matter what the degree of preference may be. Obviously this is a serious failure of the model, because it seems unlikely that subjects behave in the same way when the payoffs are 1 cent and 5 cents, or 1 cent and $100. An experiment by Siegel and Goldstein (1959) supports this common sense expectation. The authors observed three groups of 36 subjects for 300 trials in a prediction experiment with a $\pi$-value of .75. No payoffs were given to the first group of subjects. Group II was a reward group: subjects received 5 cents for each correct response and were not punished for errors. In Group III subjects also received 5 cents for correct predictions but were fined 5 cents when incorrect. The observed proportion of $A_1$ choices were .75, .86, and .95, respectively, for trials 281–300. Applying Eq. (13) we predict an asymptote of .90 for both Groups II and III. Although this prediction is not far off the observed values, it fails to reflect what is presumably an important difference in the outcome for the two payoff combinations.

This brief discussion of the scanning model was included here to show that, although stimulus sampling theory was originally developed within a conditioning framework, the notions of stimulus sampling may be successfully incorporated into information processing accounts of human behavior. Similar applications of stimulus sampling principles outside the conditioning-reinforcement framework will be encountered repeatedly throughout this book, especially in the discussion of stimulus encoding processes.

## 2.3     INTERFERENCE THEORY

Among the inheritance that psychology received from philosophy was the doctrine of associationism. Ever since Ebbinghaus it has been widely accepted that what is learned in verbal learning are associations, and that interference between associations plays an essential role in forgetting. The theory of verbal learning was for a long time a theory of the formation and extinction of associative bonds. Today, this tradition is alive in the interference theory of verbal learning. Although one of the more successful and established theories in psychology, interference theory has undergone considerable changes in the last few years and continues to do so, moving farther and farther away from pure associationism.

Until the 1950s interference theory made do with an absolute minimum of theoretical machinery: stimulus, response, and association were the only constructs thought necessary. Learning consisted in a gradual strengthening of $S-R$ associations through reinforcement. This scheme received its first major change when Hovland and Kurtz introduced the concept of response learning in 1952. These authors observed that prefamiliarization of syllables in a serial learning task facilitated learning. This observation necessitated a distinction between response learning and associative learning. The concept of response learning was important because it marked the first deviation from a strict stimulus-response conception of verbal learning. Response learning does not involve the establishment of a stimulus-response bond. Psychologists found that they had to deal with responses for which there were no identifiable stimuli. Mandler (1967a) refined the concept of response learning by pointing out a confounding in Hovland's original use of the term. In the Hovland and Kurtz experiment response learning involved both learning the identity of the set of experimental responses, as well as learning how to make the responses. Mandler suggested that the term response learning, or response integration, be reserved for learning how to make a response. Underwood and Schulz (1960) in their influential monograph have made extensive use of the concept of response learning. The recent concern with problems of response integration is also partly responsible for the preference or words over nonsense syllables as learning materials by contemporary experimenters. Words (at least high-frequency words) are never learned in the sense of response integration. The subject merely learns that a particular word is a member of the response set, but he knows the word quite well before. Nonsense material, on the other hand, requires response integration and therefore may introduce undesirable complexity into a learning experiment.

In recent years interference theory has shifted its focus of interest from a concern with the fate of individual associations to problems concerning the availability of the whole response set. Concepts like response availability and response selection are being given an increasingly important role within the theory.

## 2.3.1    TWO-FACTOR THEORY OF INTERFERENCE

Classically, interference was considered to be a matter of response competition. If an association exists between two items a and b, the learning of a new association a–c interferes with a–b because at the time of recall, the responses b and c will compete with each other when the stimulus term a is presented (McGeoch, 1942). A study by Melton and Irwin (1940) on the effects of degree of learning on retroactive inhibition (which was mentioned before in Chapter 1) provided an interesting if somewhat baffling analysis of recall errors. The concept of retroactive interference implies that forgetting occurs because the second list associations interfere with the first list associations. One might therefore suppose that a good deal of response competition between the associations from the two lists would occur, and that items from the second list would occur as intrusion errors when subjects try to recall the first list. However, Melton and Irwin reported that second list intrusions were quite rare in their experiment. Total retroactive inhibition (and hence errors in recall) increased as a function of second list trials. The number of intrusion errors, on the other hand, was higher when the interfering list was presented for only a few trials, and became quite negligible when the second list was learned well. Melton and Irwin concluded that response competition was only of minor importance in forgetting, and that most forgetting must be attributed to some "Factor X." They speculated that during the learning of the second list the first list associations might actually be unlearned.

These two factors, response competition and unlearning of associations when successive lists involve conflicting associations, have become the principal mechanisms by means of which interference effects are explained. Underwood (1948) assumed that the mechanism of unlearning was that of experimental extinction: unreinforced elicitations of the S-R bond would weaken the association. An important consequence of this assumption was that unlearning should have the same characteristics as experimental extinction, in particular, spontaneous recovery of extinguished associations. Spontaneous recovery means that after a period of rest more associations are available than immediately after unlearning: some extinguished associations recover spontaneously. To test this prediction Underwood had subjects learn two lists of 10 adjective pairs in an A–B, A–C design and tested for recall after time intervals ranging from 1 minute to 48 hours. A modified free-recall test (MFR) was used: subjects were shown the common stimulus word and responded with either the *B* or the *C* response, whichever they could remember. For brief retention intervals many more *C*-responses were given than *B*-responses. However, as the retention interval increased, the frequency of *C*-responses decreased sharply, while the frequency of first-list responses remained fairly constant. After 48 hours the original list and the interference list were equally well recalled. This finding means that there could not have been any unlearning of the first list. If the first list had been unlearned during acquisition of the second list, a more permanent superiority of second list recall over first list recall would be expected. There was, however, one way in which the unlearning concept could be saved, namely, by the assumption that the extinguished first list associations may recover spontaneously. The lack of a decrease in the recall of first list responses agrees with such an assumption: spontaneous recovery runs counter to the usual forgetting over time, and the two processes apparently balanced each other.

Barnes and Underwood (1959) put the finishing touches on the two-factor theory of interference with their experimental demonstration of unlearning of first list associations. They conducted two parallel experiments, one using an *A–B, A–C* transfer design, and one using the *A–B, A–B'* paradigm. All lists were constituted of 8 CVC-adjective pairs. In the *A–B, A–C* lists there was no apparent response similarity. Responses in the *A–B, A–B'* lists were similar in meaning, such as *insane-crazy*. All subjects learned the first list to a criterion of one correct anticipation and then were given either 1, 5, 10, or 20 trials with List 2. The recall test was a modification of Underwood's modified free-recall procedure (MMFR): subjects were given a sheet of paper with the stimulus words printed on it and were asked to write down both responses. This procedure avoids the effects of response competition, or list differentiation, and provides a pure measure of the availability of the first and second list responses. The results for the *A–B, A–C* paradigm are shown in Figure 2.5 as a function of trials on the second list. The interesting result is the decrease in recall of the responses from the first list with increasing List 2 learning. The decline in *A–B* associations seen in Figure 2.5 was a genuine unlearning effect attributable to *A–C* learning rather than simple forgetting. Barnes and Underwood demonstrated this by means of a control group that learned the first list only and then rested for a period of time equivalent to that spent in learning the *A–C* list by the group given 20 trials. Mean recall for this control group was almost perfect (7.75 correct).

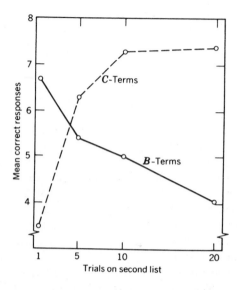

FIGURE 2.5 **Mean number of responses correctly recalled and identified with stimulus and list in the A-B, A-C paradigm. (after Barnes and Underwood, 1959)**

While first list associations became less available as second list learning increased, no loss of differentiation was observed. The term differentiation, as used here, refers to the subject's ability to tell from which of the two lists a response comes.

With the A-B, A-B' paradigm no forgetting of B was obtained. Instead, the learning of the second list was facilitated: after only one anticipation trial, recall of List 2 was nearly perfect. Barnes and Underwood interpret this result as evidence in favor of a mediational process. The subject learns a response chain A–B–B'. Thus, in the case of response similarity, an entirely new transfer mechanism is invoked. It is, of course, possible that the subject also tries to establish a response chain like A–B–C in the A–C paradigm, but fails because of the lack of association between B and C and finally extinguishes the A–B connection through lack of reinforcement. An A–B–B' chain on the other hand, will lead to correct responses and is thus likely to be established through reinforcement (Postman, 1961).

Interference at this point is regarded as an interaction between specific associative bonds, mostly in the form of extinction of old bonds during the learning of new ones, with response competition assigned a minor role. This conceptual system is supplemented by a few auxiliary terms, principally response differentiation and mediation.

## 2   TRANSFER

The results of Barnes and Underwood (1959) were extended to a number of other transfer situations by McGovern in 1964. To recapitulate, one of the conclusions of Barnes and Underwood was that first list associations become extinguished during second list learning in the A-B, A-C negative transfer paradigm. McGovern's strategy was to examine other transfer paradigms for the presence of A-B, A-C extinctive relationships. Basic to her analysis is the distinction between an associative and a response learning phase in paired-associate learning. Thus, in learning an association between S-R, there are three different kinds of associations which must be considered: first of all the forward association $S \rightarrow R$, then the backward $R \rightarrow S$ association, and finally response recall. McGovern assumed that the stimuli in response recall are environmental stimuli (stimuli emanating from the room, the experimental equipment, the experimenter, etc). Thus, response recall represents an association between contextual stimuli and the response terms. When an extinctive relationship is present in a transfer experiment for any one of these three types of associations, negative transfer will be produced. Consider the standard transfer paradigms shown in Table 1.7 of Chapter 1. In the control group A-B, C-D the forward and backward associations between A and B in the first list will not be affected when the C-D list is learned; but new response terms (D) are learned in the presence of the contextual stimuli that are already connected to the first list responses (B), and therefore the associations between the contextual stimuli and the first list responses B will be extinguished. In the A-B, C-B design the only first list associations extinguished during second list learning are the backward associations $B \rightarrow A$ (new associations $B \rightarrow C$ are being acquired). On the other hand, in the A-B, A-B_r paradigm, both the forward and backward associations of the first list will suffer during second list learning. Finally, McGovern's model predicts that forward associations and contextual associations are subject to extinction in the A-B, A-C paradigm. Thus, an obvious prediction can be derived from the model: the paradigms in which two kinds of associations are being extinguished should produce more negative transfer than paradigms in which only one type of association is extinguished during second list learning.

McGovern tested this prediction in an experiment in which subjects learned two 8-item lists. The first list was learned to a criterion of one errorless trial, and, after a 1-minute rest interval, 15 anticipation trials were given on a second list. Immediately afterward a modified free-recall test was administered: the subjects were given the first list stimuli and were asked for the first list responses. The results are shown in Table 2.5, together with the transfer paradigms used and the theoretical predictions. The finding that much more negative transfer is obtained in the first two conditions where two associative bonds were involved than in the second two groups where only one type of bond was weakened is of course what would be expected from McGovern's analysis. It shows that looking at forward associations, backward associations, and response recall as separate sources of interference is very useful in understanding the results of transfer experiments. However, it does not prove McGovern's controversial hypothesis that response recall is based upon association to contextual stimuli.

Several studies have been reported in Chapter 1 in which the similarity between the stimuli and responses of two successively learned lists was varied. Osgood's attempt to order and interpret these results in terms of his transfer surface has also been discussed (Osgood, 1949). Osgood's transfer surface was essentially an empirical generalization, and it was shown that it fails to describe adequately the very complex pattern of results obtained in transfer studies since Osgood originally proposed it. In fact, the reader who recalls the section on transfer from the previous chapter will probably agree that there appears to be very little hope for any kind of simple generalization that can account for these exceedingly complex results. However, Martin (1965) has approached the problem quite successfully via a model that distinguishes between forward associations, backward associations, and response recall. A transfer surface can be drawn separately for each of

TABLE 2.5.    **A Summary of McGovern's Experiment**

| Training Condition | | Mean Number of Correct Responses after Interpolated Learning | Nature of Extinctive— Relationships |
|---|---|---|---|
| List 1 | List 2 | | |
| A–B | A–C | 4.79 | Forward and contextual associations |
| A–B | A–B_r | 4.75 | Forward and backward associations |
| A–B | C–B | 6.42 | Backward associations |
| A–B | C–D | 6.54 | Contextual associations |
| A–B | — | 7.71 | — |

these subprocesses. Total transfer can then be expressed as the sum of these three component transfers. Sources of positive and negative transfer can be combined in this way, and, depending on the importance assigned to each component, most experimental results available can be accounted for. Additional experimental variables must be considered separately, however. The transfer surfaces take into account only the relatedness between the stimuli and response terms of the two lists. As has been shown in Chapter 1, the meaningfulness of both stimuli and responses, and the degree of learning play an important role in modifying transfer results.

## PROACTIVE INHIBITION AND EXTRAEXPERIMENTAL SOURCES OF INTERFERENCE

From the experiments already described it is clear that by introducing an interpolated interfering list marked forgetting can be produced in the laboratory. But how is the forgetting to be explained that occurs over, say, a week when the subject learns only one list? Traditionally this loss has been attributed to the interference from activities outside the laboratory during this week. This interpretation was never quite satisfactory. It meant stretching the interference hypothesis rather far to hold that the large amount of forgetting of a nonsense syllable list within a few hours was caused by interference from something that the subjects learned outside the laboratory, nonsense syllables still not being in common use. In 1957 Underwood remedied this situation by showing that most forgetting was produced by interference not from unspecified tasks learned outside the laboratory, but from tasks learned previously in the laboratory.

Figure 2.6 taken from Underwood (1957) shows that proactive interference plays a very important role in determining paired-associate recall. The very large differences in recall obtained in different experiments can be explained as proactive inhibition effects: the more lists subjects have learned previously, the poorer their recall. In constructing this figure, Underwood used the results from 16 published studies that fulfilled the following criteria: learning was continued to one perfect recitation of the list, retention was measured by a recall test after 24 hours, and finally, relatively massed practice was used during learning. The studies included had several different kinds of materials (geometric forms, nonsense syllables, words) and also differed in such factors as list length, and manner and rate of presentation. These factors are probably responsible for some of the

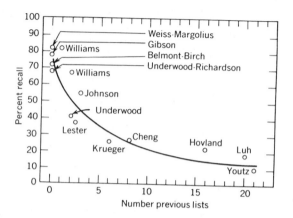

FIGURE 2.6   **Recall as a function of number of previous lists learned from a number of studies. (after Underwood, 1957)**

remaining variance in Figure 2.6, but the overwhelming effect of number of previous lists learned is clearly discernible. As Underwood points out, this makes the task of the theorist much simpler: after 24 hours the amount of forgetting still to be explained is only of the order of 25%, not around 75%, as one would conclude from Ebbinghaus' data, who, of course, had learned many previous lists.

The remaining 25% of forgetting were assigned their place within the framework of the interference theory of forgetting by Underwood and Postman (1960). The old hypothesis of extraexperimental sources of interference, which seemed a little overtaxed when it was used to explain all forgetting, now appeared sufficient for handling the reduced problem. Underwood (1957) had demonstrated the considerable power of proactive interference from lists not designed to be particularly similar to the test list. The extension from this result to forgetting without formal interfering tasks was not such a large step, especially since the interference effects of new learning during the retention interval (retroactive inhibition) could now plausibly be supplemented by the interfering consequences of previous extraexperimental learning (proactive inhibition).

The arsenal of interference theory already included sufficient mechanisms by means of which habits learned previously could interfere with present learning: learning a list requires the breaking or unlearning of previous associations, and these extinguished verbal habits may recover spontaneously in time, interfering with the retention of the to-be-learned list. Of course, if the extinguished habit is practiced again during the retention interval, its recovery would be facilitated and the interference would be maximal. One would speak of retroactive inhibition in this latter case. However, actual practice during the retention interval is not necessary, because extinguished verbal habits will recover spontaneously in the absence of practice. Underwood and Postman specified letter-sequence interference and unit-sequence interference as possible sources of extraexperimental interference. Letter-sequence interference refers to the associations established among letter sequences through ordinary language. Unit-sequence interference is produced by the preexisting associations among the words of a learning list. As an example, the authors say that if *over* is an item of a learning list, the association *over there* must be extinguished before a new association can be established. But with the passage of time, the original association will recover and interfere with retention. Furthermore, should the subject use the expression *over there* during the retention interval, the recovery of the association would be facilitated and interference increased. Some preliminary tests of this hypothesis provided positive results.

At this point interference theory was a comprehensive theory of forgetting, which adequately explained the major phenomena with which the laboratory study of forgetting had been concerned up to that time. However, the concept of interference from extraexperimental sources has come under attack, necessitating a restriction of the theory to formal retroactive and proactive inhibition designs.

The extension of interference theory to account for forgetting from extraexperimental sources of interference was made the subject of several experimental investigations. In general, the data have not supported the predictions from the theory. Several authors, e.g., Slamecka (1966) and Underwood and Ekstrand (1966), have tried to show that preexperimental associations are unlearned during laboratory learning, just as Barnes and Underwood had shown that associations formed in the laboratory are unlearned after competing list learning. The results of these studies were, however, negative, and it must be concluded that extraexperimental associations do not produce significant amounts of interference. But why are extraexperimental associations ineffective in producing interference? As yet interference theorists have not come up with a satisfactory answer to this question. Underwood and Ekstrand indicate that the concept of association might be insufficient to provide a convincing answer. Perhaps properties of association other than just strength play a role in determining the amount of interference. The lack of interference surely cannot be explained by any lack of strength of the habits learned. It may be necessary to introduce the concept of structure at this point: the associations developed in *A-B* learning by distributed practice might in some way be structured differently so as to reduce interference effects (Mandler, 1962).

### 2.3.4    SPONTANEOUS RECOVERY

Underwood's equating of unlearning and experimental extinction appears to be another weak point of contemporary interference theory. If unlearning is extinction, unlearned associations should recover spontaneously during the retention period, since spontaneous recovery is a well-established characteristic of experimental extinction.

The concept of spontaneous recovery was introduced to account for the observation that after longer retention intervals (24 to 48 hours) the first and second lists in an *A-B, A-C* design are equally well recalled. At shorter retention intervals the second list is better recalled. Underwood (1948) suggested that the first list responses that have become unlearned when the second list was learned recover strength spontaneously, so that the second list loses its initial superiority. Alternative explanations of this finding are, of course, quite possible. In fact, negatively accelerated forgetting curves alone seem sufficient to handle Underwood's results. Koppenaal (1963) has argued that spontaneous recovery is an unnecessary assumption and should be retained only if direct evidence for it can be obtained. He distinguished between absolute recovery and relative recovery of first list associations, only the first of which could be admitted as evidence for the existence of spontaneous recovery. Relative recovery refers to an increase in the availability of first list responses relative to second list responses. Negatively accelerated forgetting curves imply such a phenomenon. Absolute recovery refers to an increase in the absolute number of responses available to the subject at recall.

Koppenaal (1963) failed to find absolute recovery in his experiment, and a number of studies since have replicated this finding. The retention interval in these studies ranged from several hours to several days. With a much smaller retention interval, however, Postman, Stark, and Fraser (1968) did observe an absolute rise in correct first list responses.

On the whole, then, the evidence for spontaneous recovery is ambiguous: for the retention intervals commonly used it cannot be demonstrated, but a clear demonstration of absolute recovery exists for short retention intervals. Some intriguing questions remain as to the proper interpretation of this effect.

## ASSOCIATIVE INTERFERENCE OR RULES OF RESPONSE SELECTION?

The problem is to determine what is unlearned in negative transfer experiments. The classical answer of interference theory to this question is most clearly formulated in the McGovern study reported above: Specific associations—forward and backward associations between stimuli and responses, and associations between contextual cues and the response terms—are being unlearned. Postman, Stark, and Fraser (1968), Postman and Stark (1969), and Postman and Underwood (1973) announced some serious doubts about this classical interpretation.

Consider the following experiment. One condition consists essentially of a replication of the McGovern experiment. Different groups of subjects learn two paired-associate lists each, according to the various standard transfer paradigms. Ten item lists of letter-adjective pairs were used. The first list was learned to a strict criterion, then the subjects received 10 anticipation trials on List 2, and finally a test of List 1 was administered. The test procedure was modified-modified free recall (MMFR). In the second condition the treatment was identical, except that both learning and test employed a multiple-choice method. On each trial the subject was shown four response alternatives, one of which was the correct one, and the three others were taken from other items of the list. The reason for including this second condition was to provide a control for response recall: with a recognition procedure, response recall is not involved, and hence one would expect a somewhat modified pattern of results for the various transfer designs, using McGovern's arguments.

When learning was with the anticipation procedure and the MMFR test was given, typical transfer results were obtained; in other words. McGovern's results were replicated. However, for the recognition learning group none of the transfer paradigms produced negative transfer, except for some slight amount in the $A-B$, $A-B_r$ condition. Recognition of List 1 items was approximately the same in all other conditions and equaled the performance of the control group. This is a very striking and important result: retroactive interference seems to be a matter of response availability! Specific associations seem to be highly resistant to unlearning. Thus, interference may not work on individual associations but rather on the entire repertoire of first list responses; a process of response selection may be responsible for the results generally obtained in transfer studies.

Postman offers the following outline of the operation of this hypothetical response selection mechanism. When the subject receives his instructions, a class of response terms is selected as appropriate for the list to be learned. Within the selected response class the availability of individual responses is governed by the "spew principle"—the most frequent responses come first. When the response terms are changed, as they are in the transfer studies under consideration here, a new selection criterion must be adopted. The effectiveness of this criterion depends on the distinctiveness of the new responses: the more distinct the two response sets are, the more effective will be the exclusion of the first list responses. During recall subjects scan the available responses and match them against the criteria of selection; responses that fail this test will not be produced overtly. Thus most interference in transfer experiments remains covert. (The scanning of the response set and the editing of responses correspond to what is often referred to as *list differentiation*).

One more assumption must be made; namely, that there is some inertia in the selector mechanism. If the subject is instructed to recall List 1 while the List 2 criteria are still dominant, he may experience considerable difficulty—depending on the similarity of the criteria—and he will need some time to change his set appropriately. But the important consideration is that interference is produced not by the individual List 2 associations, but by the dominance of the most recent criterion. The strength of the List 2 associations is quite irrelevant according to this way of thinking; what is important is the degree of criterion dominance.

The results on recovery of first list associations, which were reported in the previous section, are in very good agreement with this hypothesis. Postman et al. performed a whole series of recovery experiments in which they systematically manipulated the expected dominance of the second list criteria at the end of training. Obviously if the criteria appropriate to the second list are very strong at the end of training, the subject will do poorly if he is asked to recall the first list responses; after some 20 minutes, the second list criterion will no longer be dominant, and the subject will now be able to recall more first list responses than he could right after training. Therefore, recovery of first list associations will be observed. On the other hand, if the second list criterion is weak in the first place, no further changes will take place with time, and there should be no recovery of first list associations. Postman et al. manipulated criterion strength in various ways. In the condition MMFR (1) subjects were given the stimulus terms together with the second list responses and were asked to provide the first list responses; these subjects were directly confronted with the second list terms, which should lead to a persistence of the second list criteria. In the condition MMFR (2) subjects were given only the stimulus terms and asked for both first and second list terms; under these circumstances the subject's set for recall of the second list responses did not receive external reinforcement since he is not confronted with these terms; hence it should be weaker, but it should still be present to some degree because of the instructions to recall both first and second list terms. In a final condition, subjects were asked to recall the first list terms only (as in the McGovern experiment); here set-produced interference should be minimized, and thus there should be no room for recovery of associations as a function of time. The experimental results of Postman et al. nicely confirmed these expectations: considerable absolute recovery of first list associations over a 24-minute interval was found with the MMFR (1) test, some with the MMFR (2) test, and none at all with the third recall procedure.

In conclusion, it seems that interference theory has come almost full circle (Postman and Underwood, 1973): it started out with the notion that interference was produced by response competition; later, attention shifted more and more to unlearning as the basic mechanism of interference in transfer experiments; now response competition is being reinstated in the dominant role. However, response competition is back with a difference: 40 years ago, it was the competition between individual associations that was held responsible for intereference; today, generalized response competition is thought to arise as a consequence of the inertia of the response selector mechanism. No longer is it a matter of competition between alternative responses to the same stimulus but rather between alternative response systems.

## THE ROLE OF STIMULUS ENCODING AND RETRIEVAL

Interference theory is, and always was supposed to be, a general theory of forgetting. Nevertheless, it is obvious from a perusal of the foregoing pages that much of the empirical testing of the theory has relied on one experimental technique: paired-associate learning.

There are two obvious subtasks in paired-associate learning: subjects have to learn what the responses are and they have to hook up these responses with the right stimulus terms (see the discussion on page 82). This analysis of paired-associate learning as a stimulus-response hookup has always formed an important component of the intellectual background of interference theory. The principal mechanisms of the two-factor interference theory directly reflect this emphasis: they concern the unlearning of associations and the competition between responses, either between individual items or whole lists.

In recent years, as information processing views have gained in popularity, interference theory has been criticized for its emphasis on the stimulus-response connection and its neglect of other potentially important factors. Foremost among these critics were Greeno and Martin, who pointed out the significance of stimulus encoding and retrieval processes for our understanding of interference and forgetting. Stimulus encoding and retrieval will be discussed in much greater detail in later chapters (Chapters 3 and 5, respectively). Nevertheless, we cannot leave this discussion of interference theory without anticipating some of these matters.

That paired-associate learning can frequently be described as a two-stage Markov process has already been mentioned (pages 82–86). Traditionally, these two stages have been labeled response learning and association, but Greeno (1970) has questioned this interpretation and argued that, instead, encoding and retrieval would be more accurate labels for the two stages of paired-associate learning. According to Greeno, the subject first must store a stimulus-response unit in memory as a whole (rather than merely response learning). Secondly, the subject must learn how to access this memory unit on a test trial, given only the stimulus as a retrieval cue. That is, the subject must develop a retrieval plan.

The evidence for this reinterpretation of the two stages of paired-associate learning comes from experiments in which the similarity of the stimulus and response terms was varied independently. The effect of this manipulation was noted upon the ease of first- and second-stage learning. This, of course, involved the use of a mathematical model, such as the one described in Section 2.2.1 of this chapter, because these learning stages are not directly observable. The proper dependent variables here are the learning parameters of the first and second stages of paired-associate learning, as defined by the model and estimated from the data (by methods that are somewhat more sophisticated than those outlined in Section 2.2.1). Theoretical predictions for the effects of stimulus and response similarity are easily derived from both the classical response learning-plus-association view and Greeno's encoding-plus-retrieval theory. If the first learning stage is one of response learning, similarity among the stimulus items of a list should not affect it, while both stimulus and response similarity would have an effect on the ease with which a stimulus-response pair may be encoded as a unit. These predictions are reversed for the second stage: the associative view leads one to expect that both stimulus and response similarity should be effective variables, while learning to retrieve the memory code given the stimulus item as a retrieval cue implies that only stimulus similarity should be important for second-stage learning. Greeno (1970) reported experimental results that supported the encoding-retrieval theory on both counts.

The encoding-retrieval view of memory considerably changes the interpretation of interference effects, as was shown by Martin (1971) and Greeno, James and Dapolito (1971). Encoding, according to these authors, is considered to be a process of stimulus sampling. The stimulus-response pair is represented as a set of features that differ in saliency and hence in the probability of being sampled. Saliency is determined by the relations among the feature set as a whole, which means, for instance, that if the stimulus word BALL is paired with the response word WINDOW, entirely different features of BALL become salient than when it is paired with, say, CLUB. Thus, the response determines, in part, which features of the stimulus are being sampled. This claim has important consequences for the mechanisms involved in retroactive interference. If subjects first learn a list A–B, then a second list A–C in which the same stimulus terms are paired with new responses, and are finally tested on the original list, A–B, what happens is that the feature sampling bias that was in effect during A–C learning persists into the A–B test, thus leading to retroactive interference. With time, of course, this bias would be lost, resulting in spontaneous recovery. Note that this account is not too different from classical interference theory. In both there is a notion of generalized competition, but in the Martin-Greeno theory the competition is between encoding biases, while competition in response recall is considered to be crucial in the Postman-Underwood view.

Proactive interference effects are similarly explained by Martin and Greeno as a bias to sample first-list features that carries over into second-list learning.

Although some interference effects can thus be explained as encoding phenomena, others require an explicit consideration of retrieval processes. Indeed, Greeno et al. have been quite successful in predicting the difficulty of second-stage learning from such considerations. Compare for instance, the negative transfer that occurs in an A–B, A–C design with that in an A–B, A–B$_r$ design, where the second list involves the same response terms as the first, but they are randomly re-paired with the stimulus members. A–B$_r$ should be harder than A–C since in the A–C case it is easier for the subject to differentiate the retrieval plans for the two lists.

That interference with retrieval cues is an important factor in forgetting has also been demonstrated by Tulving and Psotka (1971) in the context of free-recall rather than paired-associate learning. Tulving has introduced an important distinction between the availability of information in memory and its accessibility (see Chapter 5 for a fuller discussion). Information is available if it is stored in the Martin-Greeno sense; but such information need not be accessible—it becomes so only if there exists a successful cue for its retrieval. Tulving and Psotka demonstrated that retroactive interference in free-recall learning affects the accessibility of items, that is, it disrupts retrieval plans. In their experiment Tulving and Psotka had their subjects learn from 1 to 6 consecutive word lists. Each list consisted of 24 words, 4 each from 6 different conceptual categories (such as *animal names, items of furniture*, etc.) The results of a free-recall trial are shown in Figure 2.7. Substantial retroactive interference is demonstrated by the precipitous drop in recall as a function of the number of interpolated lists: subjects recalled 70% of the words in the absence of any interpolated learning, but less than 30% with three or more interpolated lists. The important results of this experiment, however, are the curves labeled *categories* and *words/category* in Figure 2.7. A category was scored as recalled when at least one word from it was recalled. It is obvious from Figure 2.7 that category recall was strongly affected by interpolated learning. On the other hand, if a subject recalled a category at all, the number of words that he recalled from that category was not subject to retroactive interference, but stayed right around 70% for all six groups. Tulving and Psotka interpreted this finding as interference with retrieval. Interpolated learning disrupts the retrieval plan for old lists, so that the subjects can retrieve fewer and fewer categories. But once a category has been accessed, the information stored there still remains and can be recalled independently of the amount of interpolated learning. That this interpretation is indeed plausible was confirmed by a final cued recall test that Tulving and Psotka gave to their subjects. For this test, each subject was given a list of all the category names, so that access to a category unit was now provided by the experimenter. As expected, when the retrieval process was thus sim-

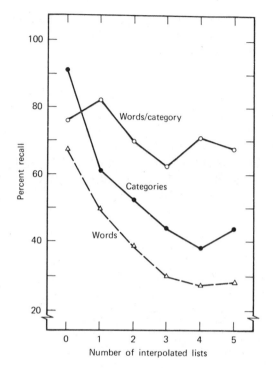

FIGURE 2.7    **The effects of the number of interpolated lists upon total free recall, category recall, and words per category recalled. (after Tulving and Psotka, 1971)**

plified, recall was unaffected by retroactive inference and subjects recalled an equal number of words in each condition, regardless of the number of interpolated lists. Retroactive interference in the Tulving and Psotka experiment made information stored in memory inaccessible, but the information was still available, as was demonstrated when proper retrieval cues were provided by the experimenter.

We have thus considerable evidence for the importance of both encoding and retrieval processes in several experimental situations. On the one hand, encoding variability serves to reduce interference effects when subjects do not sufficiently differentiate their encodings of the learning materials from two different lists. On the other hand, encoding variability may itself be a major cause of forgetting when it involves the encoding of the retrieval cue. At the time of test, the subject must encode the retrieval cue in the same way as he did at the time of study, if the cue is to make successful contact with the stored memory traces. Thus, a careful consideration of what the subject stores in memory and of the nature of the available retrieval cues may help us to gain a deeper understanding of the phenomena of interference and forgetting. The way in which these considerations will affect interference theory remains as yet uncertain. Postman and Underwood (1973) have answered Martin and Greeno (clearing up a number of misunderstandings that had arisen), but whether interference theory will survive this controversy intact, how it might be modified, or whether it will eventually be replaced by an information processing theory, only the future can tell. In any case, we shall now turn our full attention in the next chapters to the basic ingredients of such an information processing theory: encoding, memory storage, and retrieval.

# 3
# coding
# processes

Levels of human information processing are outlined; memory traces are the more or less stable products of these processes. Relatively low levels of processing are involved in sensory memory and increasingly deeper ones are involved in short-term memory and long-term memory. The role of knowledge, control processes, and inference rules in the memory system.

The next three chapters are concerned with memory. In this chapter we shall discuss the perceptual aspects of the memory system, which are concerned with initial stimulus encoding processes. In Chapter 4 we will be concerned with the investigation of short-term memory, and in Chapter 5 with long-term memory.

The view of memory upon which this division is based is outlined schematically in Figure 3.1. Sensory memory is still part of the peripheral sensory system. In the visual and auditory systems (and presumably also in the other sensory modalities) stimuli persist for a brief period of time after their termination. In this way the effective life of a stimulus is extended and thus available for further processing. This is especially important for stimuli that are presented only briefly or that were not immediately attended to.

Perceptual analyses, including feature extraction, recognition, and

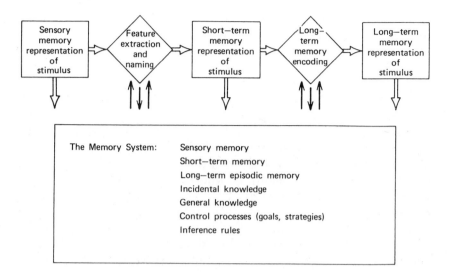

FIGURE 3.1   **An outline of the memory system.**

naming processes are performed upon stimuli residing in sensory memory. However, not every stimulus is processed equally. Processing capacity is limited, and only a few items that are perceptually available are processed to such an extent that relatively stable short-term memory representations are formed. How this selection process operates and the means by which the rich information in the perceptual system is reduced to only a few chunks in short-term memory is one of the main concerns of this chapter. Also discussed here is the question how people learn to control this selection process. Learning to encode the relevant aspects of stimuli and to disregard irrelevant ones is the main problem in many learning tasks that have been studied in the psychological laboratory, especially in discrimination learning tasks. Another area where coding processes have been shown to be very important is verbal learning, which will also be examined in this chapter.

Once a short-term memory representation has been constructed (i.e., the item has been stored in short-term memory), the nature of the experimental problem changes from an emphasis on perceptual coding to a different set of questions: what are the characteristics of short-term memory representations; how fast, and by what mechanism are they lost; what is the role of consciousness; and, eventually, how are stable long-term memory representations formed? These questions will be discussed in Chapter 4. Chapter 5, then, will be concerned with the nature and organization of long-term memory and with the problem of retrieval from long-term memory. A distinction will be made between episodic memory, that is, memory for specific personal experiences, and semantic memory, which refers to a person's store of knowledge.

The study of memory, as it is proposed here, breaks down the traditional boundaries between perception, memory, learning, and thinking. These are arbitrary, outmoded classifications that have largely lost their usefulness today (except for labeling courses), and we should not take them too seriously. It is a moot point where perception ends in Figure 3.1 and memory begins, or where the border should be drawn between thinking and memory. We have to be concerned with the functioning of the system as a whole, and there is no way to study, for instance, the organization of memory separate from thinking processes. In the same vein, we should not take the separate boxes in Figure 3.1 too seriously either. The memory system functions as a whole, and various operations may occur in parallel. The tripartite distinction between sensory, short-term and long-term memory is convenient when organizing a textbook, but it would be a mistake to think of these as three separate memory systems, like three boxes, in which one can store information and pass it from one to the other. It is impossible to talk about sensory memory without the involvement of short- and long-term memory. The perception of a word, for instance, necessarily involves long-term memory in the process of identification and naming; similarly, short-term memory is better described as the active, conscious part of long-term memory than as a separate box. What has been distinguished in Figure 3.1 are not separate memory systems, but different types of stimulus encodings, from the relatively unprocessed sensory memory representation, to the much better analyzed short-term memory representation, and finally to long-term memory representations that are connected to other items in long-term memory by means of specific, explicit retrieval cues. The rationale for these distinctions, and the demonstration of their usefulness, will be the burden of these chapters.

## 3.1    SENSORY MEMORY

When a stimulus acts upon the nervous system and is terminated suddenly some information continues to be available for a brief period of time. Stimuli like a click or flash elicit electrical activity in both the receptor and the sensory projection area of the brain which persists briefly after the termination of the stimulus itself. At a more behavioral level, such phenomena as visual after-images are well known.

When subjects are shown tachistoscopically (say for 50 milliseconds) a display of letters or digits they can identify approximately 4 to 5 items. This is a long-established result in psychology (Cattell, 1885; Erdmann and Dodge, 1898). Recently it was shown that the number of symbols perceived is underestimated with this technique. The limit is imposed by the subject's processing capacities but not by what he can see. Sperling (1963) demonstrated this with a partial report procedure. Subjects were presented 12 letters or digits arranged in three rows of four items each. Exposure duration was 50 milliseconds. Immediately after the stimulus presentation one of three signal tones (high, medium, low) instructed the subject which one of the three rows he was to report. Subjects recalled correctly 76% of the items. Since they did not know in advance which row to recall this must mean that subjects had available 76% of the 12 items, i.e., 9.1 symbols, which is appreciably more than they ever could report directly. However, if the signal tone was delayed for only one second, performance dropped to 36%, i.e., to 4.3 symbols, which is within the range of the results normally obtained with the report procedure.

Sperling interpreted these results as evidence for a visual storage system which decays rapidly, but from which the subject can extract information as long as it is available. Two kinds of evidence exist for the peripheral nature of this storage system. The first is based on the introspection of experimental subjects who often report that the physical stimulus is gradually fading out, and that they are reading items off the diminishing stimulus trace (Sperling, 1963). Secondly, Averbach and Sperling (1961) conducted an experiment in which they showed that when the visual trace was erased, no improvements in report were possible. In this experiment 18 letters were exposed for 50 milliseconds. These letters were arranged in six rows and six different signal tones were employed to tell the subject which letters were to be reported. The experimental variables of interest were delay of the signal tone (up to 5 seconds) and brightness of the pre- and postexposure field. If the pre- and postexposure fields are dark, sensory after-images may persist for several seconds; on the other hand, a light field interferes with after-images. Figure 3.2 shows the results of the experiment. Estimates of the capacity of visual storage are now increased up to about 16 symbols. More important is the striking difference between the effects of light and dark postexposure fields. It is quite obvious that a light postexposure field severely interferes with

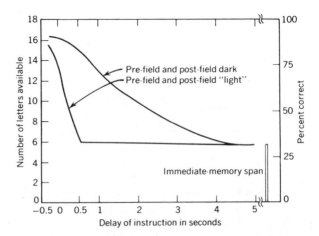

FIGURE 3.2 **Information available to one observer from two kinds of stimulus presentations. The right ordinate is the average accuracy of partial reports; the left ordinate is the inferred store of available letters. Average immediate memory span for both presentations is indicated at right. (after Sperling, 1963)**

the accuracy of partial reports. Therefore, it seems highly probable that the effect is based on a persisting visual trace.

Estes (Estes, 1965; Estes and Taylor, 1966) has used a forced choice technique for estimating the number of elements perceivable from a display of very brief duration. Sets of printed symbols in random arrangements contained either one of two critical symbols, A or B, plus noise elements. Following a 50-millisecond exposure of each set the subject had to say whether an A or a B had been included. For a display of size D the probability of a correct response corrected for guessing is given by

$$P_c = \frac{K}{D} + \left(1 - \frac{K}{D}\right)\frac{1}{2}$$

where K is the number of elements effectively processed. Since the critical elements are placed at random somewhere in the display, the probability that the critical elements are among the K processed elements is K/D. The second term in the equation is the correction for guessing: if the critical element is not detected, the subject has probability 1/2 of guessing correctly. By equating $P_c$ with the proportion of correct detections observed in an experiment with display size D, and rearranging terms we obtain an estimate of the number of elements processed by the subject:

$$K = (2P_c - 1)D$$

For instance, for a 16-element matrix one subject responded correctly 85% of the time. This implies a $K$-estimate of 11.3 elements perceived. Again we find that subjects can perceive many more elements than normally can be reported.

Most of the characteristics of the visual information store are incidental to its visual nature. An essential difference from short-term memory is that it is not subject to the same capacity limits as short-term memory. In Figure 3.2, which is based on partial reports from an 18-symbol display, capacity estimates of over 16 symbols were obtained, and there is no reason to believe that this is an absolute maximum. Evidence for an auditory sensory memory has also been obtained with a variety of different experimental procedures. Auditory sensory memory (also referred to as echoic memory or the precategorical acoustic store) resembles the visual store in that it, too, is not subject to the severe capacity limitations of short-term memory, and that information is lost rapidly (though the rate of loss is not the same as in the visual case).

One set of procedures used to demonstrate the existence of an auditory sensory store employs a sampling approach, much as in the visual case. A representative experiment is one by Darwin, Turvey, and Crowder (1972) in which the subject is presented with several acoustic messages simultaneously, so that he can no longer deal with them all. Their subject sat in a room in which three messages were played simultaneously from three distinct spatial locations. Each message consisted of three digits or letters. In the whole report condition subjects were simply asked to report as many items as they could on each trial. In the partial report conditions, on the other hand, the subject was given a visual cue to indicate which source to report. The visual cue followed the stimulus presentation by either 0, 1, 2, or 4 seconds. The results of this experiment are shown in Figure 3.3. Obviously, this figure closely resembles the previous one which shows Sperling's results with a visual stimulus presentation. In both cases the partial report curves descend toward the whole report level, though they reach it much faster in the visual case than in the auditory. In the latter case, a usable memory trace still exists after 2 seconds, and it appears that it takes about 3 to 4 seconds before it is completely lost.

Results quite in agreement with those reported above have been obtained with a variation of the sampling technique by Glucksberg and Cowan (1970). These authors had subjects perform a dichotic listening task in which two messages were played simultaneously, one into each ear. Subjects were instructed to attend to the prose that was presented to one ear, and to shadow it, i.e., repeat it out loud. A different prose message was played to the other, nonattended ear.

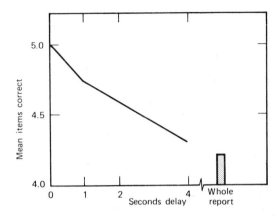

FIGURE 3.3    **Partial report by spatial location as a function of visual indicator delay compared with whole report.** (after Darwin, Turvey, and Crowder, 1972)

Shadowing is a taxing task, which ensured that very little processing of the nonattended message could occur, so that it could not be registered. At random times, single digits were embedded into the prose presented to the nonattended ear. Subjects were stopped at various delays after such a digit appeared and were asked to recall the digit. The results demonstrated that, if the subject is asked soon enough after the presentation of a digit, he can still retrieve it from his echoic memory, in spite of the fact that he never really listened to it since his attention was taken up by the shadowing task. Soon enough meant up to about 4 seconds. After that (the experimenters investigated delays up to 20 seconds), no evidence for any memory of nonattended material was found. Apparently, nonattended material enters the sensory memory store, but since it is not processed further, is rapidly lost without a trace.

A rather different approach to the investigation of sensory memory is exemplified by the work of Massaro (1970), who studied the interference effects of the decaying acoustic trace. An improvement in performance of the task that is being interfered with led him to conclude that the trace responsible for the interference was decaying. Massaro gave his subjects a short burst of a tone and had them identify its pitch. He selected his tones so that the high tone (870 Hertz) was clearly distinguishable from the low tone (770 Hertz)—if subjects were allowed enough processing time. Massaro, however, presented his tones for only 20 msec, and then blocked all further processing by a strong masking tone (820 Hertz). Under those conditions, subjects could not distinguish between the high and low tone at all. Massaro then introduced a delay between the test stimulus and the masking tone, thus allowing his subjects to continue processing the test stimulus from sensory memory. Discrimination remained at chance level until the mask was delayed for about 40 msec; thereafter performance improved steadily, becoming essentially perfect when the mask was delayed by 250 msec. This result demonstrates very nicely the functional utility of a sensory memory store: it allows the subject to continue processing a trace, if processing is still required, even if the stimulus is no longer perceptually present. The fact that the mask became ineffective after a quarter second in Massaro's experiment does not imply, of course, that the auditory trace had decayed by that time: it merely means that a quarter second was enough time to determine the pitch of the test tone. Presumably, if the experiment were repeated with complex stimuli that require more processing time, the beneficial effects of delay would extend over a longer period of time; such an example will be discussed below.

Our final demonstration of echoic memory involves the work of Crowder and Morton on the "suffix effect" (Crowder and Morton, 1969; Morton, 1970; Crowder, 1974). The "suffix effect" is a rather curious phenomenon: in digit-span experiments, where subjects are given a list of random digits to recall immediately, performance is degraded by a redundant suffix. For instance, if subjects know that every list they will hear ends with the digit "zero," one would think that they could disregard this redundant zero and concentrate only on the remaining items of the list. However, the redundant zero cannot be disregarded and it is just as much a load on memory as any other, nonredundant item. For example, if one has a list of nine digits followed by a redundant zero, this list is remembered no better than a regular, unpredictable 10-digit list. This effect depends strongly on the physical characteristics of the redundant suffix: if a buzzer is substituted for the spoken "zero," no interference occurs, and even if the "zero" differs in physical features from the other digits of the list (e.g., it is spoken by a different voice), interference is reduced. A visual suffix has no effect, either.

Why does a redundant suffix produce interference? There is, after all, no need to process such an item. But look at the role of echoic memory in digit-span experiments: items are typically presented at a rate of 2 per second, so that the subject has only .5 seconds to process each digit, except for the last one which persists in echoic memory and which, therefore, can be processed more fully. Now consider the effects of the redundant spoken "zero," coming .5 seconds after the last digit: functioning like a mask, it will interfere with the sensory memory trace of that digit, thus terminating processing and leading to poorer recall of the last item. Crowder and Morton (1969) tested this hypothesis by delaying the redundant suffix, so that after the last list item, sensory memory traces were allowed to persist for some time before the mask destroyed them; with a delay of 2 or 5 seconds, the redundant suffix produced no more interference, indicating that about 2 seconds of processing time was sufficient to store the digits in short-term memory (as compared with a quarter second for the tones in Massaro's experiment).

From the experiments discussed here, one is left with the following conclusions with regard to sensory memory. Incoming perceptual information is briefly retained in sensory memory stores that are not subject to strict capacity limitations (data are available only for the visual and auditory modalities, but presumably the other senses are similarly endowed). The persistence of the sensory memory trace permits encoding processes to be completed even after a stimulus is no longer perceptually present. Without this ability the organism could perceive nothing or very little from brief stimulus presentations, but sensory memory assures that the effective duration of a stimulus, during which the stimulus is available for perceptual processing and memory encoding, is of the order of seconds in the absence of interfering stimuli. Information is lost rapidly from sensory memory, but the rate of loss appears to be modality specific: visual sensory memory extends to not more than 1 second, while auditory sensory memory lasts for about 4 seconds. The difference between the forgetting rates for visual and auditory information also explains rather nicely the observation that auditorily presented lists of digits are recalled somewhat better than visually presented lists. The difference is in the last few items of the list. Those are the items where the longer persisting sensory memory trace for auditory stimuli permits subjects some additional processing time that is not available to the same extent for visual stimuli.

## 3.2    SELECTIVE ATTENTION

If we summarize the results reviewed in the last section, we are left with the picture of modality specific sensory memory stores retaining incoming information for a short period of time, thereby prolonging the effective life of a stimulus during which it is available for processing. These sensory memory stores appear to be unselective and not subject to the severe capacity limitations of short-term memory. That

raises the question about when and how the large amount of information that resides in sensory memory is reduced to the $7 \pm 2$ chunks,
which is all that there is room for in short-term memory.

It should be quite obvious that this reduction cannot be random,
but proceeds in accord with the goals of the individual and the task
that is being performed. It is, for instance, possible to instruct subjects
which aspects of a briefly presented stimulus are the important ones.
Subjects can report these critical attributes more accurately than
unemphasized attributes, apparently basing their reports on a more
accurate visual trace for the critical attributes (e.g., Harris and Haber,
1963). Such selection effects are not restricted to laboratory-produced
sets. In a nice demonstration experiment Erdelyi (1974) showed that
the presence of a swastica or Star of David in a visual display significantly distracted Jewish subjects. For such subjects, these were emo-
tion-charged symbols, and a set to attend to them had been firmly
established which could not be broken easily, even though it
interfered with performance in the task at hand.

## THE FILTER MODEL

Although it is easy to argue that selection effects must exist, and not
very hard to show that they do exist, the question how selection
operates is quite another matter. The problem is to determine the
mechanism that is responsible for selection effects. In terms of the
diagram in Figure 3.1, one can frame the question as follows: we know
that somewhere between the box labeled "Sensory memory
representation" and the box labeled "Short-term memory representation" selection must occur; in between are two arrows and the
"Detection" process. Does selection occur before detection, or is all
information processed, but only a small proportion stored in short-
term memory?

Broadbent (1958) outlined a model of the selection process that
introduced the concept of selective attention. In terms of our diagram, selective attention effects were localized in the arrow between
"Sensory memory" and "Feature extraction and naming." Selective
attention was conceived as a filter that lets only certain types of
information pass to the processing unit (Figure 3.4a). Only information
that possesses certain predetermined physical characteristics (e.g.,
tones of a certain frequency range, the voice of a particular person)
passes the filter and is processed; the rest is rejected. The problem is
viewed here as one of information transmission. Between the large-

capacity sensory memory and the processing unit there is a single channel that transmits information. This channel is a bottleneck, because its capacity is limited. Thus only a small part of the total available information is selected at any moment in time and transmitted for further processing. The channel can be rapidly switched to select information according to different criteria. This may produce the impression of attending to two things at a time but in fact attention always selects only one message at a time, alternating rapidly between different physical sources.

Broadbent based this model primarily on his work with dichotic listening. In such experiments subjects receive two speech messages simultaneously, one to each ear. If the subject is told to respond to one of them and to repeat it as it arrives, he remembers very little about the content of the other message. For instance, a subject might not even know in which language it had been delivered, or that the message consisted of reversed rather than ordinary speech. Not only are subjects unable to recall irrelevant messages, they also show no advantage when they later on attempt to learn the material that had been presented to the irrelevant ear. From such observations Broadbent concluded that there is a limited capacity channel and that when this channel is overloaded, only some of the information is selected for processing and the rest is filtered out. He also concluded that the filtering is done on the basis of physical stimulus attributes, because, although subjects remembered nothing about the meaning of a nonattended message, they tended to notice when the physical character of the message changed, e.g., when a female voice was substituted for a male one or when speech became pure noise. Broadbent also found that it takes time to switch the filter from one message source to another. Thus the rate at which people can switch attention is seriously limited.

Soon after Broadbent's pioneering work, experimental results were published that posed a serious challenge to the filtering model. Moray (1959) had subjects shadow one message while presenting an irrelevant message to the other ear that included the listeners' own name. The listeners noticed the occurrence of their name in the irrelevant message and could recall it at the end of the experiment. Thus Broadbent's hypothesis that messages are selected on the basis of physical cues must be questioned. Obviously, the listeners who detected their own names were processing the irrelevant message at a deeper level than that of gross physical characteristics.

A number of real-life observations agree with Moray's experimental data. It is not uncommon, for instance, that one concentrates entirely on a particular conversation at a cocktail party or in a crowded restaurant, unaware of the surroundings, only to hear one's name mentioned in some other conversation, whereupon attention immediately shifts to that other conversation. Indeed, it need not be the listener's own name; the name of someone in whom we are very interested may have the same effect, as will any topic of conversation that is important or emotionally significant to us. It seems, then, that the meaning of rejected messages is analyzed at least to some degree before the messages are rejected. Thereby, unselected channels are constantly monitored, and as something important is detected on such a channel, full attention may be shifted to it.

One may argue, of course, that cocktail party observations as reported above are hardly sufficient evidence to discredit the single channel filter model. In such situations there are no controls that the relevant conversation was fully attended to and that the listener was not, in fact, switching his attention in and out to various conversations, in the hope of finding a more congenial topic of discussion and/or partner. There are, however, a large number of laboratory studies that make the conclusion untenable that irrelevant messages are rejected without analysis.

Treisman (1964) presented identical messages to the selected and rejected ear, with various time separations, and found that her subjects noticed this identity, even if the two speakers were different, and if the messages themselves were spoken in different languages. (Her subjects, of course, were bilinguals). It is impossible that these subjects were tuning out the irrelevant message purely on the basis of its physical characteristics. Subjects must have processed such messages sufficiently to comprehend its meaning, so that when the identical message later appeared in the relevant ear, they could notice this. Of course, the processing of the irrelevant message was not sufficient to assure retention over longer time intervals, since by the end of the session the irrelevant messages were entirely forgotten, just as in Broadbent's and Moray's original experiments. Thus it seems that selection does not affect processing, but rather memory storage.

There are several other lines of evidence that indicate that selection occurs only after a certain amount of processing has occurred. A particularly interesting one involves the use of the galvanic skin response to monitor the listener's response to emotional words in the irrelevant ear (e.g., Moray, 1970). We know that if a person hears an emotional word this usually results in a galvanic skin response deflection. Moray has demonstrated that such deflections occur even when the word was presented to the irrelevant ear and the subject never consciously noticed it. Such words are not just rejected, but processed fully enough to bring the word into consciousness, or store it in memory.

These findings have led investigators to modify the single channel filter model of Figure 3.4a, creating the partial-encoding model of Figure 3.4b (e.g., Neisser, 1967). The notion of a single attention channel that is switched on the basis of low-level physical cues is abandoned in favor of a multichannel view. Each channel can be set at a certain attenuation level; thus the total channel capacity is divided

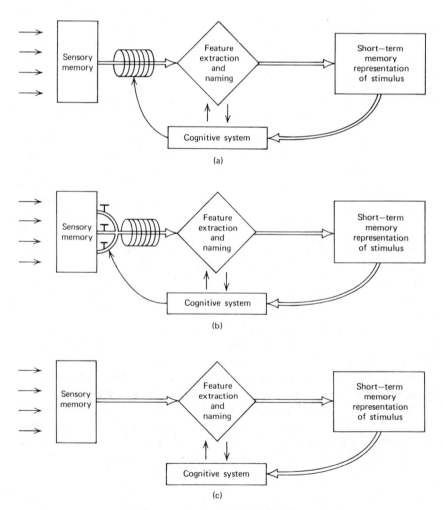

FIGURE 3.4    **Three models of selective attention.**

up among channels, usually in such a way that one channel is favored while the others are processed only partially. The main difference between diagrams (a) and (b) lies in the fate of irrelevant information: it is rejected and lost in model (a), while it is partially analyzed before it is lost in model (b). This partial analysis is what Neisser calls the preattentive process. It functions to direct attention to important channels; if a listener hears his name on an irrelevant channel, the preattentive mechanism picks up this information and switches attention to this new source.

The introduction of the preattentive mechanism solves many problems for the attention model. One of these is the problem of perceptual defense. It is known that when subjects are given emotional, bad, or dirty words, they tend to perceive such words less readily than neutral control words; subjects defend themselves against undesirable stimuli. This claim has been frequently disputed, partly because of the methodological difficulty of making it stick experimentally, but partly also because of the logical problems involved—how can anyone defend himself against the perception of a word that he has not yet perceived? Today it appears that perceptual defense is real enough (Erdelyi, 1974), and the preattentive mechanism allows us to understand how it may happen. Perceptually, a word is represented by many features, among them emotionally significant ones; all one has to suppose is that the preattentive process stops or slows down the analysis as soon as it encounters one of these disreputable features.

## THE FULL-PROCESSING MODEL

Many investigators have not been satisfied with Model (b) and proposed a more radical revision of selective attention. For instance, in the perceptual defense example just discussed, it is not obvious how the preattentive mechanism could single out the emotional meaning of a word prior to the identification of that word. Quite generally, it may be argued that there is no selective attention at all, that all stimuli are processed much more fully than had hitherto been supposed, and that a bottleneck arises not because information is transmitted through a limited capacity channel, but because of the limited capacity of short-term memory itself. This model is diagrammed in Figure 3.4c. It dispenses with the concept of an attention channel altogether, and puts no constraints on perceptual processing. The feature extraction and naming process operates on all information as long as it is available in sensory memory; within these limits all stimuli are fully analyzed. But only very little of that information can be stored in short-term memory.

The advantages of such a system are obvious: the decision about what is to be stored in short-term memory and what is to be brought to consciousness can now be made intelligently, based on a full analysis of the stimulus situation. We have come all the way from Broadbent's Model (a) where selection was based on gross physical characteristics of the stimuli, through Neisser's preattentive mechanism in Model (b) that took no more than a peek at the stimulus before deciding what to do with it, to Model (c) with a truly intelligent selection procedure. Versions of the full-processing model have been proposed by several authors, most notably Deutsch and Deutsch (1963) for the auditory case, and Shiffrin and Geisler (1973) for the visual modality. Actually, Broadbent (1958, 1971) had foreseen both Models (b) and (c), but the data available to him at that time did not require such complex models, and he felt that Model (c) had to be rejected on logical grounds: if the brain really can perform all this analysis on every incoming stimulus, why should there be any selection at all? Why reject a message after it has already been processed? This seemed a paradox to Broadbent, though it need not be, as Erdelyi (1974) and others have pointed out. Selection may be required because of storage limitations. Even though the analytic powers of the brain are large enough to continuously monitor the environment, not all of this information can, or should be stored in memory and brought into consciousness. Presumably even the human brain, with its stupendous storage capacity, would quickly run out of storage space if all perceptual processing were to leave permanent memory traces. No system has unlimited storage available, and an efficient system would need good procedures for deciding what to store and what to neglect. Complete processing of the input would appear to be optimal in this respect, because such a process could make the best informed decisions.

An experiment by Shiffrin and Gardner (1972) provides some evidence supporting Model (c) and discredits limited capacity attention theories. Shiffrin and Gardner argued that if the elements of a visual display are presented one at a time, full attention can be given to each element. On the other hand, if the whole display is presented simultaneously, the limited attention capacity of the perceiver must be divided among the several elements of the display, and hence each element should receive less processing than when it is presented singly. Attention theories predict, therefore, that sequential presentation should lead to better performance than simultaneous presentation in a detection task. They tested this prediction in a series of experiments, the basic design of which is illustrated in Figure 3.5. The visual displays contained four elements, the target element which was either an F or a T, and four distractor elements. The distractors were O's in the case illustrated, but Shiffrin and Gardner also used random shapes closely resembling F's and T's as distractors. Figure 3.5 shows the temporal stimulus sequence of a trial in this experiment. In each case, the subject sits in front of a tachistoscope, viewing a fixation point. When a start signal is given, a masking stimulus appears for .4 second. In the simultaneous presentation condition this is followed by a 50 millisecond presentation of the complete stimulus display, followed by another mask. The mask is needed to wipe out the stimulus trace in sensory memory, so that the effective processing time is, indeed, 50 milliseconds and not more. The subject responds on each trial by identifying the target stimulus (F or T) that had been presented on that trial. The sequential presentation condition is similar, except that the total stimulus presentation now requires 200 milliseconds, since each of the four stimulus elements are presented separately for 50 milliseconds.

The results of this experiment showed sequential presentation of the display to be just as good as simultaneous. As expected, there was a strong effect due to the confusability of stimuli and distractors (the detection probability was about .8 when the F's and T's were shown together with O's, but less than .7 when they were combined with the highly confusable letterlike shapes). The fact that performance did not improve when presentation was sequential implies that the initial

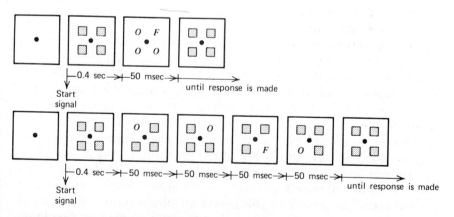

FIGURE 3.5    Presentation sequence for a single trial in the simultaneous and successive discrimination task of Shiffrin and Gardner (1972).

stages of processing up to and including letter recognition occur without capacity limitations and without attentional control, as claimed by Model (c).

The same conclusion is supported by the results of a study by Posner and Boies (1971) that employed an entirely different experimental methodology. These authors used a probe reaction time procedure to trace out a dynamic picture of the central processing demands existing during a perceptual recognition task. The rationale for such a procedure is as follows. Suppose one lets the subject perform two tasks at once, a letter matching task and a superimposed simple reaction time task to an auditory stimulus. The more capacity the letter matching task requires, the less will be left over for the reaction time task, and reactions should take longer. Indeed, by plotting reaction times continuously throughout the letter matching task, one can identify those stages of the matching task that do and do not require processing capacity. Attention theories claim that perceptual processing is limited; hence one would expect long reaction times on the probe task when a stimulus is presented. The full-processing view, on the other hand, predicts that letter recognition occurs without processing limitations, and that probe reaction times would increase only later, when capacity is taken up by the comparison process and response selection.

Posner and Boies' experimental task is outlined in Figure 3.6. A warning signal alerted the subject at Time 0. A second later a letter was presented, followed half a second later by a second letter (Condition (a)). The task of the subject was to respond "same" or "different," depending on whether or not the two letters had the same name (e.g., A and a). In Condition (b), the delay between first and second letter presentation was increased to 1 second (actually data from two separate experiments are combined here for purposes of illustration). Throughout this time, subjects' reaction times to a brief burst of white noise were sampled. All responses were key presses, the same–different judgments being made with the middle and index fingers of the right hand, the secondary task with the left index finger. Reaction times on the secondary task are shown in Figure 3.6 as a function of processing stages in the letter matching task. There was a slight improvement in reaction times after the warning signal occurred, probably an alertness effect. After the presentation of the first letter, reaction times increased gradually, peaking around the time of the second letter presentation. The important observation is the gradual increase in reaction times, which is especially obvious in Condition

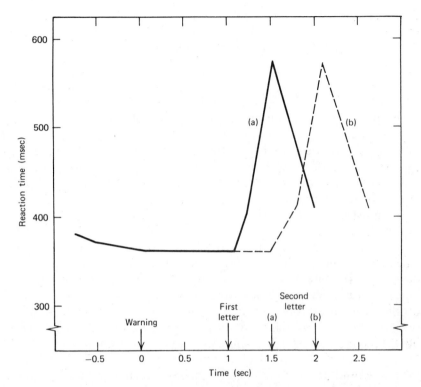

FIGURE 3.6    **Probe reaction times as a function of probe position when the second letter followed the first letter by .5 sec (a) and by 1 sec (b). (after Posner and Boies, 1971)**

(b), when there was a longer interstimulus interval: the perceptual processing of the first letter did not interfere with the probe reaction time task at all. Only later, as the subject prepared for the comparison process, presumably bringing a representation of the first letter into his short-term working memory, were interference effects noticeable in the secondary task. Subjects had trouble processing the probe during the comparison and response phases of the letter matching task, while the encoding of the letter by itself did not appear to require processing capacity.

Posner and Boies concluded that attention in the sense of limited processing capacity is not involved in perceptual identification: the contact between the sensory input and long-term memory that leads to the naming of the stimulus can be performed in parallel with other tasks, as assumed in Model (c), without interfering with performance on these tasks. The limited processing capacity attention mechanism enters only at later stages of processing, involving response selection, short-term memory, rehearsal, and consciousness.

## 3.2.3    RESOURCE AND DATA LIMITED PROCESSES

The picture that has emerged so far looks something like this: perceptual processing of stimuli, up to and including identification and naming, is done outside the central processor and is not subject to its capacity limitations; the limited capacity mechanism comes into play only when material enters short-term memory or consciousness, either for rehearsal, further memory encoding, or response selection. This almost looks as if people have two separate processing units, an essentially unlimited one for perceptual analysis and a capacity limited one for the "higher" mental processes. This is not a very appealing view, and indeed, it is probably wrong. Norman and Bobrow (1975) have argued quite forcefully that the data do not require such an interpretation, which is based on an oversimplified conception of the problems involved. Basic to their argument is the distinction between resource limited and data limited processes. Resources refer to computational processing effort, memory capacity, communication channels, etc., and they are always limited. A typical resource limited process would be the multiplication of two two-digit numbers without external aids: if we are left undisturbed and given enough time, we'll manage to do it, but few people can perform this task under unfavorable conditions. Data limited processes, on the other hand, are such that no matter how much time and effort we spend, we can do no better. Norman and Bobrow, following Gardner (1974), distinguish two types of data limited processes, signal-data limits (as in a psychophysical detection task, where the signal-to-noise ratio determines an upper performance limit that cannot be exceeded no matter how hard a person tries), and memory-data limits (as in absolute judgment tasks where subjects are limited to about seven categories for unidimensional stimuli). Norman and Bobrow plot several performance-resource functions to illustrate the rather complex problems that may arise in interpreting experimental data. In Figure 3.7, the top function illustrates a process that is data limited over almost all of its range. The bottom function, on the other hand, is resource limited throughout. Function (b), on the other hand, is resource limited for low levels of resources, but then becomes data limited, in that after a certain performance level is reached no further improvements in perform-

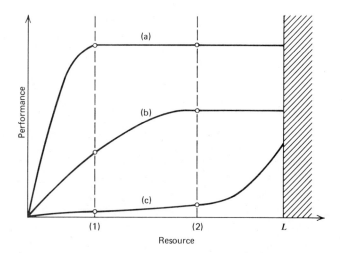

**FIGURE 3.7  Resource and data limited processes. Resources increase up to a limit _L_.** (after Norman and Bobrow, 1974)

ance can be achieved by devoting more resources to this task. Suppose an experimenter collects observations for each of the three tasks at two points, (1) and (2); he will wrongly conclude that tasks (a) and (c) are independent of the resource level, and hence independent of processing capacity limitations, while task (b) alone is sensitive to resource level. The conclusion is wrong because had the experimenter studied the three tasks over their total range, he would have found that the difference between these three tasks lies entirely in how soon data limits begin to control performance. We should not judge our unfortunate experimenter too harshly, though, because studying a task throughout the whole range of resource allocations is easier said than done, but nevertheless Norman and Bobrow's theoretical analysis points out that one must be extremely cautious about deriving conclusions about processing limitations from incomplete experimental evidence. The authors analyze several sets of data that appear to be puzzling or even contradictory in terms of resource and data limitations and are able to resolve a number of open questions. A nice example is their discussion of shadowing tasks. If a subject shadows a message that is being presented to one ear, and if his shadowing performance is high, a typical observation is that the subject will do very poorly in a word recognition task that is presented to the other ear. Indeed, this observation had originally motivated

Broadbent's filter model of selective attention: subjects were thought to filter out and reject the irrelevant message. In apparent contradiction to this result is another observation, namely, that in the same experimental situation subjects are able to detect simple tones quite well with the irrelevant ear. Why are words filtered out but not tones? Of course, we know by now that the filter model is untenable, but Norman and Bobrow's analysis of this situation permits a deeper understanding of the alternative explanation. Figure 3.8 shows some plausible resource-performance functions for word recognition and tone recognition. The latter is a much simpler task, which means that it becomes data limited at a much earlier point than word recognition. Superimposed in this figure are the resource requirements of the shadowing task. Shadowing is the primary task, and performance is high, which means that the resources devoted to shadowing $R_{primary}$ must also be high. The resources left over for the secondary task (either word recognition or tone recognition) are, therefore, the total amount of available resources $L$ minus $R_{primary}$: $R_{secondary} = L - R_{primary}$. Figure 3.8 shows quite clearly that for the resource level $R_{secondary}$, performance on the word recognition task remains quite poor, while at the same time performance on a tone recognition task would be essentially perfect, because tone recognition is a simple process that becomes data limited very early. It would be wrong, however, to con-

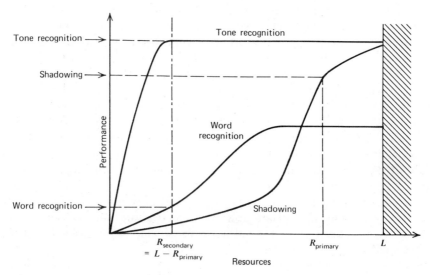

FIGURE 3.8 **Analysis of shadowing with two secondary tasks. (after Norman and Bobrow, 1974)**

clude from the fact that shadowing does not interfere with tone recognition that the two processes are independent and do not share a common processor. Presumably someone could construct a primary task that requires so much processing capacity that not enough is left over even for tone recognition.

What this means for models of attention is that we must not overinterpret data such as those of Posner and Boies (1971). Their data do not imply that the perceptual recognition and naming process is independent of the central processor and not subject to any capacity limitations; they merely mean that this type of processing is data limited over most of the resource range, so that it can be performed successfully as long as some minimal resource amount is available. There is no need for a model with two separate processing units, one for perceptual analysis without capacity limitations and one with capacity limitations for the "higher" mental operations. One central processor, with strictly limited resources, is all that is required to explain the experimental observations, if one keeps in mind that different processes become data limited at different resource levels. Many perceptual operations can be performed in parallel with good performance because these processes operate at their data limits with few resources. On the other hand, other processes such as response selection, or bringing an item into consciousness, require a great deal of the available resources, thus interfering with one another, though not necessarily with low-resource type processes. Note that in this view it is not necessary to talk about stages of information processing at all. Norman and Bobrow (1974) simply describe a pool of possible processes that become active as resources are made available for them. By drawing boxes around labels such as "Sensory memory" and "Short-term memory" one is merely identifying significant products of this essentially continuous and parallel stream of processing, as a convenience for the investigator and student.

## STIMULUS ENCODING PROCESSES IN VERBAL LEARNING

At the end of the previous chapter, winding up our discussion of interference theory, we pointed out that students of verbal learning in the tradition of Ebbinghaus have tended to neglect stimulus encoding processes. Verbal learning theory has traditionally been characterized by an emphasis on the processes of association formation and response integration. Only relatively recently has it become clear that a systematic analysis of stimulus encoding processes must be an integral part of any theoretical account of verbal learning. Of course, some psychologists have made similar arguments before (e.g., Gibson, 1940), but among our contemporaries it is Martin (1968, 1971, 1972) who has most successfully advocated such a viewpoint.

Recognition of the stimulus cue is a logical prerequisite of associative recall. The fact that an item pair A–B is associated means that there exists a memory trace a–b; if the stimulus term A is presented as a recall cue, somehow contact must be established between A and the memory trace a. Once the memory trace a is reached the response B can be produced on the basis of the associated trace b. However, somehow the stimulus A must be recognized as belonging to the memory trace a. This problem was first formulated by Höffding in 1891, its importance was emphasized by Köhler (1949), but not until very recently has this truism been given the attention that it deserves by the experimentalists and theorists in the verbal learning area.

Höffding's analysis implies that it should be possible to demonstrate empirically that stimulus recognition is, indeed, a prerequisite for successful recall. That this is so will be shown in the next section. The problem, is, however, more complex than that; it is possible that A, that is, the physical, objective stimulus, independent of the subject as part of the outside world, may not be copied faithfully by a, the memory trace corresponding to A. If one considers for a moment how complex the relationship between A and a must be, the fact that the two may differ in important ways can come as no surprise. The objective, physical stimulus that is directly under the control of the experimenter must be clearly distinguished from the stimulus that is actually effective for the subject. The first is the same for all observers; it is part of what we call the real world. Koffka (1935) called it the distal stimulus; Underwood's term for it is nominal stimulus (Underwood, 1963). The distal stimulus affects the organism through a series of transformations. For instance, the visual information about a distal object is first transformed into a pattern of light waves (Koffka's proximal stimulus), then into a retinal firing pattern, and finally into patterns of neural excitation, which have a most complex relationship to the distal stimulus. Thus, the effective, functional stimulus is the product of many transformations, some of which may be deterministic and one-to-one, while others are subjective in the sense that they depend on the momentary state of the perceiving subject; some transformations may be probabalistic and some may destroy or distort the original information, or add to it from memory.

Not only the complexity of the relationship between nominal and functional stimulus should concern us, but also its variability. Given the same nominal stimulus on two different occasions and in two different contexts, it is by no means certain that the subject will encode it in the same way on both occasions. This encoding variability may have important consequences in learning and memory. Martin (1972), in fact, claims that all effects of stimulus variables in verbal learning are determined by the degree of difficulty that subjects have in arriving at a stable encoding for the material in question. We shall return to a consideration of this "encoding variability hypothesis" below.

## STIMULUS RECOGNITION

Before a subject can retrieve the appropriate response in a paired-associate test he must be able to recognize the stimulus term. Several experiments have shown that recognition of the stimulus term is a necessary condition for the establishment of a stimulus-response connection (Bernbach, 1967; Martin, 1967). As an illustration we may take a study by Martin (1967) in which subjects learned eight trigram-number pairs. Study trials and test trials were alternated, and on each test trial the subject had to make two responses: a yes–no recognition response and recall of the response digit, guessing if necessary. On test trials the eight stimulus items were shown together with 16 distractor items in random order. Some of Martin's results are shown in Figure 3.9. When the recognition response was correct, the probability of recall increased over trials as a learning curve should; when the recognition response was incorrect, no recall learning occurred, and the probability of recall oscillated around the value of 1/8 expected by chance. Even more impressive is the finding that it does not matter how often the subject has already given a correct recall response to a particular item on previous trials: if he fails to recognize it recall performance on that trial is at the chance level. Similarly Bernbach (1967) has reported that it makes no difference how often a subject has already correctly recognized an item previously: as long as he does not recognize it on a given trial, recall performance is no better than chance.

An interesting observation with respect to stimulus recognition has been made by Wicker (1970) who compared learning with pictorial and verbal stimuli. It is well known that subjects acquire a paired-associate list with pictorial stimuli much faster than a verbal list. Wicker was able to show that this difference lies entirely in the greater recognizability of pictures. When response recall was conditionalized upon stimulus recognition in the manner of Figure 3.9, the difference between the picture and word lists disappeared!

If stimulus recognition is a necessary prerequisite of associative recall, it follows that anything that makes stimulus recognition difficult should interfere with learning. Thus, items that are well integrated and easily recognized, are encoded in the same way on different trials and in different contexts and should be easier to learn than items that the subject responds to differently every time he encounters them. This appears to be one reason why low-meaningful nonsense syllables give the learner so much trouble: on one occasion TLQ may be encoded as "something that starts with a T," on the next as "ending with a Q," and whatever is learned about one will be unrelated and independent of what is learned about the other.

## 3.3.2   ENCODING VARIABILITY IN TRANSFER

Although unstable stimulus material that encourages variable encoding retards learning, it may lead to better transfer for the very same reasons. Given a meaningful syllable like PEN as a stimulus the subject has no problem arriving at a stable encoding for it, e.g., the concept "pen," or an image of a pen. Thus, learning will be easy. However, suppose the subject is asked to learn a second response to the stimulus term PEN. Very likely, he will still encode PEN in the same way as before and start confusing the two responses. The result is negative transfer. On the other hand, suppose the stimulus term is TLQ. It is hard to find a stable encoding for such a nonsense trigram, and, therefore, original learning is slow. But now consider what happens in a transfer situation, where this trigram is paired with a new response. The same encoding variability that made original learning difficult now turns out to be an advantage. If the subject had learned the first response to the functional stimulus "something that starts with a T," but employs the code "ending with a Q" when he is learning the second response, no confusion or interference between the two responses need occur. Hence one would expect little or no negative transfer in this case. Martin (1972) has reviewed a number of experiments that test this prediction. It is indeed true that no negative transfer occurs with low-meaningful stimuli in some studies, but the effect is not a stable one. Perhaps this should be expected since we are dealing here with encoding strategies that subjects may or may not

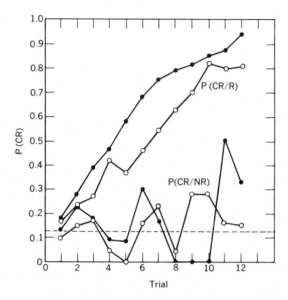

**FIGURE 3.9  Proportion of correct responses (CR) given and recognition (R) and nonrecognition (NR) of high- (full circles) and low-meaningful stimuli (open circles). The dashed line is the chance level. (after Martin, 1967)**

use, depending on how they interpret their task. Some subjects may perceive their task as encoding the second list stimuli in the same way as the first list stimuli, thus not taking advantage of the possible facilitatory consequences of variable encoding.

Similar considerations apply to another research design that has been used to investigate the encoding variability hypothesis. In several experiments (for a review see again Martin, 1972) subjects learned a first list, say A–B, but instead of the second list being a re-pairing of the same stimulus and responses as in the conventional A–B_r design, novel stimulus components were added during the transfer task, so that the second list actually corresponded to the schema AX–B_r. One would expect that subjects would take advantage of this opportunity to recode the stimuli: if they learned the first response to the stimulus A, they now could learn the second response to the stimulus component X, thus avoiding negative transfer. It is possible to determine which responses subjects learned to what stimuli by administering a final test after the learning of both lists. On this test, the two components A and X are presented separately, and the subjects' ability to produce the second list response is noted. The encoding variability hypothesis predicts that subjects will recall the second list response well in response to the $X$-cue, but poorly in response to the $A$-cue. Such results have been observed in some studies, but not consistently. Again, the data are hard to interpret, however, because of the possibility that although subjects were free to recode the stimulus on the second task, they may have felt obliged not to do so.

Perhaps the clearest support for the encoding variability hypothesis comes from an experiment reported by Martin (1972) in which the presence or absence of negative transfer was conditionalized upon whether subjects stayed with the same stimulus encoding during both first and second list learning, or whether they switched encodings. Clearly, we expect second list learning to be more difficult in the first case than in the second. Martin had subjects first learn a list in which the stimulus terms consisted of a triplet of unrelated words; the second list employed the same compound stimuli, but paired them with new responses. Schematically, the design could be represented as $(A_1, A_2, A_3) - B$; $(A_1, A_2, A_3) - C$. After learning each list, the functional stimulus was determined for both the $B$ and $C$ terms by the simple expedient of giving both to subjects and having them recall the corresponding stimulus terms. Suppose a subject recalls exactly the same stimulus components to $B$ as to $C$; this implies that the subject has not recoded the stimulus, and such a subject/item event shall be called a "stay." On the other hand, suppose a subject recalls different, nonoverlapping stimulus elements in response to $B$ and $C$; this implies that the subject has encoded the stimulus differently, and such an event will be called a "switch." All one has to do, then, to test our hypothesis is to compute separately the number of errors made during second list learning for stay and switch events. In Martin's experiment, the mean number of errors in learning the second list was 4.0 for stay events, but only 2.4 for switches. Clearly, second list learning was much more difficult when subjects did not recode the stimulus. Thus, it appears that Martin's hypothesis is, indeed, correct and that negative transfer is directly traceable to failures to recode the stimulus. There are, however, many open problems; Most importantly, we need to know when subjects will recode and when they will not. The data that we have are contradictory in this respect, and a systematic exploration of the conditions under which encoding variability occurs is one of the really important research problems today. Encoding and encoding variability are useful theoretical constructs—but we would use them with much more confidence and a better conscience if we knew more about the empirical conditions for their applicability.

## DISCRIMINATION LEARNING

On a screen before a subject two small disks of light appear briefly. The lights are carefully calibrated so that they are identical in every respect, except that one of them is brighter by a small amount than the other. The subject's task is to identify which of the two lights is the brighter one. If he performs correctly, he demonstrates that he can discriminate between the two lights. Experiments like this are called *discrimination* experiments. The procedure just described would be called simultaneous discrimination because the two stimuli that were to be discriminated were presented simultaneously. In a successive discrimination problem the stimuli appear one after the other, but the subject's task remains the same. Now consider a slight modification of this experimental procedure. Instead of asking the subject to tell which stimulus is brighter, one stimulus, called a standard stimulus, is shown first and the subject is asked to tell whether or not test stimuli are different from the standard.

*Stimulus generalization* is said to occur if the subject responds with "same" to stimuli that are actually different. Obviously, discrimination and generalization are closely related procedurally: discrimination implies differential responding; generalization implies lack of discrimination. The operational definition of concept learning or classification learning is identical with that of generalization: in a concept identification experiment the subject learns to make the same response to all instances of a concept. Membership in a concept class may be defined in terms of a common physical attribute (e.g., *blondes*) or in terms of abstract rules or relationships (e.g., *bachelor*). In either case instances of a concept may differ widely in characteristics that are irrelevant to the defining property. A distinction between concept formation and generalization is generally made in experimental psychology in spite of the lack of operational justification. This distinction appears to be historically determined: the term generalization is applied if the stimuli are relatively simple and their variability is restricted to a single known psychophysical dimension. Pure tones of different frequencies, colors, or lights arranged in certain spatial patterns are typically used in both human and animal experiments on generalization. When the stimuli are somewhat more complex (words, line-drawings, pictures) and human subjects are used, the experiments have traditionally been labeled as concept formation. However, this difference reflects common usage more than any essential operational difference. Certainly, animals can learn concepts, as for instance

Herrnstein and Loveland (1964) have shown. Herrnstein and Loveland taught pigeons the concept of the human figure using highly complex color photographs as their stimulus material.

## 3.4.1    SPENCE'S THEORY OF DISCRIMINATION LEARNING

The traditional approach to problems of generalization, discrimination, and concept identification did not involve the notion of selective coding. We shall first discuss this approach, which culminated in the theory of discrimination learning by Spence (1937), in order to illustrate its achievements and point out its limitations.

The term stimulus generalization was introduced by Pavlov (1927) who repeatedly observed instances of stimulus generalization in his laboratory. For instance, salivary responses conditioned to a pure tone of 1000 cps occurred in response to tones of different frequencies, or even to the sound made by the experimenter's footsteps, or the rattle of his key chain. Pavlov investigated generalization systematically and found that the less similar a stimulus was to the conditioned stimulus, the less likely it was to elicit the conditioned response, and the smaller the magnitude of the conditioned response became if it occurred at all. Indeed, there appeared to be a regular, monotonically decreasing gradient of generalization around the value of the conditioned stimulus. Early in training Pavlov's dogs responded to a wide range of stimuli around the CS. After extended training responsiveness became more restricted to the vicinity of the reinforced stimulus. For Pavlov stimulus generalization was one of the basic phenomena of conditioning. He attempted to explain it in terms of irradiation of neural excitation.

Hull adopted Pavlov's thesis, minus the neural theory, and introduced a distinction between primary and secondary stimulus generalization that was subsequently to become very influential. Primary stimulus generalization is essentially identical with the Pavlovian concept. It is an automatic increment in response strength to stimuli that are physically similar to the conditioned stimulus. Secondary stimulus generalization occurs through mediating responses. If the similarity between stimuli is not physical (i.e., defined in terms of common elements, or of a common dimension, such as loudness or frequency in the case of tones) generalization may occur via a common mediating response. In this manner Hull could account for what he called logical or abstract similarity. We shall use the term generalization in the sense of primary generalization at first and defer a discussion of mediation.

Stimulus generalization permitted Hull to solve what he considered a fundamental problem in learning theory. Given the variability of the human environment, two stimuli are hardly ever identical in all physical details. How, then, can a response ever become conditioned to a stimulus through repeated pairings with it, when the "same" stimulus is never repeated? Hull called this the stimulus equivalence problem and suggested primary generalization as a way out of the dilemma. Because of generalization, small variations in the conditioned stimulus nevertheless permit the build-up of habit strength to some average value.

Hull's view of the role of generalization in learning has been vigorously attacked, most notably in a famous paper by Lashley and Wade (1946). Lashley and Wade argued that generalization is nothing but lack of discrimination. They maintained that Hull's stimulus equivalence problem was a paradox only for the learning theorist, but not for the learning organism. Variability in the physical stimulus per se is relevant only if the organism actually registers this variability. At the beginning of training an organism simply does not discriminate the conditioned stimulus very well. Therefore Pavlov's dog salivated to the CS of 1000 cps, to tones of similar frequency, and even to quite unrelated noises. As training progressed salivation to noises and other tones remained unreinforced and hence extinguished. In Lashley and Wade's view, the empirical generalization gradients that are generally observed are due to the inability of organisms to discriminate precisely among stimuli, and it is not necessary to postulate a special and basic process called generalization.

Quite the opposite approach has been taken by Spence in his elegant and very successful theory which explained discrimination learning again in terms of generalization (Spence, 1937). Spence assumed that, in accordance with the views of Pavlov and Hull, a symmetric gradient of habit strength is established around the positive stimulus in a discrimination experiment, and that a similar gradient of inhibition is established around the negative stimulus. Performance is then determined by the algebraic sum of the two gradients. An example from Spence (1942) will illustrate the theory. Suppose an organism has been trained in a size discrimination task. A number of reinforcements to the positive stimulus (160 sq cm) have established a certain habit strength to that stimulus which generalizes to stimuli of similar size as shown in Figure 3.10. Extinction trials with the negative stimulus

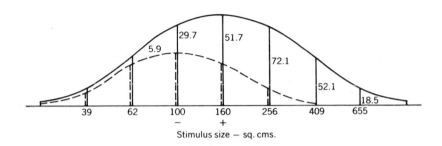

FIGURE 3.10   Hypothetical generalization gradients for habit strength after training on a positive stimulus of 160 and inhibition after training on a negative stimulus of 100. The difference between habit strength and inhibition is indicated numerically at several points. (after Spence, 1942)

(100 sq cm) have established a gradient of inhibition around that stimulus value, also shown in Figure 3.10. The total response strength for each stimulus value is determined by subtracting the inhibitory tendency associated with it from its habit strength. The theory makes a number of interesting predictions. For instance, note that the maximum difference occurs at a point to the right of the $S^+$. Therefore, the maximum response rate in a generalization test under the present conditions should be displaced from the $S^+$, away from the $S^-$. This phenomenon has frequently been observed and is known under the name of peak shift in the literature on discrimination learning.

Observe that in Spence's theory the effective stimulus is a concrete physical object: the subject learns to discriminate a square of 160 sq cm from a square of 100 sq cm. Positive habit strength is built up to the former, inhibition to the latter. On the other hand, one could maintain that what the subject really learns is to pick the larger of the two squares, rather than the particular square of 160 sq cm. In other words, the effective stimulus might be a relationship (e.g., larger) rather than a concrete physical object as Spence maintains. This notion is supported by an observation that has been termed transposition: if, after training to discriminate the two squares of size 160 and 100 sq cm, the subjects are given two stimuli of size 160 and 256 sq cm, they will choose the 256 sq cm stimulus figure, i.e., the larger one, rather than the former $S^+$! Offhand, the fact that transposition occurs seems to offer decisive evidence in favor of the relational hypothesis. However, Spence was able to show that the theory summarized in

Figure 3.10 is in complete agreement with the experimental facts regarding transposition. The theory predicts, as is seen in Figure 3.10, that the subject will respond more to the stimulus of 256 sq cm, which has never been experienced before, rather than to the $S^+$, since the habit differential is greater (72.1) for the larger stimulus than for the conditioned stimulus itself (51.7). In fact, Spence's theory wins out over the relational argument, because of another interesting implication that also can be read from Figure 3.10. Suppose we present the 256-cm square and the 409-cm square for a transfer test. Relational theory must stick to its prediction that the larger of the two stimuli will be chosen, but from Figure 3.10 the opposite prediction can be derived. The habit differential is larger for 256 sq cm than for 409 sq cm and hence the subject should not show transposition with the present stimulus pair. In addition, suppose we present two stimuli that are very large, so large that neither habit nor inhibition will generalize to them. For such a stimulus pair Spence's theory predicts random responding, while relational theory still would predict that the subject chooses the larger of the two stimuli. Empirical results support Spence in both cases: it is indeed true that transposition breaks down when the test stimuli differ greatly from the training stimuli, and that responding becomes completely random with stimuli very far removed from the training values.

Note that Spence's theory accounts for the surprising facts of transposition without invoking any new principles. Responses are still directly conditioned to the physical stimulus, and the summation of habit and inhibition gradients is all that is involved in transposition. However, one must realize the limitations of this theory. First of all, it is clear that humans can respond to relations, and even if we restrict ourselves to infra-human organisms, the victory of the absolute over the relative position is not as decisive as the discussion above may lead one to believe. Even rats can learn to respond to relational cues under appropriate conditions, as was shown by Lawrence and DeRivera (1954). It does not seem very fruitful to argue about whether organisms respond to relations or to a particular concrete stimulus. A relation between stimuli can be as good a cue in discrimination learning as more concretely definable attributes of a stimulus. This is obviously true for human subjects, while animals, especially lower ones, may be more tied to concrete objects.

A second, and even more severe limitation of Spence's theory lies in its restriction to nonverbal organisms and to experimental situations that insure that the animal is exposed and responds to all aspects of the stimulus situation. However, as will be demonstrated shortly, the most pervasive phenomenon of discrimination learning is that the subject responds selectively to different aspects of the stimulus. Coding operations and stimulus selection appear to be the central problem of discrimination learning. No satisfactory theory of discrimination learning can neglect these phenomena.


### 3.4.2    THE ROLE OF STIMULUS CODING

Stimulus objects may either be perceived as integral, unitary wholes or they may be analyzed into perceptually distinct, separate dimensions or properties (e.g., Gardner, 1974). When stimuli are analyzable, subjects tend to select one or the other aspect of the stimulus and base their response on it. As in the verbal learning experiments already discussed, it is necessary to distinguish between the nominal stimulus in discrimination learning experiments and the stimulus as it is coded by the subject. A pioneering experiment by Lawrence (1949) was the first to make this point.

Lawrence demonstrated that a good part of the difficulty in a discrimination task lies in finding the right cues to respond to. He first taught three groups of rats a simultaneous discrimination problem involving either a black-white discrimination, a discrimination between rough and smooth floors, or a discrimination between narrow and wide alleys. Then all rats learned a new discrimination problem, namely to choose one arm of a black T-maze, but to choose the other arm if the maze was white. T-mazes with both rough and smooth floors were used, but this cue was not correlated with reward. For the group trained initially on the black-white discrimination this task proved to be quite easy. Color-cues were relevant in both tasks, and therefore these subjects started the second problem with the appropriate coding responses. The problem was much more difficult for the other two groups of subjects, who at the start of the second learning task were making either inappropriate coding responses (smooth and rough floors) or were trained with an irrelevant problem (alley width no longer varied in the second problem). Since these two groups learned about equally slowly, the main difficulty seems to have been to establish the response to the color cue, which had been extinguished in the first training problem for at least some of the subjects, rather than in abandoning the inappropriate coding of the stimulus in terms of rough or smooth floors.

Similar results are obtained in studies of human concept formation (e.g., Kendler and Kendler, 1962). The learning materials in such experiments are usually drawings of simple figures, which may vary along such dimensions as shape (circle, square, and the like) or color, size, number, etc. Assuming binary dimensions the simplest kind of concept that can be defined with this stimulus material is of the form "All red cards belong to class A, all green cards belong to class B." In this case, color is called the relevant dimension, and shape, size, and numerosity are irrelevant dimensions. Once such a concept has been learned, as evidenced by a large number of correct classifications, the experimenter may change the basis of classification and begin reinforcing the subject according to a new scheme. Two kinds of changes must be distinguished: in a reversal response assignments are simply switched (red is B and green is A), but color remains the relevant dimension; in an extradimensional shift a new dimension is made relevant (e.g., large is A and small is B).

Consider a theory of discrimination learning which, like Spence's theory, assumes that during training habit strength is being built up to the $S^+$ while inhibition develops to the $S^-$. Reversal should be a much harder task to learn than an extradimensional shift according to such a theory. If an extradimensional shift involves stimulus values that are sufficiently dissimilar from the original training stimuli, few generalized response tendencies will have been formed during training and therefore interference from inappropriate responses during the learning of the shift problem should be a less serious problem than in a reversal. The results of many experiments, some of which are summarized in Kendler and Kendler (1962), indicate exactly the opposite: reversal shifts are easy to learn for adult human subjects, but extradimensional shifts may be very hard to learn. Apparently we are dealing here with the same kind of phenomenon as in the Lawrence (1949) experiment which has just been reviewed. Subjects learn a particular way to code a stimulus and base their response on the coded stimulus. When the experimenter reverses the response assignments, the coding response of the subject remains appropriate, and all the subject has to learn is to switch responses. In an extradimensional shift, on the other hand, the problem is greatly more complicated. The old coding response is now irrelevant. The subject must learn to abandon it and to acquire a new coding response. Sometimes the now-correct coding response may have already been tried during the first learning stage. Since it was inadequate then it may have become extinguished, so that the likelihood that this coding response will be evoked after a shift may be quite small.

The theoretical alternatives at this point are between theories in which there is a direct connection between the discriminative stimulus and the response and theories in which some process that is partly under the control of the subject intervenes. Various investigators have used the terms coding response, mediating response, or attention for this intervening process. A discussion of the relative merits of these terms can be deferred until the need for some such term has been unequivocally established.

Predictions from theories that assume direct connections between stimuli and responses for reversal and extradimensional shifts are complicated by the fact that the old response receives partial reinforcement after an extradimensional shift: although *red-A* is no longer correct after a shift to *small-A,* some *small* items will be *red,* and thus the subject's responses will sometimes be reinforced even though they are based upon incorrect coding responses. It is well known that partial reinforcement retards extinction, and it is possible that the poorer performance after an extradimensional shift is due to this factor rather than to the need of finding a new coding response (Buss, 1953). It was a very difficult methodological problem to design experiments in which an extradimensional shift was not confounded with partial reinforcement, without introducing some other confounding factor. However, several experimenters eventually managed to show that the superiority of reversal over nonreversal performance is retained when partial reinforcement effects are eliminated (e.g., Harrow and Friedman, 1958).

The coding responses that are employed in the simple concept formation experiments under discussion are predominantly verbal. This is implied by a series of informative developmental studies. Both rats and nursery school children find a nonreversal shift easier than a reversal shift (Kelleher, 1956; Kendler, Kendler, and Wells, 1960). Kindergarten children have about equal difficulty with reversal and nonreversal shifts (Kendler and Kendler, 1959), and college students can handle reversal problems with great ease. The more verbal an organism becomes, the easier it becomes for him to execute a reversal shift, presumably because he codes the stimulus material verbally. Kendler and Kendler (1962) have some fairly direct evidence for the importance of verbalization in explaining the developmental results. They made 4-year-old children verbalize aloud all stimuli in a concept identification experiment. One group of subjects was asked to tell the experimenter which was correct, the "large" one or the "small" one of a stimulus pair. Another group of subjects learned to say "black" or "white" in a similar way, and a control group was not required to say anything. When the cue which subjects were trained to verbalize was the relevant cue, performance was best. When an irrelevant cue was verbalized, the mean number of errors to criterion was about twice as high. The control group performed at an intermediate level. Obviously verbalization strongly influenced concept learning. The same experiment was also performed with 7-year-old children, but with somewhat different results. The interfering effect of irrelevant verbalizations was even more powerful than before, but no facilitative effect of verbalizing the relevant cue was found this time. Presumably 7 year olds are capable of making the relevant verbal coding responses themselves, and outside help is of little importance to them.

One must not conclude from these examples that all coding responses are verbal. Verbal coding responses are certainly important, but coding responses may be of a much more general nature and need be neither verbal nor conscious. The concept of coding responses is needed to explain the results of many animal discrimination learning experiments as well (e.g., Lawrence, 1949; Sutherland, 1959). Although rats have more difficulty with a reversal shift than with a nonreversal shift, previous experience with reversal shifts leads to a marked improvement in their ability to execute reversal shifts in a T-maze (Krechevsky, 1932; Dufort, Guttman, and Kimble, 1954). A similar improvement over successive reversals has been demonstrated by Harlow (1949) for monkeys. Harlow's monkeys were given a choice between two stimulus objects differing either in size, color, or shape. The monkeys learned discriminations such as "the banana is under the barrel-shaped object." Over 300 such problems were learned in succession. The performance of the monkeys improved greatly from problem to problem. For the last 100 problems the monkeys chose almost always correctly after only one learning trial. Harlow described this improvement in the ability to learn as learning-to-learn. Using the present terminology one would say that the monkeys acquired appropriate coding responses which permitted them to disregard irrelevant cues (e.g., cues associated with spatial position) and to respond quickly to changes in the correlation between the relevant cue and reinforcement.

Another significant characteristic of coding responses in discrimination experiments is that coding responses are in general not a sensitization to particular stimulus values but refer to broad classes of cues which have some common discriminative property, i.e., to attributes or stimulus dimensions. Shape, color, and size, as well as other such simple attributes, are normally used in concept formation experiments. However, attributes are not necessarily restricted to variations in a single modality (Lawrence cites as a pleasant example the dryness of a wine), nor is it necessary that there be a correlation with some physical dimension (e.g., friendliness). Simple attributes like size are used merely because they are easy to control experimentally, not because they have a status of logical priority.

An experiment that demonstrated that coding responses are not specific to particular stimulus values (red, green), but refer to attributes (color) has been reported by Johnson (1967). Johnson compared extradimensional shift and reversal shift with an intradimensional shift. In order to achieve this, Johnson used stimulus cards which consisted of two figures, each varying in four dimensions, two of which, color and form, were four-valued. One figure on each stimulus card was either red or green, the other yellow or blue. After learning the original problem (red versus green), subjects were divided into three subgroups. One group received a reversal shift (green versus red), one group received an intradimensional shift (yellow versus blue), and the third group was shifted to a new dimension (square versus triangle). As in other studies, the extradimensional shift was much harder to learn than the reversal shift. However, there was no significant difference in learning the reversal and the intradimensional shift. Johnson's interpretation of these findings is that in both cases subjects could retain their coding responses (which therefore must have been something like "pay attention to color") and merely had to change the coded-stimulus—overt-response connection. The reason for using two figures on each card in this study was that this permitted an intradimensional shift without suddenly introducing completely new stimulus values. If this precaution is not observed, novelty effects may distort shift performance, as they had in several previous studies of intradimensional shifts.

The experiments discussed so far were either animal experiments or simple concept identification experiments. However, as far as the importance of coding processes is concerned very much the same results are obtained in other types of discrimination experiments. An interesting study of what is learned when children are taught to discriminate letterlike stimuli shall serve as a final example. The study has been reported by Pick (1965).

Pick employed a transfer design in which subjects were first trained to discriminate a set of letterlike stimuli from a second set of items that were obtained by transformation of the standard items. Among the transformations used were such operations as changing lines into curves, right-left reversal, or size transformations. In the second stage of her experiment, subjects (kindergarten children) were given a new discrimination task. In the Experimental Group I the same set of standard items was used as before, but the transformations that generated the distractor items were changed. Thus, if the children had learned particular stimulus values during Stage 1 strong positive transfer would be expected. The subjects in Experimental Group II were given new standards, but the same transformations that were employed in Stage 1 were retained to produce distractor items. Thus, if the children had discovered how the forms differed in Stage 1, positive transfer would result. Finally, Pick used a control group which received both new standards and new transformations during the second stage of the experiment. Her results are shown in Table 3.1. Subjects made the fewest errors in Stage 2 when the dimensions of difference were the same in both parts of the experiment (E2). However, subjects who had to learn new coding responses to familiar standards (E1) still outperformed the group given both new standards and new transformations to learn (C). Therefore, one may conclude that coding is mostly a matter of discovering relevant dimensions of difference, although the superior performance of Group E1 over the control subjects shows that some coding was specific to particular letter shapes.

## MODELS OF DISCRIMINATION LEARNING

The idea that subjects code the stimuli in discrimination learning and respond on the basis of the stimulus-as-coded has been incorporated more or less explicitly into several theories of discrimination learning. Hull (1943) acknowledged the problem and tried to deal with it by postulating a mechanism of "afferent neural interaction." Guthrie (1959) insisted that "what is being noticed becomes a signal for what is being done." The ethologists (e.g., Tinbergen, 1951) have provided some beautiful demonstrations of the way in which coded stimuli control the behavior of animals in their natural environment. However, only in recent years has the central importance of coding processes in discrimination learning been fully recognized.

TABLE 3.1.    **Number of Errors Made in Transfer Stage by Groups With Three Types of Training (after Gibson, 1965).**

| | Type of Training | | |
|---|---|---|---|
| Group | Standard | Transformation | Errors |
| E1 | Same | Different | 69 |
| E2 | Different | Same | 39 |
| C | Different | Different | 101 |

Historically, learning theory has had a strong bias for explanations which involve only directly observable events. Therefore the suggestion that coding is mainly a matter of orienting responses is not a surprising one. The subject may modify the proximal stimulus through orienting behavior and receptor adjustments. There can be no doubt that such behavior occurs and plays a significant role in discrimination learning. Watching a rat vacillate at the choice point of a T-maze, or a person looking back and forth between the stimuli in a simultaneous discrimination task is sufficient to demonstrate this point. On the other hand, orienting responses cannot possibly be the whole story: no overt receptor adjustment can explain how the pitch of a tone, rather than, say, its loudness can become a functional stimulus. The proximal stimulus is quite independent of the subject's orienting responses in this case, or in the case of tachistoscopically presented visual stimuli, and yet stimulus coding is observed.

Theories using the concept of a mediating response have been more successful. They avoid tying responses directly to the proximal stimulus by assuming that the proximal stimulus gives rise to a mediating response. The overt response is then connected with the covert stimulus consequences of this mediating response. Schematically, we have

$$S \rightarrow r\text{---}s \rightarrow R.$$

The mediating responses transform the nominal stimulus $S$ into the functional stimulus $s$. Mediating responses are learned just as overt responses. A mediating response that is consistently reinforced because it produces a functional stimulus which is correlated with reward becomes dominant during training, i.e., it becomes associated with the proximal stimulus. When this stimulus is presented the mediating response is aroused and produces the appropriate functional stimulus. It is clear how such a theory can account for the experimental results described in the previous section. For instance, a reversal shift is clearly less complicated than a shift to a new dimension:

Reversal Shift:

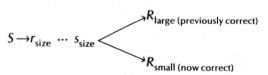

Nonreversal Shift:

$$S \begin{cases} r_{size} \cdots s_{size} \longrightarrow R_{large \text{ (previously correct)}} \\ \\ r_{brightness} \cdots s_{brightness} \longrightarrow R_{white \text{ (now correct)}} \end{cases}$$

The mediating response concept is related to stimulus coding. However, it is not as general as is required for the explanation of discrimination learning. The problem has been succinctly stated by Lawrence (1963). Mediating responses are the product of learning, and they are tied to the proximal stimulus so that, given that a certain mediating response has been acquired, a particular functional stimulus will always result until the mediating response is unlearned. It is difficult to understand the role played by sets, instructions, and attitudes within this framework. For instance, one can tell a subject (or one can teach him) to respond to the pitch of a tone and ignore its loudness. If one then instructs him to respond to loudness and ignore pitch, his behavior will change abruptly. Obviously, how a subject codes a stimulus is dependent on such factors as set and instructions, and is not simply a function of a mediating response that is elicited by the stimulus itself.

The term mediating response carries with it the suggestion that the coding process is stimulus-determined, i.e., that a mediating response is elicited by the nominal stimulus and produces the functional stimulus. A term which stresses more the contribution of the state of the perceiver would be preferable. "Coding" seems to be the most suitable term. Several authors have suggested this term. For example, according to Lawrence (1963) a sensory input is transformed by coding operations into the stimulus-as-coded, or s-a-c. The s-a-c is a product of both the sensory input and organismic factors such as the conditioning state of the organism, the set, or the instructions given in the experiment. The s-a-c is then associated with overt behavior.

Several models of discrimination learning have been suggested which may be classified as attention theories: the subject pays attention to a particular aspect of the stimulus, i.e., he codes or analyzes the stimulus in a certain way. Which aspect he attends to depends on such factors as instructions, previous experience, and the nature of the stimulus material. Sutherland (1959), Mackintosh (1965), and Lovejoy (1968) have worked out such models for animal discrimination learning. For human discrimination learning a model of this kind has been proposed by Zeaman and House (1963). The experimental task to which this model is applied is discrimination between geometric figures which vary along a number of well-defined dimensions, such as shape, color, and the like. The experimenter selects one dimension as relevant and reinforces responses according to the value of the relevant dimension. Thus it is a simple concept identification task. In describing this model the terminology of Zeaman and House has been slightly altered in order to relate it more closely to the present discussion, without, we hope, doing violence to the intention of the authors.

Figure 3.11 outlines the model for the case of four binary stimulus dimensions with *color* being the relevant dimension. Whenever an item is presented one of the four coding responses $O_i (i = 1,2,3,4)$ is elicited. Which one depends on previous experience, instructions, and the kind of stimulus material used in the experiment. A coding response produces the stimulus as coded $s_i$ or $s'_i$, depending on the value of the stimulus attribute. The stimulus as coded elicits the classification response $R_1$ with some probability $P(R_1)$. The effects of set or instructions can be represented within this framework as a bias for or against a particular coding response $O_i$. The effects of cue saliency can also be incorporated into the $P(O_i)$'s: dimensions which are very noticeable have high $P(O_i)$ values, dimensions that are less prominent have lower values. Finally, the model allows for the modification of both the coding responses, and the overt classification responses as a function of experience. Whenever the response $R_j$ based upon code $i$ is reinforced, both $P_i(R_j)$ and $P(O_i)$ increase by a fraction $\theta$, or $\theta'$ respectively, of the maximum possible increase. Whenever the response $R_j$ is made and not reinforced, both probabilities decrease by a corresponding fraction. In other words, Zeaman and House assume that on each trial both $P(O_i)$ and $P_i(R_j)$ change as a function of reinforcement according to the "linear model." Note that if a subject makes an incorrect coding response the probability that his overt classification response will be reinforced will be ½, no matter which response he makes if the stimulus items have been selected at random. This is like a probability learning situation with noncontingent reinforcement and $\pi = $ ½. We know from the results discussed in Chapter 2 that response probabilities will come to match reinforcement probabilities in such situations. Hence $P_i(R_j)$ for $i \neq 1$ should go to ½ during training, no matter what the subject's initial biases may have been. Thus, subjects will respond with $P(R_1) = $ ½ as long as they persist in making incorrect coding responses. Once $O_1$ occurs, it will be consistently reinforced and $P(O_1)$ increases. Thus, the

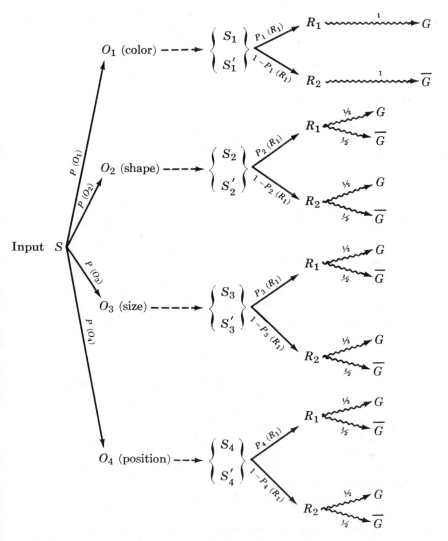

FIGURE 3.11   **Outline of a model for discrimination learning. (after Zeaman and House, 1959)**

model predicts a sharp rise in the probability of correct responses after an initial period of responding at chance level.

A study of discrimination learning in retarded children provided the data which were used to test this model. Children were presented with a tray with two stimulus objects, drawings of the kind described above. One of the stimuli was baited with a piece of candy. For instance, the experimenter might have decided to put the piece of candy always under the red stimulus; drawings of a different color were never baited with candy. The retarded children had a very hard time with such problems, some taking over 100 trials to learn, thereby providing the experimenter with a great deal of information about presolution performance.

Zeaman and House presented their data separately for fast and slow learners. Slow learners showed no improvement at all over as many as 80 trials in this task, but once they started improving they learned quite rapidly. Indeed, they learned at about the same rate as the fast learners, the difference in the two groups lying in the much shorter time during which they remained at chance level. In terms of the model, the difference between slow and fast learners in this experiment is in the rate of acquisition of the proper coding response. Once subjects start making the correct coding response they all improve at the same rate. This result strongly supports the two-process notion of discrimination learning and would be very difficult to explain for theories which do not include some kind of coding mechanism.

It is easy to see how the model of Zeaman and House can explain the results obtained when a classification is suddenly reversed, or shifted to a new basis. The dominant coding response is still appropriate after a reversal or after an intradimensional shift, and unlearning of the overt responses to the stimulus-as-coded commences immediately. In the case of an extradimensional shift a new coding response must be learned before the actual classification learning can even begin.

One of the virtues of the Zeaman and House (1963) model is the clear distinction made between the acquisition of coding responses and the classification response proper. The model has several shortcomings, though. The formal structure of the model is so complicated that one cannot derive explicit expressions and must completely rely on computer simulation, which greatly increases the difficulty of arriving at strict tests of the model. Secondly, and more significantly one would like a theory that makes more specific statements about the psychological processes involved in selecting one coding response rather than another, or about the relation between the information which the experimenter presents on a learning trial and the subject's learning processes. In Chapter 6 some similar models for concept identification will be described that are simpler mathematically and more amenable to psychological interpretations.

In addition to the purely psychological data described here, there are also some physiological results that indicate the important role of coding responses in the control of behavior. The perceptual equipment of the human organism is extremely flexible, so that man can code the world in almost any manner he desires. The situation is different for lower animals, where there are some interesting limitations on which coding operations can be performed and which are beyond the organism's capacities.

In his studies of discrimination learning in the octopus, Sutherland (1959) observed that the octopus had only a very restricted repertoire of coding responses, or stimulus analyzers as he preferred to call them. If the experimenter selected, as the relevant cue in a discrimination task, a stimulus dimension which is in the octopus' repertoire, the octopus would learn the discrimination; e.g., horizontal versus vertical lines could be discriminated, as well as deviations from horizontality. On the other hand, such cues as right versus left-sloping lines could not be detected. Sutherland concluded that discrimination learning in the octopus proceeded by attaching responses to the output of stimulus analyzers; if the appropriate analyzer was missing in the repertoire of the organism, the problem could not be solved (although later studies have shown the octopus' perceptual system to be somewhat more complex than Sutherland had originally supposed).

Sutherland believed that analyzers that permit the octopus to code certain classes of stimuli but not others are innate. Humans certainly depend on coding responses that have been acquired on the basis of experience. However, it is not clear to what extent analyzers are innate in the human case. Analyzers are clearly innate when one can specify a particular perceptual mechanism, such as in the case of color perception. When the physiological mechanisms that perform the coding operation are unknown, or when a peripheral mechanism does not exist, the distinction between innate and learned stimulus analyzers becomes more difficult to make. As a concrete example, do people learn to perceive a straight line, or are there innate mechanisms that permit us to perform this task? This problem is somewhat outside the main concern of this book, but since it is of considerable importance for the understanding of discrimination learning it will be outlined briefly.

Theories have been proposed that rely largely upon the effects of experience. An important theory of this type is Hebb's (1949). Hebb's organism starts out, like John Locke's famous blank tablet, with a huge neural network with random interconnections. Repeated stimulation of groups of neurons leads to the formation of "cell assemblies."

Once formed, cell assemblies perform as stimulus analyzers and permit the organism to solve more complex discrimination problems by becoming combined into "phase sequences." Without getting too involved in the details of Hebb's brain model, two features of this model can be pointed out: first, that Hebb was one of the first theorists explicitly to include coding notions in his treatment of discrimination learning, and second, that he tried to do this by stressing the effects of learning. Comparable with Hebb's brain theory in this respect are some attempts to build pattern recognition devices that also start out with a random net with rich but unstructured connections which are then modified by reinforcement (e.g., the Perceptron of Rosenblatt, 1958).

There are at least two kinds of arguments against random net theories. First, the mathematical probabilities that an initially random net can ever find enough properties which are correlated with reinforcement to solve nontrivial discrimination problems seem to be disconcertingly small. Secondly, evidence has been obtained from physiological studies of the perceptual system of animals that suggests that specialized innate stimulus analyzers play an important role in discrimination performance.

The lower an organism, the more specialized are its abilities for life and survival in a particular environment. A frog, for instance, appears to receive only very limited information about the surrounding world from his eyes, although the eyes are the frog's most important means of establishing contact with his environment. Modern science paints a rather dismal picture of a frog's life: the frog can do little more than sit on his lily-pad, snap at bugs that fly past, or jump into the water when an enemy approaches. At least that is what Lettvin, Maturana, McCulloch, and Pitts (1959) say that the frog's eye tells the frog's brain. Lettvin et al. came to this conclusion in a series of intriguing studies during which they presented various stimuli to the frog in a controlled experimental situation while recording the activity of single cells in the frog's optic tract. They observed that the information transmitted from the frog's retina to the brain was not about the point-by-point distribution of light and dark in the retina, but about qualitative features of the stimulus. Some cells were boundary detectors, others responded to moving curvatures, changes in contrast, or dimming. The different types of cells fell into anatomically distinct classes. Thus, the frog learns about small curved objects that move in its environment and are probably edible, and about large moving contours that may be a threat to him. His coding mechanisms limit him to information which is directly relevant to his survival. The interesting point about this is that this information was not extracted in the brain from some kind of "picture" transmitted from the retina, but was recorded only a few way stations behind the retina itself in the optic nerve.

Similar observations were reported by Hubel and Wiesel (1962) who studied the perceptual system of the cat. Hubel and Wiesel recorded from cortical locations and were able to discriminate among several types of cells which were concerned with the orientation of lines. Certain cells responded to lines in a particular orientation in the visual field, with some higher order cells responding to more general classes of lines. Hubel and Wiesel specifically note the much greater versatility of the cat's visual apparatus as compared with the frog's. In the frog very specialized processing occurs at a low level, while specialization in the cat's brain is postponed to a higher level and is carried out by a much larger number of cells.

The results of Lettvin et al. as well as those of Hubel and Wiesel show that innate stimulus analyzers play an important role in determining coding operations in the frog and in the cat. This finding has no direct implications for the human case but, together with the difficulty of conceiving of a random mechanism on purely formal grounds, it reinforces the notion that the human brain may possess much richer and more intricate innate structure than random net theories suppose.

# 4
# short-term memory

The history of the concept short-term memory, from William James to its modern revival in the 1950s; the experimental study of short-term memory.

term memory estimated by the recency effect in free-recall experiments.

At the beginning of the previous chapter we briefly described the tripartite division of memory into sensory memory, short-term memory, and long-term memory. We emphasized that this division is one of convenience; it does not imply that there are three separate, independent memory systems, and that a to-be-remembered item is put into one or the other of these memories and transferred between them as a secretary might store a letter in different filing cabinets. Instead, there is a continuum of elaboration of the memory trace, ranging from its initial perceptual processing and its availability in consciousness to its integration into a person's knowledge structure. There is only one memory system that functions as a whole. For example, we have seen that one cannot understand attentional selection processes without taking into account a person's knowledge or his goals. Nevertheless, the distinction is a conventional one in the memory literature, and indeed, the specific problems that investigators of sensory memory, short-term memory, and long-term memory are concerned with are to some extent different ones. Even more distinct are the experimental procedures commonly used in the three areas. Thus, it is a convenient organizing principle for a textbook. We employ it here without prejudging theoretical issues (such as the question whether or not separate memory stores need to be distinguished—see Section 4.4). In this chapter we first describe the phenomena of short-term retention as they have been discovered in recent years and then outline the role they play in the total cognitive system.

The distinction between a short- and long-term memory store is by no means new. James (1890) first distinguished between primary and secondary memory: information in primary memory has never left consciousness; information in secondary memory has been absent from consciousness for some time. Recall from primary memory is easy and effortless, while active search processes often characterize retrieval from secondary memory. For an item to enter secondary memory, stimulation must exceed some minimum duration, otherwise it will fail to "set" in secondary memory. Stern (1938) made a similar distinction in terms of immediate and mediate memory. He also discussed sensory memory stores, which do not involve subject's central processing capacities but consist in the continued excitation of the sense organ itself.

Ebbinghaus (1902) himself had noted that two different processes seemed to be going on when material within the span of immediate memory or when material exceeding that span was learned. There is a sharp discontinuity between memory for six nonsense syllables and memory for 12 syllables. While the former could almost always be recited correctly after just one presentation, only very few syllables, perhaps not more than the first and last, could be retained when 12 CVCs were presented. The results of an experiment, with Ebbinghaus as the only subject, that shows the relationship between the number of repetitions necessary to learn a list of CVCs to a criterion of one correct recitation and the length of the list are reproduced in Figure 4.1. Only one presentation is necessary as long as the list is within the capacity of immediate memory, which is here about six items. After that, it took Ebbinghaus approximately two repetitions per added item in order to learn the list, i.e., in order to store the added items in secondary memory. (In general, study time does not increase linearly with the amount of material to be learned, but faster: for serial recall, Derks (1974) reported that study time was a power function of the amount of material to be recalled, with an exponent of about 2.6, which means that doubling the list length requires a study time six times as long).

Although short-term memory has a sharply limited capacity, this

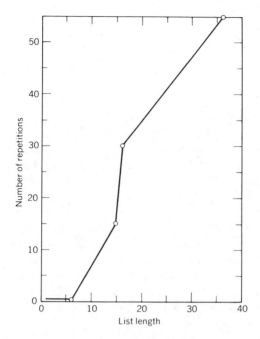

FIGURE 4.1   **Number of repetitions necessary to learn a list as a function of list length.**
(after Ebbinghaus, 1902)

limitation appears to be primarily in the number of items that can be held, but not in the size and information content of these items. This important aspect of short-term memory was stressed by Wundt (1905). Wundt observed that the capacity of immediate memory was restricted to about six items when the learning material consisted of items taken in isolation, such as random letters, digits, or isolated lines. However, if these elements were grouped into larger units (e.g., grouping letters so that they form a word) many more elements could be retained in immediate memory because the subject remembered about as many words as he could remember single letters. Müller and Schumann (1894) have investigated some of the conditions that determine the size of units in immediate memory.

In spite of these promising beginnings, the study of immediate memory progressed very little between World War I and the late 1950s. This probably occurred because the earlier studies had relied on introspective methods, at least in part, and when introspection became unfashionable with the advent of behaviorism, psychologists rejected the problem together with the methodology. That is, the importance of the problem was fully recognized: learning theory found some kind of short-term memory mechanism essential in order to explain the effects of reinforcement in establishing an S-R bond when reinforcement was delayed. Both Pavlov (1928) and Hull (1943) postulated a stimulus-trace mechanism, so that retroaction did not have to be invoked to explain the effects of delayed reinforcement. However, they were not particularly interested in this mechanism per se. Hull and his followers gave the stimulus trace concept the lofty status of an intervening variable, and turned to other problems. Nor did psychologists interested in verbal learning and memory do much more to further our understanding of immediate memory, or to follow up the interesting suggestions of prebehavioristic psychology. Most of their efforts went into two problems: the relationship between different experimental conditions and the length of the series that could be retained after one presentation (the memory span), and the distribution of errors in different serial positions.

Contemporary work on immediate memory received its impetus from a number of different sources. Neurological discoveries and theories indicated the existence of two different memory stores; information theory provided a means of dealing with the capacity of immediate memory; and the close relationship between perception and learning came to be realized. Suddenly, immediate memory turned out to be a central problem in psychology. The work and the theories of Hebb (1949) and Broadbent (1958) were especially important in stimulating this interest in immediate memory. The theoretical impetus also brought about methodological innovations. Beginning with the work of Peterson and Peterson (1959), several objective procedures have been developed for the experimental study of short-term memory.

Hebb (1949) was concerned with the physiological basis of memory. Memory, as it is usually understood, involves some structural change within the organism, the nature of which need not concern us here. Such a structural change requires an appreciable amount of time, and Hebb found it necessary to postulate some sort of a mechanism to carry memory until the structural change occurs. Anatomical and physiological evidence for such a mechanism was already available. Lorente de Nó (1938) had described fibers that were arranged in closed, potentially self-exciting circuits. Thus, a short-term memory mechanism based on a reverberating stimulus trace seemed to be both a possible as well as a necessary inference. Hebb postulated two kinds of memory: long-term memory, which is based on a structural trace and is permanent except for interference from other long-term traces; and short-term memory, based on an activity trace. Short-term memory is subject to autonomous decay. Hebb pointed out two possible reasons for this inherent instability of short-term memory: the cells in a closed, reverberating cell assembly may become refractory, or interruption through external events may occur. Activity traces are transformed into structural traces when the stimulus is presented repeatedly, or simply through consolidation: if an activity trace is not interfered with but is allowed to run its course, a stable structural memory trace is established.

Quite different considerations motivated Broadbent's distinction between a temporary and a more permanent memory store (Broadbent, 1958, 1963). Broadbent tried to infer the flow of information in the human perceptual and memory system from purely behavioral data. He did not concern himself with neurological detail, but at the same time he was not satisfied merely with a description of behavior. Just as one can describe the working of a computer in terms of a flow-diagram that identifies the function of the various subsystems without giving much thought to the electrical engineering details, one can construct and test a rough model of information processing within the organism.

Broadbent illustrated this model by pointing to our everyday experience with memory for telephone numbers. Most of us can recall our own telephone number and a few others whenever we are called to do so. On the other hand, when we look up a new number in the telephone book, memory is very frail. We can keep the number in mind as long as we need, if we can repeat it to ourselves silently. However, should we be distracted before we reach the telephone we are likely to forget the number unless we can periodically rehearse it. On the other hand, suppose we hear a new number that we want to remember and we cannot write it down. Then we try to memorize this number by some means or other. This we shall refer to as long-term storage.

The reason why Broadbent distinguished a separate short-term memory store was his belief that forgetting in short-term memory followed quite different rules than the forgetting of old, established memories.

Brown (1958) obtained some experimental results which he interpreted as evidence for spontaneous decay in short-term memory. In one of his studies, he employed a retention interval of approximately 5 seconds which was either filled with a digit reading task or empty and thus could be used for rehearsal. From one to four serially presented consonant pairs were to be remembered. He found that when rehearsal was permitted almost no forgetting occurred, except when three or four consonant pairs were used. On the other hand, when rehearsal was impossible (or at least made difficult) much less material was recalled. This result was interpreted to mean that short-term memory decays rapidly, unless it is continually reinstated through active rehearsal. Brown also found that recall was inversely proportional to the amount of material which was to be recalled.

These findings were soon extended. Peterson and Peterson (1959) provided the first systematic study of retention time in short-term recall and devised an experimental procedure for the study of the recall of single items. On each trial a consonant trigram was presented, followed by a three-place number. Subjects were asked to count backward by threes from this number until a light appeared. The subject then attempted to recall the consonant trigram. Retention intervals of 3, 6, 9, 12, and 18 seconds were studied. The results of the experiment are shown in Figure 4.2. In the same figure, the results of a replication of the Peterson experiment by Murdock (1961) are also shown, as well as a repetition of the experiment using one or three common words instead of consonant trigrams. Note that the forgetting curves in Figure 4.2 have the same shape as Ebbinghaus' curve, although the retention interval is only a few seconds. Immediately after presentation, recall is almost perfect. The few errors that did occur would normally be called errors of perception rather than memory, but the distinction between perception and immediate

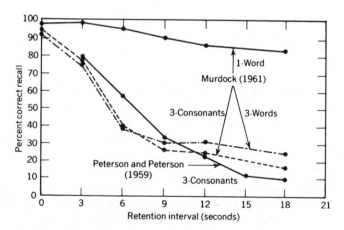

FIGURE 4.2    **Percentage frequency of completely correct recall of three-consonant trigrams (Peterson and Peterson, 1959; Murdock, 1961), and one-word and three-word units (Murdock, 1961). (after Melton, 1963)**

memory is not as clear as psychological terminology implies. Only 18 seconds after presentation recall drops to about 20% for trigrams or three-word groups. No important differences are apparent in the recall of three words or three consonants. If only one word is to be remembered, forgetting is much less, but some forgetting is clearly present even in this case. Evidently, it is the number of units or "chunks" (Miller, 1956) that determines the rate of forgetting, rather than the number of physical elements within an item, such as letters.

The Peterson procedure, which we shall also call the *distractor procedure,* has become the basis for much of the work on short-term memory, though a number of alternative experimental procedures have been developed since, involving recognition as well as various forms of cued and free recall. What these procedures have in common is that performance is studied after relatively belief retention intervals, typically just a few seconds, but sometimes going up to a few minutes; hence the terms short-term, or immediate memory. Note that this term is used here on procedural grounds: what is meant with short-term memory is merely that the memory test in question involves a short retention interval, measured in seconds rather than minutes, or hours, or even days. Anything that deals with retention intervals longer than a few minutes is conventionally referred to as long-term memory work, though sometimes an author who does not like to use the term long-term memory for a 5-minute retention interval uses such additional, vague classifications as intermediate-term memory.

There is a second sense in which the term short-term memory is used in the psychological literature, and a widespread failure to distinguish clearly between these two senses is the cause of considerable confusion. The first sense of short-term memory is operational, procedural; the second is theoretical. A distinction is made between two theoretical concepts, short-term memory and long-term memory. This is the sense in which James, Broadbent, or Hebb used the term, and many of the most influential theories of short-term memory subscribe to this position (e.g., Waugh and Normal, 1965; Atkinson and Shiffrin, 1968). However, other theorists emphasize the continuity between short- and long-term memory and reject the position that there are two separate, distinct memory stores (e.g., Melton, 1963; Craik and Lockhart, 1972). We shall discuss this controversy in Section 4.4.

To avoid confusion between the two senses of "short-term memory," we shall use the Jamesian terms *primary* and *secondary memory* for short- and long-term memory, respectively, whenever the theoretical senses of these terms are intended; "short-term memory," at least in these pages, will be reserved for memory in situations characterized by brief retention intervals.

## 4.1     FORGETTING IN SHORT-TERM MEMORY

When a to-be-learned item, say a word, a digit, or a nonsense sylla-ble, is presented and the subject pays at least some minimal attention to it, the probability that he can reproduce this item immediately thereafter is essentially 1. However, as we have already seen from Figure 4.2, this probability decreases rapidly, unless the subject is permitted to rehearse the item. Peterson and Peterson (1959) prevented rehearsal by having subjects count backward by threes from a given number during the retention interval. Under these con-ditions, recall decreases rapidly as the time between presentation and test increases, reaching an asymptote after 15 to 20 seconds.

Similar short-term forgetting functions have been obtained with other experimental procedures. A variation of Peterson's distractor procedure is the *sequential probe technique*: subjects are given a fairly long list of items to study (longer than the memory span, so that it is impossible to remember all items perfectly—e.g., 15 digits in the experiment described below), and then one item from the list is given as a probe, and the subject is instructed to respond to this probe with the next item on the list. Since the subject does not know which item will be tested, he must try to remember all of them. The list items occurring between the presentation of an item and the probe serve as distractor items. Figure 4.3 shows some results from a study by Norman (1966): as with the distractor procedure, performance starts almost at 1, but decreases rapidly as the number of interfering items increases. The data shown in Figure 4.3 were obtained with a presentation rate of 1 item per second with either a visual or auditory presentation. Note that the forgetting functions for visual and auditory presentation are essentially the same. (In the same experiment, Norman also varied the rate of presentation from 1 item per second all the way to 10 items per second, but this variation, too, had little or no effect on the forgetting rate, though the initial acquisition level decreased with the faster presentation rates).

Another popular experimental design used to study short-term memory involves the *continuous presentation* of items. For recogni-tion tests, this design was introduced by Shepard and Teghtsoonian (1961) and has already been discussed in Chapter 1. Shepard's and Teghtsoonian's learning items were three-digit numbers. These num-

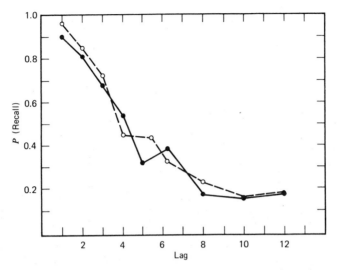

FIGURE 4.3   **Relative frequency of correct recall in a probe experiment. The abscissa is the number of intervening digits between presentation and test, including the probe. The presentation rate is one item per second; open circles are auditory presentation, full circles visual. (after Norman, 1966)**

bers were written on index cards and the subject was asked to go through a deck of such cards, noting for each item whether or not it had occurred earlier in the deck. The main variable of interest was the lag between the repetitions of an item in the deck, that is the number of other cards intervening beween the first and second presentations of each item. Figure 1.10 (page 34) shows that the short-term memory loss observed with this procedure is quite comparable to that in Figures 4.2 and 4.3, although recognition performance is higher overall than recall.

Continuous presentation paradigms are not restricted to recognition tests. They have also been adapted to the study of memory for paired-associates. Figure 4.4 shows some data from an experiment by Atkinson and Shiffrin (1968). In this experiment, sets of 4 to 8 two-digit numbers were used as stimuli and the letters of the alphabet were used as responses. Stimuli and responses were re-paired at random throughout an experimental session and the subject's task was to remember which response a given stimulus was paired with when it was presented last. One of the experimental variables of interest was the lag between the presentation of a digit-letter pair and the next presentation of the digit, in response to which the subject had to

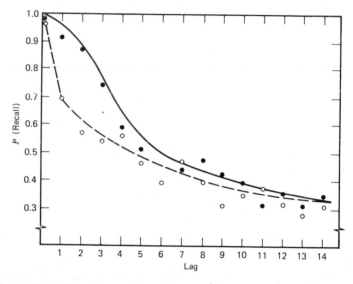

FIGURE 4.4 **Probability of correct recall in a continuous paired-associate task, for covert rehearsal (open circles) and overt rehearsal (full circles). The lines are predictions from the Atkinson and Shiffrin model, discussed in Section 4.4. (after Atkinson and Shiffrin, 1968)**

recall the appropriate letter. In each session, 220 trials were given. Each test trial (test-study-blank) took 11 seconds. This rather slow presentation rate was used because the authors were interested in studying subjects' rehearsal processes in this task. Figure 4.4 shows the forgetting functions obtained when subjects rehearsed overtly and covertly (that is, silently). Obviously, overt rehearsal improved short-term retention somewhat for the shorter lags, leading to an uncharacteristic bump in the forgetting function, but otherwise we observe the same rapid decrease in recall that was obtained with the distractor procedure, the probe procedure, and the continuous recognition paradigm.

Most of the research on short-term memory has involved verbal materials, and either visual or auditory presentation. For what is known today, it appears, however, that forgetting functions for non-verbal materials are not much different. Rapid forgetting of motor responses has been demonstrated by Adams and Dijkstra (1966) and Posner and Konick (1966), among others. Posner and Konick had subjects move a lever that was concealed from sight to a certain position and tested for retention of this motor movement after intervals ranging from 0 to 30 seconds. Tasks differing in difficulty filled the retention interval (rest, copying, addition, or classification of digits). As in the experiments with verbal materials, substantial short-term forgetting was observed. Verbal mediation could be excluded because the authors showed that subjects' verbal codes were much too vague to account for the accuracy of the motor responses. Similarly, Sullivan and Turvey (1974) found that memory for tactile stimuli decreased rapidly within just a few seconds. All the results in their experiment were analogous to verbal short-term memory studies. The exception may be short-term memory of odors: Engen, Kuisma, and Eimas (1973) reported no changes in the ability to recognize odors for retention intervals between 3 and 30 seconds; at the same time, odor recognition was far from perfect, even when free from the task of backward counting (80 to 90% hits, with over 20% false recognitions). This result is strikingly different from those obtained with other sensory modalities and invites speculation about the role that rehearsal may play in short-term forgetting (one can rehearse words, tones, and even images, but odors?).

## INTERFERENCE AND DECAY

What causes the rapid short-term forgetting observed in the studies just described? Two theoretical mechanisms can be used to explain it. First, it is possible that information is lost due to time without rehearsal; this is the *decay* theory of memory. Secondly, memory losses may occur because items in memory are being displaced by succeeding inputs; this is the *interference* theory of memory. The two theories are, of course, not mutually exclusive.

We already know (e.g., from Chapter 1) that interference is an important factor in forgetting. The question is whether decay, in the absence of any interference effects, also leads to forgetting. An experimental test of this question requires that a subject retain an item in short-term memory for varying periods of time, during which no new inputs enter his short-term memory and he does not rehearse. If forgetting occurs during such a rehearsal and interference-free time period, this could be considered as evidence for decay of short-term memory traces. If, however, no forgetting is observed, this would indicate that interference mechanisms are the only ones operative. It is not an easy task to arrange the right experimental conditions, because in the absence of any new inputs subjects will rehearse. If rehearsal is prevented in the usual way (e.g., by having subjects count backward by threes during the retention interval) the counting itself produces new inputs into short-term memory and is thus a possible source of interference. An experimental solution of this dilemma was suggested by Reitman (1974) who prevented subjects from rehearsing during the retention interval by occupying their attention with a nonverbal detection task: subjects had to detect faint tones presented over noise during the retention interval, a difficult task that distracted subjects' attention from rehearsal while producing no new inputs into short-term memory. Specifically, she had her subjects read aloud five words, which were tested either immediately or after 15 seconds. The 15 seconds were filled with a signal detection task. Anywhere from 0 to 14 tones were presented during the rention interval, and the subject was instructed to press a reaction time key whenever he heard a tone. The signal-to-noise ratio was adjusted for each subject so as to achieve a detection probability of 50%. This was a tough task, but did it really prevent subjects from rehearsing? Reitman made sure of that by a number of ingenious and complicated procedures and analyses. For instance, she instructed some subjects to try to cheat and rehearse surreptitiously, while others were asked to cooperate and avoid rehearsal as much as they could. She also asked subjects whether they had or had not rehearsed, and, finally, she very carefully inspected each subject's record for indications of rehearsal (for instance, sudden temporary drops in a subject's ability to detect the tones probably indicate that the subject was distracted from the signal detection task by surreptitious rehearsal). By such means Reitman was able to select a subgroup of 10 subjects who really did not rehearse. After 15 seconds of tone detection, recall for these subjects ranged between 65 and 88%. Thus, between 12 and 35% forgetting within 15 seconds must be attributed to trace decay, in the absence of interference effects. Decay, as well as interference, appears to be a cause of forgetting in short-term memory according to Reitman's (1974) results.

Even if Reitman's data remain unquestioned in the future, it is clear that the major cause of forgetting in short-term memory is interference, not decay. The backward counting in the distractor procedure produces verbal inputs into short-term memory that interfere with the retention of the to-be-learned items; in the sequential probe procedure, successive list items interfere with each other. The forgetting functions are qualitatively similar in these two cases, but the nature of the interference- producing activity during the retention interval is in fact an important determinant of the rate of forgetting. A systematic investigation of this factor was provided by Neimark, Greenhouse, Law, and Weinheimer (1965) who showed that the similarity of the interpolated material and the learning material affected retention. As learning material they used 16 CVCs of either high or low association value. Retention intervals of 0, 3, 9, and 18 seconds were studied. During the retention interval subjects spelled aloud at a fixed rate nonsense syllables of either high, medium, or low association value, or three-digit numbers. The high association CVCs were recalled very well and no clear effects attributable to the similarity of the intervening material were found. However, for low association value syllables, recall was best when the interpolated task involved the most dissimilar materials (numbers, and high association value CVCs), and decreased as the interpolated material became more similar to the learning material.

This result, is, of course, in agreement with the interference theory of memory. However, the authors point out another possible interpretation of the data. Pillsbury and Sylvester (1940) have held that the difficulty of the interpolated material affects retention independent of other factors. It is possible that reading unfamiliar syllables was a more difficult task than reading high association value syllables and served better to prevent rehearsal. An experiment in which the difficulty of the interpolated activity was varied independently of similarity has been reported by Posner and Rossman (1965). In their main experiment, subjects listened to an eight-digit series and performed a "transformation" task before attempting recall of the series. The transformations involved either 0, 1, 2, or 3 digit pairs in the eight-digit series, but never the first two digits. The transformations that subjects were required to perform were reversal (writing down a pair of digits in the opposite order from their presentation), addition (two adjacent digits are added and the sum is written down), two-bit classification (classifying each pair of numbers into above or below 50), and one-bit classification (the subject records A if the pair is high and odd or low and even, B for the reverse). These tasks were graded in difficulty. The results are based entirely on the analysis of the recall of the first digit pair, which was never itself transformed or recorded and was always recalled first by the subject. Thus the first digit pair was treated identically under all conditions, and only the nature and number of the transformations that intervened between the presentation of the first digit pair and recall distinguished the experimental conditions. The results are shown in Table 4.1. It is apparent that both the nature and the number of transformations performed during the retention interval strongly affected recall. The difficulty of the intervening activity does affect short-term retention, even when similarity effects are absent. In fact, in the present experiment the influence of task difficulty quite overwhelmed and reversed any effects due to similarity:

TABLE 4.1.   **Total Errors in the First Pair of Digits after Posner and Rossman, (1965)**

|         | Number of Pairs Transformed | | | | |
|---------|-----|-----|-----|-----|-------|
| Task    | 0   | 1   | 2   | 3   | Total |
| Reversal | 22  | 26  | 31  | 50  | 129   |
| Addition | 44  | 62  | 56  | 104 | 266   |
| 2/Bit    | 29  | 50  | 71  | 114 | 264   |
| 1/Bit    | 28  | 62  | 94  | 108 | 292   |
| Total    | 123 | 200 | 252 | 376 |       |

according to the Neimark et al. study, one would suppose that writing down digits would interfere more with the retention of digits than the writing of letters. However, the only tasks which involved the writing of numbers, the reversal and addition tasks, produced the least amount of interference.

In two follow-up experiments Posner and Rossman (1965) explored the interaction between the difficulty of interpolated activity and the length of the retention interval. In one experiment the total interpolated time was kept constant, but the effects of task difficulty were still obtained. In a second experiment, retention time was varied systematically. The results are shown in Figure 4.5. Effects on recall caused by task difficulty were observed for every retention interval.

Posner and Rossman interpret their results in terms of rehearsal. There is a limited central processing capacity available for the rehearsal process, and the more of it that is taken up by intervening tasks, the more forgetting will occur. A number of other experimental studies support the idea that short-term memory is a limited capacity system (Miller, 1956; Broadbent, 1958). For instance, Murdock (1965a) has shown that the difficulty of a subsidiary task that subjects perform while listening to a list of words affects recall. He used card sorting tasks of various levels of difficulty and found that the number of words recalled decreased as the card sorting task became more demanding.

The studies just reviewed suggest that interference is not so much a matter of the number of items presented during the retention interval, but rather a question of what the subject does during that time. The more an interfering task engages the subject's resources, the fewer resources will be available for the task of holding the to-be-learned item in short-term memory, and the more forgetting will be observed. Waugh and Norman (1968) have systematically explored the interference-producing factors in sequential probe experiments. They were concerned with the unit of interference in short-term memory. Is it simply the total number of interpolated items, no matter what these are? Or is the number of different items the proper measure of interference? Or are there some higher order units that must be taken into account? Their general procedure consisted of constructing strings of items according to certain constraints which will be explained below. Subjects listened to a string and immediately following the last item, one that had appeared earlier was repeated accompanied by a tone. This was the probe item. Upon this signal the subject was instructed to report the item that had followed the last occurrence of the probe item. The strings were constructed so that they differentiated among a number of possible hypotheses concerning the nature of interference effects in short-term memory. For instance, consider the hypothesis that the total number of intervening items is important, no matter what these items are, versus the alternative hypothesis that the number of different items determines interference and that items occurring twice in immediate succession function as a unit. Under the first hypothesis the following two strings should be

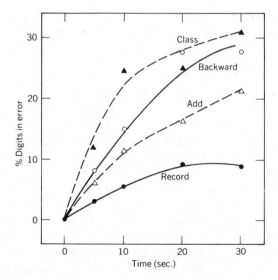

FIGURE 4.5   **Percentage recall as a function of time for various size transforms. (after Posner and Rossman, 1965)**

equivalent:

| | |
|---|---|
| . . . 7, 3, 8, 8, 4, 4 | Probe: 7 Correct Response: 3 |
| . . . 7, 3, 8, 5, 9, 2 | Probe: 7 Correct Response: 3 |

In each case four digits follow the test item. According to the hypotheses that only different items count, the first string should be recalled much better than the second string, because there are only two different items intervening. In addition to the two hypotheses already mentioned Waugh and Norman explored the idea that items may function as a unit of interference only if they are not currently stored in short-term memory, as well as a few other possibilities. We need not describe these in detail, since they all were counterindicated by their results. The only hypothesis that could account for their data was that the unit of interference is determined by a subject's expectancies: any newly presented item can displace an earlier item from short-term memory as long as it is not redundant. A redundant item is one which the subject expects to occur at a given place in a series, e.g., a 5 is expected after 1234-, or a 4 is expected after 77711199944-. Thus, regularly occurring highly predictable items do not interfere with other items stored in short-term memory.

So far, we have been concerned with retroactive interference effects in short-term memory: input that follows the to-be-learned item interferes with its retention. As one would expect from the discussion in Chapter 1, there are also proactive interference effects in short-term memory: input that precedes the to-be-learned item also interferes with its retention. The first item of a short-term memory experiment is rarely forgotten, but after just a few tests stable forgetting develops (e.g., Murdock, 1964). However, if after a few items the nature of the material is suddenly changed, the new material is retained almost as well as the items at the very beginning of the experiment. After a few trials with the new material performance returns to the old level. This effect was demonstrated first by Wickens, Born, and Allen (1963) who found that when a letter is tested after a series of digits, performance is a good as on the first trial of the session, but that performance deteriorates rapidly when several trials with the same learning material are given. In a similar study using the distractor procedure Goggin and Wickens (1971) worked with English–Spanish bilinguals. Each subject received a series of short-term memory tests. For the control subjects all tests involved the same type of materials (e.g., word triplets in Spanish, with all words belonging to the semantic category "kinds of fruit"); the experimental subjects were treated just like the control subjects for the first three test trials, but were then shifted to new materials on the fourth trial (e.g., English words from the "part of a house" category). Figure 4.6 shows the results of this experiment. We observe a steady decrease in performance for the control subjects over the four trials, a phenomenon referred to as the build-up of proactive inhibition. For the experimental subjects, however, there is a pronounced release from proactive inhibition on the fourth trial when the learning material was changed. (Similar, though smaller, effects were observed when only the language, or only the conceptual category of the to-be-learned words were changed).

Wickens (1972) has reviewed a large number of studies of this type and catalogued the kinds of shift in materials that do or do not produce release effects. The question is, of course, how to explain the proactive inhibition build-up and release in these experiments.

The first task for the theorist is to decide whether proactive inhibition is the result of a storage deficit for later items. It is conceivable that subjects store more information about an item in memory when the item is new and unexpected, but as similar items accumulate, they encode these items in a more superficial manner. Alternatively,

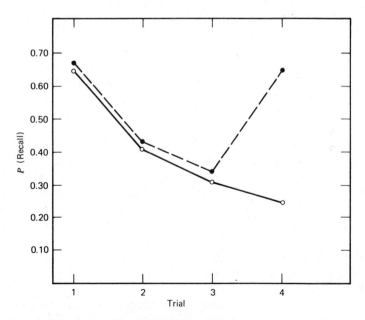

FIGURE 4.6    **Probability of correct recall for control subjects (open circles) and subjects for whom the learning material changed in the attributes of semantic category and language on Trial 4 (full circles). (after Wickens, 1972)**

storage might be equal for all items, but it might become more and more difficult to retrieve these items as the number of similar ones increases. Loftus and Patterson (1975) reported some results relevant to this issue. Their experiment involved two stages. In the first stage, subjects were given 24 trials with the distractor procedure. On each trial, the stimulus was a word triad. The subject read the words, then shadowed numbers during the 15-second retention interval, and then recalled the words. The words that made up these triads came from the same conceptual category for three trials in a row. Thus, the whole experiment comprised eight three-trial blocks. The short-term memory results were as one would expect: performance decreased over each three-trial block, but whenever a change in material occurred, release from proactive inhibition restored performance to the original level. Averaging over the eight three-trial blocks, the proportion of recall was .88 on the first trial, .70 on the second, and .61 on the last. After all 24 trials, subjects were given an unexpected final recall trial: the experimenter simply asked them to recall all the words that had been used in the experiment. If the performance decrease over each three-trial block was due to a lack of storage for the second and especially the third item in each material block, one would expect final recall to show the same decrease in performance over the three trials as short-term recall. This, however, did not occur. The proportions of words recalled on the final recall from the first, second, and third trial of each block were practically identical (.30, .30, and .28, respectively). Thus, proactive inhibition effects are not the result of storage deficits, but must be attributed to increasing retrieval difficulties in short-term memory.

Confusion between traces therefore appears to be the primary cause of short-term forgetting. The exact mechanism involved has not yet been elucidated, but its general outline seems to be clear. If, as in the previous chapter, a stimulus is represented as a set of features or attributes, one can think of encoding as a process of selecting some of these attributes for storage in memory. Thus, the memory trace may be viewed as a memorial representation of some of the stimulus elements that comprise a to-be-learned item, though by no means all possible ones. If the to-be-learned items are similar (e.g., all words from the same conceptual category), the feature sets selected for storage in memory tend to have elements in common and, as the number of items learned increases, confusions between their memory representations become more likely. The result is an increase in proactive inhibition, which is so characteristic of short-term memory experiments. The nature of the encoding process, therefore, may be the ultimate source of short-term forgetting, and to that problem we shall now turn our attention.

## ENCODING PROCESSES IN SHORT-TERM MEMORY

An outline of the memory system has been provided in Figure 3.1 (page 119). There we divided the continuum of encoding processes into three stages: sensory encoding, short-term memory encoding, and long-term memory encoding. Memory traces are records resulting from these processes. To understand the properties of the memory trace, it is necessary to study the nature of the various perceptual and cognitive analyses that are being performed on a stimulus. In Chapter 3 we concentrated on the initial perceptual analyses and on the role of attention in stimulus encoding. We shall now be concerned with the somewhat higher level of encoding that is characteristic of many of the short-term memory experiments in the psychological literature. More complex elaborations of stimulus encoding, which are required to support long-term recall, will be discussed in Chapter 5.

### PHONETIC ENCODING IN SHORT-TERM MEMORY

What is important for remembering is not so much the to-be-learned item per se, but what the subject does with it. The learning material itself determines largely, but not entirely, what the subject will do with it. It is difficult to do very much with a nonsense syllable, while a concrete, meaningful word might invite all kinds of semantic or imagery elaborations, and might readily fit into the context of other to-be-learned words, and therefore be remembered much better.

The claim that memory depends on what the subject does, rather than on the nature of the stimulus itself, is nicely illustrated by the widespread use of phonetic encoding strategies in short-term memory. Quite independently of the input modality, whether it is visual or auditory, subjects often translate the to-be-learned items into a phonetic code and retain that in memory. This is easy to do, and, if the retention interval is short, that may be all that is required for successful performance. Hence, in many short-term memory experiments subjects do not elaborate the stimulus much beyond a rather low-level acoustic code.

A large number of studies support this generalization, but the best example comes from a study of confusion errors in recall by Conrad

(1964). Conrad argued that intrusion errors in immediate recall are systematic; memory traces may decay partially, and therefore similar traces are more likely to be confused with each other than dissimilar traces. The relevant dimension of similarity along which such effects are to be expected is acoustic similarity. Conrad's experiment contained two parts. At first, he obtained a confusion matrix for the letters B C P T V F M N S X presented auditorily over noise to 300 subjects (Table 4.2). The rows of this matrix represent the input letter; columns show the subjects' response; entries are the frequency of each response, given that the row-stimulus was presented. Next, Conrad constructed a memory confusion matrix based on the recall intrusions from 387 subjects. Subjects were presented visually with a six-letter sequence and tested for recall immediately. The same 10 consonants were used. A careful scoring system was employed in order to avoid including random guesses and other noise into the data; only those sequences were scored that contained a single substitution error. In this way it was possible to maintain without ambiguity that the subject had confused a particular pair of letters. Table 4.3 shows the memory confusion matrix. The error patterns in Tables 4.2 and 4.3 are remarkably similar. The rank order correlation between the two tables is .64. It appears that although the letters were presented visually in the memory experiment, the subject recoded them acoustically, so that when a letter was partially forgotten, errors occurred which were characteristic of auditory confusions.

Conrad's results were replicated by Wickelgren (1965) with auditory presentation of the recall lists. In addition, Wickelgren made subjects

TABLE 4.2.  **Listening Confusions (after Conrad, 1964)**

| | | | | Stimulus Letter | | | | | |
|---|---|---|---|---|---|---|---|---|---|
| | B | C | P | T | V | F | M | N | S | X |
| B | — | 171 | 75 | 84 | 168 | 2 | 11 | 10 | 2 | 2 |
| C | 32 | — | 35 | 42 | 20 | 4 | 4 | 5 | 2 | 5 |
| P | 162 | 350 | — | 505 | 91 | 11 | 31 | 23 | 5 | 5 |
| T | 143 | 232 | 281 | — | 50 | 14 | 12 | 11 | 8 | 5 |
| V | 122 | 61 | 34 | 22 | — | 1 | 8 | 11 | 1 | 0 |
| F | 6 | 4 | 2 | 4 | 3 | — | 13 | 8 | 336 | 238 |
| M | 10 | 14 | 2 | 3 | 4 | 22 | — | 334 | 21 | 9 |
| N | 13 | 21 | 6 | 9 | 20 | 32 | 512 | — | 38 | 14 |
| S | 2 | 18 | 2 | 7 | 3 | 486 | 23 | 11 | — | 391 |
| X | 1 | 6 | 2 | 2 | 1 | 245 | 2 | 1 | 184 | — |

TABLE 4.3.   **Recall Confusions (after Conrad, 1964)**

| | | | | Stimulus letter | | | | | | |
|---|---|---|---|---|---|---|---|---|---|---|
| | B | C | P | T | V | F | M | N | S | X |
| B | — | 18 | 62 | 5 | 83 | 12 | 9 | 3 | 2 | 0 |
| C | 13 | — | 27 | 18 | 55 | 15 | 3 | 12 | 35 | 7 |
| P | 102 | 18 | — | 24 | 40 | 15 | 8 | 8 | 7 | 7 |
| T | 30 | 46 | 79 | — | 38 | 18 | 14 | 14 | 8 | 10 |
| V | 56 | 32 | 30 | 14 | — | 21 | 15 | 11 | 11 | 5 |
| F | 6 | 8 | 14 | 5 | 31 | — | 12 | 13 | 131 | 16 |
| M | 12 | 6 | 8 | 5 | 20 | 16 | — | 146 | 15 | 5 |
| N | 11 | 7 | 5 | 1 | 19 | 28 | 167 | — | 24 | 5 |
| S | 7 | 21 | 11 | 2 | 9 | 37 | 4 | 12 | — | 16 |
| X | 3 | 7 | 2 | 2 | 11 | 30 | 10 | 11 | 59 | — |

copy the lists as they were presented, so that perceptual errors could be excluded from the analysis. In a later study, Wickelgren (1966) showed that the confusion effect may be predicted from the linguistic structure of the different letters. Before we can understand these studies it is necessary to introduce some basic concepts from the linguistic characterization of speech sounds.

Linguists analyze the flow of sounds in natural speech into phonemes. A phoneme is a class of sound patterns, among which the native speaker of a language does not distinguish in the sense that two sounds belonging to the same class are never used to carry a difference in meaning. The smallest difference between two sound patterns which suggests to the hearer different contents is the difference of a single phoneme. By this criterion, the /r/ in rat and the /k/ in cat are two different phonemes. Sounds in the same phoneme class are acoustically similar but by no means identical. Thus there are obvious differences in the /k/ in key, ski, and caw, but these are merely free variations within one phoneme. There are 46 phonemes in English.

The phonemes of a language may be described by means of a distinctive feature system. Each phoneme can be encoded or decoded by a number of simple operations, corresponding to its distinctive features. It is somewhat arbitrary which operations are selected to describe the phonemes of a language. However, a distinctive feature system should be constructed so that a minimum number of dimensions are needed to identify each phoneme. A classification system based on the features of the articulatory system is frequently used and is shown in Table 4.4, which is reproduced from Miller and Nicely

TABLE 4.4.  **Classifications of Consonants in a Distinctive Features System (after Miller and Nicely, 1955)**

| Consonant | Voicing | Nasality | Affrication | Duration | Place |
|-----------|---------|----------|-------------|----------|-------|
| p | 0 | 0 | 0 | 0 | 0 |
| t | 0 | 0 | 0 | 0 | 1 |
| k | 0 | 0 | 0 | 0 | 2 |
| f | 0 | 0 | 1 | 0 | 0 |
| θ | 0 | 0 | 1 | 0 | 1 |
| s | 0 | 0 | 1 | 1 | 1 |
| ʃ | 0 | 0 | 1 | 1 | 2 |
| b | 1 | 0 | 0 | 0 | 0 |
| d | 1 | 0 | 0 | 0 | 1 |
| g | 1 | 0 | 0 | 0 | 2 |
| v | 1 | 0 | 1 | 0 | 0 |
| ð | 1 | 0 | 1 | 0 | 1 |
| z | 1 | 0 | 1 | 1 | 1 |
| ʒ | 1 | 0 | 1 | 1 | 2 |
| m | 1 | 1 | 0 | 0 | 0 |
| n | 1 | 1 | 0 | 0 | 1 |

(1955). Most of the features used are self-explanatory and their articulatory origin is obvious. Duration is perhaps the least intuitive feature. Note that most features are binary except for place of articulation, which is trinary (front, middle, and back). An alternative distinctive feature system is that of Jakobson and Halle (1956) who use a system of 9 binary dimensions. These dimensions were selected on the basis of more abstract and general considerations than English articulation. For instance, they use features such as vocalic-nonvocalic, grave-acute (which differentiates /o/, /u/ versus /e/, /i/, and compact-diffuse (e.g., /o/ versus /u/). We are in no position here to comment on the advantages of one system over another, but the distinctive feature analysis in general has very important consequences for our understanding of both perception and memory.

Miller and Nicely (1955) performed a study of perceptual confusions among English consonants. Sixteen consonants were presented under conditions of frequency distortion and noise. Subjects were instructed to guess at every sound. An analysis of the confusion errors showed that these were highly systematic. The more distinctive features two consonants had in common, the greater the likelihood of a confusion.

In Figure 4.7, the data from one of the conditions (S/N ratio of –6 dB) of the Miller and Nicely experiment were plotted as a function of the number of distinctive features in common between the stimulus letter and the letter given as a response by the subject. For instance, if the letter *p* was presented and the subjects gave *p* as a response, an entry is made under Distance 0. Responses *t, k, f,* and *b* are entered under Distance 1, *r* would be counted under Distance 2, *n* as 3, and *z* as 4, depending on the number of distinctive features in Table 4.4 which are different from the stimulus letters. As Figure 4.7 shows, the effect of similarity upon perception is a very strong one. However, not all features are equally affected by distortions or noise. Miller and Nicely have shown that voicing and nasality are perceived accurately even under quite adverse conditions, while place of articulation is severely affected by noise. They concluded that the perception of any of these five features is relatively independent of the perception of the others. Perception of consonants operates more like a five-channel system than one single complex channel.

Wickelgren (1966) has shown that the same holds true for short-term memory. Indeed, one can analyze the memory confusion data of Conrad (1964) shown in Table 4.3 in the same way as described above

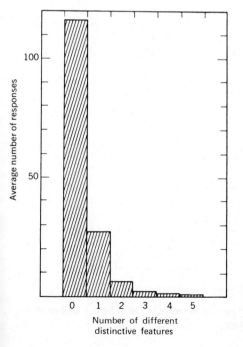

Number of different
distinctive features

FIGURE 4.7  **Perceptual confusions as a function of the number of different features between consonants. (after Table III of Miller and Nicely, 1955)**

for the perceptual confusion data of Miller and Nicely (1955). Figure 4.8 shows that the result of this analysis is almost the same as that obtained for perceptual confusions. The figure is due to Murdock (1967) who suggested this kind of analysis. Obviously the pattern of these memory results is very similar to that of the listening data shown in Figure 4.7, clearly implicating an acoustic memory code as the source of the observed confusions.

Indeed, acoustic coding has been found in many short-term memory studies. Acoustic coding is closely related to overt vocalization; it appears to be a form of "speaking to oneself." Estes (1973), for instance, obtained clear evidence for phonemic encoding of visually presented letters when vocalization was permitted at input, but not when vocalization was prevented by a categorizing task, or when the letters were presented at such a rapid rate that they could not be vocalized. Interestingly, however, phonemic encoding occurred even in these latter conditions when rehearsal was permitted following the presentation of an item. Rehearsal, too, appears to be a kind of silent speaking-to-oneself.

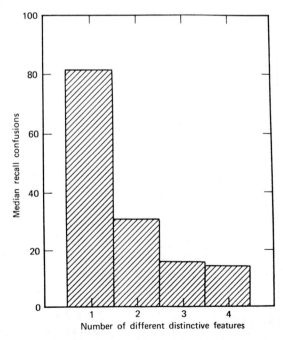

FIGURE 4.8    **Recall confusions as a function of the number of different distinctive features. Data from Conrad (1964). (after Murdock, 1967)**

Subjects use auditory encoding especially when they know that the material to be retained must be kept in memory only for a short time. It is like a person who walks to a telephone across the room repeating to himself the number he wants to dial, but for which he has no further use; in contrast, one would try to engrave that number upon memory in some more permanent fashion if one expected to use it frequently again (or supplement memory with a notebook). Thus, an acoustic code is most likely to be used for the last few items of a list, which need not be held in memory for a long time. Kintsch and Buschke (1969) have observed acoustic encoding of the last few items of the list in a sequential probe experiment. For these items, an acoustic code was sufficient to support recall, while for the early and middle items an acoustic code would have been insufficient, and subjects took recourse to more permanent semantic coding. Kintsch and Buschke's learning material consisted of strings of 16 words. After a 16-word string was presented, one of the words was repeated and the subject was asked to respond with the word that had originally followed it. There were three types of strings in the experiment: some consisted of eight pairs of synonyms in random order (POLITE-COURTEOUS), others consisted of randomly ordered homophone pairs (NIGHT-KNIGHT), and the third type were strings of unrelated words which served as controls. For the homophone strings, performance was impaired for the last few items (for which a recency effect would be expected); the acoustic similarity led to confusions and impaired encoding of these items, indicating that subjects were using an acoustic encoding strategy for these items. Recall of the early and middle items of the list, on the other hand, was unaffected by acoustic similarity, indicating some nonacoustic, presumably semantic encoding strategy. Conversely, the semantic similarity in the synonym lists produced recall decrements in the early and middle parts of the lists, but not in their recency portions.

It is, however, not the case that recency items are always coded acoustically. Subjects seem to resort to acoustic coding strategies whenever they can, and our short-term memory experiments give them ample occasion to do so, but short-term memory may also be based on nonacoustic codes, if the task requires it. Shulman (1972), for instance, showed that the recency effect may involve nonacoustic coding in a probe recognition experiment. His subjects received three types of recognition tests after being presented with a 10-word input string. The probe item was either identical with one of the list items, or was a homophone or synonym of one. Subjects were not told which type of test to expect until after the learning list was presented, so that they could not prepare differentially for one or the other type of test. Nevertheless, synonym recognition produced the same kind of recency effect as homophone recognition. If the recency effect had depended on acoustic coding, one would not have expected any recency effect at all for synonym recognition. In order to counter the possibility that subjects may have stored items phonetically but recoded them semantically when given the synonym test, Raser (1972) designed a follow-up study to preclude such a strategy. He demonstrated, in essence, that when subjects were shown a probe list containing the item BARE they correctly recognized NUDE as a synonym, but that they did not falsely identify NUDE as a synonym when the to-be-learned item was BEAR. This means that they must have held in their memory more than merely the phonemic representation of BEAR or BARE. Since Raser, like Shulman, found similar recency effects for synonym and homophone recognition, we have here a clear case of nonacoustic short-term memory.

Acoustic encoding merely represents one level of processing in short-term memory experiments. It is an important one, because subjects tend to employ acoustic coding a great deal—they even use it when such a strategy is clearly nonoptimal (for an example, see Healy, 1974)—but it is a superficial level of encoding and not very well suited for long-term retention. If one wants to remember something for more than a few seconds, deeper levels of encoding are usually more suitable.

## 4.2.2   CHUNKING AND THE CAPACITY OF SHORT-TERM MEMORY

The term "chunking" was introduced in 1956 by Miller and refers to the organization of an input string into coherent groups or chunks. As such, it is an encoding strategy. Grouping elements together to form higher order units can greatly improve a person's memory capacity. Perhaps no other single factor is more important for short-term retention than the chunking of the material.

The short-term memory function for consonant trigrams is almost identical with that for word triplets. The study by Murdock (1961) upon which this conclusion is based has already been referred to and the relevant data are shown in Figure 4.2. Obviously, separate letters are not the appropriate unit for short-term memory. When letters form a meaningful word, they are treated as a whole, so that three words are not harder to remember than three unrelated letters. Psychologists have long known that subjects group single letters, digits, nonsense syllables, or even words into clusters, which then act as units in memory. When presented with a meaningful sequence of letters, subjects perceive words, not separate letters, and words are stored in short-term memory. The perceptual processing that takes place when these chunks are formed is quite automatic and seems to require a minimum of time and effort. In fact, one of the main differences between short- and long-term memory appears to lie in the way in which material is encoded for storage. Chunks are stored in both short- and long-term memory, but the chunks of short-term memory are the result of very superficial perceptual processing, while the units of long-term memory are based on higher level analyses, which require time and often considerable effort.

Chunking is the result of the subject's perceptual coding processes. The experimenter may influence these by arranging stimuli in ways that favor the formation of particular chunking patterns. The principles of perceptual organization are not completely understood yet, but Koffka's "law of Prägnanz" (1935) is a good description of these phenomena. The law says, briefly, that perceptual organization tends to move in the direction of a regular, simple, meaningful, and stable percept. This formulation explains little, for what will happen depends entirely upon the prevailing conditions. We do not yet know exactly which principle to evoke in any given situation, as the various tendencies implied by the law of Prägnanz might well be in conflict with each other. Nevertheless, perceptual organization does occur and the factors described certainly are relevant.

Müller and Schumann (1894) showed that chunking can be induced by reading a series of nonsense syllables in a rhythmic manner. Chunks formed through an arbitrary reading rhythm can be very powerful factors in memory and may even overshadow the effects of serial associations. Visual groupings of unrelated items have similar effects. McLean and Gregg (1967) taught subjects random sequences of letters which were presented visually in groups of 1, 3, 4, 6, or 8. When a subject could recall the series perfectly, inter-response times were recorded and used to assess chunking. If a subject formed chunks of a certain size, the times between the letters belonging to the same chunk ought to be shorter than the times between letters belonging to different chunks. On the basis of this principle, McLean and Gregg could provide unambiguous evidence not only for chunking but also for the proposition that subjects use a chunk size which corresponds to the grouping used in the presentation of the learning material. Thus, most subjects who were shown letters in groups of 6, formed chunks of that size in recall, etc. Subjects who were shown the letters singly also formed chunks, but different subjects chose different chunk sizes. Again, as in the case of Müller and Schumann's results, the chunk proved to be a stronger bond than associative relations across chunks. For instance, when the (randomly chosen) letters of two adjacent groups happened to form a meaningful syllable, interrecall times were determined by the presentation group rather than the meaningful unit.

Perceptual organization is not something that is fixed once and for all. One can learn principles of organization and use them for chunking previously unorganized material. Miller (1956) describes the case of the apprentice telegraph operator, who at first hears each "dit" and "dah" separately. Then he learns to organize the sound patterns into letters, and finally into words and whole phrases. He can form larger and larger chunks as he learns more about the telegraphic code. This is greatly to his advantage because the larger the chunk he can deal with as a whole the more information he can handle in memory.

In a demonstration experiment (Miller, 1956) subjects were taught to recode sequences of binary digits (1's and 0's) into larger chunks and thereby to increase the amount of material that could be remembered. People can repeat back about nine binary digits if each digit is treated as a chunk and remembered separately. But suppose subjects are taught to recode a sequence of binary digits in terms of digit pairs: 00 is renamed 0, 01 is renamed 1, 10 is renamed 2, and 11 is renamed 3. If the subject translates a string of zeros and ones into this new code, his memory load is reduced by half. One can devise even more efficient codes in terms of triplets, quadruplets, or even quintuplets. There are $2^5 = 32$ different quintuplets and the subject must learn to give a different decimal digit name to each pattern. Once he has mastered this code he can store binary digit sequences in chunks of size five, thereby greatly increasing the capacity of his immediate memory. Miller has shown that subjects can actually use such a recoding scheme. However, it turned out that a great deal of practice was necessary before the more complicated recoding procedures could be used efficiently. It is not sufficient merely to understand the coding principles. The recoding must be almost automatic, or the subject will lose part of the next group while he is trying to remember the proper label for the last group. A well-practiced subject was able to repeat back up to 40 binary digits, by using a 4:1 or 5:1 encoding ratio.

The span of immediate memory is about 7, plus or minus 2, chunks, and is quite independent of the size of these chunks. This is a very important and curious result. It is implied by the discussion above, but there are a number of direct experimental tests which establish its validity beyond question. Wundt (1905) found the span of immediate

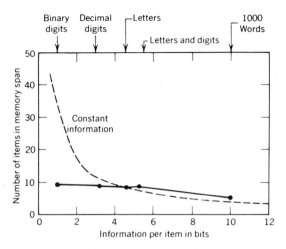

FIGURE 4.9    **The span of immediate memory plotted as a function of the amount of information per item in the test materials.** (after Miller, 1956)

memory to be about six "simple impressions," which may be isolated lines, digits, letters, words, or arhythmic metronome beats. He pointed out in this connection that the touch alphabet of the blind is limited to six binary symbols. However, the capacity of immediate memory ·can be greatly enlarged through suitable grouping of elements: While only six isolated letters may be kept in consciousness at one time, up to 10 letters can be retained if they are presented as CVCs, and from 20 to 30 letters if they form part of a sentence. In studies of subjective grouping of metronome beats six groups of beats could be retained when beats were grouped in patterns of two; when patterns of four beats were formed, five of them could still be retained simultaneously; practiced subjects managed to handle as many as five beats of size eight, for a total of 40 beats! Wundt's studies depended heavily upon the introspective report of his subjects, and it is interesting to note their substantial agreement with modern findings obtained with objective methods, such as those of Miller (1956). Miller's results (shown in Figure 4.9) demonstrate the constancy of the memory span when the size of the chunk is varied in terms of information content. To understand this figure, a brief digression into information measurement is necessary.*

---

* Excellent and clear discussions of information theory in psychology are available (e.g., Garner, 1962); we shall only attempt to introduce the basic principles of information measurement here.

Information is measured in terms of uncertainty. In a situation where many different alternative outcomes are possible and we have no idea which one to expect, uncertainty is very great, and an observed outcome is very informative, in the sense that it reduces much uncertainty. On the other hand, if there are only a few alternatives possible, or if one has good reason to expect the occurrence of one particular outcome anyway, uncertainty and hence the information value of the expected outcome is low. Telling a Californian that it will be sunny tomorrow is not very informative when it is summer and anything else would be quite a surprise.

The conventional unit of information measurement is in terms of bits. A bit is the uncertainty that exists when two outcomes are possible, each with equal likelihood, as for instance in the toss of an unbiased coin. Four equally likely outcomes represent an uncertainty of two bits, eight equally likely alternatives amount to an uncertainty of three bits, and so on. In general, if there are $n$ equal alternatives the logarithm to the base 2 of $n$ indicates how many bits of information are obtained if one of these alternatives occurs.

Suppose a subject recalls the following string of 0's and 1's: 0110010. Since at each position in this string there is a choice between exactly two alternatives (0 or 1), each such choice is worth one bit of information; there are seven choices, so that the total amount of information retained is 7 bits. Now suppose a subject is given the string 6379528 and he recalls this one, too. In the construction of this string a choice was made at each position among 10 alternatives, the digits 0 to 9. In terms of information, we have at each position $\log_2(10) = 3.3$ bits, and hence a total of $7 \times 3.3 = 23$ bits which have been retained in memory. It is clear that a string of decimal digits is much richer in information than a string of 0's and 1's. Hence, since subjects are about equally capable of recalling either one, the capacity of short-term memory is by no means constant if measured in terms of amount of information. If amount of information measured in bits were a critical variable in short-term memory recall of seven 0's or 1's should imply that only a little more than two decimal digits could be recalled, since two decimal digits amount to 6.6 bits! Instead, the capacity of short-term memory is measured in terms of "chunks" which may differ widely in their information content; let us consider Miller's (1956) evidence.

In Figure 4.9 the number of items a subject can repeat after one presentation is shown for different item populations. The population size increases from 2 (binary digits) to 1000 (words), the information per item increases correspondingly from 1 bit to 10 bits, but the memory span hardly changes at all. The number of chunks is what matters in immediate memory, but not the information per chunk. Figure 4.9 is based on an experiment using a standard memory span procedure. Lists were read aloud at a rate of one item per second and subjects were given as much time as needed for recall. The number of items that a subject could always recall plus a weighted average of the longer sequences that were recalled only occasionally were used to obtain an estimate of memory span.

Pollack's work, which is summarized in Figure 4.10, confirms the independence of chunk size and memory span (Pollack, 1953). The amount of information retained after one presentation increases almost linearly with chunk size, which implies that the number of chunks remembered was constant, irrespective of information per chunk. Note that this conclusion with respect to the span of immediate memory is at variance with the findings concerning long-term memory. In Chapter 1 we reviewed several studies that show that, in general, free recall of lists which exceed the immediate memory span improves as redundancy increases. Redundancy is a term from information theory and it refers to the difference between the actual information in a message, or any kind of learning sequence, and the maximum possible amount of information. For instance, the maximum uncertainty of a 27-letter alphabet (26 letters plus space) is 4.75 bits. However, in normal English text a letter contains only about

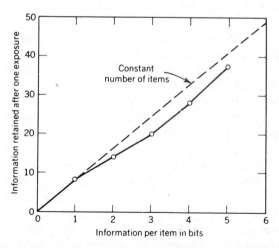

FIGURE 4.10   **The amount of information retained after one presentation plotted as a function of the amount of information per item in the test material. Data from Pollack (1953). (after Miller, 1956)**

2 bits. Thus letter redundancy in English is nearly 60%. The reason for this redundancy is that the letters in English text are to a certain extent predictable; we are much more likely to expect an H after a T than a Q, and so on. Redundancy is therefore absence of uncertainty, or information, and the studies reviewed earlier imply that the less information in supra-span sequencies, the better recall is. Memory is, however, independent of the amount of information contained in a chunk. It is the number of chunks that matter, not how complex these chunks are internally.

Miller (1956) concluded from the evidence reviewed above that the capacity of short-term memory was seven plus or minus two chunks. In actual fact, the problem is a bit more complicated than that. Miller's experimental evidence has held up quite well in the 20 years since he wrote his paper, but we must take issue with his notion of "capacity." Miller's magic number 7 $\pm$ 2 implies a short-term memory model consisting of a box of fixed sizes in which one can put 7 $\pm$ 2 chunks; these fill it to capacity, and any more will create an overflow. In Chapter 3, however, we described a rather different view of capacity limitations. We have seen that the outcome of a long series of studies of selective attention was a model that assumes parallel processing along many dimensions. For this processing task, the organism has available a limited amount of resources, which must be divided up in such a way as to fulfill the demands of the task at hand. If the task demands more resources than available, performance must suffer somewhere. Applied to the present situation, this analysis implies that capacity estimates of short-term memory must depend on the experimental task involved. If the task is an easy one, all or most of a person's resources can be devoted to keeping the to-be-learned items in short-term memory, and the number of items retained (and hence estimates of the "capacity of short-term memory") will be large. But many tasks make multiple demands on a person's resources. For instance, in a free-recall experiment, the subject on the one hand must hold input items in short-term memory, (e.g., in order to group them into suitable chunks), but he cannot devote all of his resources to short-term rehearsal. At the same time, he must encode items more deeply so that they can be maintained over longer retention intervals, because free-recall lists are typically longer than the seven or so items that a subject can retain in short-term memory. Hence in free-recall, fewer resources are available for the task of short-term retention, and one would expect fewer items to be recalled from short-term memory than in memory span experiments. An estimate of the number of items from short-term memory in free recall can be obtained from the recency effect observed in such tasks. The last few items of a list are typically much better recalled than the middle items of a list. It can be argued that these are the items still available in short-term memory at the time of recall. Hence, if one counts how many more recency items are recalled than items from the middle of the list, an estimate of the number of items in short-term memory in free-recall tasks can be obtained (a more detailed account of this estimation procedure is given below in Section 4.4.1). Typically these estimates are much lower than the 7 $\pm$ 2 estimated from memory span experiments. Glanzer and Razel (1974) have examined 32 free-recall experiments by various authors that have been reported in the literature. The studies considered used a free-recall procedure with immediate recall and 12 or more words as stimuli. For each study, an estimate of short-term memory was obtained (based on the superiority of the last six items over the middle items of the list). The frequency distribution of these estimates is shown in Figure 4.11. The mean number of short-term memory items in free recall is 2.2 (the standard deviation is .64), which is much less than the magic number 7. Nevertheless, the fact that these estimates cluster quite closely around their mean is very

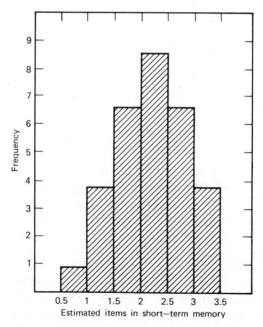

FIGURE 4.11   **Frequency distribution of the estimated number of items in short-term memory from 32 free-recall experiments. (after Glanzer and Razel, 1974)**

encouraging: in spite of large differences in the overall rate of recall in the 32 experiments that Glanzer and Razel reviewed, the number of items contributed to the recall from short-term memory appears to be fairly constant.

Miller's finding that the number of chunks, but not their internal complexity, determines short-term recall in memory span experiments has its parallel in free-recall data reported by Glanzer and Razel (1974). In one of their studies, Glanzer and Razel had subjects recall 15-item lists. The items of the list, however, were familiar proverbs, rather than words. The experiment was done with both English- and Hebrew-speaking subjects. For the former the number of items recalled from short-term memory was estimated as 2.2 proverbs, while an estimate of 2.1 proverbs was obtained for the Hebrew-speaking subjects. Note that both estimates fall at the modal value of the distribution of short-term memory estimates from free-recall studies with words as learning items (Figure 4.11). At least, this is the case if proverbs are used as the unit of analysis. In terms of words recalled from short-term memory, values of 10.1 words for English and 8.2 words for Hebrew subjects would be obtained, which are quite outside the distribution in Figure 4.11. But, of course, familiar proverbs form a chunk in short-term memory. They are encoded as a unit, and must be treated as such.

Glanzer and Razel also report an experiment concerned with the unit of short-term memory for unfamiliar, new sentences. Obviously, these could not be treated as a unit by the subject in the same sense as familiar proverbs, but equally obvious, a sentence is quite different from a sequence of unrelated words. It should be much easier to form chunks for storage in short-term memory with a sentence, even though one has never heard the particular sentence before. Thus, fewer new sentences should be retained in short-term memory than familiar proverbs, but some chunking even of new sentences would certainly be expected. This prediction was confirmed in their experiment, and their results are shown in Figure 4.12. Serial position curves from a 15-item free-recall experiment are shown for three types of materials: single words, proverbs, and new sentences (all of which were presented at a rate of 4 seconds per item). It is clear from the figure that words were much better recalled than proverbs, which in turn were much better recalled than new sentences. However, the differences are not in the short-term component of recall; the recency effects for the three types of materials are quite comparable. Indeed, if one estimates the number of items recalled from short-term memory, the following values are obtained: 1.9 for words, 2.0 for pro-

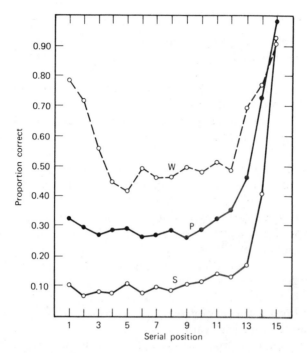

FIGURE 4.12 Serial position curves for the recall of familiar proverbs (P), new sentences (S), and words (W) which were all presented at a rate of 4 sec per item. (adapted from Experiments 4 and 6 of Glanzer and Razel, 1974)

verbs, and 1.5 for new sentences. Note that the first two are comparable to earlier estimates. As expected, fewer new sentences are recalled from short-term memory, though not much fewer (1.5 is quite within the range of the estimates shown in Figure 4.11, and still represents seven words!).

How one perceives a stimulus is therefore crucial for short-term memory. If one can encode several elements, such as the words of a sentence, as a unit, retention will be facilitated because short-term memory limitations are based on the number of units encoded, independent of how much information is contained in these units. One should be careful, however, in talking about the "capacity" of short-term memory, because there is no fixed capacity. There is the magic number 7 ± 2, which is an upper limit under optimal conditions, but in general how many chunks can be retained in short-term memory depends on the demands that a task makes on a person's resources. With most tasks, only a fraction of a person's resources are available for short-term retention.

## 4.3     RETRIEVAL FROM SHORT-TERM MEMORY

By definition, short-term memory is the conscious, available part of memory. Retrieval from short-term memory is easy and direct. Introspectively, this is about all one can say about the problem. There exist, however, experimental methods that have greatly extended our knowledge about retrieval from short-term memory.

The basic experimental paradigm was introduced by Sternberg in 1966. The subject is induced to hold a set of items in short-term memory, and then he is given a recognition test where he must decide whether or not the test item is a member of that set. The task is simple, and errors are rare; reaction times are the response measure of interest.

More specifically, the experimenter works with a stimulus ensemble, e.g., the digits 1 to 9. From this ensemble, he arbitrarily selects a positive response set. These are the items that are given to the subject to memorize. On each trial in the experiment an item from the stimulus ensemble is presented and the subject decides whether it was a member of the positive response set. The experimental variable of primary interest is the size of the positive response set. The number of items in the response set varies from one to six, but is always less than the memory span, so that the subject is able to hold the whole set in short-term memory simultaneously. For instance, a subject might be given the response set (2,3,6,8), which has size $s = 4$, on one trial, and then (4,7,8), with $s = 3$, on the next trial.

The principal results of these studies are shown schematically in Figure 4.13. This figure may be regarded as representative for the results of several dozen experiments. The important features are the following. First, mean reaction time increases linearly with the size of the positive response set. Second, the rate of increase is the same for positive and negative responses, that is, the curves are parallel. Third, the rate of increase is about 40 milliseconds for each item in the positive set. Fourth, the zero intercept for positive responses is about 400 milliseconds, while that for negative responses is slightly higher, at about 430 milliseconds. These results are idealizations, and there are exceptions to all of them in the literature, but overall they are remarkably robust and sufficiently representative that we can disregard the exceptions for our purposes.

What retrieval process is implied by these data? First of all, notice that introspection about retrieval from short-term memory did not tell the whole story; retrieval is fast, but it is not direct, because the number of items held in short-term memory affects response times.

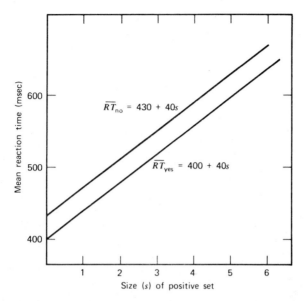

FIGURE 4.13  **Schematic results from item recognition experiments with the Sternberg paradigm.**

Either there is some sort of a search process through short-term memory, or decision processes become more complex as the number of items in short-term memory increases.

In order to understand what is going on, we must have some way of determining what the component processes are in the task at hand. Sternberg (1969) suggested that the task should be decomposed into four distinct component processes. The first subtask consists in encoding the test stimulus. Once the test stimulus is encoded, it must be compared to the contents of short-term memory. On the basis of this comparison, a decision must be made whether or not the test item is a member of the positive response set. Finally, the response decided upon must be executed. These four stages are shown in Figure 4.14.

The question that arises immediately at this point is how do we know that Sternberg's analysis is correct? It sounds reasonable, but there are undoubtedly other plausible alternatives. Psychologists are suspicious of such analyses because around the turn of the century attempts to analyze complex cognitive tasks into elementary information processes had been extremely popular and notoriously unsuccessful. Donders (1868) had pioneered a method whereby complex cognitive processes could be decomposed into their elements, based

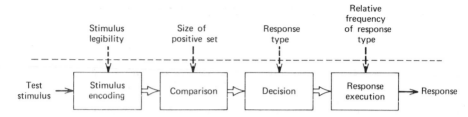

FIGURE 4.14   **Four processing stages in item recognition. Above the broken line four experimental factors are indicated that influence the stages. The factors do not interact, but affect each stage selectively. (after Sternberg, 1969)**

upon reaction time data. Wundt (1880), for instance, analyzed the process of *judging* into seven components: reflex + impulse + perception + apperception + cognition + association + judgment! Eventually this movement collapsed because the available data could not support such elaborate analyses into processing stages. Only in our time has a more powerful method been developed that permits us to discover processing stages and to verify our analyses. This is the additive factor method of Sternberg (1969). Sternberg showed that simple empirical conditions exist under which it is justified to infer a separate processing stage. These conditions depend on finding an experimental variable that affects only that processing stage without interacting with variables affecting other processing stages. For the four processing stages of Figure 4.14 such variables have been identified. For example, we can talk about a stimulus encoding stage because if one varies the difficulty of stimulus encoding in an experiment (e.g., by making the test stimulus very faint so that it is hard to read), all reaction times will increase, but all by the same amount; the curves in Figure 4.13 are simply shoved up a bit, but the pattern of results remains the same. This means that there is no statistical interaction between the effects of this variable and whatever else is going on. Therefore, one is justified in hypothesizing a separate stimulus encoding stage. Similarly, there are noninteracting variables for the other three stages, as indicated in Figure 4.14. The comparison stage is influenced only by the size of the positive response set. The decision stage depends on the nature of the particular response (*no* responses take a little longer than *yes* responses—but the curves for the two response types are entirely parallel, i.e., response type and size of the response set do not interact!). Finally, a more frequent response is executed faster than a less frequent response, but again this only shifts the curves up or down, it does not interact with the effects of other variables.

Thus, we have good reason to assume that the analysis into four stages of information processing suggested by Sternberg is empirically justified. The duration of three of these four stages according to Figure 4.13 is about 400 milliseconds, and we have no way of distinguishing how much of that time should be assigned to each stage. Only for the comparison stage do we have more detailed information, because of the regularity with which reaction times depend on the number of comparisons executed. Hence most of the theoretical interest has centered on explaining the nature of these comparisons.

An attractively simple explanation is the scanning hypothesis of Sternberg (1966; 1975). Sternberg assumes that each comparison of the test stimulus with an item held in memory requires 40 milliseconds and that the test stimulus is compared serially with all items in short-term memory. The striking feature of this model is that the search process is exhaustive; even when a match occurs, the search process continues through the rest of the items in short-term memory. This assumption is necessary, for if the search were self-terminating only half as many comparisons would have to be made on the average for positive items than for negative ones, which implies what the slope of the positive items should be only half of that for negative items. This is clearly contradicted by the data. A second notable implication of this model is the speed of the search process, which is substantially faster than the rate of covert speech (which may be one of the reasons why this search process is not open to a subject's introspection).

Before evaluating Sternberg's model in detail, there are a number of rather interesting observations to be made that relate to some of the things we discussed earlier in this chapter. For instance, there are two procedural variations of the Sternberg paradigm, the varied-set procedure, where a subject memorizes a different positive response set on each trial, and the fixed-set procedure, where the same positive response set is used for a whole block of trials. The first case is a pure short-term memory experiment; in the second case, however, the fixed set is remembered over many trials and is clearly held in long-term memory. Nevertheless, the results obtained with these two procedures are essentially identical. What this means is that with the fixed-set procedure the response set must have been held in both long-term and short-term memory. On the one hand, it was part of the subject's long-term memory (simply in the sense that it was remembered over a substantial period of time), but on each trial the subject must have "transferred" this response set to his short-term working memory, or in some sense "activated" it, so that it was ready to be compared with the test stimulus. Quotation marks were used in the previous sentence to draw attention to the fact that these

expressions are metaphors (a box metaphor for "transfer," a neurological metaphor for "activated"), and must not be taken literally.

We have seen in Section 4.2.1 that a preferred encoding modality in
short-term memory is the acoustic one, but that not all short-term
memory is acoustic, and that material in any form may be maintained
in short-term memory. This conclusion agrees well with the so-called
translation effect in item-recognition experiments. When the "languages" of the memory set and the test stimulus differ (e.g., the
response set is presented in the form of printed letters, but the test
stimulus is a spoken letter) the slopes of the reaction time functions
increase steeply (for a review, see Sternberg, 1975). This implies that
each comparison takes more time, presumably because for each comparison the item in memory must be translated into the appropriate
modality before it can be matched with the test stimulus. This is a
rather puzzling finding in itself, but note that it definitely contradicts
the idea that all items are recoded acoustically in short-term memory.
If that were the case, there would have been no need to translate
among codes in our example.

If the test stimulus and the response set are presented in the same
modality, the search rate is about 40 milliseconds. This is an average
value, and there are small variations around it. Cavanagh (1972) has
argued that even though these variations are small, they may be
meaningful. He observed that search rates for different materials correlate highly with the memory span for these materials. Just like search
rates, the memory span is remarkably constant (see Figure 4.9)—but it,
too, varies to some extent. Thus, the memory span for digits is 7.7
items on the average, for colors 7.10, for letters 6.35, for words 5.50,
and for geometrical shapes 5.30. All of these values are within the
range identified by Miller, 7 ± 2. Only when materials are used that
do not form unitary chunks, does the memory span fall below that
range: 3.8 for random forms, 3.40 for nonsense syllables. Interestingly,
these variations in memory span are mirrored quite exactly by variations in the search rates as determined in Sternberg-type experiments.
This correlation is shown in Figure 4.15, which plots the reciprocal of
the memory span against search rates. Cavanagh showed that precisely
such a relationship follows from several contemporary models of
short-term memory. Suppose, for instance, that short-term memory
has a fixed capacity and can hold only a certain number of features.
The more features necessary to specify an item (e.g., words presumably have more features than digits), the smaller the number of
items that can be contained within that fixed space. At the same time,
if recognition involves serial testing of features and each test requires

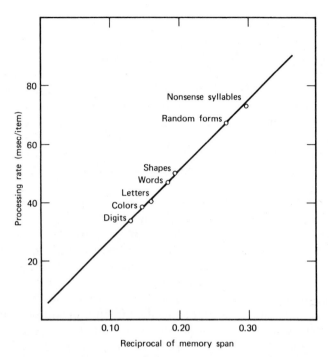

**FIGURE 4.15  The relationship between processing rates in item recognition experiments and the reciprocal of the memory span for seven classes of materials. (after Cavanagh, 1972)**

a constant amount of time, the tests will take longer for many-feature items than for items with fewer features. Hence search rates and memory span must be inversely related. Thus, the same characteristic of the memory system, the limited capacity of short-term memory, accounts for these two rather different phenomena, memory span and search rate.

The fact that Sternberg's scanning model thus relates in rather sensible ways to other aspects of short-term memory, speaks strongly in its favor. The model is, however, not without its problems. First of all, critics have accused it of being intuitively unreasonable; why should a search process continue until the whole response set is exhausted, even after a positive identification has been made? Sternberg (1975) has countered this objection very well, simply by describing several possible physical systems in which an exhaustive search would be more efficient than a self-terminating search. More serious are some empirical inadequacies of the model. In many studies with results just like those in Figure 4.13, serial position effects have been observed that the model cannot account for. Often positive responses are facilitated if the test item is identical with the first or last item in the response set. It is not at all clear how this could occur if searches are exhaustive. A second problem arises when items are duplicated in the response set; when the duplicated item is being tested, reaction times are unusually short. Finally, the model fails to explain what happens when one varies the probability with which the members of the response set are presented. High-probability items are responded to faster than low-probability items (see Sternberg, 1975, for a more detailed discussion).

Such empirical difficulties have led other investigators to propose a whole array of alternative models, with almost any combination of processing assumptions. Theios (1973) proposed a serial scanning model in which the search was self-terminating; Murdock (1974) suggested a backward serial self-terminating scan (and considered some novel sources of evidence for this model); others have worked with scanning models in which the search was exhaustive, but proceeded in parallel (e.g., Murdock, 1971), while a further group of investigators entirely abandoned the idea of a memory search and proposed direct access theories based on principles similar to those discussed in Section 1.4.1 (e.g., Corballis, Kirby, and Miller, 1972). All of these models have some attractive features, but none of them appears to be entirely satisfactory at this point. Furthermore, most of these models are entirely ad hoc, that is, they are constructed to account for reaction time data from the item-recognition paradigm, and have no direct relation to other short-term memory phenomena. Indeed, this is also a criticism that must be raised against Sternberg's original scanning model. The notable exceptions in this respect are Murdock (1974), as well as a model proposed by Atkinson and Juola (1974), which we shall discuss in some detail.

The Atkinson and Juola model can be regarded as a combination of the models of recognition memory that were discussed in Chapter 1 and Sternberg's scanning model. Thus, before proceeding, we should review some of the main ideas about the role of decision processes in recognition memory from Section 1.4.1. We assumed there that each item in memory is characterized by a familiarity value, which is simply a name for some kind of a tag that may vary quantitatively. Old items in a recognition test have, in general, higher familiarity values than new items, but under most experimental circumstances the two distributions overlap. This situation was pictured in Figure 1.12. Given a test item, the subject looks up its familiarity value in memory and on that basis makes his response; if the familiarity value is high, he says he recognizes the item as an old one, if it is low he says he does not recognize it. Because of the overlap of the distributions shown in Figure 1.12, this decision procedure will always lead to errors; if the subject assumes a very low criterion, he will correctly recognize all or most old items, but he also will falsely recognize many items he had not seen before. Conversely, if he sets up a very strict recognition criterion, he will avoid false recognitions but miss old items in the process. Usually the subject tries to avoid both extremes, missing some old items and making some false alarms. The point is that the situation constrains him in such a way that no matter how he tries, performance cannot be perfect.

In the Sternberg task, however, performance is almost perfect (errors are typically less than 2%). How is this possible, given the model just outlined? Atkinson and Juola argue that the subject's decision process is more complex than envisaged above. In their model, subjects make a recognition response only when the familiarity of a test item is either very high or very low (in the latter case the response is, of course, no). In the intermediate range, where decisions on the basis of familiarity alone would invariably lead to many errors, the subject holds his decision and searches memory, in the way described by Sternberg's scanning model. This theory is outlined in Figure 4.16. If the familiarity value of a test item is greater than the upper criterion $C_u$, the subject responds yes; if it is less than the lower criterion $C_l$, the response is no; if it falls between $C_i$ and $C_u$, memory is scanned. The memory scan is serial and exhaustive, and the response is determined by the outcome of this search.

In Atkinson's and Juola's model recognition is by direct access, hence no set size effects, such as those shown in Figure 4.13, are predicted on the basis of the recognition component alone. However, on a certain proportion of trials the outcome of the recognition test is ambiguous, and the items stored in memory are scanned as in Sternberg's model. It is this scan that produces the set size effect.

The Atkinson and Juola (1974) model has some obvious advantages. It explains all the data that the Sternberg model explains. In addition, some of the data that were incompatible with the Sternberg model are readily understandable within that framework. It is, for instance, easy to see why items that appear twice in a response set are recognized especially rapidly; they would be quite at the extreme of the familiarity distribution and only very rarely require a time-consuming memory search. Serial position effects are similarly explained. We know from many verbal learning studies that the first and last items in

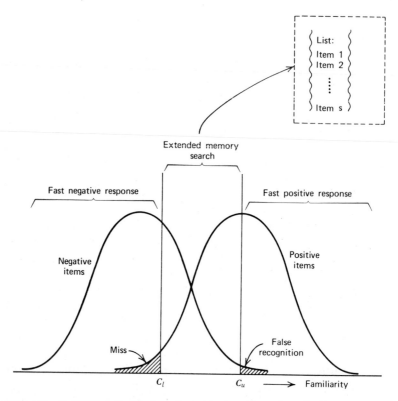

FIGURE 4.16 **Familiarity distributions for positive and negative test items, upper and lower decision criteria, associated decision regions, and corresponding actions. (adapted from Atkinson and Juola, 1974)**

a list are learned best; hence they would have higher familiarity values and would require fewer memory searches on the average than items in the middle of the list. There may be other results (e.g., probability effects) that cannot be explained by the model, or that may eventually be shown to contradict it. The main attraction of the model, however, is not merely that it explains many of the phenomena observed in item-recognition experiments of the Sternberg type, but its generality and the ease with which it can be extended to other aspects of recognition memory. The model of recognition memory described in Chapter 1 can be regarded as a special case of the theory—a situation where subjects never engage in a memory search, but always make decisions on the basis of familiarity alone. We shall see in the next chapter (Section 5.2.4) that even in conventional recognition experiments there is evidence that decisions based only upon the familiarity of test items cannot explain all of the data. Mandler (1972), for instance, reported evidence that subjects, when they are uncertain whether they had seen an item before, engage in "recall checks"; if they find they can recall the questionable item, they use this as additional evidence for a recognition response. Furthermore, the Atkinson and Juola model is not restricted to short-term memory performance as was Sternberg's theory. Similar decision processes are involved in deciding whether or not one has experienced an item before, regardless of whether it is in short-term memory or in long-term memory. Atkinson and Juola report experiments in which subjects were given long lists of items to memorize (16, 24, or 32 words). Needless to say, long-term memory must be involved in the retention of such lists, since they are much larger than the memory span. Once a list was well learned, positive and negative test items were shown to the subject, just as in Sternberg's experiments. Representative results are shown in Figure 4.17. Reaction times increase linearly with the size of the target set, but the zero intercept of the functions is much higher than in Figure 4.13, and the search rate is much lower (4.12 milliseconds versus 40 milliseconds for short-term memory). In addition, the curves

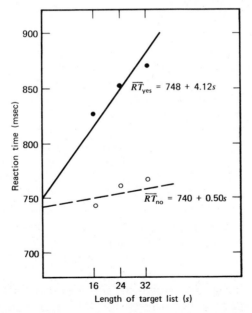

**FIGURE 4.17    Reaction time as a function of the size of the memorized target set for _yes_ and _no_ responses. (after Atkinson and Juola, 1974)**

for positive and negative items are no longer parallel; indeed, latencies for negative items are almost independent of set size. Furthermore, error rates are considerably higher in this situation than in short-term memory scanning experiments (up to 20% for positive test items in the experiment from which the data in Figure 4.17 were obtained). However the theory of Atkinson and Juola—which is a well-specified, quantitative model—can account both for the results shown in Figure 4.13 and in 4.17. In fact, the lines shown in Figure 4.17 are theoretical predictions derived from their model (rather than lines of best fit). Thus, its quantitative precision and its impressive generality combine to make the Atkinson and Juola (1974) model the best currently available explanation of retrieval phenomena in short-term memory.

## 4.4    PRIMARY AND SECONDARY MEMORY

### 4.4.1    SEPARATE MEMORY STORES

When a memory code is formed it remains for a while in an activated state, during which it is readily accessible. The person is conscious of items in this state. These available, conscious items comprise what James (1890) called primary memory. Items leave this activated state rather rapidly, unless they can be rehearsed. However, when an item leaves consciousness/primary memory, it is not necessarily forgotten, that is, lost from memory altogether. It may merely recede into a more passive, unconscious state, from which it can be retrieved, that is, returned to consciousness, although retrieval may under some conditions be difficult or impossible. These items comprise James's secondary memory.

To this date, the distinction between primary and secondary memory in terms of consciousness has been the most compelling one. However, many other lines of evidence argue for the usefulness of that distinction. Both behavioral and neurological data may be cited in its support. Milner (1967) reported an intriguing case of a specific memory deficit observed in a brain-damaged patient. A patient with hippocampal lesions suffered from an inability to form new long-term memory traces. At the same time the patient's immediate memory as well as his long-term memory appeared to be quite normal. He performed well on intelligence tests, and on other tests involving previously acquired knowledge; his motor skills were normal; there were no apparent personality changes as the result of the brain damage. However, he could not remember any new information for long. He behaved normally as long as information was held in immediate memory, but no long-term traces were formed. As soon as his attention was distracted, the contents of primary memory were lost. These observations of Milner (1967), which have since been confirmed in other cases, suggest that the neurological bases for immediate memory and long-term memory are distinct.

Quite apart from this neurological evidence, many purely behavioral results seem to require a distinction between immediate memory and long-term memory. None of these experiments is crucial in itself, but their cumulative effect gives some support to the two-store hypothesis.

If subjects are given a list of words to recall, the last items of the list, i.e., those most recently presented, will be recalled best. This is called the "recency effect" in free recall. If one wants to attribute the recency effect to retrieval from primary memory, the question arises whether there are experimental variables which affect recall of the most recent items but have no effects upon the retention of earlier items, or vice versa. Glanzer and Cunitz (1966) have shown that presentation rate is such a variable. They had 240 subjects learn eight 20-word lists with presentation rates per word of 3, 6, or 9 seconds. Rate of presentation had no effect on the most recently presented items, but giving subjects more time with each word clearly had a beneficial effect on recall of the first 15 words in the list.

Quite similar results are obtained when frequency of the words to be recalled is varied. Sumby (1963) asked subjects to recall lists of 15 unrelated words, which were either high-frequency or low-frequency words from the Thorndike-Lorge count. Overall recall was better for the high-frequency words, but the interesting result is the interaction between serial position and frequency which Sumby observed; recently presented words were recalled equally well, irrespective of frequency (on the average, high-frequency words were recalled better by one-half word in the second half of the list); the difference between the recall of high- and low-frequency words came primarily from the first half of the series (2.4 words in favor of high frequency lists).

An experimental variable that has the opposite effect, i.e., it changes the recall probability of the most recent items, but leaves the earlier items unaffected, is delay after presentation. Glanzer and Cunitz (1966), in the study already referred to, reported a condition in which subjects were shown a 15-word list, but recall was not attempted until an interval of 0, 10, and 30 seconds after the presentation of the list. The delay interval was filled with a counting task.

Figure 4.18 shows the results of this experiment. While the usual recency effect was obtained for 0 delay, the effect is attenuated for 10-second delay and completely absent when a delay of 30 seconds intervened between the end of presentation and the beginning of recall. Essentially identical results were obtained in an experiment by Postman and Phillips (1965) and several other investigators since.

When subjects recall a list of items in an experiment, the order of recall determines to a large extent what kind of a serial position curve will be obtained. Several experimental studies are available (Raffel, 1936; Deese, 1957; Murdock, 1963c; Tulving and Arbuckle, 1963, 1966) which all show that if the recall of the last items of a list is delayed by making the subject recall the early items of the list first, the usual recency effect is not obtained or at least is strongly diminished. The early and middle items of the list, which do not depend on short-term memory, are not affected by order of recall. The experiment of Tulving and Arbuckle (1963) nicely illustrates this point. In this experiment subjects learned a 10-item paired-associate list, with the numbers 0 to 9 as stimuli and nonsense syllables as responses. The order of presentation and test was arranged so that each item with a given input position was recalled in every output position. Their results are shown in Figure 4.19. Output interference does not seem to operate

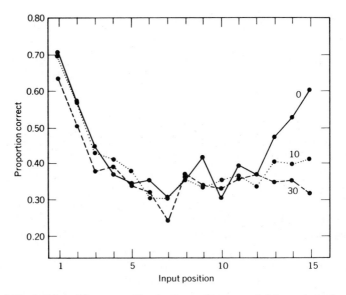

FIGURE 4.18   Serial position curves for 0- 10-, and 30-second delay. (after Glanzer and Cunitz, 1966)

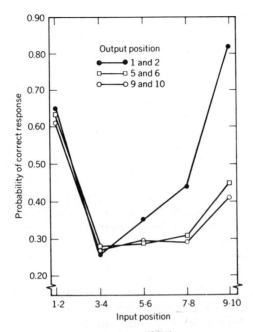

FIGURE 4.19  **Probability of recall of individual items as a function of input position as parameter, for ordered input lists. (after Tulving and Arbuckle, 1963)**

on recall of early and middle input items. The first items are recalled much better than the middle items. This primacy effect is characteristic of most free-recall and paried-associate data, except when subjects are instructed to concentrate on each item as it is presented and not to rehearse earlier items (Raffel, 1936; Waugh and Norman, 1965). Recall of items 9 and 10 depends on how long the recall attempt is delayed; recall is very good immediately after the end of presentation, but rapidly approaches the level of items 5 and 6 if it is delayed by recall attempts of other items.

The evidence from the studies reported above supports the hypothesis of two different memory mechanisms, a primary memory which contributes to recall if the retention time is relatively brief, and a more permanent memory which is less sensitive to retention time but depends on such variables as rate of presentation and word frequency.

Waugh and Norman (1965) formulated a simple quantitative model for the distinction between primary and secondary memory. Primary memory is a limited capacity system. As new items enter, old ones are displaced and lost permanently. Items in primary memory may be rehearsed. Rehearsal may be overt or implicit; what is meant by rehearsal may best be described as focusing attention on a particular item. The effects of rehearsal are twofold: it reenters items in primary memory and it may lead to storage in secondary memory. Two kinds of interference cause forgetting from primary memory: input interference, which is determined by the number of new items perceived during the retention interval, and output interference, which depends on how many old items have been recalled between the presentation and test of the item under consideration. Thus, if an item appears in position $n$ from the end of the list, and the subject attempts to recall this item after recalling $m$ other items, the total number of interfering units is $i = n + m$. Adding $n$ and $m$ implies that output interference is just as strong as input interference. The assumption is acceptable as a first approximation, though a more complicated weighting of the relative contributions of $n$ and $m$ could probably improve the model somewhat.

According to Waugh and Norman, the probability of recalling an item that has been followed by $i$ inputs or attempts to recall is given by the probability that the item can be retrieved from primary memory, secondary memory, or both. Assuming that these probabilities are independent, we have

$$(1) \qquad R_i = P_i + S_i - P_i S_i$$

where $R_i$ is the probability of recalling the item in serial position $i$, $P_i$ is the probability that it is in primary memory, and $S_i$ the probability that it is in secondary memory. The concept of primary memory implies that $P_i$ is a monotonically decreasing function of $i$ and that

$$\lim_{i \to \infty} P_i = 0$$

On the other hand, secondary memory is supposed to be relatively permanent within the experimental condition considered here. Hence we may assume that secondary memory is independent of the serial position $i$ of an item, i.e.,

$$S_i = S$$

The value of $S$ may be estimated from the asymptote of short-term forgetting curves. Whether or not $S$ is in fact constant and independent of $i$ may be determined from inspection of the recall probabilities for sufficiently large $i$. In general, the probability of recall is fairly constant after about 12 intervening items, except for the primacy effect characteristic of most free-recall studies. However, for the time being, we shall neglect this effect, and concentrate upon the properties of primary memory.

Rearranging the terms of Eq. (1), and dropping the unnecessary $i$-subscript in the case of secondary memory, we obtain

$$(2) \qquad\qquad P_i = \frac{R_i - S}{1 - S}$$

Equation (2) makes it possible to estimate the contribution of primary memory to total recall from experimental data, since $R_i$, the recall proportion of item $i$, and $S$, the asymptotic recall proportion, are directly observable quantities.

The value of Waugh and Norman's model is that it provides an analytic method for the separation of primary and secondary memory and thereby permits the direct comparison of short-term memory data from different experiments, irrespective of procedural differences that determine total recall. Waugh and Norman present some normative data for primary memory that were obtained in an experiment using a probe procedure. Subjects listened to test lists of 16 single digits which were read at a constant rate (either 1 or 4 digits per second) over earphones. No digit was repeated more than twice. The last digit was identical with one of the digits presented and served as a cue for recall of the digit that had followed it initially. This digit was the probe digit and was accompanied by a high-frequency tone. Positions 3, 5, 7, 9, 10, 11, 12, 13, and 14 of the presentation series were tested ten times each during an experimental session. Four subjects served in 12 sessions each. From the results, estimates of the probability that an item was in primary memory were obtained. The broken lines in Figure 4.20 show the 90% confidence limits for these estimates.

If the model is correct, data from other experiments under quite different experimental conditions, when transformed by Eq. (2) and plotted against the number of interfering items $i$, should fall within these confidence limits. Waugh and Norman have analyzed 24 different sets of results, taken from five published reports by different experimenters, and have found that, indeed, primary memory estimates show great consistency. Most of the data fell right between the confidence limits, and no evidence for a seriously deviant trend was found. The data analyzed came from both free-recall and paired-associate experiments, but primary memory estimates conformed quite well to the function obtained with the probe-procedure. For instance, the data from the free-recall experiment of Murdock (1962),

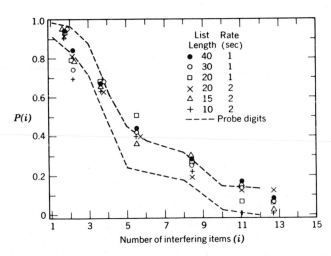

FIGURE 4.20   **Free recall data from Murdock (1962) corrected for asymptote and response interference. (after Waugh and Norman, 1965)**

the results of which were discussed in Chapter 1 and are displayed in Figure 1.4, were analyzed by means of Eq. (2). The primary memory estimates thus obtained are plotted in Figure 4.20 on top of the estimates Waugh and Norman obtained in their probe digit experiment. Obviously, the agreement is a good one. This is especially striking if one recalls the substantial differences in overall recall for lists varying in length that are apparent in Figure 1.4. These differences apparently were due to the secondary memory component, because as Figure 4.20 shows, there are no systematic differences in the primary memory components of these lists. The fact that primary memory estimates obtained from such different sets of data (free recall and sequential probes) agree so well demonstrates rather impressively the usefulness of Waugh and Norman's model.

One feature of their conceptual scheme that is often neglected is that an item may be recalled from both primary and secondary memory. In fact, Eq. (2) assumes that whether or not an item enters secondary memory has absolutely no effect on forgetting from primary memory. This point is quite crucial in evaluating studies concerned with the primary-secondary memory distinction. It means that experimental data are never pure indicators of primary memory processes. This considerably complicates the task of the experimentalist, but nothing is gained by not facing the difficulty. At least, the analytical tools of Waugh and Norman are available to indicate to what extent experimental data are influenced by each factor. Hebb (1961) performed an important experiment that gives some direct support for the hypothesis that whenever a short-term memory trace is established, there exists at least the possibility that the material will also be stored in long-term memory. Hebb had originally thought that the repetition of a digit in a memory span experiment is a pure example of an activity trace. In fact, he used the example of a calculating machine where the second string erases the first. However, an experiment he performed showed that this comparison was not justified. Subjects listened to nine digits, presented at a rate of 1 per second; 24 such trials were given. On every third trial the same string of digits was repeated. The results showed that performance on new strings did not change as a function of trials, but recall of the repeated series improved steadily. This improvement is only understandable if one assumes that some sort of a structural memory trace had been formed. Hebb's result illustrates the possibility implied by Eq. (2) of joint storage as activity trace (primary memory, short-term memory) and structural trace (secondary, long-term memory).

In this connection it is most interesting to note what happens when the Hebb experiment is performed with patients with hippocampal lesions. It will be remembered that such patients have a very specific memory deficit; the clinical evidence indicates that both their primary and secondary memories are intact, but that they are unable to store new information in secondary memory. Hence, if Hebb's experiment is repeated with such patients, no improvement over repeated series is obtained (Caird, 1964). Using a clever experimental procedure, Buschke (1968) also confirmed that patients with bilateral hippocampal lesions suffer from a learning deficit but have normal immediate memory. Buschke used a missing-scan procedure: subjects were read 12 randomly selected numbers from the set of numbers 1 to 16 and had to report which numbers were *not* read to them. Some numbers were read only once and some were read twice. The brain-damaged subjects performed as well as a control group when the numbers occurred only once, but they did significantly poorer than normals with the repeated numbers. Buschke's results nicely confirm the interpretation of the Hebb data that the improvement that occurred when items were repeated was due to storage in secondary memory— something the brain-damaged subjects could not do.

The most important extension of the primary-secondary memory framework has been provided by Atkinson and Shiffrin (1968, 1971). What is missing in the Waugh and Norman model is a description of how items can be maintained in primary memory through rehearsal.

Atkinson and Shiffrin developed a model whose central feature is a rehearsal buffer. They assume that primary memory storage in itself, without rehearsal, plays a neglible role and show that rehearsal strategies may, under certain conditions, become the dominant features of the learning process. Their model, which assumes that learning occurs when an item is rehearsed, can account for most of the empirical phenomena discussed earlier.

The importance of rehearsal will depend on the experimental conditions. Atkinson and Shiffrin designed their experiments so as to maximize the utility of rehearsal. They used sets of four to eight two-digit numbers as stimuli and the letters of the alphabet as responses. Stimuli and responses were re-paired at random throughout an experimental session and the subject's task was to remember which response a given stimulus was paired with when it was presented last; 220 trials were given per session. Reliance on long-term storage is obviously a poor strategy in this experimental situation. On the other hand, short-term memory itself decays too fast to be of much use here, since each trial (test-study-blank) took 11 seconds. This rather slow presentation rate provided ample opportunity for rehearsal.

The basic assumption Atkinson and Shiffrin make is that subjects use a rehearsal buffer of fixed size. This simply means that subjects keep rehearsing a fixed number of stimulus-response pairs throughout the experiment. Changes in the pairs being rehearsed occur according to the following rules: when an item is already in the buffer and it is shown again re-paired with a new response, it is always entered into the buffer in place of the old stimulus-response pair. This assumption is necessary, otherwise subjects might be rehearsing incorrect pairs. When an item is presented that is not being rehearsed it will be entered into the buffer with some probability $a$, replacing one of the items in the buffer at random. There may be several reasons why not every new item is entered into the buffer. Reorganization of the buffer costs time and effort, and the subject may be reluctant to give up a combination of items that is particularly easy to rehearse.

While the subject relies mostly on short-term rehearsal, more permanent information will also be stored. Atkinson and Shiffrin assume that when an item is first presented and whenever it is rehearsed later some information about it is transferred into a long-term store. This implies that the probability of retrieval from the long-term store increases monotonically as a function of the length of the time an item spends in the rehearsal buffer. Unlike other models, a provision for loss from long-term store is also made; as soon as an item leaves the rehearsal buffer, the information in the long-term store about this item begins to decrease.

The response rule for this model is simple. If an item is in the rehearsal buffer at the time of the test, the correct response will be given; if the item is not in the buffer, a search of the long-term store will be made. (Note that the retrieval model of Atkinson and Juola that was discussed in the previous section is a special case of this more general theory.) The probability of retrieving the item from the long-term store is an increasing function of the number of times the item has been rehearsed and a decreasing function of the number of trials since the item has left the rehearsal buffer.

This model has been applied to a number of different experiments, all of which were performed with the general experimental paradigm discussed earlier. The assumptions of the model have generally been supported by these experimental tests, in particular those concerning the rehearsal buffer. In one experiment the authors investigated the probability of a correct response as a function of the length of the retention interval for intervals ranging from 0 to 17 intervening items. A short-term memory function was obtained that showed a regular decrease in performance as a function of the number of intervening items. The buffer model described this function quite well. These data have already been discussed at the beginning of this chapter, and Figure 4.4 shows how good the quantitative fit of the model is. Figure 4.4 shows short-term forgetting functions for items that are rehearsed overtly and covertly. In terms of the model, overt rehearsal guarantees that incoming items will always be entered into the rehearsal buffer, while items that are rehearsed covertly can sometimes be disregarded. Hence performance is poorer for covert rehearsal at short retention intervals.

The model also predicted an interesting effect that one probably would not have noticed in the data without the model as a guideline. Let us take the case where a stimulus is re-paired with a new response whenever it is presented. Suppose an item is presented for study on trial $n$, and is shown for a test for the first time on trial $n + j + 1$. The buffer model predicts rather large differences in retention depending on the nature of the $j$ items that filled the retention interval. Suppose all $j$ items are different. In this case the likelihood is very large that the item which was shown in trial $n$ will be kicked out of the buffer. Each of the $j$ items may interfere with the item to be remembered. On the other hand, suppose that the retention interval was filled with $j$ presentations of the same stimulus which was re-paired with a new response on every presentation. According to the model, once an item enters the buffer every succeeding item with the same stimulus stays in the buffer automatically. Thus, there exists only one chance that the item to be remembered will be kicked from the buffer if the intervening items are all the same and, therefore, much less forgetting should occur in this case. This prediction of the model was confirmed by the data. The probability of a correct response as a function of lag was higher throughout when all intervening items used the same stimulus than when every intervening item used a different stimulus.

There is another implication of the buffer model which is quite counterintuitive, but which is confirmed by the data. It too depends on the property of the buffer that once an item is in it, it will stay there when its stimulus-is paired with a new response. Consider a sequence of *j* consecutive trials all involving the same stimulus, but where a new response has been introduced in the study phase of each trial. Notions such as proactive inhibition would lead us to believe that recall on trial *j* should decrease as a function of the length of the preceding sequence. However, the actual data show the opposite trend (Figure 4.21). The predictions generated from the buffer model are shown as a smooth line. It is clear why the model predicts an increase in Figure 4.21; the more often the same stimulus has been presented in succession, the more likely it is to be held in the rehearsal buffer, thus assuring its rehearsal when the response pairing is altered.

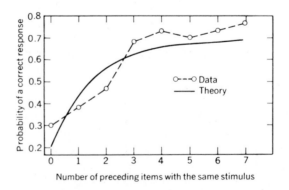

Number of preceding items with the same stimulus

FIGURE 4.21 **Observed and theoretical probability of a correct response as a function of the number of consecutive preceding items using the same stimulus. (after Atkinson and Shiffrin, 1968)**

## A CRITIQUE OF SEPARATE-STORES MODELS

The idea that there are two distinct memory stores, as outlined in the previous section, has not been without its critics. Some psychologists such as Melton (1963), Craik and Lockhart (1972), and Murdock (1974) do not find this model a useful one, and instead prefer to emphasize the essential continuity that exists between short- and long-term retention. They reject the boxes metaphor that has dominated the thinking of quite a few psychologists at one time or another—that short- and long-term memory can be compared to two separate boxes in which "information" is deposited, and between which it is transferred. With it, they tend to reject altogether the notion that short- and long-term memory are two distinct, separate memory stores. In the previous section we have reviewed the evidence for this distinction. There is quite a bit of it, but it is not totally convincing. First of all, there is the neurological evidence from observations of brain-damaged patients. However, advocates of the primary-secondary memory distinction do not want to rest their case on it. Instead, we have cited a whole range of behavioral data which showed that there are several experimental variables that affect serial position curves obtained in free-recall or probe-recall experiments differentially. We made the assumption that the recency portion of these curves includes recall from primary memory (as well as secondary memory), while the early or middle items of a list must be recalled from secondary memory, if they are recalled at all. This is certainly a reasonable assumption in terms of the two-store model. If we grant it, the evidence for the primary-secondary memory distinction is strong, indeed.

It is possible, however, to question this assumption, and Bjork and Whitten (1974) have reported free-recall data that show that the identification of recency with recall from primary memory is suspect. These authors had subjects recall lists of 13 words under four different experimental conditions. In the first condition recall was immediate; in the second condition recall was delayed by an interpolated period of 30 seconds of arithmetic. The results from these two conditions replicate those of earlier work; in fact, they are exactly like those in Figure 4.18. If recall is immediate, a strong recency effect is obtained, but a 30-second delay filled with an interfering task erases that effect. This is, of course, the kind of data upon which the identification of recency with primary memory has traditionally been based. The third and fourth conditions of the experiment, however, question this interpretation. In the third condition recall was immediate, but each word of the list was preceded and followed by 12 seconds of arithmetic; the final condition was like the previous one, except that an additional 30 seconds of arithmetic intervened between the end of the list and the recall test. One would, of course, expect the 12 seconds of arithmetic to produce sufficient interference with primary memory to destroy the recency effect. Thus, all recall should be from secondary memory in both the third and fourth experimental conditions, and serial position curves for both should look like those obtained in the second condition. There was no difference between the serial position curves from the third and fourth conditions, however, and they did not look like the second condition curve. Instead they showed a definite recency effect, one that could hardly be attributed to primary memory. This recency effect was not as large as normally observed (e.g., in Bjork and Whitten's first condition), but it was there and was unaffected by an additional 30-second delay before the test. Bjork and Whitten could show that a preference for recalling the last items on a list before the earlier ones was the probable cause of the recency effects observed in their study.

Thus, at least in the Bjork and Whitten experiment, there were long-term recency effects in free-recall that arose from retrieval strategies at the time of output, rather than from any contribution of primary memory. These data make one hesitate to accept the evidence offered in the previous section as conclusive support for separate memory stores. Perhaps at least some of the results described there must be attributed to differential retrieval strategies, rather than to primary memory.

There is a further empirical difficulty with current two-store models, and that concerns the concept of rehearsal in the theories of Waugh and Norman (1965) and Atkinson and Shiffrin (1968). This problem is central to the whole issue, and a careful consideration of the nature of rehearsal processes will greatly improve our understanding of the short- and long-term memory distinction.

According to Atkinson and Shiffrin, rehearsal serves two functions: it transfers information into long-term memory, and it recycles items in the short-term memory buffer. Atkinson and Shiffrin described in detail the control processes that select items for rehearsal and formulated a quantitative model about the accumulation of information in long-term memory that occurs as the result of rehearsal. Indeed, we have characterized their model as essentially a model of the rehearsal process. We have seen that this model successfully described recall data. Rundus and Atkinson (1970) and Rundus (1971) have shown furthermore that the rehearsal process can be observed directly, and that observed rehearsals play just the role in recall the model supposed. Their procedure was a simple one—they gave subjects a 20-word list, with 5 seconds of study time per word, and asked them to rehearse the words aloud during this study interval. Figure 4.22 shows how well the number of overt rehearsals observed with this procedure correlates with recall. The more often an item is rehearsed, the better its recall. This relationship breaks down only for the last few items on the list; although these items are not rehearsed much (indeed they are slightly less rehearsed), they are recalled very well because they still reside in the short-term memory buffer. Rundus calculated a buffer size of 3.0 to 3.5 items on the basis of his data (which, by the way, is within the range of the estimates of short-term memory capacity in free-recall experiments without obert rehearsal, as shown in Figure 4.11). The slight drop in the number of rehearsals of the last few list items leads to the prediction that if recall were based entirely on long-term memory, not only should there be no recency effect, but there actually should be a slight decline. A 30-second interval filled with arithmetic between study and test is probably not entirely sufficient to erase all items from the buffer (though it destroys the recency effect); however, if subjects are given several lists to study and recall during

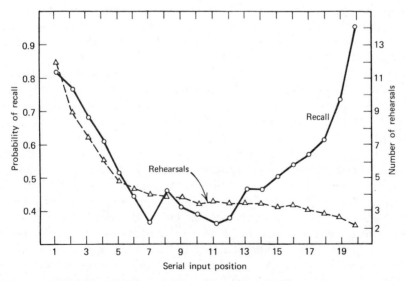

FIGURE 4.22 **Recall probability and mean number of rehearsals as a function of serial input position. (after Rundus, 1971)**

an experimental session, and are then unexpectedly asked at the end of the session to recall all the words from all the lists, this should certainly guarantee that all recall must be based on long-term memory. Under these conditions, not only is there no recency effect in final free recall, but there is a slight negative recency—exactly as one would expect from Rundus' rehearsal records. This negative recency was first observed by Craik (1970).

In spite of all that, there is something wrong with this conception of rehearsal. The problem stems from thinking of rehearsal as merely repeating an item, either covertly or overtly. There are by now several experiments available that demonstrate conclusively that merely repeating an item does nothing for long-term retention. Repetition merely maintains an item in short-term memory. For long-term retention, rehearsal must involve a better, more elaborate encoding of the item. What the phrase "better, more elaborated encoding" means will be one of the main concerns of the chapter on long-term memory. First, however, we must justify the claim that there are two distinct types of rehearsal processes: maintenance rehearsal and elaborative rehearsal.

There are several converging lines of evidence. Weist (1972) showed that the high correlation between probability of recall and the number of overt rehearsals reported by Rundus (1971) and others breaks down in multitrial recall experiments after the first trial. What becomes important is not just how often a word is rehearsed, but whether it is rehearsed together with semantically related words. That is, not repetition per se, but "organization" determines free recall. Again, we shall defer a discussion of the role of organization in memory, and turn our attention to other studies that demonstrate that repetition alone does not improve long-term recall.

One popular design consists of inducing the subject to rehearse an item for short-term retention (for that it is enough if the subject simply repeats the item to himself, without any deeper processing), and then giving him a surprise long-term memory test. Jacoby and Bartz (1972), for instance, showed subjects a 20-word list, and then, after a 15-second silent rehearsal interval, asked them to recall the list. During these 15 seconds, the subject had ample opportunity to rehearse the last few items on the list, and indeed recall after 15 seconds of rehearsal was the same as immediate recall. In one experimental session, the subject learned 10 lists in this way. At the end of the session he was given a final free-recall test. The results of this test were exactly like those obtained by Craik (1970) without the extra rehearsal of each list. There was a negative recency effect, i.e., the last items of the list were recalled worst. Thus, keeping these items in short-term memory for 15 seconds through rehearsal had no long-term effect. Similarly, Woodward, Bjork, and Jongeward (1973) had subjects recall a list of words in which after each word the subject was shown a cue that told him whether he had to remember this word or whether the word could be forgotten. Before each cue, there was a variable blank period, during which subjects had to maintain the item in short-term memory through rehearsal. Neither immediate nor final recall depended in any way on the duration of this blank period. Again, simply keeping an item in short-term memory (maintenance or primary rehearsal), without additional processing (secondary rehearsal), had no effect on long-term recall.

As a third example, consider a study by Craik and Watkins (1973). They asked their subjects to listen to a series of words and to write down the last word in the list beginning with a specified letter. For instance, suppose the subject was told that the critical letter was G, and he then heard the list *"daughter, oil, rifle, garden, grain, table, football, anchor, giraffe, candle."* In response to this list, the subject would write down *"giraffe,"* after having held this word in memory for 1 intervening item; he would also have held in memory *grain* for 3 intervening items, and *garden* for 0 intervening items. If the time that an item has resided in short-term memory is important, recall should improve with the number of intervening items between critical words. However, in an unexpected final recall test after subjects had worked with 27 such lists, the number of intervening items had no effect on the likelihood of recall (though reported items were recalled better than replaced items). Thus, as in the previous studies, we are forced to conclude that mere maintenance rehearsal, that is repeating an item to oneself in order to keep it in short-term memory, does not lead to long-term memory storage, in clear contradiction to the models of Waugh and Norman (1965) and Atkinson and Shiffrin (1968). In order to achieve long-term storage, an item must be processed more deeply and more richly than is necessary for short-term retention. In particular, it must become part of an organized memory structure. It is to these problems that we shall turn shortly.

We began this section with two types of memory stores, primary and secondary memory, and we end it with two types of rehearsal, maintenance and elaborative rehearsal. It makes sense, indeed, to call these two types of rehearsal primary and secondary rehearsal, respectively. Our conception of primary and secondary memory has changed during the last few years. Many psychologists today are no longer satisfied with the box metaphor that underlies the earlier models of short-term memory. Instead, a more dynamic conception of the memory system is evolving, with an emphasis on differential processes rather than on separate boxes for short- and long-term memory. As Melton had maintained as early as 1963, in many ways there are no essential differences between the phenomena of short- and long-term retention. More recently, Craik and Lockhart (1972) forcefully reasserted this viewpoint. Forgetting rates vary over the whole continuum—some things are forgotten very fast and others are retained very long; what determines the rate of forgetting is not the "store" from which an item is forgotten, but how well it has been encoded. Short-term memory items tend to be poorly encoded, often acoustically (perhaps because the easiest form of maintenance rehearsal is speaking to oneself?); but acoustic codes are not obligatory in short-term memory, and short-term memory may involve any other modality. Thus, the difference between short- and long-term memory is merely quantitative, rather than qualitative. The same is true when we look at the capacity of memory. As long as one thinks of primary memory as a box of fixed size that holds 7 $\pm$ 2 items, and secondary memory as an essentially infinite capacity system, the difference between the two is impressive. However, we have argued that the box metaphor is wrong in this case too. Retention in short-term memory is an active process (i.e., it requires maintenance rehearsal), and constitutes a severe drain on a person's processing resources. If all available resources can be devoted to short-term memory maintenance, the number of items maintained may be as much as the magic number 7. However, most tasks are more complex, and short-term memory maintenance becomes resource limited, with a resultant decrease in "capacity."

None of this implies that the concepts primary and secondary are useless today. The objectives raised merely concern the "stores" or "boxes" analogy. To make a distinction, as James did in 1890, between a conscious, readily available primary memory, and an unconscious secondary memory, from which items may sometimes be retrieved only with difficulty or not at all, is not only sensible but inevitable. Primary memory is the momentarily activated portion of the memory system, as sketched in Figure 3.1. The study of primary memory is the study of the nature of this activation process: its decay characteristics, the rehearsal processes that recycle primary memory contents, and the encoding processes involved, particularly the processes of chunking, whereby the units of memory are formed.

# 5
# long-term memory

We have seen in the last chapter that short-term memory is a system
where information can be maintained through a process of active
rehearsal. This rehearsal, however, is merely a maintenance rehearsal.
It does not, by itself, guarantee that an item will be remembered once
it is lost from short-term memory. For long-term retention, elaborative
rehearsal is required. What is, then, this elaborative rehearsal?

# ENCODING

## LEVELS OF PROCESSING

Memory depends on the nature of the subject's perceptual and cognitive analyses of the stimulus, and the deeper and the more elaborate these analyses are, the better retention. This view has become known in recent years as the levels-of-processing theory of memory (e.g., Craik and Lockhart, 1972). Deeper levels of processing are those involving semantic analysis. In general, we have a progression from shallow levels of processing (those concerned with the physical nature of the stimulus), through successive levels of elaboration (phonemic analysis, determination of the syntactic category of a word), to deep processing, which involves the meaning of the word. It has been demonstrated in a number of experiments (e.g., Hyde and Jenkins, 1969, 1973; Craik and Tulving, 1975) that when subjects are required to perform certain orienting tasks that require the analysis of the meaning of the words in a list, retention is as good as when they are specifically instructed to memorize the items of a list; Orienting tasks involving imagery, semantic, or affective analyses (judging the pleasantness or unpleasantness of a word) always lead to better performance than tasks involving structural or syntactic analyses. Simplifying, one can say that if one somehow can get a subject to respond to the meanings of the words in a list, he will remember them. (Similar observations have been made with respect to memory for sentences, to be discussed in Section 6.2.2).

As a prototype experiment, let us analyze the study by Craik and Tulving (1975). Their subjects performed various orienting tasks on the words of a 40-item list, which involved different levels of analysis. The subjects were told that the experiment concerned perception and speed of reaction. On each trial, a word was exposed on a screen for 200 milliseconds. Before that, the subject was asked a question about the word. After hearing the question, the subject looked at the screen with his hands on reaction time keys labeled yes and no. When the word appeared, he answered the question by pressing the appropriate key. After a series of such trials, the subject was unexpectedly given a retention test for all the words. Both recognition and recall tests were used. The experimenter's hypothesis was that the performance on the final retention test would depend on the level of processing induced by the question.

There were three types of questions, as shown in Table 5.1. A case question merely involved a decision whether or not the word was typed in capital letters. The rhyme task asked for a judgment of

TABLE 5.1.    Typical Questions and Answers in Craik and Tulving (1975)

| Type | Question | Answer Yes | No |
|------|----------|-----------|-----|
| Case | Is the word in capital letters? | TABLE | table |
| Rhyme | Does the word rhyme with *weight*? | crate | MARKET |
| Sentence | Would the word fit the sentence: "He met a _____ in the street"? | FRIEND | cloud |

whether the test word rhymed with a given word. A *sentence* question forced the subject to attend to the word's meaning in order to determine whether or not it would fit into a given sentence. At each level of analysis, half of the questions required *yes* answers and half *no*. The same pool of 40 words was used for all subjects, and each word was used in all experimental conditions for different subjects.

Some of Craik and Tulving's results are shown in Figure 5.1. Response latencies increased with levels of processing by about 200 milliseconds. At the same time, both recognition and recall performance increased very strongly with level of processing: Case-words were recognized 16% of the time, and recalled about 8%; but the same words were recognized 90% of the time and recalled 23% when in the sentence condition. Level of processing is thus a very important determinant of retention.

There are a number of questions that one would want to ask about these results. First of all, given the strong correlation between response latencies in the initial task and retention, one might ask whether Figure 5.1 is simply another demonstration that the greater the study time, the better recall. Craik and Tulving show that this is not the case, because such a position would imply that there should be a positive correlation between latencies and performance *within* each processing task, which is not the case. The important differences are between tasks, suggesting that the qualitative differences between processes are decisive. To tie this argument down, Craik and Tulving showed that a difficult, time-consuming structural task (determining the consonant-vowel pattern of a word, which takes about 1.7 seconds on the average) still leads to poorer performance than the sentence task (which took less than half as much time): recognition probabilities were .53 for the structural task, but .75 for the semantic task. Walsh and Jenkins (1973) similarly found that it is neither the effort that an orienting task requires, nor the time it takes, that is related to performance but the type of task involved; the processing must involve the item's meaning, that is "deep" levels of processing.

If deep processing occurs, it does not matter much whether learning is incidental or intentional (Hyde and Jenkins, 1973). Craik and Tulving also compared incidental and intentional learning and, although the latter was generally superior, the same pattern of results was obtained in the two cases. Whether learning was intentional or incidental, deep processing levels yielded better performance.

It has been well established that schizophrenic patients, unlike other nonschizophrenic psychiatric patients, are unable to recall a list of words as well as normals (e.g., Koh, Kayton, and Berry, 1973). However, this recall deficit can be overcome if the experimental conditions are so arranged that they ensure proper deep encoding. Koh, Kayton, and Peterson (1976) had schizophrenic and normal subjects rate 50 words in terms of pleasantness-unpleasantness, and later gave them a recall test for these words. The recall of the schizophrenics was just as good as that of normals. Thus, if one only can get schizophrenics to encode the learning items at a sufficiently deep level, their memory deficit is remediable.

Of course, to speak of deep levels of processing is to use a metaphor, and the metaphor does not fit perfectly. Some puzzling features

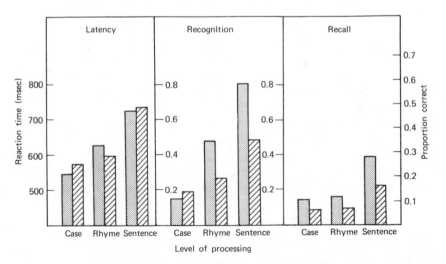

FIGURE 5.1    Initial decision latencies, recognition performance, and recall performance for words as a function of the intitial task. The dark columns represent items for which a yes response was made during initial processing; the shaded columns represent no-items. (after Craik and Tulving, 1975, Experiments 2 and 3).

in the data show that depth may not be a very good metaphor at all. If it is all a matter of depth, then why are the recall differences produced by the various orienting tasks the same for intentional and incidental processing? Subjects who know they will be tested for memory surely would analyze and perceive the name and meaning of each target word, no matter what the question asks them to do. Also, in most conditions in Figure 5.1 retention was better for items that received a yes response in the initial task than items that received a no response. There is hardly a difference in depth of processing between yes and no questions. Craik and Tulving suggest that depth of processing is not all that matters, and that the degree of stimulus elaboration, in addition to or even in place of depth of processing, needs to be considered. They suggest that high levels of retention are associated with rich, elaborate stimulus processing (rather than deep encodings). This might explain the difference in the retention of the yes and no items in Figure 5.1. Consider, for instance, sentence type questions; given "The boy met a _____ on the street" and the yes-item girl, a subject can generate a very lavish memory code, with a lot of personalized meaning, imagery, and affect. Retention will be very good. On the other hand, given this same context sentence and the no-item cloud, a less well-integrated memory code will result, and retention will be poorer. Similarly, for the rhyming task: two words that rhyme form a more coherent, integrated unit than two words that do not rhyme. Perhaps weight becomes one of the attributes in terms of which crate is encoded, leading to a richer, more stable code, while such enrichment is less likely with unrelated, nonrhyming words. The same argument does not apply to case-questions: determining that a word is typed in capital letters would not lead to a more elaborate encoding than when the word is not typed in capitals. However, it is precisely in the case condition that the usual superiority of yes over no-items was not consistently observed.

Craik and Tulving performed an additional experiment to test this argument. They arranged questions in such a manner that equivalent elaboration for positive and negative decisions would be expected. For instance, if the question is "Is the object bigger than a chair?" then it does not matter whether a yes-response is given to some item (e.g., house) or a no—response (e.g., mouse); both should lead to equivalent degrees of elaboration. Under these conditions, the difference in the retention of yes and no items that was observed earlier dutifully disappeared; words given yes responses were recalled with a probability of .36, those given no-responses were recalled with a probability of .39.

Extending this line of thought, the authors also demonstrated that more complex, elaborate sentence frames lead to better recall than impoverished ones. Thus, "He dropped the _____" produces recall of about 40% for the target word *watch*, while for the same word the sentence "The old man hobbled across the room and picked up the _____ from the mahogany table" leads to over 80% recall. Even though the target words are processed semantically in both cases, there are still large recall differences. It is not only the nominal level of processing that matters; the elaboration of a code within a level is equally significant.

In addition to depth and richness of encoding, we have already discussed the importance of the variability of encoding in verbal learning (Section 3.3). Whenever an item is repeated so that more than one memory code must be formed, it becomes very important whether the second encoding merely duplicates the first, or whether it enriches it.

## ENCODING VARIABILITY

The more often an item is presented for study, the better the overall performance. However, improper spacing of item repetitions can greatly reduce the efficiency of repetitions. A paired-associate experiment by Greeno (1964) demonstrates this point. Greeno arranged his items in blocks of 30 trials. Spaced items were presented once in each block; each massed item was presented twice in each 30-trial block, with either zero or one item between the two presentations. Thus, massed items were presented twice as often as spaced items. In spite of that, performance on spaced items and on the first presentation of massed items in each block of trials was practically equal, as Figure 5.2 shows. Performance on the second presentation of the massed items was very good, of course. But this effect was transitory. The second presentation, following immediately after the first, seemed wasted as far as later performance was concerned. The effectiveness of a study trial depended on the length of the presentation interval. If two study trials followed each other closely they were hardly more effective than a single trial.

Several studies in which continuous paired-associate tasks have been used, instead of list learning as in Greeno's experiment, confirm and extend this finding. Word-digit pairs were presented twice with either 0, 1, 2, 4, 8 or 16 other pairs between the successive presentations in a study by Peterson, Wampler, Kirkpatrick, and Saltzman

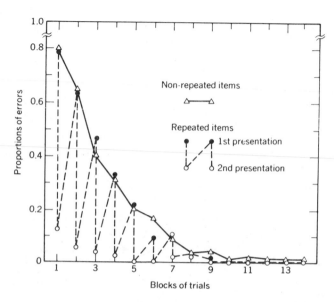

FIGURE 5.2    **Mean learning curves for repeated and non-repeated items. (after Greeno, 1964)**

(1963). Eight filler items followed the second presentation, and then the word was shown alone for a test. All items were presented at a 2-second rate. In Figure 5.3 the results of this experiment are shown. Greeno's results are confirmed insofar as an interpresentation interval of about eight items was considerably more beneficial than very brief intervals. However, the probability of a correct response does not increase monotonically with the length of the interpresentation interval but shows a definite drop for very long intervals. Young (1971) has replicated all essential features of the Peterson et al. experiment as part of a larger investigation. His results are also shown in Figure 5.3 and are almost identical with those of Peterson et al. Note that Young's subjects remembered as much after just one presentation as after two massed presentations.

Spacing effects like those shown in Figure 5.3 have also been obtained in multitrial free-recall experiments (e.g., Melton, 1970) and recognition experiments (e.g., Kintsch, 1966). In general, massed repetitions are less effective than spaced repetitions, with the optimal spacing somewhat dependent on experimental conditions, but generally between 10 and 20 items.

How are these spacing effects to be explained? Melton (1970) has proposed an explanation in terms of encoding variability. If two presentations of an item are massed, the encoding context for the two items will be the same, and hence the two encodings will be largely the same and redundant. Thus, two such memory codes are little better than a single one. If two presentations are spaced far apart, the encoding context will differ for the two presentations and different stimulus attributes are likely to be encoded on the second trial than on the first trial. In effect, this is like forming a single, richer memory code.

This explanation of the greater effectiveness of spaced repetitions asserts that spacing effects occur because of correlated context changes. It is therefore implied that if context can be changed by other means without affecting the spacing between repetitions, a similar facilitation should be observed. Gartman and Johnson (1972) biased their subjects so that they would differentially encode homonyms presented twice in succession, and observed the predicted improvement in performance. They also biased the encoding of spaced items by presenting them both times in the same context. As expected, these items were not recalled as well as spaced items normally are, presumably because they were encoded in the same way on both trials.

It should be obvious that this explanation of spacing effects in learning is in complete agreement with the notion that the degree of elaboration of a memory code is a crucial determinant of retention. Craik and Tulving (1975) biased subjects to encode an item presented

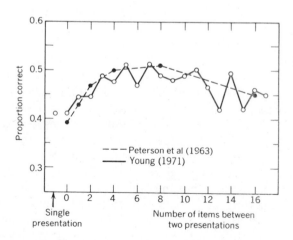

FIGURE 5.3    **Recall as a function of the lag between two presentations of an item. (after Peterson et al., 1963, and Young, 1971)**

once more or less richly and observed correlated performance changes. In the work discussed above, the richness of the memory code is determined by the encoding variability on two repeated presentations of an item. In both cases, the more different stimulus attributes that are stored in memory, the better retention. What one must do in order to remember well, is to encourage encoding variability and rich, elaborate memory codes.

### 5.1.3    STIMULUS ATTRIBUTES IN ENCODING

A stimulus item may be regarded as a potential set of features, or attributes, that may be used for encoding in memory. The process of encoding consists in selecting a sample of features from this set and storing this sample, as a unit, in memory. From the preceding discussion it appears that the richer this sample, that is, the more different features it contains, the better retention will be. Furthermore, it is very important that meaning-related stimulus attributes form part of a memory code. In the present section we shall discuss the role that stimulus attributes such as modality, order, and recency play in retention.

Suppose a subject is shown the list "BOOK, LAMP, JAR, BOOK, SHELL, BOOK." Not only will this subject be able to recall these four words, he will be able to tell us a number of other things about this list. He will probably know the order in which the words were presented, he will recall that he had seen these words, rather than listened to them, and he will know that BOOK was presented three times, while the other words were shown only once. In other words, the subject had encoded in memory order, modality, and frequency information.

We know (from the previous section) that items encoded in terms of their meaning are better retained in memory than items encoded in terms of their physical attributes. One might be tempted to conclude, therefore, that physical attributes are lost from memory more rapidly than meaning attributes. However, this is not the case. Semantic processing does indeed improve retention over nonsemantic processing, but physical features that become part of a memory code are as resistant to forgetting as semantic features. One must think of the memory code for an item as a whole set of features, many of which are semantic (and these are the ones that support retrieval well) but some of which are residuals from more shallow processing levels, e.g., from the perceptual analysis. The latter allow the subject to remember the input modality of the item. Such modality-specific attributes are stored as part of the memory code, even when the experimental task does not demand retention of the input modality (e.g., Hintzman, Block, and Inskeep, 1972). Furthermore, memory for the physical features of a stimulus is not merely short-term, but can be long-term. That is especially true under intentional rather than incidental learning conditions (Jacoby, 1975).

In many cases, especially when the learning material consists of sentences or text, very little encoding of physical features occurs: under normal circumstances, readers concentrate on the meaning of a text and process words and their physical features only in so far as it is necessary to arrive at their meaning. In these cases, memory for physical features is minimal and fleeting (see the closely related discussion in Section 6.2.3). In list-learning studies, however, modality attributes typically appear to be an integral part of the memory code. In a study by Bray and Batchelder (1972) subjects could recognize the modality (auditory or visual) in which words had been presented equally well whether they had been forewarned that such a test would be given or not, and whether the test was given immediately or after a 15-minute delay. Memory for modality appeared to have no function in this experiment (subjects could recognize the modality of an item even when they could not recall it)—it was just there. Similarly, in a free recall experiment with bilingual subjects Kolers (1966) found that his subjects could recall the language in which the words were presented without really trying. They found it no harder to recall the words-plus-language than the words alone, presumably because they processed the words in a specific language anyway. If one remembers that memory traces are the residuals of the perceptual and cognitive processes that a subject engages in when studying a list, these results are not surprising. Subjects remember what they have been doing.

While memory for modality is a natural byproduct of the perceptual analysis, memory for order requires the specific encoding of order cues as part of the memory code, and thus rests on quite different processes than the memory for the item itself. A subject can form a very good and elaborate memory code for such an item as BOOK, but not remember its position in an input list. Special associations either to its serial position or its list context are required for order information.

A number of experimental observations support the claim that item and order information in memory are based on different processes. First of all, Estes (1972) has shown that the two types of information are forgotten at different rates. Estes showed subjects four consonants, followed by a series of digits of varying length. Items were presented at a rate of 2.5 per second, and subjects were asked to pronounce them aloud. At this rate, this was a fairly taxing task and sufficient to prevent rehearsal. After each series, subjects attempted to recall the initial four consonants. The data were scored in terms of two types of errors: transposition errors and nontransposition errors. Transposition errors are indicators of the loss of order information, but not item information: a transposition error occurs when a subject recalls the correct letters of a string, but transposes them. For instance, a transposition error would be scored if the study series NTCD is recalled as NDCT. Estes found that at very short retention intervals subjects made mostly transposition errors, but that with increasing retention intervals nontransposition errors came to predominate.

There exists considerable further evidence that item and order information in memory are based on distinct processes. One line of evidence comes from studies demonstrating that some experimental variables affect item and order information in different ways. For instance, Watkins, Watkins, and Crowder (1974) studied the free and serial recall of phonetically similar and dissimilar lists. If we disregard the last few recency items in their lists, their results can be summarized quite simply: phonetic similarity was beneficial in free recall (a test of item information), but interfered with serial recall (a test of item as well as order information). Healy (1974) managed to separate item and order information even more cleanly. In one of her experiments, all trials involved the same four consonants; all the subject had to do was remember the order in which they were presented. In a second experiment, the subject knew beforehand the position in which a particular consonant could appear, so that he only had to concentrate on item information (e.g., if he remembered a $K$, he knew $K$ must have been the third letter). The results of these two experiments were quite different: in the first experiment, testing order information, typical bowed serial position curves were obtained, but the serial position curves were flat when only item information had to be remembered. Bowed serial position curves therefore result from processes connected with order information, while the retention of item information makes quite different demands on the memory system. Different sets of stimulus attributes must be selected to encode order and item information.

Finally, consider the attributes of recency and frequency and their role in retention. Numerous studies have shown that subjects are quite good at remembering how often they have seen an item, or when they saw it last. Traditionally, it was suggested that frequency and recency judgments are based upon the strength of an item in memory. The greater the "associative strength" of an item, the more frequent and recent it will be judged. It is indeed logically possible to derive frequency and recency judgments in this way, but it appears to be empirically false. Wells (1974) has reviewed the literature in this area and made a compelling case against the strength theory of frequency judgments. Instead, she views frequency judgments as the result of multiple memory representations of an item. Each of these is a complex, distinct, multi-attribute encoding, much as we have argued above, with some relationship between them; frequency judgments are based on a count of these multiple representations. Wells could not reject strength interpretations of recency with equal confidence, but there, too, she made a good case for the notion that recency judgments are normally based on encoded information about serial position or temporal order, though in the absence of such specific information it is possible that recency judgments might be based on more global features of a memory code: a good, elaborate code without time information might be judged more recent than a poor, deficient code without time information.

## IMAGERY

Frost (1972) gave subjects simple line drawings of 16 common objects to study. The objects could be classified in two ways: in terms of semantic categories (e.g., there were four pictures of animals, four pictures of vehicles, etc.), or in visual terms (the main axis of the picture was horizontal, vertical, or slanted either right or left). Half of Frost's subjects expected a recognition test and half expected a recall test. All, however, were asked to recall the pictures. The subjects who prepared themselves for a recall test clustered items in their recall by semantic categories. Subjects who were led to expect a recognition test, however, recalled the pictures either in semantic or shape clusters. That is, these subjects had stored in their long-term memory information about the visual shape of the stimulus items and had grouped these items in terms of their shapes.

This study demonstrates that visual representations may be retained in memory, which should, of course, surprise no one. We have mentioned recency, frequency, and modality information in memory, as well as acoustic and semantic cues; clearly memory must also contain visual information. It is, however, true that until recently the study of how visual characteristics are represented in memory has been relatively neglected, given the preoccupation of psychologists with verbal materials. A change in this state of affairs was brought about largely through the work of Paivio, whose "dual coding theory" of memory has been a major stimulus for work in this area (e.g., Paivio, 1971, 1975a).

Paivio maintains that there are two independent but interconnected memory systems; an imagery system that contains holistic analogues of things, and a verbal memory that bears no resemblance to things. The evidence that he cites for this position is rather impressive.

Linguistic memory and processing appear to be localized in the dominant hemisphere of the brain (usually the left one). Nonlinguistic memory and processing (e.g., spatial relations and music) are localized in the right or nondominant hemisphere. The two systems appear to be quite independent, in that a person with lesions in one half of the brain may show very specific linguistic deficits, while his nonlinguistic performance remains unimpaired, and vice versa (e.g., Gazzaniga, 1970). It is even claimed that normal subjects process verbal inputs better with their right hemisphere, while the opposite is the case for nonlinguistic processes (Kimura, 1973).

The neuropsychological data that suggest separate storage and processing for words and imagery are in good agreement with a large body of test data that show people's verbal and nonverbal abilities to be relatively independent (e.g., Guilford, 1967). Behaviorally, the imagery and verbal systems are also independent to some extent. We have already reviewed the considerable evidence that the ease with which subjects can form an image or a word (i.e., its "imagery value") is one of the most powerful determinants of learning: words that are easy to image are easy to learn (see Section 1.1.4). If learning is incidental, pictures are generally remembered better than words—except when the words are imaged during learning, in which case they are retained as well as pictures, as was demonstrated by Paivio and Csapo (1973). The same authors also showed that when an item is repeated first as a word and then as a picture the effect of this repetition is significantly greater than when it is repeated twice as a word or twice as a picture. What is involved here is, of course, another instance of encoding variability: presenting once a picture of a zebra and then the word zebra leads to more variable encoding (and hence better retention) than presenting the same stimulus twice.

Further evidence for the independence of imagery and verbal components in memory has been obtained in studies that showed that one can selectively interfere with imagery and words. Reading interferes more with the simultaneous representation of spatial relationships, while listening interferes more with verbal memory (Brooks, 1968). Atwood (1971) gave subjects 35 imaginal phrases such as "Nudist devouring a bird" to study. Thirty-five other phrases were abstract ones, such as "The intellect of Einstein was a miracle." After each phrase either a visual or a verbal interference task had to be performed: a digit, either 1 or 2, was presented either visually or auditorily, and the subject had to execute a reversal response, that is, press Key 1 if a 2 was presented and press Key 2 if a 1 was presented. A control group, without an interference task, completed the design. Finally, a cued recall test was given to all subjects (e.g., recall "bird" given the cue "nudist"). The principal results of this study are shown in Table 5.2. For both abstract and concrete sentences, recall was best when there was no interference. Visual interference had a large effect on memory for imaginal phrases; auditory interference disrupted, above all, abstract phrases—a clear indication that imagery involves visual processes!

Paivio's dual coding theory postulates not only the existence of independent verbal and imagery systems, but also makes a qualitative distinction. While verbal representations are discrete (such as a set of features or attributes), imagery representations are analogue in nature. The memory trace of an image is not just some arbitrary symbol that stands for or represents the image (as for instance in a computer, where we would quite arbitrarily stipulate that activation of a certain area in the computer's memory—say area, 14,764—stands for the feature "red"). Instead, the memory trace of an image is analogous, it bears a direct resemblance to the object from which it derives. Paivio insists that one should not think of this as "a picture in the head." Images can be much more abstract, that is, contain less detail than pictures, and they are more like active perceptions than static pictures. Nevertheless, images are analogue in nature and not discretely representable; the image of an elephant in memory is in some quite direct sense "greater" than the image of a mouse.

TABLE 5.2. **Proportion Correct Recall for Imaginal and Abstract Phrases as a Function of the Nature of Interference (after Atwood, 1971)**

|  | Visual Interference | Auditory Interference | No Interference |
|---|---|---|---|
| Imaginal phrases | .58 | .76 | .82 |
| Abstract phrases | .60 | .44 | .70 |

There exists considerable evidence for analogue representations in memory. Common sense almost demands that there be such representations. Try to tell someone how to ski a steep slope in deep powder, or how to hit a backhand volley. We just do not have the words for it. You will end up by demonstrating. It is very easy to show a child how to build a little tower with her blocks, but almost hopelessly difficult to tell a computer how to do it.

Impressive experimental demonstrations of what appear to be analogue-type processes can be found in the work of Shepard on mental rotation (e.g., Shepard and Metzler, 1971; Cooper and Shepard, 1973). Shepard and his co-workers asked subjects to determine whether pairs of perspective line drawings depicted objects of the same shape or not. On half of the trials the objects were the same, on the other half they were mirror images of each other. On all trials, however, the objects were shown in different rotations. The striking finding was that when the two objects were of the same three-dimensional shape, the time it took subjects to decide that they were the same increased linearly with the angular difference between the pictured orientations. If the orientation were the same for the two objects, reaction times were on the order of 1 second; reaction times increased to about 4 to 5 seconds as the difference in orientation between the pictures increased to 180°. Shepard explains these results in the following way. First, the subject creates an image of the portrayed object; he then internally rotates this image, analogous to how he would rotate an external object held in his hand, until the image becomes congruent with the other member of the pair. Subjects cannot carry out this imagined rotation faster than at the rate of about 60° per second. Hence reaction times increase linearly with the angle of rotation.

It is perhaps possible to account for Shepard's results without postulating an analogue process (after all, digital computers perform such tasks), but Shepard's explanation is certainly the simplest and most elegant. Furthermore, it agrees fully with the subjects' introspections in these problems. In any case, there are other results in the memory literature that are hard to explain without assuming that people have analogue processing capacities. There are several experiments showing that when people are asked to make comparisons along some continuous perceptual or semantic dimension, a large "distance effect" is observed: the farther away the to be compared objects are, the more rapid is the decision. The first of these studies was done in 1967 by Moyer and Landauer. They showed that subjects can respond faster that 8 is greater than 2, than that 8 is greater than 7. This is a strange result if one assumes that people have in their head something like the sequence $1 < 2 < 3 < 4 < 5 < 6 < 7 < 8 \ldots$, plus a transitivity rule; in that case the decision $7 < 8$ should be the fastest, while other decisions would involve computations and should therefore be slower. Instead, Moyer and Landauer's results suggest that subjects have stored the number sequence as an array in memory and can inspect it internally much as one can look at an external array. Large perceptual differences are detected faster than small differences; the same is true for memory comparisons, suggesting that the memory comparison involves processes analogous to the perceptual comparison. The distance effect is not restricted to digit comparisons. It is also found with alphabetic comparisons (e.g., Lovelace and Snodgrass, 1971), size comparisons (*mouse* smaller than *squirrel* is slower than *mouse* smaller than *elephant*; e.g., Moyer, 1973; Paivio, 1975b), items that are arbitrarily ordered in a linear array (subjects learn the ordering of five different cars in terms of their speed; e.g., Potts, 1972), as well as comparisons along semantic dimensions (e.g., it is easier to say which is warmer in the case of hot-frigid than hot-tepid; e.g., Holyoak and Walker, 1976).

We conclude with Paivio (1971) that the evidence for an imagery system, independent but interrelated with the verbal system and analogue in nature, is overwhelming. Nevertheless it appears that his dual coding theory may still be unsatisfactory. First of all, Paivio concentrates on two modalities, imaginal and verbal. What about acoustic memory codes, and other sensory modalities? Most importantly, what about abstract, conceptual memory traces that are neither words nor images? (The evidence for such codes will be discussed at length in Section 6.2.3). It seems that what is needed is not a dual-coding theory, but a multiple-coding theory! Secondly, proponents of imagery are very insistent that imagery is not a picture or a "reproduction of reality," but other than that, they are vague about what an image is. In actual practice, the properties images are said to have are those of pictures: images must somehow look like the objects they represent. Pylyshyn (1973) and Anderson and Bower (1973) have strongly criticized this notion, insisting that a code is always a description. Indeed, the only workable descriptions of images in artificial intelligence programs today employ a descriptive language essentially the same as they use for the descriptions of verbal messages. As we learn more about the nature of analogue processes, this situation may change, but the basic point seems incontrovertible that the memory trace for a sensory stimulus, be it a visual image, a sound, or something else, must indeed be a code, that is a description of the event, not a look-alike copy. We have some notion what verbal codes might be. We can think of them, for instance, as attribute or feature sets, as we have frequently done in these pages. Likewise, we understand the propositional representations of meaning which will be discussed in Section 6.2.4 at least to some extent. On the other hand, what a look-alike but not a picture image might be, is not at all clear.

## 5.2    ORGANIZATION OF MEMORY

The importance for long-term retention of generating a rich, elaborate memory code for a to-be-remembered item, especially one that involves meaning and imagery elements, can hardly be overstated. However, there is another aspect to the encoding problem that has not yet been examined in depth. The most effective encoding does not stop with the single item, but organizes the to-be-remembered items into higher-order units. The formation of higher-order units in short-term memory has been called chunking; what forms a chunk in short-term memory is largely determined by principles of perceptual grouping and organization. In long-term memory, the processes of organization are more varied. Items can be organized into complex, interrelated structures on the basis of interitem associations, categorical relationships among items, or other, more elaborate cognitive processes. Materials that can be organized readily by any one of these means are remembered better than materials that are difficult to organize. However, even if a set of to-be-learned items has no obvious organization subjects will invent some sort of structure for it. If something is to be remembered well, it must be organized and, conversely, organizing guarantees remembering. Thus, "organization" appears to be ultimate, deepest level of encoding.

There are, indeed, cases where deep processing alone, be it semantic or imaginal, does not improve recall. These cases always involve learning materials that consist of several independent elements. Deep processing of the elements is not of much help here; what is necessary, first of all, is that the elements be organized into some coherent unit. Sematic processing may sometimes presuppose organization: as long as the items are not ordered into higher units, deep processing can't take place. For instance, Kintsch, Crothers, and Jorgensen (1971) gave subjects three randomly selected words to study. The study period was followed by a short period of backward counting, and by a recall test. On some trials, subjects merely read the three words aloud, just as in the standard Peterson and Peterson experiment; on other trials subjects responded to the meaning of each word, but each word was considered separately (subjects were asked to determine whether a given word was a category name, e.g., *animal,* or a category instance, e.g., *donkey);* on the remaining trials a nonsemantic processing task was used (for each separate word, subjects had to estimate whether the number of letters was odd or even). After a 24-second retention interval performance was about the same under these three conditions, varying between 24 and 30% recall of the word triplets. Thus, it did not really matter what the subject did with each word, as long as each word was treated separately. (Of course, quite different results are obtained when already unitized learning materials are used, as in the studies reviewed in Section 5.1.1). However, semantic processing of an integrating nature was highly effective: when subjects were asked to form a sentence or phrase employing all three study words, performance after 24 seconds was 79% correct!

Parallel results were reported by Bower (1970) for imagery. When subjects were given random word pairs to study, performance on a later paired-associate test was about the same whether subjects used a rote learning strategy (36% correct) or formed separate images of each word (34% correct). Only when an interactive image was formed ("visualize the objects denoted by the words interacting in some vivid way in an integrative scene") was recall improved (61%).

Just like chunking in short-term memory, organization plays a similarly crucial role in long-term memory. We need, therefore, to take a closer look at organizational processes and their interaction with other encoding activities.


## ASSOCIATIVE AND CATEGORICAL ORGANIZATION IN RECALL

Several studies concerning the effects of objective organization of the learning material on free-recall learning were described in Chapter 1. It is sufficient merely to mention these studies here and to restate their conclusions. They were all concerned with demonstrating that the more redundant a list is, the easier it is to recall. Miller (1958) constructed a set of meaningless letter combinations according to simple generating rules and showed that these rule-generated items could be recalled better than random combinations of the same letters. Garner (1962) and Whitman and Garner (1962) presented systematic investigations of the effects of statistical redundancy on free recall. They showed that not only the amount of redundancy but also the exact nature of the redundancy affect recall. Simple contingencies are much easier to learn than complex interactions. Finally, a number of studies, starting with the classical paper of Miller and Selfridge (1950), provided evidence that the more a string of words approaches the statistical structure of English, the easier it is to recall the string.

Another important determiner of recall is the associative structure of a list of words. It is well known that if a large group of subjects is asked to give a free association to a stimulus word there will be a high degree of communality in the response. Kent and Rosanoff (1910) have collected the associations of 1000 adult subjects to 100 familiar English words. They instructed their subjects to respond with the first word that occurred to them, other than the stimulus word itself. The resulting tabulation of response words provided the basis for most work on the effects of associative structure in recall. For each stimulus word Kent and Rosanoff reported the number of subjects who responded with a particular word. For instance, for the stimulus word NEEDLE the three most frequent responses were THREAD, PIN, and SHARP with frequencies of 160, 158, and 152, respectively. Examples of associations given only once in response to the stimulus word NEEDLE are DILIGENCE, PINCUSHION, and WOMAN. Palermo and Jenkins collected extensive word association data in 1964, and most recent workers have used their tables.

The first investigations of associative relationships in recall were reported by Jenkins and Russell in 1952, and Jenkins, Mink, and Russell in 1958. These authors gave subjects associated word pairs to learn, followed by a recall test. They found that related words tended to cluster in recall, and that the stronger the associative relationships between the word pairs in a list were, the better was recall.

Instead of merely working with associatively related word pairs, Deese (1961, 1965) calculated the average relative frequency with which all words in a list tend to elicit each other in free association tests. This index can be obtained from a matrix such as that of Table 5.3. This table shows the associative relationships among the 15 words of one of Deese's lists. All of the words in this list happen to be high associates of BUTTERFLY. However, they are quite highly related to each other, in addition, as the table shows. Rows in Table 5.3 give the stimulus words, and columns give the response words. Entries are the percent of subjects who gave the column word as a free associate to the stimulus word. Since subjects may respond with associates that are not members of the list, the percentages in each row do not have to add up to 100%. Deese suggests as a measure of the strength of the

TABLE 5.3. Interitem Associative Matrix for 15 High-Frequency Associates of BUTTERFLY (after Deese, 1961)

| | Moth | Insect | Wing | Bird | Fly | Yellow | Net | Pretty | Flowers | Bug | Cocoon | Color | Stomach | Blue | Bees | Average |
|---|---|---|---|---|---|---|---|---|---|---|---|---|---|---|---|---|
| Moth | | 2 | 2 | | 10 | | | | 2 | 10 | | | | | | |
| Insect | 4 | | | | 18 | | | | | 48 | | | | | | |
| Wing | | 6 | | 50 | 24 | | | | | | | | | | | |
| Bird | | | | | 30 | | | | | | | | | 2 | | |
| Fly | | 10 | | 8 | | | | | | 18 | | | | | | |
| Yellow | | | | | | | | | 3 | | | 11 | | 16 | | |
| Net | | 2 | | 2 | | 2 | | | | | | | | | | |
| Pretty | | | | | | | | | | | | | | | | |
| Flowers | 2 | | | | | | | | | | | 2 | | | 2 | |
| Bug | 2 | 36 | | 2 | 4 | | | | | | | | | | 4 | |
| Cocoon | 16 | 6 | | 4 | | | | | | 10 | | | | | | |
| Color | | | | | | | | | | | | | | 20 | | |
| Stomach | | | | | | | | | | | | | | | | |
| Blue | | | | 15 | | | | | 5 | | | 10 | | | | |
| Bees | | | | | | | | | | | | | | | | |
| | 24 | 56 | 8 | 81 | 86 | 2 | 0 | 0 | 10 | 86 | 0 | 23 | 0 | 40 | 8 | 28.3 |

associative interrelationships in a list the index of interitem associative strength; this index is simply the mean of the column sums in Table 5.3. In practice the index has a maximum around 30%. Therefore, the list shown in Table 5.3 has a relatively high interitem strength.

Deese constructed 18 different lists of 15 words each and computed their interitem associative strength. Associative frequencies were obtained from a sample of 50 subjects. A different group of 48 subjects then studied and recalled each list. The obtained recall scores correlated very highly with the index of interitem associative strength: $r = .88$. The more the items of a list tend to elicit each other, the better the list can be recalled. Deese also observed that the stronger the interitem associations were, the fewer recall intrusions occurred: $r = -.48$. In another experiment Deese (1959) showed that intrusions can be predicted quite accurately from the associative structure of a list. Suppose we want to predict the probability that BUTTERFLY occurs as an intrusion error in the recall of the word list shown in Table 5.3. The average of the frequencies with which each word of the list elicits BUTTERFLY may be used to predict its intrusion probability. The average associative strength of an intrusion, as defined above, correlated .87 with observed intrusion frequencies across 36 different lists in Deese's experiment.

Associative relationships not only predict total recall and intrusions, but also can account for some of the sequential phenomena observed in a free-recall experiment. It has already been mentioned that Jenkins and Russell could predict clustering from measures of interword association. Similarly, Rothkopf and Coke (1961) reported that if two words were recalled in sequence, the second word tended to have many associations with the first word. In Rothkopf and Coke's experiment both the probability of recall and the sequence of recall could, to some extent, be predicted from word association measures.

The studies discussed so far have only been concerned with the associative relationships among items of a list. It may happen, however, that items of a list are not associated with each other, but nevertheless cluster in recall because they all are associated with a word which itself is not a list member. For this situation Deese (1962) has devised his Index of Associative Meaning. This index is not restricted to the words appearing in a list, but is a count of the number of associates that any two words of the list have in common. For instance, none of Deese's subjects gave SYMPHONY as a response to PIANO, but the two words are still associatively related because both are associated with NOTE, SONG, SOUND, MUSIC, NOISE, and ORCHESTRA. The index of associative meaning does not predict the tendency of two words to elicit each other as does the index of interitem associative strength, but it measures the likelihood that words are being used in the same linguistic environment. The index of associative meaning is therefore closely related to our next topic, the role of conceptual categories in recall.

In 1953 Bousfield described a phenomenon which he labeled category clustering. Bousfield studied the recall of subjects who learned a 60-word list composed of 15 instances of each of four conceptual categories. The categories were animals, names, professions, and vegetables. The words were presented one by one in random order at a 3-second rate. Unlimited time was given for recall. Bousfield observed that words belonging to the same category tended to cluster together in the subject's output. The number of repetitions that a subject made in his recall was taken as a measure of clustering. A repetition was counted when a subject recalled two instances of the same category in succession. Bousfield's subjects made many more repetitions than would be expected on the basis of chance. They clearly were grouping words according to category in their output.

Bousfield had selected the words for his categories according to his best judgment. Most later investigators have made use of norms collected by Battig and Montague (1969). These authors compiled responses from 442 subjects to 56 categories, such as FISH, SHIP, BUILDING, VEHICLE, etc. Their subjects were told to write down the first four specific instances they could think of for each category. The responses for each category were then tabulated according to the frequency with which they occurred. For instance, TROUT, BASS, and SHARK were the three most frequent responses in the FISH category, with frequencies of 216, 195, and 176, respectively. CARP, SHELL and WATER give some idea about the words that occurred only once in this category. Bousfield, Cohen, and Whitmarsh (1958) have used such norms to investigate category clustering. They compared a highly organized list (15 frequent responses in each of four categories) with a low-organization list (15 infrequent responses in each of four categories). Words were presented in random order. Lists with high probability category members were recalled better, and clustering was more pronounced.

A number of empirical relationships concerning category clustering have been investigated so that we now have a fair amount of empirical knowledge about the recall of categorized word lists. Bousfield and Cohen (1953) have studied clustering as a function of repeated study trials. From 1 to 5 trials with a 60-word, four-category list were given to independent groups. Total recall improved from 24 words recalled after one trial to 38 words after 5 trials. At the same time, the number of repetitions doubled.

Cofer, Bruce, and Reicher (1966) have reported that recall of a categorized word list is better if all the items from the same category are presented in blocks than when the presentation sequence is completely random. In the same study recall improved and clustering increased when the subjects were given more time to study each item.

It seems that categorized word lists are recalled better because categorized words are somehow more available. This conclusion is suggested by the observation of Bousfield et al. (1958) that lists composed of high-frequency category members are recalled better than lists composed of low-frequency category members—a result that has been replicated repeatedly (e.g., Cofer et al., 1966).

If the response availability of category instances is more or less controlled, most of the variance in recall of categorized word lists can be attributed to category recall, rather than to forgetting of category instances. Cohen (e.g., Cohen, 1966) has shown that if at least one word is recalled from a category, subjects recall a fairly constant percentage of the words remaining in the category under a wide variety of conditions. For instance, in one of his experiments Cohen manipulated list length. He had lists of 10, 15, and 20 categories, each composed of 3 or 4 words. If a category was recalled at all, i.e., if at least one word was recalled per category, the mean number of words recalled per category was around 60% and apparently invariant with respect to list length. In another experiment no differences in mean words per category were found when the rate of presentation was varied. How many words a subject recalls is primarily dependent on how many categories he can remember. Subjects either recall a high percentage of the words in a category or none at all.

## 5.2.2    SUBJECTIVE ORGANIZATION

If the learning material is organized in some way the subject uses this organization in learning to recall. This manifests itself in two ways: organization facilitates recall and leads to clustering in the subject's output that corresponds to the input organization. However, even if the input material is not organized by the experimenter, the subject imposes his own organization upon it in learning to recall. It appears that the major problem that a subject is faced with in a free-recall experiment is to organize the material for himself so that it can be retrieved later. If a list is already objectively organized the subject's task is facilitated, but in either case long-term recall usually involves organization of the learning material.

The first experiment that showed that subjective organization occurs in the learning of a list of unrelated items was reported by Tulving in 1962. Tulving defined subjective organization as the tendency to recall words in the same order on successive learning trials, even if there are not experimentally manipulated sequential dependencies among the words of a learning list. For his experiment he used a list of 16 disyllabic nouns that were not related to each other in meaning, according to the best judgment of the experimenter. Each subject was given 16 recall trials, with a different order of presentation on each trial. The presentation rate was one word per second, and the recall period was 90 seconds. This rate is rather fast so that subjects did not have time for elaborate processing. The average number of words recalled as well as an index of the amount of subjective organization are shown in Figure 5.4. The index is a measure based on information theory which depends on pairwise depen-

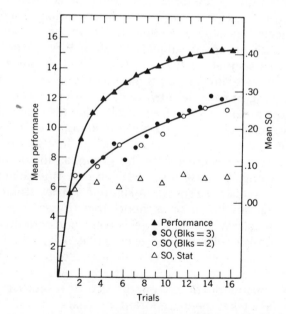

FIGURE 5.4 **Mean performance (upper curve) and mean subjective organization (lower curve) as a function of trials. Mean subjective organization for blocks of 2 trials from 16 statistical subjects are shown for comparison, open triangles. (after Tulving, 1962)**

dencies in successive recalls. If the index is low the order of recall from one trial to the next is unrelated. The statistical subjects whose "data" are also shown in Figure 5.4 serve to show how much organization may be expected on the basis of chance alone. The increase in the subjective organization index that characterizes the performance of the actual subjects means that recall order became more and more stereotyped from trial to trial. As the figure shows, total recall and subjective organization correlate highly.

Considering the high correlation between subjective organization and recall the hypothesis suggests itself that organization is not merely an epiphenomenon of recall learning, but that there is actually a causal relationship between recall learning and subjective organization. Of course, in order to demonstrate that one learns to recall because material is organized subjectively, more than a correlational analysis is necessary. An experiment by Bower, Lesgold, and Tieman (1969) suggests that if subjects are prevented from achieving a stable organization they learn very little from successive presentations. Bower et al. presented a list of 24 unselected nouns in 6 groups of 4 words each. Each group of words was shown for 12 seconds and subjects were told to make each four-tuple into a visual image. For one group of subjects the same four-tuples were presented on each of 4 trials; for another group of subjects the four-tuples were changed from trial to trial so that no two words appeared in the same four-tuple more than once. Bower points out that if free-recall learning is a process of learning of each item by itself, no differences between the groups should be expected. If free recall depends primarily on the number of associations existing between items, the second group might be expected to perform better than the first group. The total number of associations is greater for this group, although the associations are less strong, because they received only one reinforcement. The results of this study are shown in Figure 5.5. They strikingly agree with the expectations based on a theory that stresses organizational factors in free recall. When the subjects were not permitted to form stable organizations hardly any improvement at all occurred from trial to trial. Interference with a subject's subjective organization negates learning effects.

Another demonstration of the importance of subjective organization for free recall has been reported by Mandler and Pearlstone (1966). The principal purpose of their study was to compare free versus constrained conceptualization. Subjects were given a deck of 52 cards, each of which had a word printed on it, and were told to sort these cards into from 2 to 7 categories according to any system they

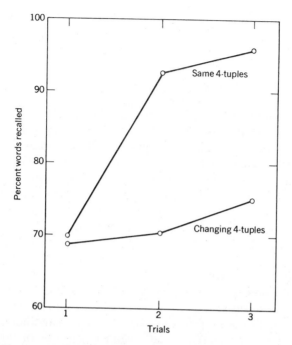

FIGURE 5.5  **Percentage of words recalled with constant or with changing four-tuples.** (after Bower, Lesgold, and Tieman, 1969)

wished. They were also told that they would be given sorting trials with the same deck of cards until they achieved a stable organization, i.e., until they sorted the cards in exactly the same way twice in a row. Mandler and Pearlstone called this a free concept-utilization task: subjects could use any basis they cared to for their sorting, but some kind of stable system had to be achieved. A second group of subjects was given a constrained conceptualization task: these subjects had to sort the 52 cards according to an experimenter-defined scheme, which is the usual procedure in concept formation experiments. In order to equate the difficulty of the sortings made by the free and constrained groups each subject in the constrained group was yoked with a free subject. The constrained subject's task was to sort the cards in the same way as the yoked free subject. Immediately after reaching the criterion of two identical sortings subjects in both groups were asked to recall as many of the words that they had just sorted as possible.

Not unexpectedly, the free subjects needed fewer trials to reach a stable sorting than the constrained subjects. Indeed, the latter took twice as long as the subjects who could choose their own basis of classification. In spite of this difference, the subjects in the two groups could recall an about equal number of words. The constrained subjects had twice as many sorting trials and hence twice as many opportunities to learn, but they were able to recall only 20 words on the average, just like the free subjects. Therefore, it is not the number of learning trials that matters for free recall, but the level of organization achieved on these trials. Both groups reached the same sorting criterion and hence recall was identical, although one of the groups needed twice as many trials to reach criterion as the other.

Although trials to criterion in the sorting task were not related to free recall, the number of categories used in sorting was highly correlated with recall ($r = .95$). This relationship is shown in Figure 5.6 for the 10 free subjects. Total recall is a direct function of the number of categories used in sorting. The subjects in Mandler and Pearlstone's experiment remembered a little over five words for each category. This relationship between the number of categories used (C) and recall (R) can be expressed formally by fitting a linear equation to the data. The best fitting equation is also reproduced in Figure 5.6, together with the scatter diagram of the data. Mandler (1967b) has explored the category-recall relationship in a series of other experiments. In all of these, a high correlation between the number of categories used in sorting and total recall was obtained (median $r = .70$). On the other hand, trials to criterion in the sorting task and recall did not correlate significantly (median $r = .16$), and the category recall relationship remained essentially the same when the number of sorting trials was controlled through partial correlation (median $r = .73$). Thus it is clearly the number of categories, not the number of trials, that determines recall performance in Mandler's experiments.

A similar finding has been noted above: when they are given a categorized word list subjects seem to recall the items in each category quite well if they recall a category at all. Certainly there must be experimental limits to this category-recall relationship, but these have not yet been explored adequately.

Mandler (1967b) also showed that sorting instructions and recall instructions are approximately equivalent for the task described above. In one of his experiments all subjects received five sorting trials, so that any differences in recall between the different groups used in this experiment must be caused by factors other than the number of trials. Half of the subjects received recall instructions and half did not. Both groups were further subdivided according to their

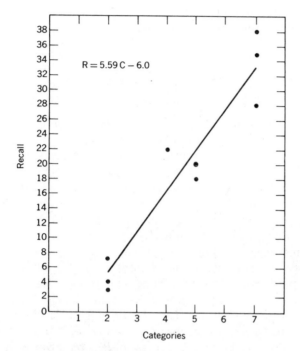

$$R = 5.59\,C - 6.0$$

FIGURE 5.6  **Recall as a function of the number of sorting categories.** (after Mandler, 1967b)

instructions for the sorting task: half of the subjects were asked to sort into from two to seven subjective categories, as described above, while the other subjects were merely instructed to place the words one after the other into seven columns. Subjects who received either organization or recall instructions, or both, recalled about equally many words. Subjects who were not instructed to recall, nor forced to organize the material, recalled significantly fewer words. Thus instructions to recall and instructions to organize had equivalent effects, in agreement with our hypothesis that free-recall learning essentially involves subjective organization of the learning material.

Once again we have seen that what a subject does is the important determinant of memory. Intent to remember per se is irrelevant; if we get the subject to do the right thing during the study period, he will remember, whether this is organization as in Mandler's studies, deep processing as in Craik and Tulving's (1975; see Section 5.1.1), or discrimination to support later recognition (as in Estes and Dapolito,

1967). If the subject takes the right approach to the learning material, it makes little difference whether learning is incidental or intentional (Postman, 1964).

### 5.2.3    ORGANIZATIONAL PROCESSES IN RECALL

So far we have only shown that organization is important for long-term memory and that certain types of materials are easier to organize, and hence to remember, than others. Now we must turn to some investigations of the process of organizing itself: How are items interrelated? It appears that a necessary condition for interrelating items is that they be held conjointly in short-term memory. Short-term memory serves as the working memory in which organization occurs; organization is a type of elaborative encoding, which is not directed at encoding features of a single item, but consists in encoding relations among items. Frequently, these relations are not established de novo, but are copied from already existing structures in semantic memory such as associations among words based on the use of language, or semantic category relations (see Section 5.6). Thus, a preexisting association between items held in short-term memory may be detected and marked (e.g., *play-ball*), or common category membership (e.g., *lion-tiger*), or some idiosyncratic relationship between items will be established (e.g., *cow-moon* is encoded as an image of a cow jumping over the moon).

It follows from this account that the perceptual grouping factors that determine chunking in short-term memory (see Section 4.2.2) are important for organizational processes. Items that are chunked together in short-term memory *may* be subject to further organizational encoding. Thus, we have already seen that when a series of letters is presented, chunking is determined by the pattern of pauses in the series; Bower and Springston (1970) have shown that if within such a pause-induced chunk there happens to be a phonemically legitimate letter sequence (that is, a sequence of letters that can be pronounced in English, not necessarily a word), such sequences form organizational units in long-term memory. Similarly, Glanzer (1976) found that if a sequence of words was read with an intonation pattern that coincided with the pattern of semantic relationships among the words, recall was facilitated; semantically related words were chunked together in short-term memory, and this relationship could be used as the basis for long-term memory organization. On the other hand, when the innovation pattern was out of phase with the semantic grouping, recall was lowered; semantically related words did not occupy short-term memory at the same time, and hence this relationship could not be used in the process of organizational encoding.

If, as is the case in most laboratory experiments, a word list is presented without a distinct intonation pattern, short-term memory chunking is less predictable. However, it is obvious that on the average the closer together two words are on the input list, the greater the likelihood that they will be held in short-term memory at the same time, and hence that any existing relationship between them might be detected and used in the encoding process. Thus we can derive the prediction that words that are closer together on a list should be more likely to be organized together as a long-term memory unit than words that are separated by many other list items. One indication of what forms a long-term memory unit is, as we have seen, output order; when items are recalled together we infer that they might have been stored together. An obvious confirmation of this prediction is the well-known finding discussed above that categorized word lists are recalled better, and recall is more strongly clustered by categories, when the presentation order is blocked by categories than when it is random. However, it is by no means the case that input adjacency is a necessary condition for encoding as a long-term memory unit. The learner has a certain amount of control over the content of his working memory; in trying to organize a list for long-term retention he typically brings back into working memory earlier items from the list that he still remembers in order to check whether these items would fit into the encoding scheme that he is presently working on. This gives the encoding process a great deal of flexibility and liberates it at least to some extent from the severe constraints that input order would otherwise impose on it (e.g., Kintsch, 1970). Indeed, this process of "looking back" in memory can be brought under at least partial experimental control. Jacoby (1974) had subjects learn a list of words and asked them to make a decision, as each word was presented, whether that word belonged to the same semantic category as the word $n$-items back in the input list. By varying the value of $n$, Jacoby could induce subjects to process implicitly items presented earlier in the list. Such implicit processing greatly facilitated the effectiveness of semantic cues as evidenced by later recall. Interestingly, it did not help at all when the words were related by acoustic similarity. Acoustic cues are just not subject to much encoding variability; they will be encoded in more or less the same way regardless of context. Semantic cues, on the other hand, provide a much richer encoding potential, and how they will be encoded is very context dependent (e.g., *sofa* in the context of *sleep* versus the context of *chair*). It is not that acoustic relations among words cannot be used for long-term encoding (in general, acoustic similarity in a list improves long-term retention over unrelated control lists; e.g., Glanzer, Koppenaal, and Nelson, 1972), but that acoustic encoding is relatively unique, context independent, and hence cannot profit as much from encoding variability as semantic encoding.

The position taken above that the encoding of interrelationships among items is crucial for long-term recall has been challenged by Slamecka (1968). Slamecka argued that storage in memory is not organized, but that traces are stored independently. He reported that on a free-recall test, when subjects are given part of a learned list of items as recall cues, their performance on the remaining items is not better (and sometimes worse) than when no cues are given at all. Theories of free-recall learning that assume that interitem dependencies are formed during learning imply that a list item should be able to cue recall of other list items and hence are contradicted by this result. The phenomenon is a stable one and has been replicated by several other experimenters. However, there are some methodological problems with Slamecka's experimental procedures.

In one experiment, Slamecka had subjects study a categorized word list; for a test, each subject received a recall sheet with half of the words printed on it in random order. One problem with this procedure is that the randomly arranged words on the recall sheet did not correspond to the way subjects had organized the list, and hence produced interference. Secondly, in free recall the subject typically reports first the items he still holds in short-term memory. Giving subjects earlier items as recall cues may interfere with this efficient recall strategy and result in a loss of items held in short-term memory. If these factors are controlled, cueing with part of the list can facilitate recall of the remaining list items. In an unpublished study from the Colorado laboratory Kintsch and Kalk had subjects study a list of 20 categories, each containing four words. Recall occurred under three conditions: in the random-half group, subjects received half of the study words in a haphazard sequence on the recall sheet; in the two-per-category group, subjects received two words from each category in the same order in which they had appeared on the study list, blocked by category; finally, a control group had to recall all 80 words. For all groups, short-term memory was eliminated by means of a brief backward-counting period between study and test. Under these conditions, a sizeable facilitation of recall was obtained when subjects were given two words from each category in an orderly way.

On the other hand, Slamecka's results were also replicated: if a random half of the words were given as cues in a manner not corresponding to the subject's list organization, no recall facilitation was observed. Interestingly, the facilitation was entirely one of greater category recall, while differences in the number of items recalled per category were only minor. Subjects learned some 70 to 80% of the words in each category on the first trial; their problem was to gain access to all the categories. As Figure 5.7 shows, this was effectively provided in the two-per-category condition, but not by merely cueing with random half of the words.

Other investigators (e.g., Allen, 1969; Wood, 1969) have made similar arguments and reported similar results. Thus, we are probably quite safe at this time in rejecting Slamecka's independent storage hypothesis. The formation of interdependencies during learning appears to be an integral part of long-term memory encoding; organization is the key word. Here it should be stressed that the terms organization and association are closely related, and are by no means contradictory. They differ in their connotations (organization being a

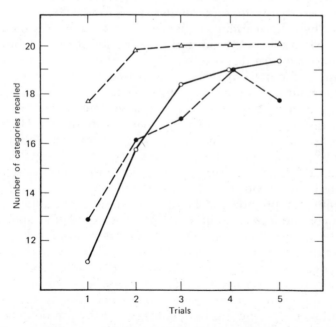

FIGURE 5.7    Number of categories from which at least one word was recalled as a function of trials and retrieval cues: random half of the items (filled circles), two items from each category cues (triangles), and no retrieval cues (open circles).

somewhat more general term), but operationally they are concerned with the same problem: the formation of interitem dependencies in learning (e.g., Postman, 1972).

### 5.2.4    ORGANIZATION IN SERIAL RECALL

In the first chapter (Section 1.2.1) we discussed in some detail one of the classic problems in verbal learning: how does serial learning work? We have seen that the search for the functional stimulus in serial learning was a misguided one. We can now subsume the problem of serial learning under the organizational theory of recall. Martin and Noreen (1974) have shown that subjects learn a series of words by dividing it into a sequence of subsequences, learning the internal structure of these subsequences, and finally learning the correct order of these subsequences. In other words, subjects do very much what they do in free-recall learning, except that, in addition, they must encode order information. When the sequences that subjects are asked to learn have no a *priori* basis for ordering, subjects impose their own structure upon them, just as they subjectively organized the unrelated word lists in such studies as Tulving (1962) or Mandler (1967b). When the learning sequences have their own structure, for example, when they are produced by some set of rules, subjects use this rule structure as the basis for their organization. This latter case is discussed in Section 7.2.2; here we are only concerned with the organization of unstructured serial lists.

The task of the subject is to learn to anticipate the next word in a series in response to each list item. Martin and Noreen (1974) have shown that if one plots correct responses on successive trials in such a serial anticipation experiment, clusters of items emerge such that performance within a cluster is good, but errors accumulate at the transitions between clusters.

A number of phenomena in serial learning are clarified by this analysis. For instance, Martin and Noreen showed that anticipation errors (a response that is wrong for the current position but correct for a later position) occurred most often at the leading-edge word of a subsequence; words inside a chunk are less likely as anticipation errors, although these items are much more available (in the sense that they are given more frequently as correct responses). Secondly, the item just preceding a subsequence, which by the definition of a subsequence is one on which anticipation errors occur, is closely integrated with the subsequence that precedes it: if subjects are given a free-recall test after serial learning, that item is recalled well and clusters together with the preceding items; similarly performance is good on a backward anticipation test. The problem is that the item just before a subsequence that is never correctly anticipated is part of the preceding cluster, and the link between the two clusters has not yet been established. Thus we have an interesting case of an item (the last one in a cluster) that is highly available in memory (as indexed by free recall and backward serial recall) but is not retrieved on the forward serial test. On the other hand, another item (the first one in a cluster) is not very available but it is frequently retrieved when it should not be, thus leading to anticipation errors. Indeed, by a comparison of clustering in free recall and serial recall Martin and Noreen could demonstrate that the list is learned from the inside out: within cluster order is learned first, then the recall order of the groups.

## RECOGNITION AND RECALL

Although recall, as we have seen, depends very much on how well the learning material is organized, recognition performance does not rely primarily on organization. In a recognition test it makes very little difference whether the material is organized or not, or whether subjects are induced to organize the material for themselves.

A large number of experiments have been reported in the literature that support this conclusion (for reviews see Kintsch, 1970, or McCormack, 1972). In a prototypical experiment, Kintsch (1968b) used lists of 40 words, 10 each from four conceptual categories as learning material. A high-organization list was constructed from the most frequent reponses in the category norms, and a low-organization list was constructed from the least frequent responses. On a recall test, subjects recalled 22 words from the high-organization list, but only 15 from the low-organization list. When a recognition test was given memory strength as estimated by the $d'$ statistic was nearly identical for the two lists. In a second experiment the learning material consisted of CVCs that were constructed so that letter combinations were highly predictable in one condition (high-structure), and unpredictable in the other (low-structure). In addition, intralist similarity was varied by using either 5 or 10 different consonants to construct the set of CVCs. The results of the experiment are shown in Figure 5.8. High intralist similarity decreased performance for both recognition and recall, but did not interact with list structure. List structure significantly facilitated recall, but had little effect on recogni-

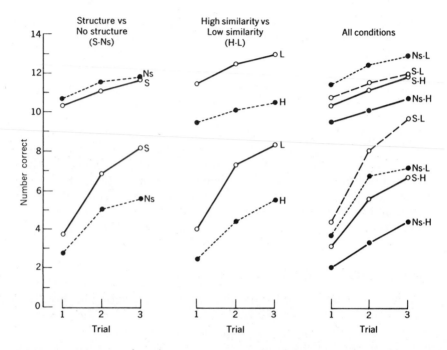

FIGURE 5.8   **Mean number of correct responses minus incorrect responses. The upper curves refer to recognition, the lower to recall. (after Kintsch, 1968b)**

tion. A procedural detail of these experiments must be noted. When a study list consisted of high-frequency words from each of four conceptual categories, the distractor items were also high-frequency words from the same four categories. If unrelated distractors had been used an effect of organization due to class recognition would certainly have been obtained. However, as long as one is concerned with item recognition proper organization of the learning material is a less important variable.

What does the differential effect of organizational variables on recognition and recall imply about the nature of these two processes? Why is organization so important for recall, but not for recognition? First of all, subjects encode items differently when they expect a recall test than when they expect a recognition test. It has been shown, for instance, that when subjects expect a recall test, but are given an unexpected recognition test, their performance is poorer than when they prepare themselves for a recognition test (e.g., Carey and Lockhart, 1973). Indeed, recall and recognition are independent of each other to a surprising extent. Tulving and Wiseman (1975) reviewed a number of paired-associate studies by different authors in which both recall and recognition tests were given and plotted recognition performance on all items against recognition performance on only those items that were recalled correctly. Their plot is shown in Figure 5.9. If recall and recognition are entirely independent, the points should fall along the main diagonal; if successful recall implies that a subject can also recognize the item, all points should fall along the top border of the graph. Clearly the results are much closer to the former prediction, implying that recognition and recall processes either use memory traces in different ways or are based on different types of information in memory, at least in paired-associate learning.

This, of course, raises the question what it is that subjects do differently when they recall and recognize, or when they prepare themselves for recall and recognition. A number of studies have explored this issue, and they agree quite well that for recall subjects try to organize items, to interrelate them, so that they can be later retrieved, while for recognition subjects try to discriminate each item from the others, so that they later can tell them apart from distractor items. Note that only instructions that insure that the subject orga-

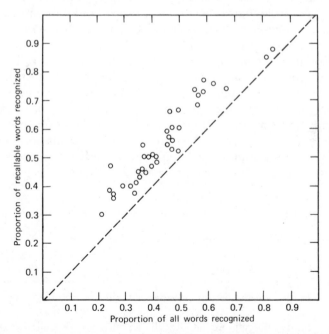

FIGURE 5.9    **Relation between overall recognition and recognition of recallable words. The data are from 12 different experiments. (after Tulving and Wiseman, 1975)**

nizes the material are effective for recall, while almost any instruction is adequate for recognition, as long as the subject makes some kind of a differential response to the learning items. For instance, Estes and DaPolito (1967) tested the retention of paired-associates after incidental and intentional instructions by both recognition and recall. In the incidental condition the subjects were asked to abstract the principle by which specific numbers were paired with specific nonsense syllables. Subjects who received intentional recall instructions performed significantly better than subjects with incidental instructions, but no corresponding difference was obtained in recognition performance.

The amount of time an item is studied determines recognition performance much more than recall. In Section 4.1.2 of the previous chapter we discussed an experiment by Woodward and Bjork (1973) that helps establish this point. These authors gave subjects a list to learn under somewhat unusual experimental conditions: after each word, there was a variable blank time period (during which the subject had to maintain the word in memory), followed by a signal to either forget or remember that item. We have discussed earlier the finding that recall was independent of the amount of rehearsal an item received. Indeed, this observation was one of the reasons for distinguishing between maintenance rehearsal, which merely keeps an item in short-term memory but does not improve long-term recall, and elaborative rehearsal, which is what long-term recall requires. Woodward and Bjork also gave subjects a recognition test, however, and quite unlike recall performance, recognition was better for those items that had been rehearsed more. Thus simple maintenance in short-term memory was sufficient for later recognition, but not for recall. An experiment by Hogan and Kintsch (1971) supports this conclusion. Table 5.4 outlines the design of the study. One group of subjects received four study trials with a 40-word list and was then given a

TABLE 5.4.  **The Effects of Study- and Test-Trials on Recall and Recognition (after Hogan & Kintsch, 1971)**

| | | Session 1 | | | | | Session 2 (48 hr later) | |
|---|---|---|---|---|---|---|---|---|
| Group 1: | Study | Study | Study | Study | Recall 15.6 | — | Recall 8.2 | Recognition 34.0 |
| Group 2: | Study | Recall | Recall | Recall | Recall 12.0 | — | Recall 8.2 | Recognition 30.4 |

recall test; a second group of subjects was given only one study trial followed by four recall tests on which no response feedback was provided. The first group of subjects did significantly better on the last recall trial, recalling 15.6 of the 40 words on the average, versus only 12 words for the second group. However, when both groups were retested after a two-day delay, performance was identical: both recalled on the average 8.2 words. This means that forgetting was 47% for the group receiving four study trials, but only 32% for the group receiving four test trials. Practicing retrieval thus helped long-term retention more than additional study trials. In contrast, when both groups of subjects were given a final recognition test, better performance was observed for the subjects who had received four study trials than for the subjects who received four test trials. Recognition thus depended on total study time, while recall was influenced by the nature of the training—retrieval practice being more useful than regular study trials.

Retrieval schemes do not play the same role in recognition as in recall. On a recognition test, a test item is given to the subject, and his task is to determine whether this test item matches one of his memory codes. This process is basically one of pattern matching: a perceptual pattern is matched with memory codes. The model of recognition memory outlined in Section 1.4.1 assumes that a test item on a recognition test somehow makes contact with the corresponding representation in memory (this is the process we have named here "pattern matching") and that an old-new decision is then made, depending on the "familiarity value" associated with that memory code. If the familiarity is high, the item is recognized as "old"; if it is below criterion, a "new" response is made. One may think of this "familiarity value" as some kind of a tag associated with a memory code, but different interpretations are possible. For instance, it may simply be an indication of how well the process of pattern matching succeeded: if a test stimulus matches a memory code perfectly, familiarity will be high; if it does not match at all, familiarity will be low; partial matches will produce intermediate familiarity values (e.g., Kintsch, 1974).

Note that the process of pattern matching is context dependent. If the stimulus work BARK is encoded in the context of DOG, the memory trace will consist of attributes that have to do with *barking;* on the other hand, an almost completely different set of attributes will be stored in memory when BARK occurs in the context of TREE (except for the graphic-phonological attributes, which remain the same in the two cases). Thus, the *tree*-BARK will not match very well a memory code based on the *dog*-BARK, and recognition failures will occur. This is, of course, precisely what happens (see the discussion in Section 1.4).

Nevertheless, pattern matching processes alone cannot explain all of the phenomena of recognition learning. Typically, what happens is that subjects shift to a different response strategy when decisions upon the basis of familiarity cannot be made with confidence. That is, they operate not with one decision criterion (as in Figure 1.12) but with two (as in Figure 4.16): if the familiarity value (or alternatively, the goodness of the pattern match) is high, they respond "old"; if it is low, they respond "new"; but if it is intermediate they do not risk a likely error, but try to retrieve the item from memory as on a recall test. Mandler (1972) calls this a "recall check." This is precisely what is assumed in the Atkinson and Juola (1974) model discussed in Section 4.3. The experimental evidence that supports this assumption comes partly from latency data. For example, Murdock and Dufty (1972) have found that response latencies are directly related to the distance from the yes-no criterion in a recognition task. In this experiment, subjects were asked whether or not they recognized each test item. The latency of their response was measured, and in addition confidence ratings were obtained. Subjects had to rate on a three-point scale how confident they were that their response was the right one. Figure 5.10 shows that the more confident subjects were, the shorter was their response latency. The longest latencies were obtained when subjects were uncertain of their responses; presumably these latencies were so long because subjects performed time-consuming recall checks. The memory search data of Atkinson and Juola (1974) are, of course, further examples of this response strategy.

If subjects make recall checks when they cannot reach a decision on the basis of an item's familiarity alone, organizational variables should affect recognition performance to the extent that such recall checks are made; recall checks should be more successful when the material is well organized than when it is poorly organized. This prediction was confirmed in a study by Mandler and Boeck (1974). Mandler and Boeck first had subjects sort 100 words into 2–7 categories, as in a previous study (Mandler, 1967b). Eleven subjects used only 3–4 categories (and thus were poor organizers, who, as we know, recall the words poorly), while 10 subjects used 6–7 categories (and thus were good organizers, who recall the words much better). Then, Mandler and Boeck gave a recognition test to these 21 subjects. The latency of each recognition response was recorded and used to divide the data into

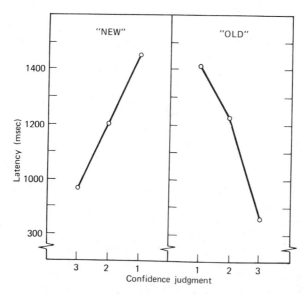

FIGURE 5.10  **The relationship between response latencies and confidence judgments in a recognition memory study. (after Murdock and Dufty, 1972)**

two groups: trials on which a fast response occurred and trials on which a slow response occurred. Since fast and slow are relative terms, the authors successively counted the most extreme 10%, 30%, and 50% of the responses as fast or slow, as shown in Figure 5.11. Recognition performance for the two groups of subjects, the good and the poor organizers, was considered separately on fast and slow trials. On fast trials, there was no difference between good and poor organizers: recognition apparently was based on the familiarity of an item, and whether the material was organized well or not played no role, as in the majority of the studies reviewed by Kintsch (1970) and McCormack (1972). On slow trials, however, that is, on trials during which a recall check occurred, those subjects who had organized the material well (by using a sufficient number of categories in the sorting task) did much better than those who had not (by using too few categories in the sorting task).

Mandler and Boeck's study thus provides a very clear indication of the role of organization in recognition. As long as recognition responses are based merely on a process of pattern matching (or, which amounts almost to the same thing, a familiarity check), organization is irrelevant. Organization becomes important, however, to the

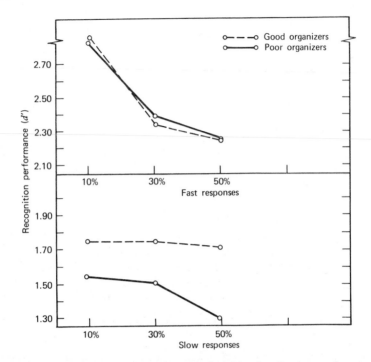

FIGURE 5.11  **Recognition performance, as indexed by the d' measure, for good and poor organizers, separately for fast responses (with 10, 30, and 50% of all responses defined a fast) and slow responses (with 10, 30, and 50% of all responses defined as slow). (after Mandler and Boeck, 1974)**

extent that recognition responses involve recall checks; a recall check amounts to trying to recall the item, and thus organization becomes important because of its effects upon recall.

## 5.3    RETRIEVAL

It is not clear whether anything is ever forgotten in the sense that it is lost from memory, once it has ever entered long-term memory. It is quite possible that the information is simply irretrievable: it is still there, and if we knew how, we could recover it. Whether or not such speculations are correct, it is certainly the case that one frequently cannot recall something and then remembers it later; such information has not been lost from memory, but merely could not be retrieved temporarily. In this respect, memory is like a huge warehouse in which all sorts of things are stored but which is less than perfectly organized, so that it is not always easy to find a given item upon demand.

In recall experiments, many errors are caused by retrieval problems. Memory traces may be available but inaccessible. Nice illustrations of this fact are obtained with the "selective reminding" procedure of Buschke (1973). Unlike the usual multitrial free recall experiment, Buschke showed subjects the words of a to-be-recalled list only up to their first recall. Once an item had been recalled, it was never shown again, but the subject was given further recall trials. One subject learning a 20-word list under these conditions made 34 errors before he mastered the list. Sixteen recall failures occurred before the first recall, indicating that the word had not yet been stored in memory. The remaining 18 recall failures occurred after an item had already been recalled once. Eventually the subject retrieved all of these items without further opportunity to study them. In one case as many as eight recall failures occurred between the first recall and final mastery. Clearly, these recall failures represent failures to retrieve the item; the item must have been in memory, because eventually it was retrieved and learned without being shown again. Thus, the problem of recall learning is not only one of storing an item in memory, but of storing it in such a way that it can be retrieved, given its proper retrieval cue.

How retrieval cues work has been investigated in an experiment by Tulving and Pearlstone (1966). They constructed nine categorized word lists which differed in length (12, 24, and 48 words) and in the number of words per category (1, 2, and 4). Items in each category were grouped together and each group of items was preceded by its category name. The lists were read to subjects and subjects were told to memorize the words, except for the category names that did not need to be memorized. For the recall test half of the subjects were asked to write as many words as they could remember on a blank sheet of paper, while the other half of the subjects were given a recall sheet with all of the category names printed on it. Afterwards, a second recall attempt was made, for which all subjects were given recall cues. The results were clearcut: the cues greatly facilitated recall. As an illustration we shall use here the results of the 48-item list which consisted of 12 categories of 4 words each. With cues subjects recalled about 30 words. Without cues recall was only 20 words. However, when the subjects who received no recall cues on the first test were given recall cues on their second attempt, they could retrieve about 28 items. These additional items were clearly "there," but the subjects needed some help before they could find them. In this context it is interesting to note that merely forcing the subject to recall more items is of little use. Cofer (1967) reported some experiments in which subjects were given 15-word lists to recall. If they could not recall all words they were told that so-and-so many words were missing and to write down additional words as well as they could to fill up the list. Cofer's subjects performed rather poorly in this forced recall.

The improved recall in Tulving and Pearlstone's cue-condition was entirely due to better category recall. For instance, for the 48-4 condition subjects on the average recalled words from 11.4 categories when they were given the cues, but only from 7.3 categories when they were not. However, if at least one word from a category was recalled a constant proportion of the remaining words was recalled. The mean number of words recalled per category was 2.61 for the cue-condition, and 2.65 for the no-cue condition. These data are, of course, in complete agreement with the results of Cohen (1966) which were discussed earlier, and imply that there are two rather different processes in recall. One has to do with the accessibility of higher-order memory units, categories in this case; the other deals with the retrieval of items within these higher-order units. The latter process seems to be largely independent of the experimental variables that were manipulated in the studies discussed here.

Psychoanalysts have long known that one way to retrieve a person's repressed experiences is through the use of free associations. Free associations may also be used to recover otherwise unavailable memories in laboratory experiments, as has been demonstrated in a long series of studies going back about 40 years. We shall briefly outline a recent report by Haber and Erdelyi (1967) which included better controls than earlier studies. A fairly complex picture was shown briefly and the subjects were asked to recall its contents immediately. Some prompting was used to make sure that subjects reported everything they knew about the picture. The subjects in the experimental condition were asked to give free associations to the picture for 35 minutes. Subjects in the control group played darts during this time. A second recall trial concluded the experiment. The recall protocols (the subjects drew pictures together with identifying labels) were rated as to their overall correspondence to the original picture. In immediate recall there were no significant differences between the reproductions of the experimental and control groups. However, after free associations subjects were able to recall significantly more details and came closer to the theme of the picture than on their first recall trial, while subjects in the control group could not improve their scores. This result was not merely a consequence of a tendency on the part of the experimental subjects to add highly probable but unperceived detail, or of indiscriminate embellishment as a result of the free associations. A second control group excluded that possibility: subjects in this group were never shown the original pictures at all, but instead were given the first drawing of a yoked subject in the experimental group. Otherwise these subjects were treated exactly like experimental subjects. No significant change in the recall scores following free associations occurred for these control subjects. Therefore Haber and Erdelyi concluded that free associations alone are ineffective; but if something has been perceived more is stored in memory than the subject can retrieve under ordinary circumstances, and free associations can help the subject to recover initially unavailable material.

## ENCODING SPECIFICITY

The studies reviewed above point to the importance of processes occurring at the time of retrieval. When subjects are given retrieval cues they can recall things that they could not otherwise. However, what happens at the time of storage is equally important. Retrieval presupposes storage: a retrieval cue will only help if the material had been organized appropriately at the time of storage. Tulving and Osler (1968) have demonstrated this important point. Their subjects recalled 24-word lists. During presentation the words were shown either alone or together with a retrieval cue which was a weak associate of the to be learned word. With these two training conditions two methods of testing were combined factorially: half of the subjects were given the retrieval cues and half were not. The results of the experiment were quite unambiguous: Retrieval cues facilitated free recall if and only if they were present both at the time of storage and at the time of recall. Cues present only at the time of storage or only at the time of recall did not improve performance; if anything they resulted in somewhat lower scores.

Tulving and Thomson (1973) have provided some dramatic demonstrations of the specificity of encoding. They arranged situations in such a way that subjects had a good retrieval cue which enabled them to recall the test item, but without which they failed to recognize the test item. Schematically, their experiment comprised four phases. In the study phase, subjects were shown a series of word pairs such as *ground* COLD. They were told to remember the capitalized word, but also to look at the accompanying cue because it might help them to remember the test word. The second phase of the experiment was a free-association test. Subjects were asked to free associate to stimulus words selected so as to maximize the likelihood that the to-be-remembered words from the study phase would be generated as responses. For instance, if subjects were asked to free associate to the stimulus word *hot,* the to-be-remembered word COLD was frequently given as an associate. The third phase of the experiment was a recognition test in which each subject was asked to circle among the associates they had just produced all the words that were to-be-remembered items from the earlier list. Subjects did very poorly on this recognition test: only 24% of the to-be-remembered words were recognized! In contrast to this poor recognition performance when subjects were given a cued recall test during the last phase of the experiment, performance was quite good. When given the cue *ground,* subjects recalled COLD 63% of the time! Thus, with its proper retrieval cue, subjects could recall COLD quite well, while on the preceding recognition test they frequently failed to recognize the same word.

On the basis of these data and the earlier results of Tulving and Osler (1968), Tulving has formulated the "encoding specificity principle." The principle states "that a retrieval cue can provide access to information available about an event in the memory store if and only if it has been stored as part of the specific memory trace of the event" (Tulving and Thomson, 1973, p. 16). Thus, given the retrieval cue *ground,* which was stored as part of the memory trace of COLD, subjects could recall COLD very well; but they often could not recognize in the COLD they produced as a response on the free association test the same COLD that had appeared on the study list. It must be assumed that somewhat different attributes of COLD were stored in memory on the two occasions (those associated with *ground-cold* in one case and those associated with *hot-cold* in the other), so that the pattern matching process upon which recognition is based frequently was led astray.

Watkins and Tulving (1975) have shown that the results reported above are quite robust: essentially identical results are obtained even if the recognition test involves an experimenter-prepared list, rather than the subject's own associations, or if a forced-choice recognition test is used rather than yes-no decision. However, others (e.g., Postman, 1975; Reder, Anderson and Bjork, 1974) have questioned the generality of the phenomenon and argued that the retrieval system, just like the encoding process, is flexible and adaptable. If the right retrieval route is blocked, a detour will be tried; if the right cue is unavailable, various search strategies may be used to recover the target item. At the time of this writing it is not clear whether the encoding specificity principle is as general and inviolable as Tulving believes or whether there are other means of accessing a memory trace in the absence of a specific retrieval cue, or what these means might be. It is clear, however, that specificity of encoding is a very important determinant of retrieval.

The encoding specificity principle was formulated in the context of cued recall experiments, using a paired-associate procedure. It is not clear how it applies to free recall, but assuming that it is indeed a general principle, the theoretical consequences are far-reaching. The encoding specificity principle rules out a whole class of explanations of memory retrieval, the so-called tagging models (e.g., Anderson and Bower, 1972; Bahrick, 1970, Kintsch, 1970). What these models set out to explain is why it is so much easier to recall a well-organized list than an unorganized one. Tagging models start with the observation that "learning a list" really does not mean that one learns the words of the list; the subject already knows the words; all he does is learn that these particular words were presented together as the to-be-remembered experimental list. Saying that the subject already knows a word means that the subject has stored in his memory the corresponding word concept (e.g., a set of attributes that in some sense defines the word—we shall have more to say about the nature of word concepts in Section 5.5.) Tagging models assume that for each word in the to-be-learned list the subject puts a familiarity or list tag on the corresponding word concept that is stored in his memory. Retrieval is understood as a generation-recognition process: the subject implicitly generates various word concepts and looks for the right list tag. If a word is tagged, it is overtly recalled; if not, it is rejected and the memory search continues. The virtue of this theory is that it explains why organized lists are recalled better than random lists. Saying that a list is organized means that the corresponding word concepts are interrelated in memory. Thus what is tagged in free-recall learning is an interrelated structure. Upon retrieval, the search process is guided by this preexisting memory structure and is thus able to locate the list items. The tag is detected and recall occurs. On the other hand, with an unorganized list, the search process does not have the guidance of a preexisting memory structure, never contacts some list items, and hence no recall can occur.

The trouble with such tagging models is that they violate the encoding specificity principle. If learning in a typical free-recall experiment consists of associating a list tag with a word concept already stored in memory, then it is not easy to see why this list tag is not detected independent of context. Specifically, suppose the word is COLD. In memory (we shall call this part of memory "semantic memory") there is a word concept COLD, that is part of a complex system of interrelations: for instance, it stands in an antonym relationship to another concept HOT, and in an associative relationship with such concepts as ICE, DRINK, and GROUND. If COLD receives a list tag in one context, it should be possible to detect that tag in another context because the same semantic memory node COLD is accessed in both cases. The findings of Tulving and Thomson (1973) show that this is not necessarily the case, and hence contradict the model.

Recall learning is not simply a process of tagging semantic concept nodes. Rather, we should liken it to a process of establishing new, context dependent memory traces. Given the word COLD in the context of GROUND, the learner selects a set of attributes from the semantic concept COLD, emphasizing its relationship with GROUND, and forms a new context specific memory trace. Given the stimulus word COLD in the context of HOT, a somewhat different memory trace will be formed. Although both are related to the semantic concept COLD (in both contexts the subject understood the meaning of the word COLD), they are not necessarily directly related to each other. Hence given one memory trace, the information associated with the other does not automatically become available.

## 5.3.2   CONTROL PROCESSES

Suppose a subject has learned a list of animal names, and then learns a second list consisting of names of cities. When the experimenter asks him to recall the first list, the subject will do so without giving any intrusions from the second list. We say that the subject has a set for recalling animal names and therefore avoids inappropriate intrusions. Experimental investigations of the concept of set have frequently been reported in association experiments, reaction time experiments, and in studies of problem solving and thinking, but in the area of memory they have been rare.

Müller (1913) believed that the role of set in memory can be explained in purely associative terms. The task establishes a set or constellation that favors one association over the other. The general constellation determines the particular constellation: a cue like "large" may evoke "elephant" in the context of animal names, but it will evoke something like "Los Angeles" in the context of city names.

Bühler (1908) pointed out that semantic meaning is often a more powerful determinant of retrieval than association by contiguity. In remembering sentences the particular words in which a sentence was expressed are easily lost while the meaning of the sentence is still retained. Subjects often can reproduce the meaning of a sentence correctly without using the words employed in the previous formulation of the sentence. There is of course no reason to suppose that association by contiguity and meaning mutually exclude each other as regulators of the reproductive process. What seems to be important are the instructions that a subject receives. The subject normally obeys the instructions the experimenter gives him and searches his memory along whatever lines are indicated. Thus, he may try to remember the meaning of a sentence, or he may try to recall the particular words which were used to form the sentence. Ach (1910) has introduced the term "determining tendency" to designate the control which instructions and task characteristics exert over a subject's behavior. If a subject in a typical memory experiment has learned a list of paired-associates, like DUS-NEF, and is then given the stimulus terms of the pairs, he is set to reproduce the corresponding response members. However, the experimenter may change the determining tendency that controls the subject's behavior by giving him different instructions. Suppose the experimenter asks the subject to reverse the consonants in each syllable as it is presented instead of reproducing the associated syllable. Thus the proper response for the stimulus DUS would be SUD, rather than NEF. Obviously subjects will be able to comply with such instructions, even after strong associations between DUS and NEF have been formed. It is not the strongest association that occurs in a given situation, but that response which is appropriate to the subject's set.

An experimental investigation of set was undertaken by Ach (1910). Ach not only demonstrated the importance of determining tendencies but also suggested an operation to measure their strength. One of his subjects was taught three sequences of eight nonsense syllables. The first sequence consisted of unrelated syllables; the second sequence was constructed so that all even members of the sequence rhymed with the preceding odd syllables; in the third sequence the even items were obtained by inverting the consonants of the preceding syllables. These three sequences were presented 70 times each, distributed over 6 days, thereby insuring that the subject had learned them very well. On days 7 to 14 only the odd numbers of the sequence were shown and the subject was asked either to reproduce the first word coming to his mind in response to each syllable, or to invert the syllable, or to find a rhyme for it. Different tasks were given on separate days. A number of new syllables were also included in the test period. The basic measure of the experiment was the subject's reaction time. Median reaction times are shown in Table 5.5, together with the percent correct reactions. Apart from the fact that the activity of inverting was obviously much easier than rhyming, both with respect to speed of reaction and correctness, Ach manages to demonstrate his point: when the association acquired during the 6 days of training agrees with the determining tendency established by the instruction, errors are rare and reactions are fast. When the response set and the previous association disagree, errors occur more frequently and the reaction times become longer. Responses to new syllables tend to have a rather long reaction time, but were always correct.

Both Ach's experimental methodology and his theoretical concepts have been subject to criticism. Lewin (1917) objected to Ach's use of association as a baseline in his experiments. Rightfully, Lewin argued that there is nothing automatic about the tendency to reproduce the response member of a syllable pair when the stimulus syllable is presented, but that the subject is simply behaving under the control of the experimental instructions to associate, just as he does when the instructions are to rhyme, or to invert. The tendency to associate is therefore just as much a set as other response sets are. Nevertheless, this tendency has a peculiar characteristic that makes it particularly interesting: the experimenter can vary the strength of an association very easily by controlling the number of learning trials.

A deeper reason for the neglect of the concept of determining tendency or set by experimental psychologists in recent years lies in the vagueness and inherent difficulty of the concept. What is a

TABLE 5.5.  **Median Reaction Times in Seconds and Percent Correct Reaction; Subject A (after Ach, 1910)**

| Task | Construction of the Four-Syllable Pairs: | | | |
| | Rhymed | Inverted | Unrelated | New series |
|---|---|---|---|---|
| Reproduce | .87 | .77 | .88 | 1.08 |
| Rhyme | .78 | .89 | 1.13 | 1.05 |
| | (83%) | (25%) | (75%) | (100%) |
| Invert | .80 | .66 | .84 | .83 |
| | (50%) | (100%) | (92%) | (100%) |

tendency? What do we mean when we say that there is a tendency to respond with THREAD, PIN, and SHARP to the stimulus word NEEDLE, other than that these words frequently occur as responses to NEEDLE? Does an airplane have a tendency to fly with the utmost possible speed and noise? Problems like these are responsible for the preference of many experimental psychologists to regard the concept of determining tendency (or set) as a rather loose analogy, which should best be avoided. However, there is really nothing mysterious about the determining tendency. It plays in human behavior very much the same role as an executive program does in the operation of a computer. It performs essentially a message switching and control function. Depending on the high-level goals and policies of the organism it controls the input that the organism receives, and calls up the appropriate subroutines for processing it. "Calling up a subroutine" is computer language, and merely another language, but one that helps to understand the functioning of determining tendencies. Depending on task characteristics, instructions, and motivation a subject predetermines his response. For instance, the memory system associated with the concept ANIMAL may be searched, rather than CITIES. Or, the subject instructs himself to rhyme by making those areas of his memory accessible in which his previous experiences with the activity of rhyming are stored.

The concept of control processes plays a significant role in present theories of memory (e.g., Atkinson and Shiffrin, 1968). Obviously, there are limits on how effective a subject's control is over his memory system. We know, for instance, that subjects perform very well on the first trial of a short-term memory experiment, but that proactive inhibition builds up quickly, and performance deteriorates. If subjects had complete control over their memory processes, they could avoid the build-up of proactive inhibition: there is no need to retain in memory anything at all about the earlier trials in the typical short-term memory experiment, and the perfect subject should simply erase from memory all information about past trials, and hence would not suffer any proactive interference. As we know, subjects are unable to do that. On the other hand, explicit cues to forget, given right after the presentation of an item, are quite effective in this respect. Bjork and others have shown that under certain conditions subjects can be directed to forget (e.g., Bjork, 1972) and such directions can negate the build-up of proactive inhibition. Consider the following paired-associate experiment. Nonsense syllables were paired with words, and after each list a single probe test was given. After some items, a forget cue was presented by changing the color of the stimulus display from green to yellow. Subjects were instructed that those items that turned yellow needed not to be remembered. Subjects could follow these instructions very well, so that forget-items behaved as if they had never been presented in terms of their effect upon the to-be-remembered items of the list. Specifically, forget-items did not produce proactive inhibition, as is shown in Figure 5.12. Performance on items that were preceded by forget-items only was the same as performance on items that were not preceded by other items at all. In both cases performance was substantially better than for items that were preceded by other to-be-remembered items, which suffered from the effects of proactive interference. (Performance on all items in Figure 5.12 decreases as a function of the number of items intervening between the presentation of an item and its test—in other words, there are retroactive interference effects).

What happens when a subject is told to forget an item? Does he erase it from his memory? Apparently not, because Bjork (1972) reports a number of findings that contradict an erasure hypothesis.

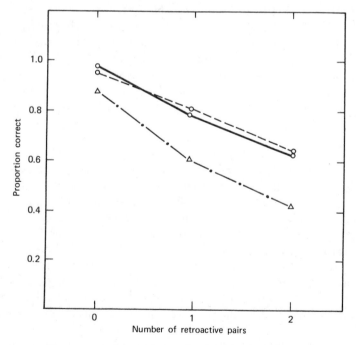

FIGURE 5.12 **Proactive and retroactive interference for pairs preceded by one or two to-be-remembered items (triangles), one or two to be forgotten items (open circles), and pairs not preceded by other items (black circles). (after Bjork, 1972)**

For instance, if an item is cued to forget, and the subject is later given a recall test for both the to-be-remembered and the to-be-forgotten items, his recall is quite poor (except while the to-be-forgotten item is still in short-term memory). However, the subject still can recognize forget-items as well as remember-items! Thus, a memory trace for the forget-items must still have existed in memory, though it could not be retrieved. Bjork argues that subjects use two control processes in this task: first, they stop all rehearsal of forget items; second, they differentially group the to-be-remembered items and the to-be-forgotten items in memory. Only the former are rehearsed and organized, and can therefore be retrieved later. For the forget-items, only an unelaborated memory trace is formed that is just sufficient for recognition.

## MNEMONICS

Memory can be vastly improved by applying some of the principles discussed in the previous sections to the task of memorizing. Rules of learning that improve recall are called mnemonics, or mnemonic devices. Some of these are simple to use and follow in a straightforward manner from the general principles of memory; others are exceedingly complex and are mastered only by a few memory artists. They help us to realize how fragmentary our understanding of memory still is and how much mnemonics are still an art rather than a science.

If one wants to improve performance on memory span tests the obvious mnemonic is chunking. For instance, if one is asked to remember a series of digits, one can try to remember them in chunks of fours, e.g., by treating each quadruplet as a "year." This trick improves memory span somewhat over the usual range of five to nine digits, but only in unusual people (Hunt and Love, 1972), or with an unusual amount of effort (Miller, 1956) is the improvement a large one.

If the to-be-remembered material consists of a list of items that are well organized, the order of presentation significantly affects memory. Bower, Clark, Lesgold, and Winzenz (1969) have shown that for the right kind of materials hierarchical organization schemes can be highly effective. Their learning list consisted of 112 words organized into four hierarchies. An example for one of their word hierarchies is shown in Table 5.6. In the control condition (random—all words) the 112 words were presented in random order for four trials. In the

TABLE 5.6    **The Hierarchy for "Minerals" from the List of Bower** *et al.* **(1969)**

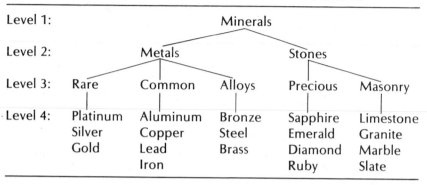

| Level 1: | | | Minerals | | |
|---|---|---|---|---|---|
| Level 2: | | Metals | | Stones | |
| Level 3: | Rare | Common | Alloys | Precious | Masonry |
| Level 4: | Platinum | Aluminum | Bronze | Sapphire | Limestone |
| | Silver | Copper | Steel | Emerald | Granite |
| | Gold | Lead | Brass | Diamond | Marble |
| | | Iron | | Ruby | Slate |

experimental group only the level 1 and 2 words were shown on the first study trial. On the second study trial these subjects received the level 1, 2, and 3 words, and only on the last two trials were all words presented. Thus, subjects first learned the superordinate category labels before studying the category members. Note that the level 4 words (there were 74 of them) were shown four times in the control group, but only twice in the experimental group. A second control group (random-progressive) received the same number of words on each study trial as the experimental group, but these words were randomly selected from the total word pool. The average number of level 4 words recalled per trial is shown in Figure 5.13. Obviously, teaching the subjects how to organize a list first by presenting a hierarchy of category labels into which later items may be fitted is much more effective than merely showing the items themselves. We may conclude, therefore, that in free recall the optimum presentation schedule is one that maximizes the probability that the subject utilizes whatever objective organization or structure exists in the learning list.

Atkinson (1975) investigated an interesting mnemonic device in paired-associate learning called the key-word method. His problem was to teach college students the vocabulary of a foreign language in the best possible way. The key-word strategy turned out to be of considerable help. It involves associating the sound of a foreign word with that of an English word, and then constructing an image relating the key word and the English translation. For instance, in Russian *zdanie* is the word for *building;* when pronounced it has some similarities with the English word *dawn.* Subjects were told to form the acoustic link *zdanie-dawn,* and then form an image relating *dawn* and *building,* for instance a large building with many windows glowing pink in the first dawn. Interestingly, Atkinson obtained his best results when he gave subjects the key word together with the Russian word, but let the subjects generate their own images. The use of imagery was crucial in this method; just a sentence relating the two words instead of an image, e.g., "The building glows in the pink dawn," was not nearly as effective.

Frequently the problem in memorizing is to remember the material in the right order. Peg word systems are frequently used mnemonics for this case. Suppose a subject is first taught the rhyme: "One is a bun; two is a shoe; three is a tree; four is a door; five is a hive; six are sticks; seven is heaven; eight is a gate; nine is a line; ten is a hen." This rhyme can be very helpful in remembering up to ten words in their correct order. For instance, given a list starting with *piano, dog, shell,* the learner associates the first word with *bun* (perhaps by imagining a piano squashed by a giant bun), the second with *shoe* (a dog tearing up a shoe), the third with *tree* (shells growing on a tree), and so on for the remainder of the list. During recall the peg words are recited, and the words associated with them are thereby retrieved in the correct order.

On a much grander scale, this method has been used widely by orators in classical antiquity. It was known as the method of *loci,* or the method of places (Yates, 1966). Orators in classical Rome and Greece were called upon daily to perform what we would consider today pro-

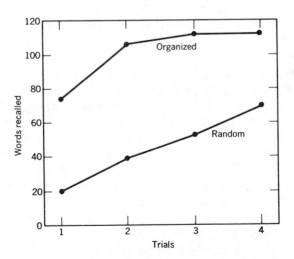

FIGURE 5.13  **Mean number of words recalled from a 112-word list as a function of ordered, hierarchical presentation or random presentation. (after Bower, et al., 1969)**

digious feats of memory. Lacking paper to write notes on, speeches for all occasions had to be given from memory. In the ancient schools of rhetoric orators were specifically trained in the "art of memory." This training is very interesting because it was based on rather profound insights about the nature of memory. First the orator was told to provide himself with a system for serial organization. Specifically, he was asked to visit a large house with many and varied rooms and to walk through it in a particular order. In each room a few easily discriminated objects were noted, also in a particular order: a windowsill, an arch, or a statue. The rooms and the objects in the room were committed to memory through much exercise until the whole series was mastered completely, forward, backward, and from any arbitrary starting point. When something was to be memorized the orator went in his mind through his house, depositing at each place an image constructed from the to-be-learned material. Upon recall, he revisited in his mind the places in the house in their proper order, retrieving from each the image which had been left there. The fixed sequence of places prevented him from forgetting his position in the sequence.

It was considered absolutely necessary that images be constructed from the learning material, because the Greeks knew that images could be retained much better than words or sentences. The more concrete, the more vivid, and the more affective these images were, the better. Indeed, the orator was advised to choose his "places" carefully; the light there should be neither too dim nor too glaring, so that it would not distract from the clarity of the images that were to be deposited (for modern research with this method see Wollen, Weber, & Lowry, 1972).

What we have discussed so far are applications of reasonably well understood psychological principles to memorization (though in most cases the techniques greatly anteceded the principles). There are, however, occasional individuals with incredibly good memories, or incredibly good memorization strategies, whose performance still baffles the scientist. On a few occasions such cases have been studied extensively by well-qualified scientists. The most famous such case was S., who was observed systematically by the Russian psychologist Luria for almost 30 years (Luria, 1968). When S. was given a 13 × 4 matrix of digits, he could recite it without errors after studying it for 3 minutes. He recited it equally well by columns, rows, in reverse order, by diagonals, or by making one long 52-digit number out of it. He had an image in his mind from which he could read the numbers at will.

Other memory artists who perform similar feats (e.g., Hunt and Love, 1972) do not work with imagery, but remember each row of the matrix as a date and then remember what they did on that date! S., however, was entirely dependent on imagery. When told the word *elephant*, he saw a *zoo;* when he heard *America*, he saw an *Uncle Sam*. In addition to imagery, S. possessed a marked degree of synesthesia: sounds for him spontaneously gave rise to visual sensations. As a three-year-old boy he recited the words of Hebrew prayers that he did not understand, each word appearing to him as a little puff. When a person said something, he saw the words as well as a color for the tone of his voice.

S.'s memory was by no means an unmixed blessing for him. S. was not very intelligent. On first impression he appeared dull and disorganized. If he listened to a story, sometimes he would become confused: each word called up images, they collided with each other, and he could no longer understand what was said in the resulting chaos. He could not think abstractly: "I can only understand what I can visualize." He could not tell what was important and what was a trivial detail that should be forgotten rather than remembered, which made it hard for him to function in daily life. His imagination was so powerful that he sometimes confused his images with reality, as when he did not want to get up in the morning as a little school boy and continued to "see" the clock hand point to 7:30 until his mother found him at 9 o'clock.

## SEMANTIC MEMORY

When a subject in a psychological experiment learns to recall a list of words, he is not learning the words themselves. He already knows the words. What he is learning is merely that these particular words were shown to him by the experimenter at a certain time and in a certain place. That is, most experiments on memory study memory for personal experiences, as distinguished from the acquisition of knowledge, which is impersonal. That a particular word means what it does, or that $7 \times 4 = 28$ are items of knowledge rather than personal memories—we no longer know under what conditions or when this knowledge was acquired, nor does it matter.

Tulving (1972) used the terms episodic and semantic memory for this distinction. Episodic memory, according to Tulving, receives and stores spatially and temporally marked information about episodes or events. Episodic memory always has an autobiographical reference: "it happended to me" is always implied, and when and how it happened is often as important as what it was.

Semantic memory is the organized store of knowledge that a person possesses, about the world as well as about language and its use. As such it includes rules or programs for actions or operations. It is generative in the sense that it permits retrieval of information that was never stored in it, but is the product of inferences (e.g., the fact that Napoleon had 10 toes). Semantic memory is necessary for the use of language. Indeed, it is necessary for storing information in episodic memory—words need to be understood, materials need to be organized, which presupposes an interaction between knowledge and perceptual experience. What we experience is always in part determined by our knowledge; on the other hand, knowledge is either totally or largely a product of our experience. Hence the two systems of episodic and semantic memory interact, and it is not always entirely clear where one ends and the other begins. Nevertheless, the distinction is a very useful one—if for no other reason than to point out that psychologists, surprisingly, have concentrated their research efforts almost entirely on the study of episodic memory. No wonder we find it difficult to develop a technology of education: schools are concerned with the acquisition of knowledge, not with the episodic memory that has been studied in our laboratories!

Even now most studies that deal with semantic memory are not concerned with the acquisition of knowledge—how personal experiences, through processes of abstraction and generalization, turn into general items of knowledge, and how they are integrated into the existing knowledge structure. Instead, they are concerned with retrieval from semantic memory.

Various aspects of the retrieval process have been subjected to psychological study. Psychologists have been most interested in drawing inferences about the structure of semantic memory from observations of the speed with which people can retrieve familiar facts (Section 5.5.1). A related problem concerns the manner in which the names of semantic concepts are stored as part of our total knowledge of the concept. Rather frequently it happens that one can remember a concept without immediately recalling its name: the name is on the tip of the tongue but can't be produced. Brown and McNeill (1966) were the first to investigate this phenomenon experimentally. It is familiar to everyone from his own experience: a word of which one has knowledge cannot be recalled. The evidence of knowledge is either an eventual successful recall or prompt recognition if the word is provided by some other means. If a word that a subject has not been able to recall is given to him, the subject often recognizes the word without any additional training. In the same vein, if a wrong word is given to the subject, he is frequently able to reject it, and may even be able to tell how similar it is to the target word. Brown and McNeill have shown that when complete recall is impossible but is felt to be imminent the subject can often recall the general type of the word, its meaning, its sound pattern, or the correct number of syllables. They did this by reading dictionary definitions of relatively uncommon words to a large number of subjects and asking them to provide the corresponding word. By this means they elicited several hundred instances of the tip of the tongue phenomenon. Whenever such an instance occurred the subject wrote down all words he believed to be similar in sound or meaning to the target word and also guessed the number of syllables in the target word and its initial letter. Unambiguous evidence for partial recall was obtained. Subjects could indeed recall the first letter, or the number of syllables of a word which was on the "tip-of-the-tongue."

This finding is important. It implies that words are not recalled as units, but as a bundle of different aspects which are only loosely tied together, such as general meaning, sound pattern, first letter, etc. When a sufficient number of aspects are retrieved the word is reconstructed. In the tip-to-the-tongue phenomenon the pronunciation of the word is missing: the subject knows what he is searching for but he cannot find access to the necessary phonetic information to produce the word. The phonetic information must exist somewhere in his memory because he will recognize the correct word immediately if it is presented; however, for some reason which is not yet understood it is temporarily inaccessible.

Semantic knowledge, in this case word knowledge, appears therefore to be functionally similar to epidosic memory traces: both may be represented as a set of features or attributes. Retrieval in the case of episodic memory traces is governed by the principle of encoding specificity (Section 5.3.1); only those features will retrieve an episodic memory code that have in fact been stored as part of it. Retrieval from semantic memory is much more flexible, though perhaps only because the encoding is necessarily much richer in the case of knowledge than episodes. Each person's semantic memory may be compared to a complex structure. How retrievable items are in that structure depends on their relationships to other items in the structure. The nature of this structure has interested psychologists a great deal during the last few years.

## 5.5.1   SEMANTIC STRUCTURES

In 1969 Collins and Quillian suggested that semantic memory was organized as a hierarchical network, and at the same time proposed an experimental technique to investigate this network. Figure 5.14 shows a tiny excerpt from a semantic memory organized according to their model. The structure is basically a noun hierarchy: the nodes *asparagus, carrot, parsley,* are all connected to the superset node *vegetable,* which in turn is connected (together with *grass, tree,* and others) to the superset *plant.* Properties are stored in an economical way, that is at the highest possible node. Thus the property *is edible* is stored with *vegetables* rather than directly with *asparagus* or *parsley.*

Collins and Quillian assumed that retrieval from semantic memory consists in searching such networks along the available pathways. Suppose subjects are asked to verify the sentence *Parsley is a plant;* they would need to make a connection between *plant* and *parsley* via the *vegetable* node. Hence this is called a level 2 sentence. On the other hand, *A carrot is a vegetable* would be a level 1 sentence, because a direct connection exists between the two components of the sentence. *A carrot is a carrot* is a level 0 sentence, since it merely involves an identity match. Likewise, an example of a level 0 property sentence would be *Asparagus has scalelike leaves,* which merely involves a look-up of a property stored at the *asparagus* node. *Carrots are edible,* on the other hand, first requires a connection between the nodes *carrot* and *vegetable* (level 1), while *Parsley has seeds* involves a double connection between *parsley* and *plant,* via the vegetable node (level 2). If one assumes that moving up and down in this hierarchy

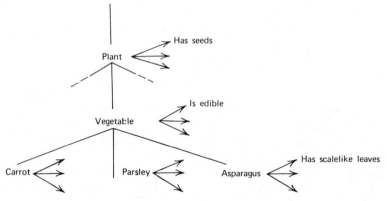

**FIGURE 5.14   Portion of a semantic network according to Collins and Quillian (1969).**

requires time, a number of predictions can be made regarding the time it should take to verify the sentences described above. Verification times should increase the farther apart in the hierarchy the subject and predicate of the test sentences are.

In Collins and Quillian's experiment subjects were given a large number of sentences of levels 0, 1, and 2, both set-inclusion statements and property statements. The subjects' task was simply to verify each sentence as fast as they could by pressing appropriate response buttons. False sentences were of course also included in this experiment. The results of their study showed verification times to increase as a function of level (Figure 5.15). Traversing each node added about 75 milliseconds to the verification time. In addition, property sentences took longer than superset sentences, indicating that extra time was needed to retrieve a property from a noun node.

Collins and Quillian constructed the noun hierarchy upon which their experiment was based by intuition. Later investigators showed that Collins and Quillian's levels were confounded with other variables, notably sentence frequency. Wilkins (1971) showed that when category norms were used to determine the conjoint frequency of subject and predicate, reaction times were faster for the more frequent sentences. For instance, *robin* is a high-frequency response in the category *bird* in the Battig and Montague (1969) norms, while *goose* is a low-frequency response in that category. Correspondingly, it takes subjects less time to respond "true" to *A robin is a bird* than to *A goose is a bird*. Conrad (1972) obtained similar results. She had subjects generate descriptions of words and selected from these descriptions high- and low-frequency statements. Statements of different levels were included among these tests sentences. Her results replicated Collins and Quillian in that she, too, found a levels effect, but she could show that this levels effect was confounded with sentence frequency. Higher-level sentences were less frequent (people just don't say very often *Carrot is a plant*), and hence subjects took longer to verify such sentences.

These results seriously question the interpretation of the Collins and Quillian results as the effect of levels: Wilkins showed that nouns within the same category vary widely in accessibility, and Conrad has shown that high-frequency sentences are verified faster than low-frequency sentences, independent of level. Finally, Rips, Shoben, and Smith (1973) reported an experiment that made the original Collins and Quillian (1969) model entirely untenable. Rips et al. used 12 bird names in the sentence frames (*X is a bird* and *X is an animal*), 12 names of mammals in the frames (*X is a mammal, X is an animal*) and 12

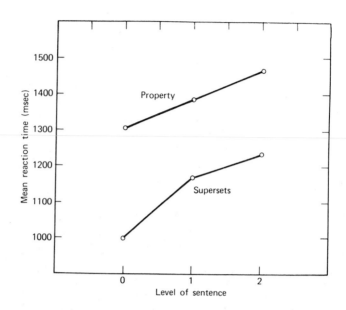

FIGURE 5.15    **Reaction times to verify superset and property sentences as a function of the level of the sentence in the semantic hierarchy. (after Collins and Qullian, 1969)**

names of cars in the frames (*X is a car, X is a vehicle*). Large within category differences in verification times were obtained. Subjects decided very quickly that *cows* were *mammals,* but needed 200 milliseconds longer to determine that *pigs* were *mammals.* More importantly, in some of the sentences the levels effect was reversed: while *bird* was always faster than *animal,* and *car* almost always faster than *vehicle,* deciding that *X is a mammal* took subjects 88 milliseconds longer than deciding that *X is an animal*! Level obviously did not predict verification time in this case. Instead, Rips et al. could show that their data are reasonably well predicted by ratings of the semantic distance between the words. Subjects simply were given the word pairs *cow-mammal, whale-mammal,* etc., and asked to rate their semantic distance. For *cow-mammal* this distance is small, since *cow* is almost the prototypical *mammal; whales,* on the other hand, are rather less typical and the rated distance is large. These distance ratings correlated $r = .63$ with the obtained verification times.

That semantic distance rather than level in a hierarchy is the important variable has also been demonstrated in a number of other experiments using different experimental tasks. Schaeffer and Wallace (1969) showed subjects two words and asked them to decide as quickly as they could whether the two words belonged to the same semantic category. Given the stimulus pair *lion-tulip* the subjects would respond "yes" because both were members of the category *living things*. Reaction times in this task depended on how similar the words were semantically, that is, on semantic distance: for semantically similar word pairs, such as *lion-zebra* reaction times were faster than for semantically distant word pairs, such as *lion-tulip*. Semantic distance affects reaction times even when all subjects have to do is to decide whether two letter strings presented to them are both words or not: if the words were related in their meaning, such decisions could be made more rapidly than for unrelated words. In this situation subjects were not even required to evaluate semantic distance—all they had to do was determine whether something was a word or not; nevertheless, semantic distance effects were observed (Meyer and Schvaneveldt, 1971). Finally, a study using a restricted association paradigm should be mentioned, in which semantic distance was one of several variables that were investigated. Loftus and Suppes (1972) gave subjects a category name together with a restricting letter and required them to produce an instance of that category that began with the given letter. For example, a proper response for *vegetable—a* might be *asparagus*. Semantic distance in this experiment was defined operationally as category dominance, as in the Wilkins (1971) study; responses to the category name in the Battig and Montague (1969) norms were ranked in terms of their frequency, and the rank of each response was used as the dominance measure (for instance, *asparagus* is the most frequent response to the category name *vegetable*). In addition to dominance, Loftus and Suppes investigated 11 other structural variables in their experiment. Of these, dominance, which may be considered a measure of semantic distance, was one of three variables that proved to be a good predictor of reaction times. The other two variables were childhood frequency measures: frequency of the stimulus category in children's vocabularies, and frequency of the most likely response in children's vocabularies. These three variables together accounted for 61% of the production time variance.

For true sentences, reaction times are faster the more closely related the subjects and predicates are. The opposite is the case for false sentences, as was demonstrated in several studies, e.g., Rips et al. (1973), and Kintsch and Crothers (1974). In both of these studies semantic distance for false sentences was manipulated by violating the animate-inanimate distinction. For instance, the distance between *robin-mammal* is smaller (and the reaction time to say "false" to *A robin is a mammal* is larger) than between *robin-car* (and, correspondingly, subjects say "false" more rapidly to *A robin is a car*).

Summarizing the empirical results discussed above, we see that semantic distance plays an important role in various reaction time tasks involving sentence verification, same-different judgments, and restricted associations. A common component of all of these tasks is retrieval of word pairs from semantic memory. Semantic distance effects are obtained for both positive and negative cases. Positive judgments are facilitated if the concepts are closely related semantically. Negative judgements are easiest when the concepts are semantically unrelated. Semantic distance has been defined in various ways in these studies: as steps separating concepts in a hierarchy, category dominance, definitional frequency, associative relationships, rated distance, or by the experimenter's intuitions. As yet, we have no satisfactory theory of semantic distance and no way of telling which of these definitions of semantic distance is the best one. We know that for some domains (e.g., *animal names*; see Rips et al., 1973) semantic distances can be scaled in a multidimensional Euclidean space, but this is certainly impossible for the semantic system as a whole. Nevertheless, at an empirical level the generalization that semantic distance is a crucial variable in these experiments can be offered with confidence.

What this all means for the Collins and Quillian (1969) hierarchical model of semantic memory is that the model is much too simple and much too logical to capture the semantic relationships as they exist in the memory system. Hierarchical structures may very well be important in semantic memory, but not everything that can be organized in that way is, in fact, so organized. In other words, efficiency of storage is not the overriding consideration in semantic memory. There is a trade-off between storage efficiency and the amount of computation necessary in a memory system. It is certainly much neater to store only once the fact that *Plants have seeds,* than to store it separately with each *flower, tree, grass,* etc. However, given the statement *Sunflowers have seeds,* we must then go through a whole chain of inferences (from *sunflower* to *flower,* from *flower* to *plant*) before we can verify this sentence. Thus, storage efficiency is paid for with extra computations. Whether the trade is worthwhile depends on the relative costs of storage space and computations in the system. Collins and Quillian's mistake was that they thought only in terms of storage efficiency and disregarded the cost of computations. It may very well be more efficient to store frequently used facts directly with each concept node, even though they could be inferred. Thus, *Sunflowers have seeds* may very well be stored at the *sunflower* node (that is, it would be part of the definition of the concept *sunflower*), rather than inferring it every time one makes use of this relationship. On the other hand, *Carrots have seeds* for anyone except a gardener is a fact rarely used and it may very well have to be inferred in the manner Collins and Quillian hypothesized.

An alternative to Collins and Quillian's network model is a feature model of semantic memory. Proposed by several authors, the feature model has been developed most fully by Rips et al. (1973) and Smith, Shoben, and Rips (1974). Feature models assume that a concept is represented in semantic memory by a set of features. The semantic distance between two concepts is given by the amount of overlap in the corresponding feature sets. A sentence of the form *A (instance) is a (category)* is evaluated, according to this model, in a two-stage process. The first stage consists in computing the semantic distance between subject and predicate, that is in calculating the overlap in the two feature sets. If the two sets overlap very much or not at all, that is, if semantic distance is either very small or very large, a response is made without further processing. Thus, sentences that are strongly related are accepted quickly, and sentences that are quite unrelated are rejected quickly. If the semantic distance is intermediate, further processing occurs. This processing requires time, and hence true sentences that are not closely related semantically, as well as false sentences that are related semantically, are verified relatively slowly. There is some controversy about exactly what this second-stage processing involves. In the model of Smith et al. (1974), the second-stage processing is restricted to a comparison of a subset of the features sets in question: only if the "defining" features of the two concepts agree will a positive response occur; if the concepts are related only in accidental ways (e.g., *A cup is a coffee*), the sentence will be rejected as false. On the other hand, Kintsch (1974) has argued that this is too static a view of memory and that the second-stage processing is essentially one of inference making For some of these inferences, the model of Collins and Quillian (1969) applies: presumably the sentence *Napoleon had toes* is verified via the inference chain *Napoleon was a man, A man has toes.* Semantic memory certainly includes a set of inference rules; exactly what these are and how they are applied is today one of the major unsolved problems in the field of cognitive psychology.

Note that the two-stage model described above for the retrieval of information from semantic memory bears a close similarity to the model for retrieval from episodic memory discussed in Section 4.3. This model (Atkinson and Juola, 1974; also Wescourt and Atkinson,

1976) assumes that recognition in episodic memory is a two-stage process: in the first stage, a decision is made on the basis of an item's familiarity value: a positive recognition response occurs if this value is very high, a negative response occurs if it is very low, and the decision is delayed for further processing if the familiarity value is intermediate. The second-stage processing consists in searching memory and attempting to recall the item. Only if this attempt is successful will the item be accepted. The present model is functionally similar: a semantic distance judgment replaces the familiarity judgment, and an inference process rather than a memory search constitutes the second stage of the process. The conception of memory in terms of feature sets applies equally to both episodic and semantic memory. This kind of convergence of models is highly desirable and holds the promise that eventually a unified theory of memory will be possible.

## 5.5.2    FUZZY CATEGORIES

We have seen in such studies as Wilkins (1971) and Rips et al. (1973) that considerable differences may exist among the members of the same conceptual category: *carrots* and *parsley* are both called *vegetables,* but subjects take less time to verify *Carrots are a vegetable* than *Parsley is a vegetable.* Indeed, some people will argue that *parsley* should not be considered a member of the category *vegetable* at all. This points out a very important fact about natural categories: most of them are not well defined, but are basically fuzzy in nature; class membership is a matter of degree. When do we classify someone as a "University of Colorado student"? We don't go to the dean's office and look up whether he is enrolled; instead we make our classification on the basis of fuzzy criteria: mostly location (on or near the campus), behavior (goes to class), but also age and dress. Each of these criteria is unreliable. If they are all satisfied, we have the typical, ideal CU student: the prototype for this class. The farther a given person deviates from this prototype, the less willing we are to classify him as a class member. Lakoff (1973) has pointed out that there are linguistic devices called hedges to indicate degree of class membership. John may be a *regular* CU student, meaning that he possesses most of the characteristics of a typical student. On the other hand, someone may say that *loosely speaking,* John is a CU student, meaning probably that although John acts like a student, he is not really a member of that class (just as one can say that loosely speaking, a whale is a fish). If John is in fact enrolled as a student but has not left the ski slopes for weeks, there is another way to indicate this kind of marginal category membership: John is *technically* a CU student.

Lakoff's point was that one cannot understand the meaning of such hedges unless category membership is considered to be a matter of degree rather than all or none. A number of psychological studies by Rosch (e.g., Rosch, 1973) provides further evidence for this claim. Rosch showed that natural categories, both perceptual and conceptual, are defined only ambiguously by typical members, and that various degrees of category membership exist. In one of her experiments Rosch asked subjects to rank category members as to their degree of category membership. Subjects agreed rather well among each other. For the category *birds,* Rosch's subjects named *robin* and *eagle* as most typical, *chicken* and *ducks* as less typical, while *penguins* were considered as marginal cases, and *bats* hardly as birds at all. For *vegetables, carrots* and *asparagus* were considered to be typical class members, *parsley* or *pickle* as peripheral members. Rosch showed that these ratings are important in that they predict how well subjects can operate with the concepts involved. If subjects in a standard concept identification experiment (see Section 7.1) are given sets of typical category instances to discriminate, they learn much faster than when the categories are composed of marginal category members. Learning rates directly reflect the degree of category membership.

Semantic categories are not like well-defined mathematical sets, but are inherently fuzzy. Inferences people make, therefore, must be fuzzy. A whole new formal discipline, fuzzy set theory, has been developed to deal with fuzzy categories, mostly by engineers who deal with human-like, that is, fuzzy, systems (Zadeh, Fu, Tanaka, and Shimura, 1975). What does it mean to say that Hans is *very* kind, that *X* and *Y* are *approximately* equal, or to tell a subject to place a mark *far* to the right of a line? Clearly, all of these cases involve fuzzy categories and fuzzy operations. As yet very little work has been done by psychologists on these important problems.

Semantic memory, thus, is not a clean, logical structure but a rather messy one, with a great deal of flexibility. Concepts in semantic memory are not precisely defined, but instead their use is indicated in a loose way. We have frequently claimed that concepts are represented in memory by a set of features, or attributes. These are not, however, defining features, in the way a mathematician might use them ("*X* is the set of all elements *x* such that *x* has the property $f(x)$"); Rather, they must be considered as more or less reliable indicators that a certain classification is appropriate. Labov (1973) suggests that the concept *cup* is characterized by a set of 10 features: (1) concrete,

(2) inanimate, (3) upwardly concave, (4) is a container, (5) has a handle, (6) made of earthenware or similar material, (7) set on top of saucer, (8) used for consumption of food, (9) which is liquid, (10) and hot. However, none of these features is really critical; one or the other feature may be missing and people still call an object a "cup." Furthermore, when something is called a cup is strongly context dependent. Labov demonstrated both these points in a series of ingenious experiments. First, he made drawings of a large number of objects that were distortions of a prototypical coffee cup: he systematically varied the width-depth ratio in the drawings, deleted the handle or added a second handle, and changed the shape in various ways. Then he gave this set of drawings to subjects with the instructions to name each drawing. This naming was done in four context conditions: in a neutral context without further instructions; in the "coffee" context, where subjects were told to imagine that someone was holding the object in his hand, adding sugar and stirring it with a spoon, and drinking coffee from it; in the "potato" context, where subjects were told to imagine the object on the dinner table, filled with mashed potatoes; and finally in the "flower" context, where subjects imagined the object sitting on a shelf filled with cut flowers. The data were scored simply according to whether the subject used the word *cup* in naming the object (even if he said "a funny cup," or a "cup with a long stem"). Figure 5.16 shows the results for five of these objects. Note first of all that the category "cup" is fuzzy: there are no discrete boundary lines that separate objects that are always (or almost always) called *cup* and objects that are never (or almost never) called *cup*. Secondly, what is called a cup is context dependent. Object 1 is a typical cup, and it is called so in all contexts. Objects 2 and 3, however are called *cup* in the coffee context and out of context, but not when they contain mashed potatoes or flowers. Object 4 is sort of a cup in the coffee context, but not at all in the potatoes and flower context. Finally, Object 20 is rarely called a cup, even if someone drinks coffee out of it.

Features interact. If an object has the property "used to drink coffee from," people are ready to forgive odd shapes, or the lack of a handle. On the other hand, if the object contains a bunch of roses, it is only classified as a cup if its shape is just right. Similarly, a dot on top of the letter *i* is just a dot; the same dot, however, becomes an eye if it is put into the context of the drawing of a face. The features that characterize (*not* define!) a concept are always only potential features. Which features will be activated at any given time depends on the context. Therefore, which features are stored in memory will be

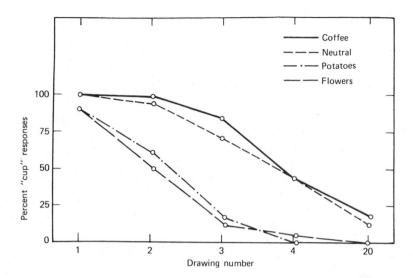

**FIGURE 5.16  Percent of subjects calling a drawing a "cup" in four different contexts. The results are shown for five different drawings (out of 20 used in the experiment). (after Labov, 1973)**

equally context dependent. We already know that if a subject sees the word *jam* in the context of *strawberry*, he will recognize it only poorly in the context of *traffic* (Section 1.4). However, *jam* is a homonym, that is, it is a word with two distinct meanings, and one does not need to invoke the fuzziness of semantic memory to account for this result. Similar results are obtained, however, with words that have only one meaning. Particular aspects of words can be made salient by the context in which the word is presented. Barclay, Bransford, Franks, McCarrell, and Nitsch (1974) had subjects study sentences like *The man lifted the piano* or *The man tuned the piano*. Later, two kinds of recall cues were provided: either *Pianos are heavy* or *Pianos make nice sounds*; the subjects' task was to recall the predicate of the study sentences (i.e., either *lifted* or *tuned*). Depending on which form of the study sentence subjects had received, one or the other of these cues was appropriate. Appropriate cues led to significantly better recall (80%) than inappropriate cues (61%). Similar results were obtained by Anderson and Ortony (1975) who found that *appliance* was a very good recall cue for the sentence *Television sets need expert repairman*, while for the sentence *Television sets look nice in a family room* the best recall cue was *furniture*. Clearly both *appliance* and *furniture* are potential features of *television set*, but which of these features is activated and stored in memory depends on context. According to the principle of encoding specificity (Section 5.3.1) only retrieval cues actually stored with the to-be-recalled word are effective; The results of Barclay et al. (1974) and Anderson and Ortony (1975) follow.

The philosopher Wittgenstein (1953) has been the foremost proponent of the view of semantic memory as a flexible, context dependent system. He maintained that natural concepts are not "defined" in any strict sense. Semantic memory merely indicates how to use a concept; it does not specify it precisely. Concepts used in different contexts are never quite the same, but bear only a "family resemblance" to each other. Modern psychology agrees with Wittgenstein, but has barely begun to elucidate the mechanisms by which context modulates meaning.

## 5.6    THEORETICAL CONSIDERATIONS

A single, generally accepted, well-formulated theory of memory does not exist today. There is, however, considerable agreement among students of memory about what the essential ingredients are from which such a theory should be constructed. Four issues appear to be crucial in this respect: the short- and long-term memory distinction; the episodic-semantic memory distinction; encoding and organization; and retrieval. I shall briefly review these concepts here, not with the intent of formulating a theory of memory, nor to add new information to what has been said in the previous pages, but simply to clarify some general points that might have been submerged in the welter of experimental results presented.

The distinction between short- and long-term memory as two separate stores is somewhat misleading. This box model of memory characterized theories of memory in the 1960s, but today the view prevails that there is only one memory store rather than two (or three, if one includes sensory memory). Nevertheless, the concept of short-term memory is still a valuable one. It is used very much in the Jamesian sense: as that part of the memory which is momentarily activated, accessible, and conscious. In this view, which was elaborated in Chapters 3 to 5, cognitive processes are limited, on the one hand, by what is available, that is, stored in memory. On the other hand, the central processing system itself is limited in its resources. Keeping things active in short-term memory requires some of these central processing resources. Therefore, how much can be retained in short-term memory depends on the resources that can be devoted to this task. Sometimes the term working memory is used to refer to the totality of cognitive processing, most of which is unconscious; working memory is therefore a much broader term than short-term memory. However, it does not appear to be very useful to introduce a new kind of "memory," when all that is meant with it is cognitive processing.

Although the distinction between episodic and semantic memory is a handy one, we shall emphasize again that one must not think of it in terms of two separate memory stores. All it means is that some memory traces are particular, personal experiences with time and place tags, while others are impersonal and generalized in nature. Clearly, the latter must somehow derive from the former, and there must be intermediate stages between them. However, as yet psychologists have done very little research on the acquisition of knowledge, that is, semantic memory. More work has been done on retrieval from semantic memory, and it is noteworthy that the models for retrieval from semantic memory are formally similar to models for retrieval from episodic memory, in spite of some important differences (e.g., the role of inferences in knowledge retrieval). Indeed, some theorists prefer not to make a distinction at all between semantic and episodic memory, but explain all knowledge on the basis of particular experiences (e.g., Anderson and Bower, 1973).

At the same time as psychologists stopped thinking of memory in terms of stores into which "information" is put, and became less interested in the nature of the material that was to be learned, they turned their attention to the processes involved in remembering: encoding and retrieval. Increasingly, the to-be-remembered item has ceased to be regarded as a unit but rather as a set of features or attributes. An important problem for research has become the encoding of such attribute sets. Stimulus sampling theory (see Chapter 2) was an obvious precursor of this view. The first memory model of this type was proposed in 1967 by Bower. Later, a number of investigators have helped to develop this viewpoint (e.g., Underwood, 1969; several of the papers in Norman, 1970, and Melton and Martin, 1972; Kintsch, 1974; Tulving and Watkins, 1975). There is still disagreement about the nature of attributes (are all attributes abstract descriptions—as in Anderson & Bower, 1973—or do we admit imagery attributes as in Section 5.1.4) and about the precise mechanism of the encoding process. On the other hand, many psychologists agree that the depth and richness of encoding is the primary determinant of how well something will be remembered; furthermore that the encoding process is highly context dependent (Craik and Tulving, 1975; Jenkins, 1974). Organization, that is, the elaboration of interrelationships among items, is regarded as an especially important form of encoding (e.g., the papers in Tulving and Donaldson, 1972).

Together with the emphasis on encoding processes we have witnessed an intensified study of retrieval processes. The encoding specificity principle of Tulving and Thomson (1973) expresses the context dependence of encoding and retrieval: retrieval is successful only in so far as the context of encoding can be reinstated. Models of the retrieval process in recall have to be modified to account for this insight (e.g., Anderson and Bower, 1972). Kintsch (1974) has suggested that a process of pattern-completion may be basic to retrieval: the pattern of the retrieval cue (i.e., the specific set of stimulus attributes characterizing the retrieval cue) must match a part of the pattern stored in memory; this memory code contains not only the attributes corresponding to the retrieval cue but also those corresponding to the to-be-recalled item. Hence the process is one of pattern completion and the cue is able to retrieve the to-be-recalled item (see also Horowitz and Prytulak, 1969, on redintegrative memory). The retrieval processes in recognition, on the other hand, are simpler by comparison: a process of pattern matching involving the attribute set corresponding to the test stimulus and that corresponding to the memory code appears to be basic to recognition. However, if the match is inconclusive, additional processing occurs (Atkinson and Juola, 1974). Such a model describes not only data from standard recognition experiments, but also reaction times in memory scanning experiments, and, with some modifications, the verification times in experiments concerned with retrieval from semantic memory.

Many models of memory have been mentioned here but no unified theory. This is characteristic of the state of affairs in the field of memory today (see also Murdock, 1974). However, this does not mean that the field lacks a consistent viewpoint: the emphasis on encoding and retrieval processes is what gives memory research its unity. Memory and its complement, forgetting, are explained by the interaction of these processes.

# 6

# language comprehension and memory

The development of psycholinguistics. Chomsky's generative grammar and the competence-performance distinction. The modern emphasis on meaning and language use. Interdependence of the work in cognitive psychology, linguistics, and artificial intelligence.

The material discussed in this chapter could have been worked into
the three earlier ones, because basically we are again dealing with
how people encode and retrieve information. The topics that we have
studied there will appear again: attention and short-term memory,
levels of processing, and organization. However, it is pedagogically
useful to treat list learning research and research employing sentences
and texts in separate chapters, partly as an orientation aide to the
reader, partly because there are some new aspects emerging with the
latter types of materials that are lacking or are present only in rudimentary form in list learning research. The structure of sentences and
texts is much more complex than that of word lists; before, the most
tightly organized material that we dealt with was a list containing
words from several semantic categories; now we want to ask how
people comprehend and remember typical passages of English text.

The experimental study of memory started with Ebbinghaus' decision to avoid the structural complexities of meaningful materials
through the use of neutral verbal materials: the nonsense syllable.
That was in 1885; gradually, psychologists began to move away from
this position, first from nonsense syllable lists to word lists, then in
more recent years from word lists to lists of unrelated sentences. At
present, there are indications that the movement will not stop there,
and that the sentence lists will eventually be abandoned for natural,
that is, coherent, texts. This movement away from the Ebbinghaus
tradition is motivated by the growing insight that the nonsense syllable
does not simplify the psychologist's work, but makes it more difficult:

the less meaningful the material the less predictable the manner in which the subject will encode it (and hence how he will remember it). Words make better experimental materials for the psychologist, sentences are better than words, and texts better than sentences, because the more complex the material the more constraints are imposed on the encoding process. If we know the structure of a text we can predict much better what a subject will do with it than with, say, a word list that has little or no organization. Thus, modern cognitive psychology may eventually reverse Ebbinghaus' order of preference.

The crux of this argument is, of course, that we need to know the structure of sentences or texts; Ebbinghaus did not, and that is why he chose the nonsense syllable. Today, our knowledge is still a long way from adequate, but progress has been made, and psychologists need no longer abstain from the study of natural language materials.

The original impetus in this area came from linguistics, from Chomsky's generative grammar movement. Chomsky (1957, 1965) revolutionized linguistics by developing a new type of grammar, a generative rather than merely a descriptive grammar. A generative grammar consists of an ordered set of rules that can be applied to generate all grammatical sentences in a language (and no ungrammatical sentence). Some simple examples of such rules will be described below; here it suffices to note how much this notion of generating sentences by a system of rules appealed to psychologists. True, Chomsky did not talk about the psychological processes in sentence generation. He specifically distinguished between the processes involved in sentence generation, which he considered to be outside the domain of linguistics, and the idealized linguistic competence of a speaker. Chomsky's theory was a theory of competence, not a process theory. Competence, according to Chomsky, is unaffected by grammatically irrelevant conditions such as memory limitations, the speaker's interest and motivation, attention, shifts of attention or distractions, or errors in applying knowledge. In other words, Chomsky effectively isolated his theory from the real world. Actual performance, he maintained, reflects competence only in indirect ways; knowing the linguistic rules to generate a sentence does not necessarily tell us anything about how an actual speaker generates a sentence. In spite of these warnings, psychologists were intrigued and set out to determine whether the rules linguists talked about had any psychological reality. This was the origin of modern psycholinguistics. At first, psychologists were subservient to linguists: the latter provided the ideas and the psychologists went to their laboratories to test them. Much of this work in the 1960s was done essentially without any contact with traditional experimental psychology. As we shall see, all of this has changed in the last few years. Chomsky's theories no longer dominate linguistics. As in any successful revolution, the second stage has destroyed the first one. Chomsky's almost exclusive concern with syntax has been replaced by an interest in the meaning of texts, that is, semantics, and in the communicative function of messages in their situational contexts, that is, pragmatics. The competence-performance distinction has become untenable along the way, and many linguists today realize that one cannot talk about language without taking into account a person's intentions, beliefs, short-term memory, or how he uses his knowledge. At the same time, psycholinguistics have moved back into the mainstream of human experimental psychology (not without rechanneling it in the process). Its methods have been broadened, and its theories have matured and become more independent of the linguistic tutelage. Psychologists, linguists, and computer scientists interested in artificial intelligence today work side by side on the common problem of understanding language behavior. Each has his own methods and his special problems, but their progress is increasingly interdependent.

## SYNTACTIC AND SEMANTIC ISSUES

The earliest experiments on the role of grammar in verbal learning simply attempted to demonstrate that grammatically organized material is easier to learn and to perceive than material without this organization. Two examples will suffice. In Miller and Isard (1963) and Marks and Miller (1964) five-word sentences were constructed as follows: (a) grammatical sentences (e.g., "pink bouquets emit fragrant odors"); (b) semantically anomalous sentences in which the syntactic structure was retained but the meaning destroyed (e.g., "pink accidents cause sleeping storms"); and (c) ungrammatical strings (e.g., "around accidents country honey the shoot") for the first experiment (1963). For the later experiment (1964) there were two final groups: (d) anagram strings, the original grammatical sentences with scrambled word order in which the semantic components were retained but the syntactic structure was destroyed (e.g., "bouquets pink odors fragrant emit"); and (e) word lists in which both the semantic and the syntactic components were destroyed (e.g., "accidents pink storms sleeping cause"). The first experiment (1963) was a perception task in which the sentences were presented over noise. The second experiment was a learning task. The results confirmed the prediction that disruption of semantic and syntactic rules would hinder learning and perception. The anagram strings and semantically anomolous strings had fewer errors than the strings with both disrupted syntax and meaning (i.e., the word lists). In the learning experiment (1964) certain characteristic errors occurred; most errors in the semantically anomalous strings were of a semantic nature (intrusions, i.e., misplacing words from one string to another), while the anagram strings were characterized by syntactic errors (inversions, i.e., incorrect word order, and morpheme errors, i.e., omitting or supplying wrong affixes). The authors concluded that both syntactic and semantic rules are involved in language processes and must be taken into account.

These studies, like the many others that have been described in these pages, show that greater redundancy, that is, greater organization, facilitate recall. The special interest in language materials arises because with such materials it is meaningful to inquire as to exactly what the nature of this organization is. Hence syntactic, that is, grammatical organization shall be our first concern.

## 6.1.1 SYNTACTIC CHUNKING

Generative grammarians following Chomsky (1957, 1965) distinguish two types of syntactic rules that are involved in the generation of sentences. These are *phrase structure rules* and *transformational rules.* Phrase structure rules chunk sentences into phrases and subphrases and explicate the relationships among these phrases. Consider, for example, the sentence *The tall boy saved the dying woman.* It consists of a noun phrase *The tall boy* and a verb phrase *saved the dying woman;* the latter includes another noun phrase, namely *the dying woman.* Both noun phrases in this sentence have the same structure: they consist of the definite article *the,* a modifier (*tall* or *dying*), and a noun (*boy* or *woman*). Sentences such as *The bad wolf ate the little lamb* have identical phrase structures, and we shall indicate below how one can write a system of rules to generate sentences of that type.

In addition to phrase structure relations we shall be concerned with transformational relations among sentences. Consider, for instance, the sentence triplet *The tall boy saved the dying woman, The dying woman was saved,* and *Did the tall boy save the dying woman?* Clearly these are related syntactically, although their phrase structures are quite different. The relationship here is a transformational one. If one assumes that there is an abstract underlying phrase structure common to all three sentences (Chomsky calls it the *deep structure* of the sentence), we can think of the first sentence being derived from that deep structure via an active affirmative transformation, the second via a passive transformation (including agent deletion), and the third via a question transformation. According to Chomsky (1965), phrase structure rules generate deep structures, and transformational rules then produce the actual verbal expressions.

Obviously this account of generative grammar is greatly oversimplified, but for our purposes we need only a very general idea of the principles involved so that we can understand the psychological work based on them. First, we want to look at the role that phrase structure rules play in language comprehension and memory.

Phrase structure rules are rewriting rules. Starting with the initial symbol $S$, phrase structure rules elaborate $S$ in terms of an intermediate vocabulary (which consists of terms such as noun phrase, verb, preposition, and the like) and specify how English words as the terminal symbols of the system can be substituted once the desired phrase structure of a sentence has been developed. For instance, the first rule used in both examples in Figure 6.1 is (*i*) $S \rightarrow NP$ (noun phrase) plus $VP$ (verb phrase). The noun phrase itself can then be broken down into determiner plus modifier plus noun by rules ii and v or, in Example b, into noun phrase plus prepositional phrase by iii. The rules which introduce the terminal vocabulary are of the form (ix) $D \rightarrow the$, (x) $N \rightarrow boy$ / *woman* / *house* / *street,* etc. The examples given are clearly oversimplified; for instance, we have not shown how the past tense of the verb in (a) is obtained, and similarly the progressive form of the verb in (b), but they suffice to illustrate how phrase structure rules work. In the present context it is most important to realize that phrase structure rules quite naturally organize a sequence of words into groups or chunks. For instance, sentence a is divided into two parts: ((*The* (*tall*(*boy*))) (*saved*(*the*(*dying*(*woman*)))))); sentence b has major breaks after *house* as well as after *street.*

The way phrase structure rules divide a sentence into chunks determines, in part, both the initial perception of a sentence and memory for it. In studies by Ladefoged and Broadbent (1960) and Fodor and Bever (1965), subjects listened to sentences with superimposed auditory clicks. They were then asked to indicate where the clicks occurred in each sentence. The prediction was that subjects would tend to hear the noise not where it actually occurred but in such a way that it would not interrupt a perceptual unit, hence

(i)    $S \rightarrow NP + VP$

(ii)   $NP \rightarrow D + MN$

(iii)  $NP \rightarrow NP + PrepP$

(iv)   $NP \rightarrow D + N$

(v)    $MN \rightarrow M + N$

(vi)   $PrepP \rightarrow Prep + NP$

(vii)  $VP \rightarrow V_1 + NP$

(viii) $VP \rightarrow AUX + V_2$

(ix)   $D \rightarrow the$

(x)    $N \rightarrow boy/woman/house/street$

(xi)   $M \rightarrow tall/dying$

(xii)  $V_1 \rightarrow saved$

(xiii) $V_2 \rightarrow burning$

(xiv)  $AUX \rightarrow is$

(xv)   $Prep \rightarrow across$

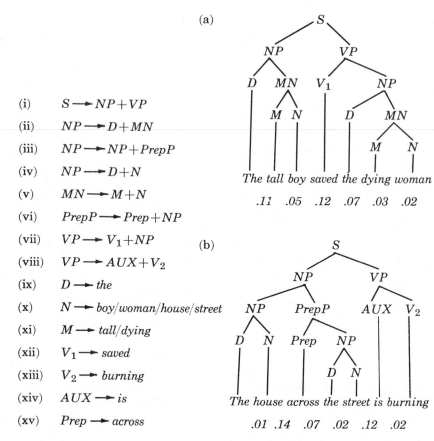

FIGURE 6.1  **A fragment of the rules for a generative grammar of English and phrase structure trees for two sentences which can be produced by these rules; below each sentence are shown the transition errors obtained in the recall experiment of Johnson (1965, see page 309).**

between the boundaries marking off these units. The magnitude of errors in displacing the clicks could then be used as a measure of the size of the perceptual unit. The results of both experiments indicated that subjects were processing more than one word at a time. In addition, Fodor and Bever found that significantly more click displacement occurred at major syntactic boundaries than within segments, thus providing evidence for the hypothesis that the perceptual units correspond to the segments marked off by formal phrase structure analysis. In a follow-up experiment, Garrett, Bever and Fodor (1966) showed that this effect did not depend on acoustic correlates of the phrase structure of a sentence. For instance, consider the following sentences in which the common part can be made acoustically identical by using the same tape recording in both cases:

(a) (*In her* hope of marrying) (Anna was surely impractical)

(b) (*Your* hope of marrying Anna) (was surely impractical).

By placing the same acoustical material into a different linguistic context the major syntactic break can be made to occur either before or after *Anna*. Clicks which coincided with *Anna* appeared to subjects displaced either before or after *Anna,* depending on the location of the syntactic break. Since the two passages were acoustically identical, this displacement cannot depend wholly on the intonation and stress pattern of the sentence, but implies that in some sense the subject reconstitutes the phrase structure of a sentence to which he is listening.

There are some interesting limitations on when this phenomenon occurs. First of all, the data are complicated by a prior-entry bias for expected clicks: in general, expected stimuli are always perceived sooner than unexpected ones, so that the clicks tend to be heard earlier than the corresponding words. In addition, there are a number of studies in which clicks showed no tendency to move into the phrase boundaries at all, which puzzled experimenters for a while until Seitz and Weber (1974) showed that whether or not click migration into phrase boundaries will be observed depends on the response requirement in the experiment. If subjects listen to a sentence and then write it out, marking the syllable when they heard the click, the Fodor and Bever results are obtained. However, if subjects are given a prepared script on which to mark where they heard the click, they are quite accurate and unbiased. Giving them the sentence apparently eliminates for them the need to process it, and hence no phrase structure effects are obtained. Only when subjects have to remember the sentence, at least long enough to write it down, is the perception of the click biased by the phrase structure of the sentence.

Phrase structure also determines chunking in short-term memory. Subjects appear to hold the current phrase in short-term memory, quickly getting rid of it when the next phrase arrives. Moreover, memory for the current phrase is always verbatim, in contrast to previous phrases. A study of Jarvella (1971) illustrates these points. Jarvella used the same test sentence, but by embedding it into different contexts he established different syntactic boundaries for it. For instance, suppose subjects hear the following texts:

*The confidence of Kofach was not unfounded. To stack the meeting for McDonald, the union had even brought in outsiders.* (A)

*Kofach had been persuaded by the international to stack the meeting for McDonald. The union had even brought in outsiders.* (B) The last two phrases are identical in these texts, but different syntactic groupings are achieved by means of the context sentence. Right after listening to these sentences, subjects were asked to recall them word-for-word. The results are shown in Figure 6.2. For B-type sentences, recall was essentially perfect for the last seven words, which formed a separate sentence, while the previous sentence was recalled much less well. This pattern is quite different for the A-type sentences: there, the last phrase was recalled almost perfectly, but the middle phrase which is part of the same sentence was also recalled quite well; in contrast, recall was again very poor for the first sentence. Thus, the contents of short-term memory in these tasks were largely determined by the phrase structure of the sentences in this experiment.

When subjects are asked to memorize sentences they use the natural grouping provided by the sentence structure for chunking. When they recall the sentences, they make most errors at the chunk, that is, the phrase boundaries. Johnson (1965) was the first to notice

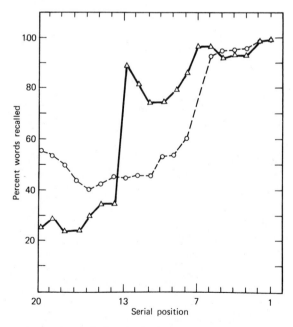

FIGURE 6.2   **Percent words recalled verbatim for type A and B sentences (triangles—A, circles—B). (after Jarvella, 1971).**

this phenomenon. He reasoned that material within a chunk should be relatively coherent and there should be a tendency to recall chunks as a whole. Errors should be most likely in the transition from one chunk to the next, hence at the major syntactical breaks. Johnson's subjects learned sentences such as (a) and (b) in Figure 6.1 as responses in a paired-associate experiment in which the stimulus terms were digits. The results of principal interest are the conditional error probabilities in learning the sentences which are also shown in Figure 6.1. Given that the first word of a sentence was recalled correctly, the probability of making an error in recalling the second word (*tall*) was .11; given the correct recall of *tall*, the probability of not recalling *boy* was .05, etc. The probability of a transition error was highest at the major grammatical subdivisions in both sentences, in agreement with the experimental hypothesis.

The relatively high error probability for the first transition in sentence (a) shows that learning does not depend solely on syntactic structure. There is no large syntactic break between *the* and *tall,* but the high error rate here is understandable if one considers the meaning of the sentence. The meaningful core of the sentence is clearly something like *Boy saves dying woman.* The word *tall* is not very closely related to the main theme of the sentence and hence it is not remembered as well as it should be.

Not only are there other nonsyntactic factors that determine how subjects group the words of a sentence (we shall discuss many more of these below), subjects often do not chunk sentences at all. It is only when they are trying to remember the words of the sentence that phrase structure grouping is employed. We have already seen that if the memory requirement is eliminated from the click location task, no syntactic biases are observed. Similarly, if there is no memory requirement subjects do not seem to pay much attention to phrase boundaries in reading. Aaronson and Scarborough (1976) gave subjects sentences to read one word at a time and recorded the time subjects took to read each word. When subjects had to remember the sentence, they took disproportionately more time with the last word of each phrase; presumably this time was spent in grouping the words together to form a chunk. In addition, the more phrases accumulated in reading the sentence, the more reading time was required at the phrase boundaries; presumably, late in a sentence subjects not only had to worry about chunking the current phrase, but also about relating it to the preceding sequence of phrases. However, none of these effects were observed when subjects read the sentences with instructions merely to comprehend rather than to remember them. Syntactic structure did not affect reading time at all. However, the semantics of the sentence did: in the comprehension condition subjects spent more time reading those words that were crucial in determining the meaning of the sentence, without much concern about the syntax (which in their sentences was fairly uncomplicated anyway).

We can therefore conclude that phrase structure rules are often important in determining how subjects encode a sentence. Basically, such rules provide subjects with a convenient guide for organizing sentential materials. However, it is not at all the case that sentence processing always involves chunking according to the phrase structure: only if subjects are trying to remember the words of the sentence will they resort to this strategy. With different task demands syntactic processing is much less important.


## 6.1.2   THE DERIVATIONAL THEORY OF COMPLEXITY

So far we have only been concerned with psychological processes that mirror linguistic phrase structure rules. Transformational rules have also been investigated in the psycholinguistic laboratory. The hypothesis was tested that the processes involved in sentence comprehension directly reflect the transformations of generative grammar; the more transformations in the derivation of a sentence from its deep structure, the greater the processing difficulty. This hypothesis was named the derivational complexity hypothesis. Although some early experiments appeared to support it, the derivational complexity hypothesis is no longer tenable today. Nevertheless, it was an important episode in the early history of psycholinguistics that helped a great deal to clarify the relationship between psychology and linguistics. For this reason it is quite instructive to take a brief look at what happened.

Early psycholinguists tended to look for the psychological reality of linguistic rules. Chomsky had described the role of transformational rules in linguistic theory, so psychologists set out to demonstrate transformational operations in sentence comprehension. A typical experiment is by Miller and McKean (1964). These authors gave subjects a sentence, asked them to transform that sentence grammatically (e.g., transform an affirmative sentence into a passive, a negative into a negative-passive, a passive-question into an affirmative, etc.), and then locate the transformed sentence on a list of sentences. How much time subjects needed to find a particular sentence was the dependent variable. Their results were encouraging. They found that the transformations they investigated (affirmative, negative, passive, and question) required different amounts of time, and that multiple transformations were additive. For instance, a negative-passive transformation took about as much time as a negative transformation alone plus a passive transformation alone. Concretely, this means that the time it takes to transform the sentence *The boy hit the girl* into *The girl wasn't hit by the boy* can be predicted from the time it takes to transform *The boy hit the girl* into *The boy didn't hit the girl,* plus the time it takes to transform *The boy hit the girl* into *The girl was hit by the boy.*

Later experiments confirmed and extended these findings. Subjects were given a list of study sentences and were then given a recognition test containing these sentences, various transformations thereof, and unrelated control sentences (e.g., Clifton and Odom, 1966). While control sentences were falsely recognized only 3% of the time, transformed sentences produced false alarm rates between 17 and 85%. Moreover, a modified version of Miller and McKean's additive model accounted for the data quite well. The same pattern of results was also obtained from similarity ratings of transformationally related sentence pairs.

The derivational theory of complexity was further supported by some memory data reported by Savin and Perchonock (1965). Their study is based on the capacity limitations of short-term memory. They proposed to measure the amount of memory storage taken up by a given sentence type by seeing how much material a subject could remember in addition to the sentences. If the syntactic features are encoded separately, then each should occupy a characteristic amount of space. The sentences used were in the form of simple active sentences and ten transformations: passive, negative, question, negative-question, emphatic (E) (e.g., "the boy DID hit the ball"), negative-passive, passive-question, passive-negative-question, emphatic-passive and wh-question (wh) (e.g., "who has hit the ball?"). The subject was given a sentence followed by a string of words and was then asked to recall the sentence verbatim and as many of the words as possible. It was predicted that sentences with more transformations would be more difficult to remember and, hence, fewer words would be recalled after them. The results showed this to be the case: significantly more words were retained after simple active sentences than after any of the other versions and likewise more words were recalled after single-step transformations than after the more complex ones (i.e., N > NP; P > NP, PQ, PQN, EP; Q > PQ; E > EP; also QN > PQN). No predictions were made about·the relative difficulty of the individual single-step transformations. An additive relationship was found in the more complex transformations whose distance from the simple active sentence could be computed from additive combinations of the distance A-E, A-P, A-N, A-Q and A-QN. This, then, would seem to indicate that the various transformations do occupy a characteristic amount of space in the short-term memory dependent on their relative complexity, which in turn agrees with the hypothesis that transformations are stored independently from the content of the sentence. The authors point out that the length of the sentence in number of words was not a factor since neither the Q transformation nor the E transformation lengthens the sentence; yet both increased the difficulty of remembering the sentence.

In spite of such impressive experimental support, the derivational complexity hypothesis is generally considered disproven today. There are both logical and empirical difficulties. First of all, the predictions that psychologists derived from linguistic theory are incorrect because they do not take into account the full complexity of the theory. Chomsky's transformational rules must be applied in a certain order (otherwise ungrammatical sentences are derived). Psychologists have simplified the theory by neglecting this requirement—with the result that their predictions are quite different from those actually derivable from Chomsky's theory. Fodor, Bever, and Garrett (1974) showed that if derivational complexity is computed correctly, it does not predict data such as Miller and McKean's (1964) at all. As if this were not enough, Fodor, Bever, and Garrett also reviewed a series of experiments and thought-experiments that clearly contradict the derivational complexity hypothesis at an empirical level. This point is simply that transformations do not necessarily result in greater psychological complexity. *Fred phoned the girl up* is not more complex psychologically (as measured in a Savin and Perchonock type task) than *Fred phoned up the girl,* though the former is transformationally more complex because it has undergone the transformation of particle movement. *Fred runs faster than the girl* is in fact easier to perceive than *Fred runs faster than the girl runs,* from which it is derived by a deletion transformation. Whether passives are more complex than actives depends entirely on the semantics of the sentence: reversible passives like *The boy was chased by the dog* are difficult, but nonreversible passives such as *The steak was eaten by the dog* are no harder than simple active sentences. *The dog which was big chased the boy who was little* is transformationally closer to the deep structure of that sentence than *The big dog chased the little boy,* but surely the latter sentence must be easier to comprehend and remember. Fodor, Bever, and Garrett cite other such examples that clearly indicate that sentence comprehension must be quite unlike a process of running off linguistic transformations in reverse order. Whatever the fate of transformational rules will be in linguistic theory, psychologists must develop an understanding of the process of sentence comprehension that is quite independent of the formal syntactical rules of linguistics. Clearly, linguistic complexity is not directly related to processing difficulty; the comprehender is not a transformational grammarian in disguise.

## SENTENCE COMPREHENSION STRATEGIES

If not the formal rules of linguistics, then what does guide the process of sentence comprehension? Bever (1970) suggested that people develop certain strategies of sentence comprehension. Strategies are rather different from formal rules. A mathematical rule or algorithm, when applied correctly, always guarantees a correct answer. A strategy, on the other hand, is a heuristic device; it is a good thing to try, but it is by no means 100% successful. Strategies work some of the time; when they don't, they are exchanged for new ones. Furthermore, the goal of Bever's strategies is not a syntactic one at all. People are interested in comprehending a sentence, that is, in constructing its semantic representation; most of the time they don't care at all about its syntactic make-up. Thus, comprehension strategies are designed to infer a sentence's meaning, and syntactic analyses are performed only to the extent that they are necessary for that purpose.

Several sentence comprehension strategies have been identified by psychologists. Bever (1970) described the tendency of English sentence comprehenders to assume that the first noun-verb-noun phrase they hear is the main clause of the sentence. Frequently, this guess is right; sometimes it does not work. In cases such as *The lady presented the diamond lost it* a more thorough syntactic analysis of the sentence is required. Sometimes the verb in the N-V-N clause is marked to indicate that this strategy is inappropriate, as in *The lady given the diamond lost it,* which saves the listener an incorrect hypothesis.

Another way to avoid falsely interpreting an initial N-V-N phrase as the main clause of the sentence is by using a cue word such as *that, who, whom,* or *which: The lady who was presented the diamond lost it.* One of the comprehension strategies of listeners is to assume that words such as *who* mark the beginning of a relative clause. Thus, sentences in which the relative clause is marked with such a word should be easier to comprehend than sentences lacking this cue. This is indeed the case. Fodor and Garrett (1967) showed that sentences such as *The boy whom the dog chased ran* are easier to paraphrase than *The boy the dog chased ran*. Hakes and Cairns (1970) came to the same conclusion using a different experimental method. They had subjects listen to the test sentences and at the same time perform a phoneme monitoring task: whenever they heard a word beginning with a certain specified phoneme, they were to press a response key as rapidly as possible. The more resources that are taken up with the sentence comprehension task, the fewer there are left for the monitoring task, and hence the longer reaction times should be. In the example above, for instance, subjects would be asked to respond to an initial /d/: without the *whom* subjects took on the average 595 milliseconds to react to the /d/ of *dog,* but in sentences with a *whom* reaction times were only 459 milliseconds, indicating that this sentence was easier to process.

A similar strategy that subjects apparently use involves the *that* in complement constructions. Some verbs may either take merely a direct object (*Fred believed the girl*), or they may take a sentence complement (*Fred believed the girl was the most beautiful in the whole world*). Subjects interpret a *that* after verbs like *believe* to be a signal for the presence of a sentence complement. Therefore, complement constructions containing a *that* are easier to comprehend than sentences without it. Hakes (1972) demonstrated this fact, again using the phoneme monitoring method. Response times to target phonemes—the g of *girl* in our example—were 198 milliseconds in sentences containing a *that,* but increased to 239 milliseconds when no *that* signalled the presence of a complement construction.

A rather different comprehension strategy is the order-of-mentioning strategy. In sentences describing a temporal sequence of events subjects tend to assume that the order in which these events are expressed in the sentence corresponds to the order of events in time. Violations of these expectations make a sentence difficult to understand. E. Clark (1971) has investigated this comprehension strategy with sentences containing the terms *before* and *after*. She could show that *The boy kicked the rock before he patted the dog,* is easier than *Before the boy patted the dog, he kicked the rock*. Clark's subjects were children of ages 3 to 5 who acted out sentences such as these with toys. It was clear from her results that the youngest children employed a first-order-of-mention strategy in carrying out the instructions they received. Clark's middle age group responded correctly to sentences containing *before,* but relied upon the order of mentioning in sentences containing *after*. Only her oldest subjects understood both terms correctly, whether or not the order in which the events were mentioned in the sentence corresponded to their actual order.

The order-of-mentioning strategy nicely illustrates the fallibility of strategies: usually people tell a story in its natural order, and, assuming they do so, the listener can disregard the cues indicating the order of events. However, when the story deviates from the natural order of events the listener must use the linguistic structure to recover the natural order. Novels or movies are easier when the natural order of events is maintained than when they are full of flashbacks and reversals, but since the latter invite deeper processing they are more interesting to read or watch.

## SEMANTIC AND LEXICAL CUES

The purpose of comprehension strategies is to extract meaning, not syntactic analysis. It is therefore not very surprising that semantic cues play an important role in sentence comprehension. In many simple sentences, especially when they are not isolated from their context, the semantic constraints alone are sufficient to ensure comprehension. Thus, given *dog, steak,* and *eaten* we can dispense with the grammar and nevertheless know who ate what. Semantically well-integrated sentences, that is, sentences whose constituents are strongly related associatively, such as *The doctor cured the patient* are easier in every respect than semantically poorly integrated sentences, such as *The doctor fired the janitor.* Rosenberg (1968) showed that such sentences are remembered better, and Rosenberg and Jarvella (1970) showed that such sentences are easier to shadow over noise. Presumably this effect arises because listeners do not have to apply much of their processing resources to the task of syntactic analysis.

Under some special conditions, however, semantic redundancy may invite shallow processing of a sentence, and hence results in poor recall. Some verbs, for instance, imply certain modifiers. Thus, if someone *yells,* he is usually *angry;* telling us that he is angry is redundant and subjects sometimes disregard such redundant information. Ehri and Muzio (1974) gave subjects sentences of the form

(1)   The angry waitress yelled at the actor
(2)   The angry waitress served the actor
or
(3)   The barber washed the dirty mirror
(4)   The barber gazed into the dirty mirror

Subjects received either sentence 1 or 2, and either 3 or 4. Later they were given the subject noun of each sentence as a cue and were asked to recall the sentence. Recall of *angry* was 16% better for sentences of type (2) than type (1); similarly recall of *dirty* was 58% better for sentence of type (4) than type (3). Evidently the semantically redundant modifiers in sentences (1) and (3) were often not encoded by subjects.

Some words are semantically more complex than others and hence a source of comprehension and memory difficulty. A particular type of complexity that has been studied extensively concerns the marking of comparatives. In comparative sentences such as

(5)    Giraffes are taller than goats
(6)    Goats are shorter than giraffes

*taller* is the unmarked and *shorter* the marked member of the adjective pair. Linguists (e.g., Bierwisch, 1967) base the distinction between marked and unmarked adjectives on two criteria. First, one can only use the unmarked member of a pair to ask a neutral question. Thus, one can ask *How long is the board?* without presupposing that it is either short or long, while *How short is the board?* presupposes that the board is short, and we are asking exactly how short it is. Secondly, the name for the underlying dimension is always derived from the unmarked member of an adjective pair. Therefore, we talk about *depth, length,* or *width,* while the English language has no corresponding words derived from *shallow, short,* or *narrow.* This linguistic evidence makes one think that *long* is semantically simpler than short, and hence should be easier to comprehend and remember. H. Clark (1969) was the first to show that this is actually the case and many studies since have confirmed his results. A study by Carpenter (1974) is particularly instructive. Carpenter's subjects performed three tasks, verification, recognition, and recall. In the verification task they were merely given a sentence and asked to indicate whether the sentence was true or false by pressing a response key. In the recall task subjects were given the main noun of each sentence as a prompt and had to recall the sentence verbatim. A recognition test was also included in the experiment. There were four types of sentences, as shown in Table 6.1: sentences containing marked and unmarked adjectives, as well as true and false sentences. The main results of her study are also shown in Table 6.1. First of all, unmarked sentences were verified significantly faster than marked sentences, the means being 2.4 seconds and 2.7 seconds, respectively. Secondly, the same difference reappeared in the recall task: unmarked sentences were recalled with a .44 probability, marked

TABLE 6.1. Verification Times, Recall and Recognition Probabilities for Four Types of Sentences (after Carpenter, 1974)

| | | Verification Time in Seconds | Recall Probability | Recognition Probability |
|---|---|---|---|---|
| True—Unmarked | Mares are older than fillies | 2.4 | .47 | .67 |
| False—Unmarked | Sons are older than fathers | 2.5 | .42 | .54 |
| True—Marked | Tadpoles are younger than frogs | 2.6 | .34 | .62 |
| False—Marked | Teachers are younger than pupils | 2.7 | .34 | .56 |

with only .34 probability. Interestingly, however, there was no difference in how well subjects could recognize marked and unmarked sentences: the recognition rate of 60% for unmarked sentences was quite comparable to that of 59% for marked sentences. This observation suggests that marked sentences are more difficult to retrieve than unmarked sentences.

What is marked are the words *short, shallow,* or *narrow.* One can expect a marking effect to appear when subjects are dealing with these words, that is, in comprehension tasks and in memory tasks such as Carpenter's where verbatim recall was required. However, the final purpose of comprehending a sentence is to extract its meaning, at least in most nonlaboratory situations. Hence what the subject remembers is the meaning of the sentence, not necessarily the wording. Whether or not a marked or unmarked adjective is used in a sentence, the subject will tend to retain the correct meaning in memory. Brewer and Lichtenstein (1974) gave subjects lists of comparative sentences using such adjective triplets as *long—not long— short.* The task was a recall task. On 4% of the sentences a shift occurred from a marked to an unmarked adjective form, or vice versa. Most of these shifts (61%) were from the marked form to the unmarked form. This bias in favor of unmarked form agrees with the observations of Clark (1969) and Carpenter (1974). However, most of these shifts were also meaning preserving (73%), that is, they were shifts from *short* to *not long,* but not from *short* to *long!* In a second experiment these authors presented only sentences with *long* or *short* (and similar comparative pairs), but no forms with *not,* thus making meaning preserving shifts impossible. In this experiment, shifts simply did not occur any more. The bias for unmarked forms was clearly subordinated to the goal of meaning preservation. Thus, whether or not marking effects are observed depends a great deal on the level of processing involved. At the word level, marking is important; at the conceptual level other considerations predominate. When people are concerned with words or with syntactic structures, quite different variables are important than when they are concerned with meaning. We shall return to this issue in more detail in the next section.

## 6.2    SENTENCE PROCESSING

The studies discussed in this section are not primarily concerned with how comprehenders parse a sentence syntactically, or not even with how they use syntactic cues in deriving the sentence meaning.

Rather they concentrate on the problem of meaning itself. The main point of interest here concerns the question of how meaning is represented in memory and what psychological processes are involved in cognitive operations at the semantic level.

## SENTENCE VERIFICATION

An experimental design that has been used with much success in recent years is sentence verification. Frequently, a sentence is verified against a picture. For instance, a simple picture consisting of a star and a plus, one above the other, might be shown together with a test sentence like *The star is above the plus,* and the subject is asked to decide as quickly as possible whether the sentence is true with respect to the picture or not. In other experiments one sentence is verified against another. For instance, the subject might read the sentence *Fred forgot to let the cat out* and is then asked to verify *The cat is in.* The data of interest in these tasks are the verification latencies. The analysis of these tasks involves the concept of stages of information processes, much as in the Sternberg type tasks discussed in Section 4.3, or the concept learning tasks described in Section 7.2.1. Sentence verification data are, in general, quite orderly, and a number of models have been developed that give some insight into the process of sentence comprehension.

Consider the following prototype experiment. A subject sees a row of four dots which are either all red or all black. Then he is shown the sentence *The dots are red,* or the sentence *The dots aren't red,* and asked to respond true or false as rapidly as he can. The verification latencies obtained in such an experiment have three characteristics. First of all, negative sentences take longer to verify than affirmative sentences. Secondly, true affirmatives are verified faster than false affirmatives. Thirdly, this relationship is reversed for negatives: false negatives are verified faster than true negatives. Among the models that can account for these effects are those of Clark and Chase (1972) and Trabasso, Rollins, and Shaughnessy (1972). We shall discuss the Trabasso et al. model in Chapter 7 in a somewhat different context; here we shall describe the simplest and most elegant of the models that predicts the pattern of results obtained in sentence verification experiments. It is the constituent comparison model of Carpenter and Just (1975).

The model is basically a pattern matching model; the assumption is made that each pattern matching operation adds a constant amount of time to the process. Thereby differences in verification times are explained. The patterns matched are propositions. Propositions are abstract representations of the meaning of elementary sentences. For instance, the meaning of *The star is above the plus* is represented by one proposition, the meaning of *The dots are red* is also represented by one proposition, while the meaning of *The dots are not red* is represented by two propositions: *The dots are red* requires one proposition, and the negation another. We shall concern ourselves in much more detail with the nature of propositions in Section 6.2.4; for present purposes the few examples given suffice, except that we need a notation. Propositions do not contain words, but abstract concepts, which for convenience we designate by means of words. To mark this difference, we shall write concepts in capital letters: *red* is the English word by means of which we express the concept RED. Furthermore, we shall adopt the convention of writing the relational term (or predicator) of a proposition first, and then the argument or arguments that are being related. Thus we write (ABOVE,STAR,PLUS) to designate that the *star* (which is one argument of the proposition) is *above* (the relation, or predicator) the *plus* (which is the second argument), or (RED,DOTS) to predicate *red* of *dots*. Frequently a proposition may be the argument of another proposition. This is the case with negation, where the predicator *negation* (we shall write NEG) operates upon a whole proposition, e.g., (NEG,(RED,DOTS))—*The dots are not red*.

The Carpenter and Just model assumes that in verifying a sentence against a picture both the sentence and the picture are represented propositionally. The two propositional representations are then compared with each other proposition by proposition. If a match is obtained, the process proceeds. If a mismatch occurs, the whole comparison process starts again from the beginning, and the mismatched component is tagged, so that on subsequent occasions it will be treated as a match. If one mismatch is detected, the sentence will be called false; however, if two (or any even number) of mismatches occur in processing the sentence, the sentence will be true, because two negations have the same net effect as an affirmation. Verification times are predicted by the total number of constituent comparisons necessary in this matching process.

The details of this model are shown in Table 6.2. First, consider the *true affirmative* case. The sentence *The dots are red* and the picture of red dots are represented in the same way, (RED,DOTS). The matching process detects the match (designated by a plus in the table), then detects another match in that neither the sentence nor the picture representation is negated, and the response "true" is made. Let us

TABLE 6.2. A Psycholinguistic Processing Model of Sentence Verification. The Sentence is Either "The Dots are Red" or "The Dots aren't Red"; the Picture is Either a Row of Red Balls or a Row of Black Balls. (after Carpenter & Just, 1975)

| | True Affirmative | False Affirmative | False Negative | True Negative |
|---|---|---|---|---|
| Sentence Representation: | (RED,DOTS) | (RED,DOTS) | (NEG,(RED,DOTS)) | (NEG,(RED,DOTS)) |
| Picture Representation: | (RED,DOTS) | (BLACK,DOTS) | (RED,DOTS) | (BLACK,DOT) |
| Matches: | $+$ $+$ | $-$<br>$+$ $+$ | $-$ $+$<br>$+$ $+$ | $-$<br>$-$ $+$<br>$+$ $+$ |
| Response: | True | False | False | True |
| Number of Comparisons: | $k$ | $k + 1$ | $k + 2$ | $k + 3$ |

assume that the total operation involved *k* steps (including the two matching operations).

For *false affirmatives* the situation is different: the proposition (RED,DOTS) and (BLACK,DOTS) do not match, the mismatch is tagged and the truth index for the sentence is set to "false." Then the match is attempted again, and this time everything works, because the tagged mismatch is counted as a match. The total operation requires one more step than in the previous case, that is $k + 1$ comparisons.

*False negatives* at first lead to a match in the proposition (RED,DOTS), but then a mismatch is detected because the sentence representation but not the picture contains a NEGATION. Again, the mismatch is tagged and the process is restarted. Two matches occur, bringing the total number of comparisons to $k + 2$. Because of the one mismatch that was detected, a "false" response is made.

*True negatives* require the most complex operations according to this model. First the initial propositions mismatch; on the second try the NEG produces another mismatch; and only the third attempt is successful. The total number of comparisons involved is $k + 3$, three more than for true affirmatives. The response is "true" because the two mismatches cancel each other.

The prediction of the model is that verification times increase proportional to the number of comparison operations. Figure 6.3 shows a set of experimental results that is in excellent agreement with this prediction. Each comparison in Figure 6.3 took 215 milliseconds, and the model predicted quite precisely the number of comparisons involved

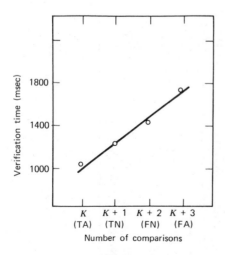

FIGURE 6.3  **Sentence verification times as a function of the number of comparison operations. (after Carpenter and Just, 1975)**

in the different sentence types. Carpenter and Just cite further data to support their model. By using more complex expressions they were able to obtain more stringent tests of their theory. For instance, denials such as *It isn't true that the dots are red,* which are represented as (NEG,(AFF,(RED,DOTS))), allowed them to extend the function shown in Figure 6.3 up to $k + 5$. They also reported some experiments in which reading and representation times were excluded (by timing only from the onset of the picture), without changing the qualitative character of the results.

There are a number of other cases to which the model has been applied. Consider for instance the verification of counterfactuals:

$$\text{If Judy had not left, } \ldots \rightarrow (\text{NEG},(\text{LEFT},\text{JUDY})) \ldots$$
$$\text{Probe: Judy left.} \rightarrow (\text{LEFT},\text{JUDY}),$$

or of implicit negatives:

$$\text{Fred forgot to close the door} \rightarrow (\text{NEG},(\text{CLOSED},\text{DOOR}))$$
$$\text{Probe: The door is open} \rightarrow (\text{OPEN},\text{DOOR})$$

The last example is interesting because in cases like this subjects may recode the sentence before comparing it to the probe. That is, the proposition (NEG,(CLOSED,DOOR)) may be recoded as (OPEN,DOOR); this recoding takes time, but once it is accomplished the comparison process is simplified.

It is doubtful, however, that all sentence verification tasks can be described by this model. The Carpenter and Just model is probably restricted to relatively simple sentences. The strategies used with more complex materials have not yet been investigated in as much detail, but we know, for instance, that the comprehension of sentences with four or five negatives cannot simply be described as a straightforward extension of sentences with one or two negatives. Sentences with multiple negations are very difficult to understand and in fact are incomprehensible without a conscious, elaborate reasoning process.

A rather interesting complication for the model arises from the very nature of memory. What is remembered are traces of processing operations, and the processing of a sentence necessarily occurs simultaneously at different levels. One cannot understand the meaning of a sentence without analyzing the actual physical stimulus event (the graphemic pattern in the case of a written sentence, the acoustic wave form in the case of a spoken sentence), or the words and phrases used in expressing this meaning. These analyses need neither be complete nor very detailed, but to some extent they must be there. Thus, the memory trace of a sentence consists not only of its meaning, but also of various surface features—its linguistic or physical realization. Thus, matches may occur at different levels, in addition to the propositional one, greatly complicating the picture.

Sentence verification tasks involving active and passive sentences provide good illustrations of this interaction between propositional and surface traces. Consider an experiment in which the subject is shown sentences such as *The car was hit by the truck,* and is then given a question *Did the truck hit the car?* The matching model discussed above can easily be extended to this situation, but now it becomes crucial to distinguish at which level the match occurs. Consider first the propositional level. The sentences *The truck hit the car* and *The car was hit by the truck* are both represented by the same proposition (HIT,TRUCK,CAR). They mean the same, they differ merely in their surface structure for pragmatic reasons. The active voice is neutral with respect to what the speaker wants to emphasize as new in the sentence (though a speaker may use other linguistic devices such as intonation to indicate what he regards to be the important component of the sentence). The passive voice, on the other hand, is used for emphasis: the speaker has reasons to assume that his listener is already aware of the object of the sentence and wants to tell him what happened to that object. Thus, passive sentences highlight the new information they contain. At the propositional level, however, they are no different than their corresponding active sentences. Thus, matches at the propositional level should be independent of whether the target sentence and the question agree in voice. Passive questions are harder to decode (there are more words than in active questions), so one might expect passive questions to produce longer reaction times than active questions, but whether the target sentence was active or passive should make no difference. These predictions are shown graphically in the right-hand panel of Figure 6.4.

A quite different situation is obtained if we consider matches at the surface level, that is between the actual sentences rather than the underlying propositions. An active sentence requires only one comparison when the question is in the active voice; if the question is in the passive voice a mismatch is produced and the process must be restarted. A similar argument can be made for passive target sentences: if their voice is congruent with the question, the surface level comparison succeeds and reaction times are short; if the voices of target and question mismatch, reaction times increase. Thus, an interaction between target and question voice is predicted, as shown in the left panel of Figure 6.4.

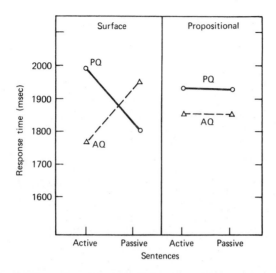

FIGURE 6.4  **Predicted response times for active and passive sentences and active and passive questions (AQ and PQ) when the comparison process involves surface constituents (left panel) or propositional constituents (right panel). (after Garrod and Trabasso, 1973)**

Experiments by Garrod and Trabasso (1973) and Anderson (1974) have reported precisely such an interaction. Garrod and Trabasso had subjects read four sentences that were either in the active or passive voice. Then a question was asked about one of these sentences. The voice of the question was varied orthogonally with the voice of the target sentence. Depending on whether or not subjects had surface information available about the sentence, the interaction predicted in the left panel of Figure 6.4 was or was not observed. When the test question referred to the last presented sentence, that sentence was still available in memory in terms of its surface structure; hence incongruent questions required more time to answer, as shown in the left panel of Figure 6.5. When the question referred to the second or third item, the matching process operated primarily upon the propositional representations of the sentence-question pairs, and no congruence effects were observed, as shown in the right panel of Figure 6.5. Obviously Figure 6.5 corresponds very well to the predictions shown in Figure 6.4. The data in Figure 6.5 are only from true sentences, but the results for false sentences were very much alike, except that false sentences were always answered more slowly than true sentences. Anderson (1974) reported results very similar to those of Garrod and

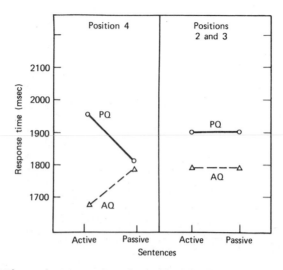

FIGURE 6.5    **Observed response times for active and passive sentences and active and passive questions (AQ and PQ) when the sentence was the last of four input sentences (left panel) and when it was either the second or third of the input sentences (right panel). (after Garrod and Trabasso, 1973)**

Trabasso, but used more input sentences and asked more than one test question, so that the interval between reading a sentence and being asked a question about it could be as long as 2 minutes. The conclusion from both of these studies is clear: models of sentence comprehension must not restrict themselves to the meaning or propositional level, but must also take into account memory traces rising from the various processes involved in constructing the meaning of a sentence. In the next section we shall turn to an explicit discussion of these levels of processing.

## 6.2.2    LEVELS OF PROCESSING

In Chapter 5 we discussed in some detail the importance of the kind of processing that a to-be-learned item undergoes, as well as the richness of that processing. The deeper the level of processing and the richer the processing, the better retention. These results were based on list learning experiments, but they hold equally well for sentence memory. A study in which the level of processing of sentences was varied in an incidental learning task, much like the experiments with word lists reviewed in Section 5.1.1, has been reported by Mistler-Lachman (1974). Subjects were given a list of sentences and asked either to judge the meaningfulness of the sentence, or to determine whether the sentence fitted into a given context, or to follow up the sentence with a continuation. The second and third tasks require a deeper level of processing than the first. As in the word list experiments, recall was directly related to the level of comprehension.

Similar results have been obtained by Treisman and Tuxworth (1974), who also confirmed another finding from word list experiments: relatively shallow processing levels, e.g., acoustic coding, are often sufficient for short-term comprehension, but deeper levels of processing are required for long-term memory. Treisman and Tuxworth had subjects perform one of two tasks: phoneme detection, or semantic anomaly judgment, thus inducing a superficial, acoustic coding of the sentences in one case and a deeper, semantic encoding in the other. Sentence recall was equal in the two conditions when the retention interval was short (84 versus 86%), but superior in the semantic condition when the retention interval was long (67 versus 83%). They also demonstrated that the qualitative difference between the semantic and acoustic tasks was responsible for this result, and that processing difficulty could not account for the data: various internal analyses showed that the difficulty of the phoneme detection and semantic judgment tasks were equal. The reader will perhaps remember entirely parallel arguments with respect to task difficulty and the levels of processing phenomenon in Section 5.1.1.

We can therefore assume that the memory trace for a sentence, just like the memory trace for a word, consists of multiple levels: they are the persisting effects of the processing operations performed at the time of study—including the physical processing of the visual or acoustic stimulus, word identification, syntactic analyses, and whatever semantic analyses are performed. The latter type of traces are more suited for long-term retrieval than the more shallow traces.

Saying that, for words as well as sentences, semantic cues are better for long-term retention than acoustic cues does not imply that the latter are only stored in short-term memory, while long-term memory is semantic. A great deal of evidence was presented in Section 5.1.3 that physical features of the stimulus are remembered over long retention intervals. Exactly the same is true for sentence memory. Kolers and Ostry (1974) have shown subjects texts in various forms: normal typography, upside down, mirror reversed, etc. After 32 days, the subjects were given a recognition test for these sentences, with either the same or changed typography. Even after this very long retention interval, subjects could recognize reasonably well whether they had seen a particular sentence upside down or in normal form. Kolers argues that what the subjects remember are the analyzing activities performed during encoding: reading a strange typography requires considerable effort at the visual decoding level, and hence this type of information is strongly represented in memory. Analogously, a child will remember whether she has read "Snowwhite and the Seven Dwarfs," seen the movie, or had someone tell her the story.

Begg (1971) has provided some evidence that the memory traces at different levels are independent of each other. He used a continuous sentence recognition paradigm, with tests for both meaning and wording. Whether or not subjects recognized the correct wording of a sentence was unrelated to their ability to recognize its meaning. In a later experiment with a similar procedure, Begg and Wickelgren (1974) found that semantic information, as tested by recognition of sentence meaning, was learned better initially than syntactic-lexical information (as indicated by recognition for the wording of sentences). Furthermore, the rate at which lexical-syntactic information was lost was about 50% higher than that for semantic information.

Levels of processing considerations are even more important with sentences or texts than with word lists, simply because the processes involved in reading a text are so much more complex than those involved in studying a word list. Kintsch (1975) has described the processing that occurs when someone reads a story. A simplified but slightly expanded version of this model of the reading process is shown in Table 6.3. We have there eight levels of processing, each giving rise to a particular kind of memory trace. Undoubtedly finer discriminations could be made, or additional levels may be involved, say in the form of visual imagery not for the printed text but for the content of the text. Since we are talking about reading, the analysis must begin with the visual processing of the text. Frequently, though not necessarily (see Gibson, Shurcliff, and Yonas, 1970) reading is accompanied by implicit speech, giving rise to phonetic cues. At the lexical level, words must be identified, then at the syntactic-semantic level the words are strung together to form phrases and sentences; this is the kind of processing described in Section 6.1. We stressed there that syntactic analysis is not a goal in itself in sentence comprehension, but is subordinated to the goal of determining the meaning of the sentence. The product of this process is a representation of the meaning of the sentence. Later, in Section 6.2.4, we shall suggest various possible models for representing the meaning of sentences, involving the notion of propositions. Finally, understanding a text does not end with the meaning of separate sentences, but these sentences must be organized into larger units. The result of these organizational processes is a representation of the gist of a text, which

TABLE 6.3. An Outline of Stages of Comprehension in Reading, the Memory Traces Arising from these Processes, and Their Selection for Encoding in Memory. The Thickness of the Arrows Indicates the Likelihood that Particular Types of Memory Traces Will be Encoded in Memory for Long Term Retention under Standard Reading Conditions. (after Kintsch, 1975)

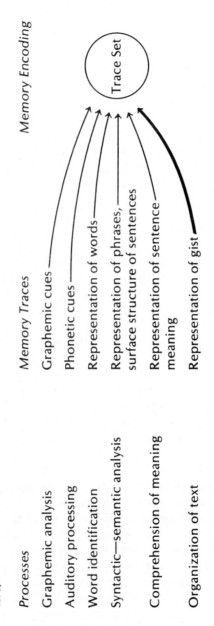

| Processes | Memory Traces | Memory Encoding |
|---|---|---|
| Graphemic analysis | Graphemic cues | |
| Auditory processing | Phonetic cues | |
| Word identification | Representation of words | |
| Syntactic—semantic analysis | Representation of phrases, surface structure of sentences | |
| Comprehension of meaning | Representation of sentence meaning | |
| Organization of text | Representation of gist | |

is something quite different from the meaning of the separate sentences that make up the text. We shall turn to this problem in Section 6.3.4.

It is important to note that the levels of processing in Table 6.3 are not strictly serial processing stages. It is not the case that a complete visual analysis of a letter string is made first, that this leads to the word identification, that once the words are identified the syntactic analysis begins, to be followed by the semantic process, etc. Instead, these processes are highly interactive and occur largely in parallel. It is not necessarily the case that the lower level analysis is completed before the higher one. If this were the case phonemes would have to be processed before syllables, but Savin and Bever (1970) found that when subjects had to locate a target in a string of syllables, they were between 40 and 250 milliseconds faster when the target was a syllable than when it was a phoneme. Thus phoneme identification does not precede syllable identification in listening. Similarly, Johnson (1975) found that subjects perceived words before they could identify the letters in the words. Readers frequently comprehend a word without noticing the misprinted letter in it, or comprehend a sentence without being aware of each word. Rapid reading essentially consists of inferring the gist of a text, with a minimum amount of lower level analysis of words or even sentences. Indeed, the higher level analysis often facilitates the lower level analysis, so that it is easier to identify a letter if that letter forms part of a word than when it stands alone (Reicher, 1969; Estes, 1975).

To the extent that the processes described in Table 6.3 occur during reading, they all have some memorial consequences. They leave memory traces behind. Kintsch (1975) has argued that two things may happen to these memory traces: they may be lost after relatively short time periods, either through interference or decay; or they may be selected for encoding in memory. What is retained in memory is, therefore, a selection of all the memory traces that are generated in processing a text. The selection process is a biased one, that is, not all types of traces are equally retained. What the subject's purpose is in processing the sentence determines at least partly the selection of traces for memory storage. Usually, a reader's interest is primarily in what we call the gist of what he reads. Therefore, the representation of the overall structure of the text, that is, its gist, will be preferentially retained. In reading a list of active and passive sentences, the syntactic feature sentence voice would be a highly salient characteristic and would be encoded preferentially. On the other hand, in reading a newspaper article the likelihood that the voice of sentences would be encoded, and hence retained, would be exceedingly small. In reading a mirror reversed sentence, subjects are quite concerned about this visual property of the sentence and remember it for as long as they remember the sentence, while details of typography might often be neglected in other reading situations. What is retained from the myriad possible processing traces that are formed in reading is not entirely controlled by conscious selection though: readers hardly ever try to remember where on a page they read this or that, but nevertheless incidental memory for such information is often surprisingly good (e.g., Rothkopf, 1971). Thus, which traces are remembered and which are disregarded appears to be partly random, partly purposeful.

Table 6.3 is no more than an outline. Some of the processes involved can only be sketched today, and many more research results are needed to fill in the details, or to modify the whole structure. There exists, however, a fair body of experimental work that demonstrates the necessity of including as one level of processing in Table 6.3, the analysis of sentence meaning. In order to understand sentence processing, we need to concern ourselves with the abstract representation of the meaning of a sentence, independent of its verbal, linguistic realization. To this problem we shall turn next.

## MEMORY FOR MEANING

A study that suggested that memory for the meaning of a sentence must be distinguished from memory for the linguistic expression itself was reported in 1967 by Sachs. Sachs read subjects a paragraph of normal English text. One of the sentences in the paragraph was selected as the test sentence. Subjects were given a recognition test after listening to the paragraph with either the sentence in its original form, a formally changed sentence, a syntactically changed sentence, or a semantically changed sentence. The subject was asked to tell whether the test sentence was the same as one in the original passage or not. For instance, suppose the original sentence was *He sent a letter about it to Galileo, the great Italian scientist*. A formal change of this sentence consisted merely in a permutation of the word order: *He sent Galileo, the great Italian scientist, a letter about it*. A syntactic change involved a passive transformation: *A letter about it was sent to Galileo, the great Italian scientist*. A semantic change touched upon the meaning of the sentence: *Galileo, the great Italian scientist, sent him a letter about it*. Sachs' results were quite clear: when the test sentence was embedded somewhere in the middle of the paragraph, subjects' memory for both syntactic changes and formal changes was minimal; at the same time, they were still very good at detecting changes in meaning. Her subjects obviously did not transfer to memory inessential information about the form of the sentences. Interestingly, if the test sentence was the last sentence in the paragraph all kinds of changes could be detected. Presumably subjects still retained the sentence in primary memory, and had available sufficient information to detect any kind of change.

What do we mean when we say that subjects remember the meaning of a sentence as distinct from its wording? First of all we should note that comprehension involves integrating information from different sentences, organizing and supplementing it through inferences from what one already knows, rather than merely interpreting what is directly expressed by a sentence. A series of studies by Bransford, Franks, and Barclay supports this claim. In their first report, Bransford and Franks (1971) told subjects a simple story consisting of four basic ideas. In one case, all four ideas were expressed in separate sentences. An example would be

The ants were in the kitchen.
The jelly was on the table.
The jelly was sweet.
The ants ate the jelly.

In another case, two, three, or all four of these ideas were combined into longer sentences. Examples of two-, three-, and four-idea sentences would be, respectively,

The ants in the kitchen ate the jelly.
The ants ate the sweet jelly which was on the table.
The ants in the kitchen ate the sweet jelly which was on the table.

Subjects were presented some combination of such sentences, but not all of them: just enough to expose them to all four ideas. There were four such idea sets used in their experiment. Following acquisition, subjects were given a recognition test. The sentences in the recognition test came for the most part from the four idea sets used in the acquisition phase of the experiment. However, most of them were sentences that were true but subjects had not actually experienced them (NEW sentences), while some test sentences were repetitions of study sentences (OLD sentences). In addition, there were some test sentences that were unrelated to the four idea sets used in acquisition (NON-CASE sentences). The subjects' task was to indicate which of the sentences they had actually heard before and which they had not. In addition, subjects indicated their confidence in the correctness of their responses on a five-point confidence scale, which ranged from very low confidence (1) to very high confidence (5). The two main results of the experiment are both shown in Figure 6.6. First of all, note that subjects recognized as "old" those sentences that integrated the elementary ideas into larger units. They were quite sure that they had in fact heard the four- or three-idea sentences, uncertain about the two-idea sentences, and tended to think that they had not heard the one-idea sentences. The only sentences where they were sure were new were the NON-CASE sentences, that is sentences that did not fit thematically into any of the idea sets. The second important point about the Bransford and Franks result is that these judgments were almost the same for OLD and NEW sentences. Whether or not they had actually experienced a particular sentence, subjects judged it to be old in proportion to how much of the total information it contained. Clearly, these subjects did not remember words or sentences, but had formed a unified representation of the meaning of each idea set, perhaps by means of imagery, and were comparing test sentences against this wholistic memory trace.

Sentences are the vehicles by means of which information is transmitted. The vehicle itself is less important than what it contains.

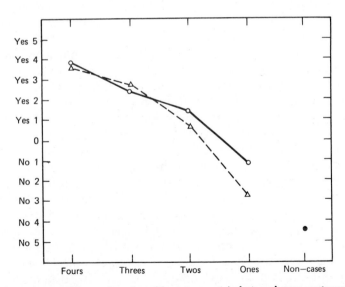

FIGURE 6.6  **Recognition ratings for old sentences (circles) and new sentences (triangles) as a function of the number of propositions in the test sentence. Noncase (black circle) are sentences that do not fit the meaning of the study sentences. (after Bransford and Franks, 1971)**

The meaning of a sentence, but not necessarily its wording, is retained in memory. Bransford, Barclay, and Franks (1972) provided a further demonstration of this point. They had subjects listen to one or the other of the following sentences:

(1)    Three turtles rested beside a floating log, and a fish swam beneath them.
(2)    Three turtles rested on a floating log, and a fish swam beneath them.

After presenting sentences such as these, a recognition test was administered. The recognition set contained the old sentences (which were recognized well), unrelated filler items (which were rejected without much trouble), and two types of more interesting test items:

(3)    Three turtles rested beside a floating log, and a fish swam beneath it.
(4)    Three turtles rested on a floating log, and a fish swam beneath it.

Those subjects who had heard sentence (1) were able to reject sentences (3) and (4) on the recognition test. However, subjects who had heard sentence (2) could reject sentence (3), but not sentence (4): sentence (4) is a correct inference derivable from sentence (2), because if the fish is beneath the turtles and the turtles are on the log, the fish must also be beneath the log. Subjects recognized what they knew was true, not what they had actually seen. The same observation was made in studies by Potts (1972) and Barclay (1973). In both of these experiments, subjects were taught a linear array, such as "*The hawk is smarter than the deer, who is smarter than the wolf, who is smarter than the bear.*" One can teach such an array in various ways: e.g., by presenting the three adjacent pairs in the relation, but not the three remote pairs such as "*The hawk is smarter than the bear.*" The general finding is that once subjects have learned the array, they do not remember any more the specific input sentences, but they tend to recognize as old sentences all true statements and reject sentences incongruous with the ordering they have learned.

Thus far, the inference that sentence memory involves an abstract, nonverbal meaning level has been supported mainly by demonstrations of recognition confusions on the basis of meaning. A rather different approach was taken by Kintsch and Monk (1972) and King and Greeno (1974). These authors argued that if what is stored in memory is the meaning of a text, it should not matter in which form that text was presented when at a later time subjects are asked to make use of that meaning in an inference task. Therefore, they constructed two versions of experimental materials (simple stories or descriptions in the case of Kintsch and Monk, arithmetic problems in the case of King and Greeno): in one version the syntax was kept as simple as possible, while in the second version the same text was written as one long sentence, containing various syntactic complexities. Care was taken that the two versions of each paragraph were strict paraphrases, that is, they contained the same information, in spite of the syntactic differences. Subjects took longer to read the syntactically complex texts than the simple texts, indicating that it was easier to decode the meaning of simple sentences than complex constructions. However, once the decoding process was performed, the differential difficulty of the texts disappeared: when subjects were asked questions about the text that involved an inference from what they had read, they were equally accurate and equally fast in responding, whether they had read the simple or the complex version of a paragraph pair. This indicates that the memory representation that was accessed in performing the inferences was independent of the wording of the input; it was a conceptual rather than a linguistic structure. Whether something was said in a complicated way or in a straightforward way did not matter once it was understood.

The relationship between the meaning of a sentence and its surface form may sometimes be quite an indirect one, as in proverbs. Honeck (1973) has exploited this fact to show that the repetition of the meaning of a sentence with totally new words can be just as effective as the repetition of the actual sentence. Honeck used proverbs as the learning material in his experiment, and repeated each proverb in one of three manners, as illustrated by these sentences.

(5)     Industry is fortune's right hand and stinginess her left.
(6)     Stinginess is fortune's left hand and industry her right.
(7)     You must work hard and spend money carefully to make a fortune.
(8)     A fortune is made or lost nearly every day.

Sentence 5 is the to-be-remembered proverb. In one experimental condition, this proverb itself was repeated. In another condition the proverb was followed by a repetition with a word order change, such as sentence 6. In the third condition, a meaning paraphrase was used instead, as in sentence 7; here only the meaning of the proverb is repeated, while entirely different words as well as syntax are used. Finally, in a control condition, sentence 8, differing both in meaning and wording, was used instead of a repetition. The test in this experiment was a cued recall test, with the subject noun of the proverb serving as the recall cue. If we take recall in the control condition as 100%, the number of words recalled in the exact repetition and transformed repetition groups did not differ much from that value:

110% and 98%, respectively. The best recall was obtained in the meaning paraphrase condition, 145%. Thus, a meaning paraphrase was even more effective than an exact repetition of the proverb. Honeck finds that the best explanation of this result is the same one we offered for the other experiments discussed here: that the proverb and its paraphrase have a common conceptual representation in memory. The proverb-plus-paraphrase combination is so effective because it provides both for the repetition of that common conceptual base and an enriched, variable verbal context (see Section 5.1.2 on encoding variability).

Together these studies make a forceful argument: one cannot understand sentence comprehension and memory without dealing with the problem of meaning. Some of the processes occurring in sentence comprehension are at an abstract conceptual level, and are to some extent independent of the shallower levels of analysis concerned with physical stimuli, words, or even sentences or texts as linguistic entities. These studies demonstrate persuasively the psychological reality of this conceptual level. Now we must face a much harder problem: what can we say about how meaning is represented in memory? We shall examine several suggestions with respect to that question shortly, but first we must resolve what many readers will have regarded as a contradiction between our previous discussion of levels of sentence memory and some of the results on memory for meaning discussed above.

In the previous section we claimed that the memorial consequences of comprehending a sentence are always multilevel, ranging from memory for the actual physical stimulus and the linguistic form of a sentence to its meaning. In several studies just discussed only memory for meaning was found, and subjects often could not tell which particular sentence they had seen or had not seen, as long as it was part of the meaning structure they had acquired. It must be emphasized that this finding depends entirely on the particular experimental procedures used in these experiments and is not a general one. Several follow-up studies of the Bransford and Franks (1971) experiment have shown that subjects can integrate separate ideas into a unified whole while still remembering the original input items; indeed, recognition response biases favoring integrated sentences over part statements can be established without an ideational basis with arbitrary, unrelated input sentences (e.g., Small, 1975). Similarly, the finding that the actual input sentences are entirely forgotten in such experiments as Bransford et al. (1972) or Barclay (1974) is restricted to the special conditions of these experiments. In these studies subjects were given many input sentences that were highly similar. Thus, interference with the surface form of the sentences was at its maximum. It is not very surprising that if subjects hear a whole set of sentences all of the form "The hawk is smarter than the bear," "The wolf is smarter than the bear," "The wolf is less smart than the hawk," etc., little or no memory for surface form results. The only way the subject can avoid becoming totally confused is by trying to disregard all these similar sentences, mapping the information contained in them upon some linear array of "smartness." This does not mean, however, that he will not remember its surface form when he hears "The hawk is smarter than the bear" as part of a discourse consisting of a variety of formally dissimilar sentences, e.g., in the context of a conversation, or of a fairy tale.

A series of studies by Keenan and Kintsch (1974), and McKoon and Keenan (1974) explores this interaction between memory for the surface form of sentences and memory for meaning. When one reads a paragraph, memory for surface form, in general, is lost more rapidly than memory for meaning. Shortly after reading both memory traces are readily available; after a sufficient delay interval, filled with an interference producing task such as further reading, memory for the surface form of sentences should be weakened, while memory for meaning remains intact. This prediction was tested in the following way. Suppose a subject reads this short paragraph:

(9)    A carelessly discarded burning cigarette started a fire. The fire destroyed many acres of virgin forest.

and then is asked to verify as true or false the sentence:

The discarded cigarette started the fire.

Errors in such a task are negligible, but the verification times provide a sensitive indicator of the information processing involved in this task. If the test sentence follows the paragraph right away (up to about 30 seconds), verification times are approximately ½ second shorter than if a 20-minute delay filled with reading other unrelated paragraphs intervenes. With no delay, the subject can perform the task in two ways: either by matching the surface form of the test sentence against his memory for the surface form of the text, or by matching the meaning of the test sentence against the meaning of the text. After a delay, memory for surface form is weakened and no longer useful in this task, and the match must be performed at the meaning level. If we furthermore assume that meaning matches are slower than surface matches (or perhaps just that two matches in parallel are faster than one alone, independent of the nature of the memory trace involved), the data are accounted for.

In an additional part of this experiment subjects read the following paragraph (or, actually, several paragraphs of this kind):

(10)    A burning cigarette was carelessly discarded. The fire destroyed many acres of virgin forest.

The subjects were then given the same test sentence to verify as before. Note that the test sentence is not explicitly stated in (10). However, if the text is to make sense, it must be inferred during reading. In fact readers have no trouble making such an inference (though it is not at all a logical inference!): they say that *The discarded cigarette started the fire* is true with only 4.5% errors, as opposed to 3% errors after reading the explicit version of the text. This is not very surprising, because inferences of this kind are commonplace in everyday conversations, or reading a newspaper. Clearly, however, the verification must have involved an operation at the level of meaning, rather than a pattern match of surface forms, because the test sentence is never actually presented in text (10). Reaction times are entirely in agreement with this argument: they are longer than when the test sentence had actually been presented as in (9), and they do not change much with delay. The whole pattern of results is shown in Figure 6.7: reaction times are approximately equal when the verification task involves an operation at the meaning level (that is, either when the test sentence was never explicitly presented and had to be inferred during reading, or, if it was presented explicitly when the memory for the surface form of the sentence was weakened by the delay). The absence of a difference in reaction times between the explicit and implicit conditions after a delay implies that the inference that the cigarette had caused the fire was indeed made during the reading of (10). If the inference had been made only when verifying the test sentence, one would expect the time required for this inference to lengthen the reaction times in the implicit condition beyond those in the explicit condition, even after a delay.

Note that in this experiment subjects discriminated very well whether or not they had actually read a particular sentence or had to infer it, quite unlike the subjects of Barclay. However, the task here was not a very confusing one: subjects read standard English prose, rather than a whole set of formally similar sentences.

The results shown in Figure 6.7 are not restricted to reading and memory for the surface form of sentences. Precisely the same pattern of results is obtained when subjects are told a story by means of a sequence of pictures, and are then asked to verify one of these pictures. Baggett (1975) has repeated the Keenan, McKoon, and Kintsch

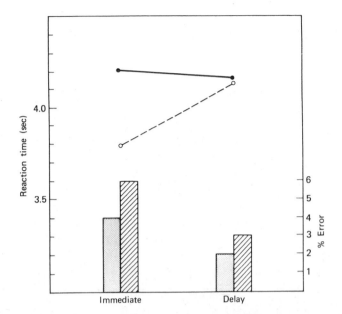

FIGURE 6.7  **Reaction times to verify explicitly presented (open circles) and implicitly presented sentences (filled circles) and error rates (white for explicit, shaded for implicit condition), for immediate and 20-minute delayed tests. (after Keenan and Kintsch 1974, Exps. I and II, short paragraphs)**

work with pictures and found essentially the same results. Instead of a story, a sequence of four cartoons was shown to subjects. In one case, the sequence included the critical test item, just as paragraph (9) includes the test sentence. In the implicit picture series the test item had to be inferred, just as in paragraph (10). The cartoons told simple stories, e.g., of a long-haired boy entering a barbershop, sitting down, the barber cutting his hair, and the boy leaving the shop with a crew cut. For the implicit version of this story, the picture showing the barber actually cutting the boy's hair was omitted. That picture was then used as the test item. Again, subjects were faster in calling the test picture "true" when they had actually seen the picture than when the picture had to be inferred, but this difference disappeared after a delay. Because recognition memory for pictures is so notoriously good, a much longer delay interval (3 days) was used than in the sentence memory experiments. Baggett's results are shown in Figure 6.8, and the similarity to the verbal data shown in Figure 6.7 is certainly striking.

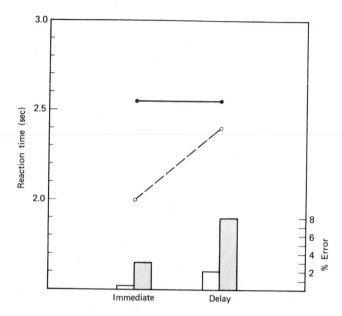

FIGURE 6.8 **Reaction times to verify explicitly presented (open circles) and implicitly presented pictures (filled circles) and error rates (white for explicit, shaded for the implicit condition), for immediate and 72-hour delayed tests. (after Baggett, 1975)**

## 6.2.4   THE REPRESENTATION OF MEANING

Data such as those reviewed in the last section have convinced many psychologists that they must be able to deal directly with the meaning of sentences. In order to tell whether or not a subject has correctly recalled the meaning of a sentence, one must be able, somehow, to tell what that meaning is; in order to determine how the meaning of a passage affects its comprehension, one must be able to represent that meaning. Research with meaningful sentences and texts is stymied unless we have some model for the representation of meaning to work with.

Philosophers have traditionally disagreed on the question "What is meaning?" and even on the usefulness of the concept of meaning itself. They have approached the study of meaning, that is, semantics, in two rather different ways. Some philosophers prefer to ignore the notion of meaning altogether (e.g., Quine, 1961); for others, the concept of meaning is a basic one, and semantics is conceived as an answer to the question "What is meaning?" The former approach is called extensionalism, the latter intensionalism. Intensionalism is characterized by the belief that words and sentences have an underlying meaning that is conceptual rather than linguistic in nature. Different languages are regarded as different means of expressing the same underlying meaning: horse, Pferd, and cheval are just different words for the same concept. Extensionalism, in the behaviorist tradition, has no use for a separate substratum of "meaning," apart from the words or objects themselves. Quine (1961, pp. 47–49) finds that there are two ways in which the word meaning might be employed, but that in both cases nothing is gained by using it—except a dangerous illusion of having explained something. The first context is that of "alike in meaning." This, for Quine, reduces to the problem of synonymy: it is sufficient to state that the word X is synonymous with the word Y, and quite unnecessary to say that the word X means A, and the word Y also means A, hence they are synonymous. In the same way Skinner (1957) would be content to state that an organism makes a certain response R to a discriminative stimulus $S_D$, and the same response R to another stimulus $S_{D'}$, without feeling it necessary to talk about the meaning of $S_D$ at all. The second context that Quine describes is that of "having meaning." For Quine, all that is involved here is the notion of significant sequences, which is entirely a grammatical one. The grammarian's task is to determine which sequences of the language are significant, and according to Quine this can and should be done without a prior notion of meaning, just as synonymy did not require the concept of meaning. Many modern linguists, as well as psychologists and philosophers, find this behavioristic approach too restrictive and have chosen to work with the concept of meaning, rather than to disregard it, but at the same time to explicate this difficult concept in a precise and detailed way.

The oldest theory of meaning is the referential theory: the meaning of a word is its reference. Frege (1952) destroyed that idea with his famous evening star example: since the morning star and the evening star both refer to the same object, the following two sentences must be synonymous according to the referential theory:

The morning star is the evening star.
The evening star is the evening star.

However, the latter sentence is logically true, while the former is not: telling someone who does not know it that the two stars are the same object is quite informative. Hence the two sentences cannot be synonymous. The referential theory of meaning fails because of problems such as this one.

Two important alternative intensionalistic theories of meaning within philosophy are the semantic theory of Katz and Fodor (1963) and the meaning postulate approach of Carnap (1952). Katz and Fodor represent the meaning of concepts as a set of features, or semantic markers. Thus, the meaning of the concept "bachelor" might be represented by the feature set {(physical object), (living), (human), (male), (adult), (never married)} (e.g., Katz, 1966). Since memory representations in terms of feature or attribute sets are very common in psychology, as we have seen in the previous chapters of this book, the Katz and Fodor theory fits quite well into current psychological thinking. Nevertheless, most psychological models for the representation of meaning are closer to Carnap's approach, using predicates rather than features (for an example see Table 6.6). Carnap's meaning postulates for the psychologist become a system of inference rules that permit one to derive new sentences from a set of given sentences, much as a logician derives theorems from his axiom sets. However, not only logical truths are derivable in such a system, but all kinds of sentences. Thus a formal, pseudo-logical system of great flexibility and power is obtained. Below we shall attempt to explain how such systems are supposed to work.

We shall be concerned here with three proposals for the psychological representation of meaning: Anderson and Bower (1973), Kintsch (1974), and Norman and Rumelhart (1975). These models were developed for somewhat different purposes, and they differ in some important respects, but their overall goals and their basic approaches are the same. We shall briefly sketch the principles involved and discuss some of the differences among these models. Then, in this and the following sections, we shall show how the models make feasible psychological research with natural language materials and compare them to some closely related computer models of artificial intelligence.

Some examples from Kintsch (1974) will introduce the basic concepts common to these models for the representation of meaning. The theory is concerned with texts and the meaning of texts. A *text* is a sequence of connected sentences in a natural language; the meaning of a text is its *text base*. The text base consists of a sequence of *propositions*; propositions in turn are composed of *concepts*. Each proposition consists of one *relational term* and one or more *arguments*. For instance, consider the proposition (HIT,GEORGE,JOHN) in Table 6.4. It consists of three concepts, the relation HIT and the arguments GEORGE and JOHN. We shall write concepts in capital letters, to distinguish them from the corresponding words which are

4.    **Examples of Propositions from Kintsch (1974)**

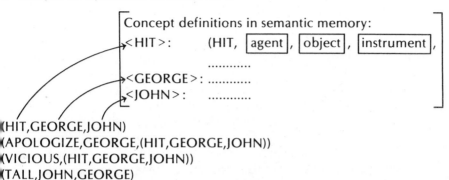

Concept definitions in semantic memory:

<HIT>:    (HIT,  [agent] ,  [object] ,  [instrument] ,

............

<GEORGE>:    ............

<JOHN>:    ............

(HIT,GEORGE,JOHN)
(APOLOGIZE,GEORGE,(HIT,GEORGE,JOHN))
(VICIOUS,(HIT,GEORGE,JOHN))
(TALL,JOHN,GEORGE)
(CONCESSION,(TALL,JOHN,GEORGE),(STRONG,GEORGE,JOHN))

italicized; furthermore, a proposition is always enclosed in round brackets, and the relational term is written first. (HIT,GEORGE,JOHN) can be realized linguistically by the English sentence *George hit John* or, in the right context, by *He hit John,* or some other such expression. The concepts appearing in this proposition are defined in semantic memory. HIT, for instance, is defined, in part, by a frame showing the case structure appropriate for propositions with HIT as a relation: the HIT-frame has slots for an *agent,* an *object,* and an *instrument*; in our example, the instrument slot is empty, but part of the definition of *HIT* also includes the information that if the agent of HIT is a person, likely instruments are HAND, STICK, etc., so that although it is not said with what George hit John, the comprehender can make some reasonable assumptions about it. The definition of HIT further includes the information that if someone is hit, he will be hurt, get angry, hit back, etc. These consequences of HIT correspond to the meaning postulates in Carnap's theory and form the basis for the inferential capacity of the system.

Continuing in Table 6.4, we note some different types of propositions. Example (2) shows how a proposition is used as an argument of another proposition: *George apologized for hitting John.* This capability of embedding one proposition into another is a crucial feature of propositional systems and greatly increases their power. A similar example is (3), except that here the relation is expressed in English by means of an adverb: *George hit John viciously.* The next example introduces the concept TALL in the context of the sentence *John is taller than George.* Note that the proposition (TALL,JOHN) also must be interpreted as a comparative statement, but one in which the comparison is not made explicit: John is tall for the class of persons he belongs to, e.g., four year olds (see Section 5.5.2). Finally, we have an example in which the relation is a sentence connective, the concept CONCESSION, and both arguments are propositions. CONCESSION is expressed in English by means of a *but*, or *however*, so that the English version of (5) might be *John is taller than George, but George is stronger than John*, or *John is taller than George. George, however, is stronger than he*. How a given proposition will be expressed linguistically depends on pragmatic factors, e.g., assumptions that the speaker makes about the listener's knowledge, or the speaker's desire to emphasize certain aspects. For now we shall neglect pragmatic factors, but we shall return to this important problem in Section 6.3.

The examples shown in Table 6.4 introduce the most important types of propositions. In each case the definitions of the concepts in semantic memory determine which concepts can be combined to form propositions, and how they are to be combined. Thus, a proposition such as (HIT,STADIUM,SHARK,SKY) would be semantically impossible, because stadium is not a possible agent for HIT, nor is SKY a possible instrument. The next step is to show how the propositions themselves are strung together to form text bases. Before that, however, we need to make a few comparisons among the different propositional systems that have been mentioned above. Propositions in the Norman and Rumelhart (1975) theory are constructed in much the same way as in Kintsch (1974), except that Norman and Rumelhart use a graphic notation. Table 6.5 shows how *George hit John* would be expressed in their system. Obviously (a) and (b) are merely notational variants. Both systems are based on the notion of *semantic cases*: the relational term in a proposition stands in a certain case relationship to its arguments, such as agent, object, instrument, or goal (after Fillmore, 1968). Propositions in these systems are treated as wholes, and as the basic units of meaning. Anderson and Bower's (1973) theory contrasts with these two systems in this respect. Their theory—called HAM, for human associative memory—is an associationistic one, in which a sentence is analyzed into a sequence of binary nodes. The labels on the associations between the nodes are derived from standard syntactic theory. A sentence consists of a *Subject* and *Predicate*, and the latter is subdivided into a *Relation* and *Object*. Thus, the same information is represented in (c) as in (a) and (b), but instead of treating propositions as units (c) breaks them down into their elements, the concept nodes.

The difference between the models in which propositions are treated as units (*a* and *b* in Table 6.5) and associationistic models (*c* in

TABLE 6.5.   **The Propositional Representation of** *George Hit John* **According to Kintsch (1974), Norman and Rumelhart (1975), and Anderson and Bower (1973).**

(a)        (HIT, GEORGE, JOHN)

(b)

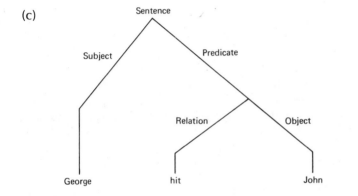

(c)

Table 6.5) is not merely one of notation. Substantive psychological issues are involved: are propositions Gestaltlike units, or is it sufficient to talk about the concepts themselves and their associative connections? Suppose we give a subject a list of unrelated sentences to read and then let him recall the sentences as well as he can. The wholistic theory would maintain that propositions should be recalled as units, even when they contain many arguments. The associationist theory would not predict any particular tendency to recall propositions as units. An experimental test of this prediction is, however, complicated by the fact that the experimenter does not have complete control over the subjects' encoding processes: hence, if subjects do not recall a given proposition as a unit, we do not know whether this is because they did not encode the proposition the way the experimenter wanted them to, or whether this observation represents a true failure of the wholistic theory. Specifically, suppose we give our subject the sentence *The settler built the cabin by hand.* According to wholistic models, this sentence is based upon one proposition containing the relation BUILD, an agent SETTLER, an object CABIN, and an instrument HAND. Now suppose our hypothetical subject recalls this sentence as *The settler built a cabin;* is this because he never encoded the instrument HAND, or is it a case of partial recall? We certainly cannot assume that a reader always encodes a sentence in the way we want him to; the nominal and functional stimulus are in general no more identical in sentence memory experiments than they are in paired-associate experiments. Therefore, the mere occurrence of partial recall does not contradict the notion that propositions are the units of recall.

Kintsch and Glass (1974) have suggested a way out of this dilemma: they compared recall for sentences derived from a single proposition with sentences that had the same number of content words but were derived from two or three propositions. Wholistic theories predict more complete sentence recall in the former case. An example would be a sentence pair such as *The settler built the cabin by hand* versus the three-proposition sentence *The crowded passengers squirmed uncomfortably* (the three propositions being *The passengers squirmed, The passengers were crowded,* and *The squirming was uncomfortable*). Although about 91% of the total recall (i.e., the number of content words recalled from each sentence) came from complete sentence recall when the sentences were based on a single proposition, only 74% of total recall came from complete sentence recall when the sentences were based on three propositions. Thus, there definitely appeared to be a tendency to recall propositions as units, at least more so than the control sentences used in this experiment.

Sentence recall data from experiments in which subjects were given lists of sentences to study and in which recall was cued with one or more words from each sentence are also relevant to the issue. Anderson and Bower (1973) have reported some findings that strongly support their associationistic memory representations. Table 6.6 explains their argument and experimental design. According to HAM, cued recall is possible only when the connections between the recall cue and the to-be-recalled word exist in memory. Thus, if the test sentence is *The child hit the landlord,* and the recall cue is *child,* the object of the sentence can be recalled if and only if the path from *child* to *landlord* is intact. If $a$ is the probability that the section of the path from *child* to the relation node (V) is complete, and $c$ is the probability that the path from the relation node to *landlord* is complete, the probability that both exist, and hence that *landlord* can be recalled in response to the cue *child,* is $ac$. Similarly, if the recall cue is

TABLE 6.6.  **HAM's Memory Representation in the Cued Sentence Recall Experiment (a) and the Crossover Experiment (b). (after Anderson and Bower, 1973)**

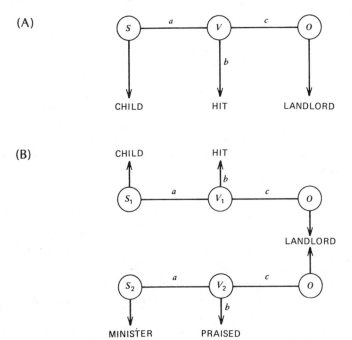

*hit* and we let *b* be the probability that the path from *hit* to the relation node (V) exists, the probability of recalling the object *landlord* to the verb cue *hit* is *bc*. Now consider part (b) of Table 6.6. Here we have two sentences that share the same object, *landlord*. If we assign probabilities that certain sections of the path exist between *landlord* and the cue words in the same way as before, we can make some interesting calculations. First of all, we have as before

$$P(O/S) = ac$$
$$P(O/V) = bc$$

where *O,S*, and *V* stand for object, subject, and verb, respectively, and the slash denotes that the probability of recalling the object is conditional from the *S* (or *V*) cue. The interesting case arises when we give both *S* and *V* as a recall cue. Suppose we give the subject and verb from the same sentence as a recall cue (denoted $S_1$ and $V_1$). In order to calculate the probability of recalling the object in response to that cue, we must take into account three possibilities: the probability that the $S$ cue is effective, the probability that the $V$ cue is effective (both of which we have already calculated), and the probability that both $S$ and $V$ are effective simultaneously, which we have to subtract from the sum of the first two terms according to the general formula for summing probabilities

$$P(X \text{ or } Y) = P(X) + P(Y) - P(X \text{ and } Y)$$

Since the probability that both $S$ and $V$ are effective is simply the probability that all of the paths for that sentence are intact, we have

$$P(O/S_1 V_1) = ac + bc - abc$$

Now consider what happens when the subject of one of the sentences and the verb from another sentence is presented as a recall cue. According to HAM

$$P(O/S_1 V_2) = ac + bc - acbc$$

because in this case both links labeled $c$ must be intact for both $S_1$ and $V_2$ to lead to the recall of *landlord*. However, $acbc$ is always less than $abc$, so that we arrive at the counterintuitive prediction that $P(O/S_1 V_1)$ $< P(O/S_1 V_2)$. Certainly, if propositions form wholistic units, one would expect a crossover cue to be less effective than when both subject and verb come from the same sentence.

Anderson and Bower performed such a crossover experiment and found the results predicted by HAM: $P(O/S_1 S_2)$ was .58, but $P(O/S_1 V_2)$ was .61. They concluded that "there is no further information in the same cues than that contained in its parts, $S$ and $V$." It looked as if for once someone had found an experimental design to finally decide the age-old controversy between elementaristic and wholistic theories in psychology. However, Anderson and Bower's results did not remain unchallenged for long; Foss and Harwood (1975) successfully reopened the case. First of all, they reported an experiment that was essentially a replication of Anderson and Bower's experiment but which yielded rather different results: the same sentence cues were much better (40%) than the crossover cues (25%). Secondly, they could explain why their results differed so much from Anderson and Bower's: if the overall level of recall in experiments of this type is high (as it was in Anderson and Bower's case), the mathematics of the situation work out in such a way that HAM-like results must always be obtained; only if the overall recall is low (as it was in the Foss and Harwood experiment) is it possible to obtain data that contradict HAM.

In summary, it seems fair to say that the data of Kintsch and Glass and Foss and Harwood argue more in favor of a wholistic theory than for associationistic conceptions.

The issue of elements versus wholes is, however, not the only one that distinguishes between the models in Table 6.5. Another related problem concerns the role of semantic decomposition in sentence comprehension and memory. The ideal of many semantic theories is to decompose the meaning of all concepts into a small set of meaning elements. All word meanings can then be constructed by combining these semantic elements in suitable ways. Just as the chemist constructs all matter by compounding a relatively small number of chemical elements, so the semanticist wants to construct all concepts by compounding the semantic elements. The semantic markers of Katz and Fodor (1963) were supposed to be such a set of basic meaning elements. Computer scientists who work on artificial intelligence programs usually share this ideal. They, too, tend to view operations with meaningful materials as a calculus of semantic elements. Ideally, one would know how to decompose complex semantic expressions into their elements. One could then operate with these elements (e.g., to derive inferences) and, since the number of these elements would be relatively low, a fairly simple rule system might be sufficient to govern these operations. Once the necessary computations have been accomplished, the semantic elements are then reconstituted into complex expressions. The work of Schank (1972) is an excellent illustration of such an approach. For the psychologist the problem is more complicated because he must decide whether, or rather under what circumstances, people analyze complex concepts into their elements: it is not sufficient to assume that thinking occurs at the level of semantic elements, merely for the sake of an elegant theory.

Table 6.7 shows how decomposition is employed in the theories of Norman and Rumelhart (1975) and Kintsch (1974). Norman and Rumelhart represent the sentence *Mary gives Fred a book* by (a). They claim, however, that only a superficial level of comprehension is involved in (a). A deeper level of comprehension results in the representation (b), in which the complex concept GIVE has been decomposed into its constituents: some act of Mary causes Fred to get the book. An even deeper analysis yields (c), in which the concept GET itself is decomposed into its semantic primitives, a change from one state of possession to another state of possession. In Kintsch (1974) the same effect is achieved through the use of meaning postulates as shown in (d).

There is no question that the analysis of GIVE in Table 6.7 is

TABLE 6.7.    **The Decomposition of** *Mary Gives Fred a Book* **According to Norman and Rumelhart (1975), and the Meaning Postulate for GIVE According to Kintsch (1974).**

(a)

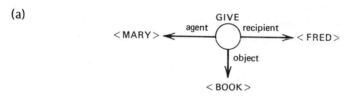

(b)

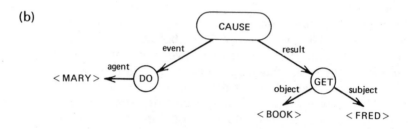

(c)

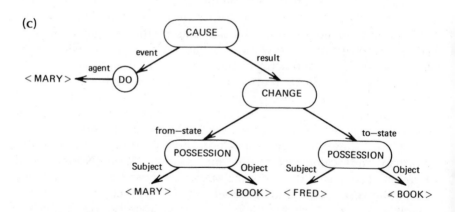

(d)    (GIVE,AGENT,RECIPIENT,OBJECT)=
(CAUSE,(DO,AGENT),(GET,RECIPIENT,OBJECT))=
(CAUSE,(DO,AGENT),(CHANGE,(POSSESS,AGENT,OBJECT),
(POSSESS,RECIPIENT,OBJECT)))

psychologically meaningful. For instance, Gentner (1975) has shown that it predicts the order in which children learn such words as *give, take, trade, buy,* or *sell.* Each of these words requires that the child be able to operate with a certain number of basic semantic concepts. The semantic elements of GIVE are DO, CAUSE, and TRANSFER; other words such as *trade* or *sell* require additional semantic elements for their use, and are therefore more complex semantically. Gentner tested whether children between the ages of 3 and 8 years could understand these verbs by having them act out instructions with some toys. She found that the children almost always understood the conceptually simpler verbs before the more complex ones. The order in which the children acquired the verbs and the errors they made could be explained by the nature and number of the semantic elements necessary for the comprehension of each concept.

Obviously, people are able to decompose concepts like GIVE; they know it involves an act of causation resulting in a change of possession. After reading *Mary gives Fred a book* they have no trouble answering questions like *Who has the book?* Upon demand they are certainly able to decompose GIVE. But that does not imply that all comprehension necessarily involves semantic decomposition. Indeed, this does not appear to be the case. Instead, people treat complex semantic concepts as units, without decomposing them, unless the task demands it. Kintsch (1974) has reported a series of experiments in which he tried to measure the difficulty subjects have in comprehending sentences that contain a complex semantic concept versus control sentences containing a simpler concept. For instance, if the comprehender always decomposes concepts, a sentence with the verb *accuse* should be more difficult to process than a sentence containing *guilty: John is accused of stealing* must be decomposed into *Someone says John is guilty of stealing,* and hence should be harder than *John is guilty of stealing.* However, Kintsch (1974) was not able to detect differences in processing difficulties for sentence pairs of that kind. Similarly, it appears that *John is guilty of stealing* is no easier to remember than *John is accused of stealing,* though the decomposed version of the latter sentence is surely more complex and would be less likely to be stored correctly in memory. Hence it appears that subjects store in memory meaning representations like (a) in Table 6.7, rather than (b) or (c)—unless there is some special reason to do so.

The problem is to decide what the set of circumstances is under which complex semantic concepts are decomposed. In some sentence verification experiments subjects apparently employ a decomposition strategy (Section 6.2.1). Furthermore, answering questions and making inferences frequently requires decomposition. Even the mere comprehension of a sentence may sometimes involve decomposition. Sherman (1976) had subjects judge the reasonableness of sentences containing multiple negations. He used the speed with which such judgments were made as an index of the difficulty of comprehension. He was particularly interested in whether marked adjectives (e.g., *sad*) and negatively prefixed adjectives (e.g., *unhappy*) were treated as units or were decomposed (i.e., *not happy*). In an otherwise affirmative context such adjectives had no effect on reaction times, indicating that they were treated as units. However, in sentences with more than two negatives *sad* and *unhappy* increased comprehension times, indicating that they were decomposed semantically: negatives always increase the processing time for a sentence (Section 6.2.1). Thus, in simple sentences *sad* and *unhappy* are comprehended as unitary concepts; if they occur in a sentence that is very difficult to comprehend because it already contains several negatives, they are decomposed into *not-happy*. It is as if in this latter case the normal comprehension process is no longer able to deal with the complexity of the sentence, and instead the sentence meaning must be calculated by counting the number of negatives.

On balance it appears that we definitely do not want a system in which semantic decomposition is obligatory; people frequently operate with complex concepts as chunks. On the other hand, precisely when decomposition is used is as yet not well understood.

Although many questions remain about the psychological representation of meaning, enough progress has been made to ask what one can do with such models. The three models discussed here have been put to rather different uses. Kintsch is oriented toward the study of discourse, which will be discussed in the next section. Norman and Rumelhart are as much interested in developing a viable artificial intelligence program as in purely psychological questions. Anderson and Bower's HAM is the only one of the three with an explicit psychological processing model for a wide variety of experimental problems: encoding of sentences in memory, sentence recognition and recall, fact retrieval, question answering, as well as list learning. HAM recognizes sentences by means of a process called MATCH. Suppose that HAM's memory structure includes the sentence *George hit John* in the form shown in Table 6.5 (c). If HAM is given that sentence again, it will recognize that it already has a representation of it in memory by matching the sentence representation against its memory. Starting from the words *George, hit,* and *John,* HAM matches the terminal nodes connected to these words in memory and then examines the paths leading away from these nodes. A match will be obtained if there is a path in memory connecting the same terminal nodes such that all the labels on this path occur in the same sequence as in the input sentence. One experimental prediction that immediately follows from this model is that the more different paths that have to be examined from a word, the longer it should take to retrieve the target path. If there is only one path in HAM's memory from *George,* it is easier to find than when there are many. Indeed, Anderson and Bower (1973) have reported some experimental results supporting this prediction.

As described, the MATCH process would always complete a match, if a sentence is stored in HAM's memory; that is, the model would predict that no recognition failures occur. To get around this problem, and also to make the search process more efficient, the paths leading from each terminal node in HAM are not all equivalent but are ordered according to their recency. For instance, all the paths leading away from *George* would be ordered in a pushdown stack, such that the most recent one is at the top of the stack, pushing all the others down a step. The MATCH process does not examine all the paths in a stack, but only a certain number on the top of the stack. Thus, the more recent connections will be examined first, and very old ones not at all, leading to recognition failures. Anderson and Bower have shown that this rather simple mechanism can account for an astonishing variety of phenomena in word and sentence learning.

There are two ways of testing such complex theories as HAM: by comparing their predictions against the results of psychological experiments in the conventional manner, or by writing computer programs to see whether they work at all. If one can write a program that recognizes sentences and answers questions one has, of course, no guarantee that the computer does it the same way as the human subject would, but at least one knows that the theory upon which the program is based works. It may not work the right way, but, with theories as complex as those discussed here, just to know that it does what it is supposed to do is not in the least trivial. Furthermore, our experience with artificial intelligence programs tells us whether or not they were originally conceived as simulations of human processes or simply to get a job done, the better they function the more human they appear to be. One is almost tempted to speculate that for a really complex operation such as language comprehension or chess playing there is only one good way to perform it, namely the human way. However this may be, it is clear today that the distinction between artificial intelligence models and psychological theories is becoming less and less obvious; artificial intelligence appears to be on its way to becoming a branch of cognitive theory (Bobrow and Collins, 1975).

As yet there is no artificial intelligence program that can compete with the human intellect; but then there is no psychological theory either that could account for the full range of cognitive processes. The progress that has been made is nevertheless impressive in both fields. It has already been mentioned that Norman and Rumelhart's (1975) work is an excellent example of the modern hybrid that is both psychological theory and artificial intelligence program. However, they were more interested in the principles that must be incorporated into a computer program that is to exhibit intelligent behavior than in actually constructing a working program. Other examples of this type of work are found in Schank and Colby (1973) and Bobrow and Collins (1975), but the most impressive program that is actually functioning today is that of Winograd (1972).

Winograd's program allows one to interact with a computer (by means of a typewriter) as one would with another person. One can ask it questions, get intelligent answers, give it instructions, teach it new words—as long as the interaction is confined to the computer's world. This world consists of some blocks (cubes, pyramids, etc.) of different sizes and colors, a box to put things in, and a support surface. Actually, it is realized only as a picture on a CRT screen, and the computer can move objects about in this world by means of a pointer. However, within that restricted world one can engage in sophisticated conversations with the computer, several examples of which are given in Winograd's paper. The computer obviously understands this conversation adequately and responds in an intelligent manner.

Winograd achieved this rather impressive feat with a program that consists of three interacting components: a syntactic parser that analyzes the input sentences (and generates the output sentences), a program for the representation of knowledge and inference making, and a semantics program that serves as a bridge between the other two.

Let us consider how this program would understand some simple sentences, such as *The block is red,* or *The box contains the block.* Winograd's parser is a sequence of programs that are applied recursively. A very simplified version is shown in Table 6.8. The sentence program first calls the noun phrase and verb phrase programs. The noun phrase program looks for a determiner (*the* in our example) and a noun (either *block* or *box*). Having found what it was looking for the noun phrase program returns control to the sentence program, which now calls the verb phrase program. The verb phrase program has two

**TABLE 6.8.   A Simple Parsing Program after Winograd (1972)**

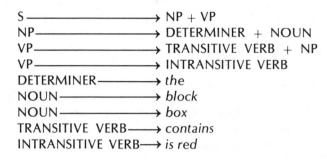

S ⟶ NP + VP
NP ⟶ DETERMINER + NOUN
VP ⟶ TRANSITIVE VERB + NP
VP ⟶ INTRANSITIVE VERB
DETERMINER ⟶ *the*
NOUN ⟶ *block*
NOUN ⟶ *box*
TRANSITIVE VERB ⟶ *contains*
INTRANSITIVE VERB ⟶ *is red*

options: it either finds a transitive verb (e.g., *contains*) in which case it will call back the noun phrase program to analyze the rest of the phrase, or it finds an intransitive verb (to keep our example simple, we shall consider *is red* as such an instance). Obviously this syntactic parser will correctly accept sentences such as *The block is red* or *The box contains the block*.

At this point, the semantics program takes over, and given such a phrase as *red block* it applies procedures to identify such an object in the world. Sometimes, however, the semantic program will censor the output of the parser. Note that the rules in Table 6.7 would also accept the sentence *The block contains the box*. The semantic program would tell the computer that such a sentence cannot be true.

Information that is syntactically and semantically analyzed is then stored as part of the computer's knowledge base. Knowledge is represented propositionally, and part of the knowledge base consists of inference making programs. The latter permit the computer to answer questions like *Is the block inside the box?* after hearing *The box contains the block.* Furthermore, the computer keeps track of the referents of phrases throughout a conversation, as well as of the current scene in the blocks' world. Thereby, it can identify pronouns: if asked *Is it inside the box?* the computer would identify the *it* with the object most recently mentioned, in much the same way as people do in a conversation.

As impressive as it is to talk to Winograd's program, it certainly is not the last word in artificial intelligence. As psychologists we must object to the excessive dependence on syntax in understanding sentences. The program could not understand a simple nonsyntactic phrase such as *eat-dog-steak,* though as we have seen in Sections 6.1.2 and 6.1.3 people generally use semantic comprehension strategies and pay relatively little attention to syntax, if they can get by without it. Most important, however, is the restriction to the block world. Programs that can deal with a broader section of the world will probably not be straightforward extensions of the blocks' world program. New, more powerful theoretical approaches will be necessary to handle large data bases.

Winograd's program answers questions very well, as long as they refer to the blocks' world. Humans however, not only know many more answers, they can also determine what kind of an answer the questioner wants. Norman (1973) has pointed out that what the answer will be to the question "Where is the Empire State building?" depends quite strongly on context: if the question is asked in Russia, an appropriate answer might be "In the US"; in New York City, an answer like "On 34th street" would be better. Or, if the question is asked in the New York subway, the answer would not be a location at all, but instructions how to get there. A really intelligent question answering system must take into account the total context in which the question is asked. Not single sentences, or isolated items of knowledge, but whole texts or dialogues in their pragmatic context must become the objects of psychological inquiry.

## 6.3    TEXT PROCESSING

We have repeatedly pointed out the importance of context in sentence comprehension. Neither experimentally nor theoretically can much progress be made unless larger units than the sentence become the basis of analysis. On the one hand, a sentence must be viewed within its linguistic context. That is, texts rather than sentences must be studied. On the other hand, the nonlinguistic, pragmatic context cannot be neglected either. The speaker's and listener's beliefs and intentions, the conventions they observe, are inseparable from the meaning of a text.

Several experimental demonstrations of the importance of context have already been discussed. Of the many others that could be added, consider just two illustrative ones. It is known that when subjects recall a list of sentences, the tenses of the verbs are very poorly recalled. In one study by Harris and Brewer (1973) 45% tense shifts were observed, However, these authors could show that the poor tense recall can easily be improved: all one needs to do is to provide a temporal context (by means of temporal adverbs, such as *yesterday* or *tomorrow*) to the sentences, and tense is recalled very well. A similar demonstration was made by Brewer and Harris (1974) concerning deictic sentence elements (e.g., words such as *here, now, this, the,* that are defined only in an appropriate context). In isolated sentences deictic words are very hard to remember; embedded in an appropriate context, however, subjects recall them as well as other words. Clearly verb tenses and deictic elements are a problem only out of context, when they have no meaning by themselves.

The question is not whether sentences should be studied in their context but how. Research with prose materials has been hampered by the lack of a theoretical foundation for dealing with the structure of texts. Hence the emphasis has been on the nature of the subjects' activities during comprehension, rather than the characteristics of the text itself. A great deal of important information has been acquired in these studies about how instructions affect what subjects learn from a text (e.g., Frase, 1976), about the influence of the subjects' goals on memory for a text (Frederiksen, 1975), or about how questions before or after reading a text affect its processing (Anderson and Biddle, 1976). Rothkopf (1972) has developed a systematic account of how the reader's activities determine what is learned. These studies are reminiscent of the experiments on "task variables" in verbal learning that were discussed in Chapter 1. What is lacking here is a concern with the "materials" variable. Indeed, in some cases investigators went so far as to deny the importance of materials variables in learning from prose (e.g., Frase, 1976), because the materials variables manipulated in their studies had demonstrably little effect. However, the text characteristics investigated in these studies were things like the syntactic complexity of sentences, or word frequency. There was no way of studying the complexity of the content of a text itself, nor of dealing with such concepts as context, theme, or gist, which must be the basic concepts of a theory of text processing.

The models for the representation of meaning discussed above provide us with the necessary theoretical apparatus that makes the psychological study of text processing possible. We shall first discuss research on the effects of the content and structure of relatively short texts and then look at some more recent work with longer texts.


## TEXT BASES, READING, AND RECALL

Of the models for the representation of meaning discussed above the one that was developed specifically for work with texts rather than sentences is that of Kintsch (1974). We have already outlined this model as it applies to the representation of sentences. It remains to be shown here how the meaning of a whole text is represented by means of propositional text bases. A very simple example is shown in Table 6.9. The meaning of a two-sentence text of 21 words is represented by a text base of eight propositions. Each proposition is written on a separate line and numbered for convenience of reference. Thus, Proposition 5, which reads (WHEN, 3,4) is simply a shorthand for (WHEN,(CONQUER,ROMAN,GREEK), (COPY,ROMAN,GREEK)). The examples in Table 6.4 should enable the reader to understand the notation used here. There is only one new aspect that has not yet been discussed: how does one distinguish between an unrelated list of propositions and a coherent text base? Kintsch (1974) has argued that a necessary condition for coherence (though not a sufficient one) is argument repetition. The propositions of a text base must be interconnected through the repetition of arguments. For instance, 2 is connected with 1 because of the repetition of the argument ART; the relationship between 2 and 1 is one of subordination. Similarly, 3 and 4 are subordinated to 1 because of the repetition of GREEK; 5 is subordinated to 3 and 4, because 3 and 4 are embedded in 5 as arguments. Propositions 6, 7, and 8 are subordinated to 3 because of the repetition of ROMAN in 6 and 8, and of 3 itself in 7. Thus argument repetition creates a structure of interconnections in a text base, as shown in Figure 6.9. Proposition 1 is the topical proposition in this text base; propositions 2 to 4 are subordinated to it, and form the next

TABLE 6.9. **An Example of a Text and its Text Base. The Level of a Proposition in the Text Base is Indicated by Indentation (after Kintsch, et al. 1975)**

*Text:*
The Greeks loved beautiful art. When the Romans conquered the Greeks, they copied them, and, thus, learned to create beautiful art.

| *Text base:* | 1 | (LOVE,GREEK,ART) |
|---|---|---|
| | 2 | (BEAUTIFUL,ART) |
| | 3 | (CONQUER,ROMAN,GREEK) |
| | 4 | (COPY,ROMAN,GREEK) |
| | 5 | (WHEN,3,4) |
| | 6 | (LEARN,ROMAN,8) |
| | 7 | (CONSEQUENCE,3,6) |
| | 8 | (CREATE,ROMAN,2) |

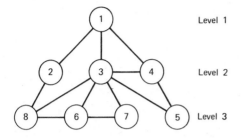

Level 1

Level 2

Level 3

FIGURE 6.9  **The hierarchical structure of the text base shown in Table 6.8. Propositions that are related via argument repetition are connected by a line.**

level in the propositional hierarchy. Propositions 5 to 8 are at the lowest level in this text base. Note that the level of a proposition is defined objectively by the repetition rule, given the choice of one or more topical propositions for a paragraph. Although the theory requires text bases to be connected via argument repetition, texts may be disconnected as in *It is snowing and the streets are slick,* but in the underlying text base there must be a connection between the two propositions expressed in this sentence, e.g., a relation CAUSATION that was deleted in the actual text. A listener who hears such a sentence must therefore infer the connecting proposition—as we have already seen in Section 6.2.3.

Given text bases like the one in Table 6.9, one can ask how various characteristics of the text base affect comprehension and recall. Kintsch and Keenan (1973) have shown that there exists a lawful relationship between the time subjects take to read a text and the number of propositions they process, independent of the number of words in the text. Subjects were given sentences to read that were 14 to 16 words long, but were based on text bases containing from 4 to 9 propositions. For example, *Romulus, the legendary founder of Rome took the women of the Sabine by force* is based on only four propositions; *Cleopatra's downfall lay in her foolish trust of the fickle political figures of the Roman world* is derived from a text base with eight propositions. Subjects read these sentences and their reading time was recorded. Immediately after reading they tried to recall each sentence as well as they could, not necessarily verbatim. The number of propositions represented in each recall protocol was noted, and correlated with the time it took the subject to read the sentence. The results are shown in Figure 6.10. Note that in this experiment the number of words read was the same for all sentences. Nevertheless, a reader who recalled only four propositions from a sentence (say either all four in the *Romulus* sentence cited above, or four of the eight in the *Cleopatra* sentence) studied the sentence for about 11 seconds. To

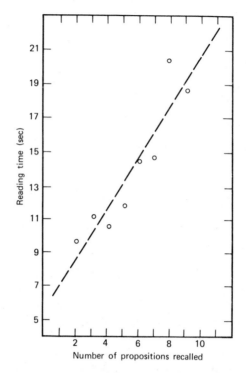

FIGURE 6.10   **Reading time as a function of the number of propositions recalled for 16 or 17-word sentences with different numbers of propositions in their bases. (after Kintsch and Keenan, 1973)**

get all eight propositions of the *Cleopatra* sentence correct, a reading time of around 17 seconds would typically be required.

There are of course other text base variables that affect reading in addition to the number of propositions in the text base. If the number of propositions in a text is controlled, but the number of arguments employed in these propositions is varied, reading times are longer when many different arguments appear in the base than when only a few arguments are repeated (Kintsch, Kozminsky, Streby, McKoon, and Keenan, 1975). Kintsch et al. constructed paragraphs about 70 words long, and always composed from the same number of propositions (about 24), but in one case the text base was constructed from only 7 or 8 arguments that were frequently repeated, and in the other case they were constructed from twice as many arguments that were less frequently repeated. Introducing many new arguments produced comprehension difficulties: reading times became longer, or if reading times were fixed, recall decreased. This effect occurred in spite of the fact that if only a few arguments can be used in texts with a fixed number of propositions, many embeddings of one proposition as an argument of another must occur, and that such texts are structurally quite complex. Frequent repetition of arguments, however, appears to overcome whatever problems might be produced by this complexity. Indeed, Manelis and Yekovich (1976) reported that recall for sentences that are connected via argument repetition (e.g., *Arnold lunged at Norman. Norman called the doctor. The doctor arrived*) is better than for much shorter sentences in which the connecting words have been deleted (e.g., *Arnold lunged. Norman called. The doctor arrived.*) With repetitions recall was 51%, without repetitions it was only 43%.

Whether a proposition is recalled depends most of all on its position in the text base hierarchy. High-level propositions are recalled much better than low-level propositions. The data shown in Figure 6.11 are representative: the difference in recall probability between the most superordinate and the most subordinate propositions is of the order of .50! The finding that superordinate propositions are recalled much better than subordinate ones also has been observed by Meyer (1975). Meyer inserted a paragraph into a longer text either in such a way that it was high in the text hierarchy or low. Recall of the paragraph in the low position was only 72% of the recall when the paragraph was high in the structure. After a one-week delay, this effect was even more pronounced: recall in the low position was now reduced to only 27%

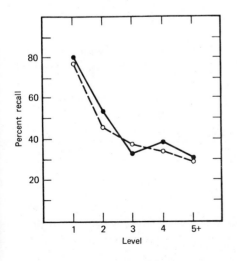

FIGURE 6.11 **Recall probability as a function of the level of a proposition in the text base hierarchy. The data are for 70-word paragraphs about history (filled circles) and science (open circles). (after Kintsch et al., 1975)**

of recall in the high position. Kintsch et al. have obtained similar results for delayed recall, suggesting that superordinate propositions are not only processed preferentially, but may also be better retained.

Wanner (1974) showed that the effectiveness of a word from a sentence as a recall cue depends on the number of propositions that word is involved in. Consider the sentence pair

$$\text{The governor asked the detective to } \left\{ \begin{array}{l} cease \\ prevent \end{array} \right\} \text{ drinking.}$$

which has the corresponding text bases

(ASK,GOVERNOR,DETECTIVE,(CEASE,DETECTIVE,
(DRINK,DETECTIVE)))
(ASK,GOVERNOR,DETECTIVE,(PREVENT,DETECTIVE,
(DRINK,SOMEONE))).

In the *cease* sentence the detective is involved as an argument in all three propositions; in the *prevent* sentence it is involved only in two propositions. Hence *detective* should be a better recall cue in the first case than in the second. Indeed, Wanner reports that the recall likelihood was .39 for sentences of the *cease* type but only .30 for sentences of the *prevent* type when *detective* was the recall cue. Since the sentences were not recalled with different probabilities when *governor* was the recall cue (.27 and .25, respectively), we conclude that they did not differ in overall difficulty, and that the greater involvement of *detective* in the base of these sentences accounted for the differential recall.

The experimental results discussed here suggest that it is quite profitable to view the process of comprehension as one of constructing text bases from texts. Knowing the text base of a text permits us to predict quite well how long subjects will study it, and which propositions will be recalled. In other words, our structural theory of the text permits us to say something about the way subjects process this text—something that could not be predicted from the text alone. However, in the account presented so far we have not emphasized sufficiently the constructive nature of this comprehension process.

## 6.3.2  CONSTRUCTIVE PROCESSES

In the above studies only reproductive recall was scored: the recall protocols generated by a subject were compared with the propositions in the study material and each proposition represented in the protocol was scored as recalled, whether recall was verbatim or not. This procedure has the advantage of considerable objectivity and reliability, but it neglects some important features of prose recall: all partial recall of propositions is disregarded and, more importantly, all nonveridical recall is neglected, that is, cases where the subject says something that was not stated in the text. Some of these cases are errors or elaborations of the text material. Others, however, are not errors at all but occur when the reader constructs a text base that deviates somewhat from the one actually intended by the speaker. The reader makes some inferences that are not made in the text, he overgeneralizes in some places, or he summarizes portions of the text. These are processes that occur during comprehension, and we shall call them constructive processes. Another source of nonveridical recall are reconstructive processes that occur at the time of recall. These are especially prominent when fairly long texts are being recalled for which the reader remembers only the gist or some details. Frequently, he then proceeds to fill out this detail with plausible reconstructions.

There has been an unfortunate controversy among students of prose memory as to whether recall is reproductive, constructive, or reconstructive. Bartlett (1932) studied how his subjects, English college students, recalled some rather obscure Indian folktale called "The war of the ghosts." He found that their recall was characterized by substantial error. The folktale usually was quite distorted in recall and subjects appeared to be making much of it up at the time of recall. Bartlett concluded that prose recall was more than the reproduction of the input and was above all reconstructive. Later investigators, however, failed to replicate Bartlett's finding. Gomulicki (1956), Zangwill (1972) and Cofer (1973), using less exotic learning materials, found recall to be quite accurate, with very few reconstructions and elaborations of the kind Bartlett had described. Furthermore, when multiple recall trials were given, there was considerable consistency between what was recalled on one trial and the next (see also the work of Frederiksen described below). Constructions or inferences, if they occurred at all, were part of the comprehension process, not the recall process. Therefore, Gomulicki argued that recall was reproductive and constructive, but not reconstructive, and others since have taken either his or Bartlett's side.

Prose recall is, however, neither reproductive nor constructive nor reconstructive, but all three, and the problem for the psychologist is to explore what is involved in these processes and to determine the conditions under which one or the other becomes dominant. Suppose a subject reads a 70-word paragraph about the Biblical story of Joseph and his brothers in Egypt. If he is asked to recall the paragraph immediately, his recall will be primarily reproductive; his main error will be omission of subordinate material. Suppose, however, that he is asked to recall the paragraph after a 1-day delay. In this case his recall will include some reproduction, but most of all it will be reconstructed from his knowledge of the Joseph story. He does not remember very well what the paragraph said and instead responds with other information that he has about this story. Sulin and Dooling (1974) and Kintsch et al. (1975) have described this phenomenon. Thus, we have both reproductive and reconstructive recall for the same passages, depending on the time of testing.

Quite in general, it can be asserted that the nature of recall depends on many factors, such as delay and familiarity of the text (discussed above), the length of the text (reproductive recall for very long texts is poor—in recalling a long story such as a novel one tends to summarize it rather than to reproduce it, as we shall see in Section 6.3.4), and the instructions given to the reader (e.g., Brockway, Chmielewski, and Cofer, 1974). Inference processes during reading were described in Section 6.2.3, but these inferences were of a special kind: they were necessary for the comprehension of the text. Readers frequently make other inferences that are not necessary for comprehension, but that are invited by the text to some degree or another.

A study that establishes the point that inferences may occur during reading rather than at the time of recall is one by Frederiksen (1975). Frederiksen's subjects recalled a 500-word descriptive essay, and Frederiksen scored their protocols not only for veridical recall but also for several types of constructions and errors. Instead of treating propositions as units, Frederiksen scored separately for concepts and relations, but since the two gave similar results we shall only discuss the combined data. Three types of constructions were considered: overgeneralizations (e.g., a subject recalls *best administrators* as *administrators*), pseudodiscriminations (e.g., *administrators* is recalled as *successful administrators*) and inferences (e.g., given *senators are ranchers* and *senators are rich, rich ranchers* is recalled). Finally, Frederiksen distinguished a response class called elaborations consisting of new material introduced by the subject into the recall protocol. In a way Frederiksen's elaborations are also inferences of a sort, but less direct ones, e.g., when a subject recalls that *senators were elected by the majority of the people,* although nothing at all was said about elections in the text.

Frederiksen scored 43% of all responses as veridical, 40% as constructions, and 17% as elaborations. Veridical recall increased considerably over the four recall trials in Frederiksen's experiment, while constructions remained essentially constant and elaborations decreased. Constructions are not errors, and once a subject makes one he apparently retains it on later trials. The number of constructions correlates positively with the number of veridical responses in Frederiksen's protocols, though not very highly. If these responses were the product of reconstructive processes at the time of recall, one would have expected a negative correlation: as more veridical information becomes available the need for reconstructions decreases. Thus, we seem to be justified in maintaining that overgeneralizations, pseudodiscriminations, and inferences are constructive responses occurring during the comprehension process itself. Elaborations are different. They are more like errors, they decrease over trials in frequency, and their number is negatively correlated with the amount of correct recall. Thus, elaborations probably represent reconstructions during recall, and as recall improves over trials, they are discarded.

Which inferences from among the many possible ones actually occur during comprehension is another important problem. There are various ways that texts invite inferences. For example, Loftus and Palmer (1974) showed subjects a film about an auto accident and asked them a biasing question about it: "*About how fast were the cars going when they smashed/collided/bumped?*" A week later the subjects were given a recognition test. Among the test items was *Did you see broken glass?* (There was no broken glass in the film). More subjects answered *yes* to that question who had been given the "smashed" question during study than who had been given the "collided" or "bumped" question.

Loftus' and Palmer's experiment is an example of how language biases memory through the presuppositions that we associate with certain words. Their subjects never saw broken glass, but those who were given the question with "smashed" inferred that there must have been considerable damage to the cars, and therefore later reported seeing broken glass.

Whether someone says *The girl opened the door* or *The girl did not open the door,* he implies in either case that the door was closed. Statements that are implied by both an assertion and its negation are called presuppositions. Normally both a speaker and a hearer assume presuppositions as given. If someone says *Richard stopped getting drunk every night,* we assume that Richard indeed was in the habit of drinking too much every night. The presuppositions of a sentence are not scrutinized as much as what the sentence asserts (in this case that *Richard stopped*), and hence are good for lying. Hornby (1974) had subjects verify sentences against pictures. The sentences were either cleft or pseudo-cleft sentences such as *It is the girl that petted the cat,* or *The one that is petting the cat is the girl.* In either case the sentence focuses on the girl and presupposes that she is petting a cat. The picture, which followed 1 second after the sentence, was presented only for 50 milliseconds, and showed either a girl petting a cat, in which case the subject was to respond *yes,* or a boy petting a cat, or a girl petting a dog, in which case the proper response was *no.* The interesting result of the study was that many more errors occurred when the picture misrepresented the presupposed part of the sentence (i.e., a dog rather than a cat was being petted) than when it misrepresented the focus of the sentence (a boy rather than a girl). In fact, errors were almost doubled when presuppositions were misrepresented (2.16 for presuppositions, 1.17 for focus).

Presuppositions are a kind of invited inference. Such inferences are made during the comprehension process, and they have consequences for the memory representation of a sentence, too. A study by Offir (1973) shows that subjects are quite good on a recognition test at detecting changes in sentences when a presupposition is affected. Offir constructed her sentence materials from two propositions

(A)     I know a man.
(B)     A man (the same one) embezzled $1,000,000.

If one wants to communicate these two propositions to a listener who is ignorant of both, the following two relative clause sentences would be equally appropriate

(1)     I know a man who embezzled $1,000,000.
(2)     A man I know embezzled $1,000,000.

However, consider how one would tell a listener who already knows that there is some man who embezzled $1,000,000, that I know this man:

(3)     I know the man who embezzled $1,000,000.

(3) asserts proposition (A), but presupposes (B). Conversely, if someone knows about my knowing a certain man, and I want to tell him what that man did, we have

(4)     The man I know embezzled $1,000,000.

(4) asserts (B) and presupposes (A). Thus, (3) and (4) differ in their presuppositions in a way that (1) and (2) do not. Offir showed that more recognition confusions occur between (1) and (2) than between

(3) and (4), demonstrating that what was stored in memory were not only the propositions (A) and (B) themselves, but also some information about the presuppositions of each sentence. If (3) or (4) occur within a larger context, that context will determine what is presupposed and what is new information in the sentence. Out of context, the subject must remember such information separately.

The relative clauses in (3) and (4) are syntactic devices to signal to the hearer which parts of the sentence are new information and which are old. Speaker and hearer adhere to the same set of conventions in this regard: the speaker syntactically marks the new information in his sentences, and the listener analyzes the sentence on the assumption that the speaker has done so. His strategy is to identify the part of the sentence marked as old or given information. The listener thereby obtains access to the relevant area in his memory and is able to integrate the new information in the sentence with the information already in his memory. Haviland and Clark (1974) have called this the Given-New Strategy of sentence comprehension and provided some impressive experimental evidence for it. This strategy probably underlies the facilitatory effect of repetitions of concepts in a text that was discussed in Section 6.3.1. Repeated concepts identify old information in a sentence and thereby make it easier for the listener to assign that sentence to its right place in the memory structure. Haviland and Clark collected comprehension time data that are entirely in agreement with this conclusion. In their experiment subjects were given two sentences to read in succession; the experimental variable was the time subjects took to comprehend the second sentence (they simply pressed a button when they thought they had understood the sentence). The first sentence either provided a direct antecedent for the experimental sentence, that is, there was an argument repetition in the underlying propositions, or it did not:

(5)    We got some beer out of the trunk. The beer was warm.
(6)    We checked the picnic supplies. The beer was warm.

Comprehension times were 835 milliseconds for sentences like (5), but 1016 milliseconds for sentences like (6). In order to comprehend (6), an inference had to be made to establish the coherence of the text base, namely that beer was among the picnic supplies. This inference significantly increased comprehension times.

Haviland and Clark obtained evidence that subjects operate with the Given-New Strategy also in other types of sentences. Consider, for instance, the presuppositions implied by *again*: it is simply that whatever is being talked about has happened before. If there is a context sentence, as in (7), that directly refers to this presupposition of *again,* the sentence containing *again* should be easier to understand than if an inference is necessary for this presupposition, as in (8):

(7)     Last Christmas Eugene became absolutely smashed. This Christmas he got very drunk again.

(8)     Last Christmas Eugene went to a lot of parties. This Christmas he got very drunk again.

Sentences like (7) where the first part spells out the presupposition of the second, are comprehended in 984 milliseconds, while 1040 milliseconds are required for the comprehension of sentences like (8), where some computations need to be done to establish the correctness of the presupposition established by the *again.* Haviland and Clark reported similar results for *still, either,* and *too.* Their results are, therefore, clear evidence that subjects actually make the inference invited by the *again,* and thus for constructive comprehension processes.

So far, most of the inferences occurring in comprehension were semantic inferences. Their basis lies in people's knowledge about the meaning of words such as *close* or *again.* There is, however, also a class of pragmatic inferences that is very important in human communication. People frequently do not say what they mean, and yet, within the system of conventions that guides human communication, they are readily understood. At a dinner party, if someone is asked *"Could you pass me the salt?"* he responds to this question as a request; if the hostess remarks to her husband that the guest's wine glass is empty, she is not merely describing what she sees on the dinner table, but is similarly making a request. Grice (1967), Searle (1969), and Gordon and Lakoff (1971) have described in some detail the conventions that govern the interpretation of these sentences. Grice discussed four "conversation postulates" that permit the listener to understand what the speaker intends, even though what he actually says may be quite different. Whenever one of these conversation postulates is violated, the hearer interprets the utterance not literally, but looks for its implied meaning. The four postulates are

*Quantity:*   provide as much information as necessary but not more.
*Quality:*   information must be of sufficiently high quality.
*Relevance:*   information must bear directly upon an issue.
*Manner:*   information must be expressed clearly, and concisely.

If someone asks whether you can pass the salt, or lend him a million dollars, he can't be serious (but not if he asks whether he could borrow a quarter!), because conversational conventions prevent questions for which the answer is known; hence the question must be interpreted in some other way. Both Searle (1969) and Gordon and Lakoff (1971) have discussed ways in which this might be done.

H. Clark and Lucy (1975) have studied experimentally whether the account given above correctly describes the processes involved in comprehending the conversationally implied force of a sentence. At issue in their experiment was the question whether people first process the literal meaning of a sentence and then infer its intended meaning. If a listener first constructs the literal meaning of a sentence, checks it for plausibility, and then applies conversation rules to derive its conveyed meaning, a number of predictions can be made concerning people's behavior in comprehending such sentences. First of all, people should of course act in accordance with the conveyed requests. However, it should take them longer to comprehend conveyed requests than direct requests, because of all the extra processing involved. These predictions were tested by having subjects read a sentence which was either a direct or a conveyed request of the form *Color the circle blue,* or *Can you color the circle blue?* and then judge as fast as possible whether a given circle had been colored according to the request. Both predictions were confirmed by the pattern of judgment times. Clark and Lucy could, however, go one step further in their experiment. Consider the sentence pair

(9)     I'll be very happy if you make the circle blue.
(10)    I'll be very sad unless you make the circle blue.

Both sentences have the same conveyed meaning, and subjects responded *yes* when the circle was actually blue. However, reaction times were 500 milliseconds longer for (10) than (9). The additional 500 milliseconds required for the comprehension of (10) are readily understood if the literal meaning of each sentence is processed before the conveyed meaning, because (10) contains two negatives—*sad* and *unless*—and it is well known in sentence verification studies that negatives require extra processing time (see Section 6.2.1). Thus we can conclude that conversationally implied requests are understood by first computing and rejecting their literal meaning, and then inferring their intended meaning.

We have discussed two types of inferences in comprehension: semantic implications and presuppositions, and pragmatic, that is, conversational implications. As we have seen, these are inseparable from the comprehension process. In the next section we shall investigate inferences that occur at the time of recall rather than during comprehension itself.

### 6.3.3   RECONSTRUCTIVE PROCESSES IN RECALL

When asked to recall a sentence, subjects frequently reconstruct the sentence on the basis of only partial information. Such recall is comparable to speech; the subject remembers some main ideas and makes up the rest of the sentence to fit these ideas. An illustrative experiment has been reported by James, Thomson, and Baldwin (1973). These authors first analyzed normal speech production and found that is was biased in several respects. For instance, people showed a preference for using the active voice over the passive, and they tended to begin sentences with the most salient nouns. Precisely the same kind of bias also occurred in the recall of sentences. In cases when people remembered only the meaning of sentences but not their surface form, surface forms were reconstructed at the time of recall, and hence were subject to the same influences as normal speech.

The reproductive character of recall is especially pronounced when subjects are not given unrelated sentences to recall but stories or pictures. In the famous investigations of recall by Bartlett (1932) both constructive and reconstructive processes were evident. In one series of experiments Bartlett read his subjects a short story (about the length of a paragraph) and then had them recall it at various later dates. In analyzing the recall protocols of his subjects Bartlett noted two main features. First, memory for even the simple stories used in this experiment was extremely inaccurate. Often not more than the outline of a story was remembered, while details as well as the style of the story changed greatly, usually in the direction of becoming more stereotyped. Secondly, Bartlett was impressed by the large amount of construction he could observe in the subjects' response protocols. Subjects often did not remember more than a vague impression or attitude, but proceeded to construct a story around it. Some subjects remembered nothing but an isolated detail, but then invented a plausible story as a rationalization for this detail.

In some of Bartlett's experiments subjects were tested repeatedly for recall of the same story. This procedure rapidly produced profound changes in the story. Proper names and titles were altered; individual characteristics were lost; the story tended to become abbreviated and more concrete. But the most interesting phenomenon observed in serial reproduction was the subjects' tendency to rationalize, to give the story some meaning or coherence, even when memory had become quite distorted. Sometimes elaborate connections were invented when some unfamiliar or improbable detail was remembered; at other times descriptions of a familiar setting and incidental features were deleted. Bartlett's subjects were clearly not reporting just what they could recall about a story, but were making up the story as well as they could from the often meager information they had been able to retain.

Similar observations have been made in studies of memory for form. In an influential experiment Wulff (1922) showed his subjects line drawings of abstract forms. The subjects were asked to draw the figures as they recalled them 30 seconds after presentation, and again after 24 hours, after a week, and two months later. Wulff analyzed the reproductions and identified several systematic changes in the drawings. Subjects either exaggerated characteristics of the original figure, which he called sharpening, or they neglected individual peculiarities, which he called leveling. Furthermore, Wulff found that these changes were progressive. Small errors on the first reproduction tended to become larger on successive reproductions. Wulff believed that he could identify three causes for the changes that he observed in his subjects' recall protocols. One was a tendency to normalize, i.e., to make the reproduction look more like a familiar object. This occurred especially often when subjects remembered a name or a verbal description of a figure. The second cause of errors of memory was a tendency to overemphasize a single notable feature of a figure. Both of these errors have their counterpart in Bartlett's descriptions of the distortions which occur in memory for stories. Wulff also reported an autonomous change of the memory trace as a function of time in storage. The memory trace itself was supposed to change gradually into a more simple and regular pattern. This third proposal attracted a great deal of interest in Wulff's experiment. In the years since Wulff's original study many experimenters have tried to test the hypothesis of autonomous change in memory with increasingly sophisticated techniques. Their efforts remained unsuccessful because Wulff's hypothesis is stated so vaguely that it simply is not testable. It has never been specified with sufficient clarity exactly what changes are to be expected under what conditions. Riley (1962) has described this interesting episode of psychological history, which combines great sensitivity to methodological problems with completely inadequate theorizing. However, if we disregard the hypothesis of autonomous change in memory, Wulff's experiment and the many succeeding studies serve quite well to demonstrate the reconstructive character of recall. Leveling and sharpening seem to be characteristic of free-recall performance for both pictures and stories.

Wulff had already noted that verbal labels have a strong effect on the recall of pictures. Carmichael, Hogan, and Walter (1932) conducted a study to assess the importance of this effect. Some of their test figures are shown in Figure 6.12. One group of subjects received Word List 1 together with these figures, and one group received Word List 2. A control group was given no labels at all. Two judges rated the deviations from the stimulus figure in the subjects' reproductions. They found that about three-fourths of the major changes were in the direction of the verbal label. For instance, subjects who were told that the first figure was a diamond in a rectangle tended to close the figure at the bottom, while subjects who were told to remember this as a curtain in a window tended to draw it more like a curtain.

The experiment of Carmichael et al. leaves one important point unclear: when do the changes in the figure occur, at the time of perception, during memory storage, or at the time of reproduction? That the perception of a figure is in part determined by its name, its context, and the subject's expectancies is of course nothing new and it is possible that the Carmichael et al. experiment could be entirely explained by perceptual factors. Hanawalt and Demarest (1939) have shown that this is not so, but that changes occur at the time of reproduction, independent of how a subject perceived the figure originally. Their method was a simple modification of the procedure of Carmichael et al. Instead of giving subjects the verbal labels along

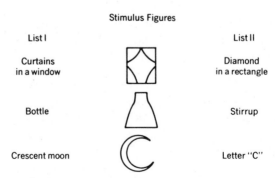

Stimulus Figures

List I               List II

Curtains in a window           Diamond in a rectangle

Bottle                  Stirrup

Crescent moon          Letter "C"

FIGURE 6.12 **Three figures and labels for the study of the effect of language on the reproduction of visually perceived forms. (after Carmichael et al., 1932)**

with the stimulus figures, the figures were shown alone and labels were supplied only at the time of recall. Thus the labels could not have a systematic influence on perception, although subjects will, of course, sometimes use their own labels. Effects on the material stored in memory are also excluded, and changes that occur in the direction of greater similarity of the reproductions with the figures suggested by the labels must be caused by processes occurring at the time of reproduction. Hanawalt and Demarest found that the subjects' reproductions were indeed partly determined by the suggestions given at that time. Not surprisingly, this effect was strongest at the longest retention interval (7 days in their study).

Apparently what happens in recalling pictures or stories is that the subject remembers an overall theme and then reconstructs the rest. Details, single features of a story or of a drawing, are easily forgotten, but the theme of a story is much less susceptible to forgetting.

Bower and Clark (1969) have shown how one can use the fact that the theme of a story is relatively easy to remember to dramatically improve memory for single words. They gave subjects 10 unrelated nouns and asked them to weave a story around these words, using every one of the 10 nouns. This task was self-paced and subjects took about 2¼ minutes to make up their stories. Control subjects were given the same nouns for the same amount of time with instructions to memorize them for later recall. An immediate recall test was given at the end of the 2½ minutes, and all subjects in both the experimental and control groups recalled perfectly. Twelve such lists were given in succession. After the twelfth list, subjects were unexpectedly asked to recall all 120 words. The subjects who simply memorized the 12 lists in succession did very poorly. As one would expect, the effects of retroactive interference were powerful: they recalled only 14% of the words. On the other hand, subjects who made stories recalled 93% of the words, that is 6 times as much as the control subjects. Organizing the 10 nouns into a story, however artificial and silly it might be, apparently protected the words from retroactive interference, and since subjects could fairly easily recall the themes of their stories they thereby gained access to the individual words of each list.

## SCHEMA THEORY

When people comprehend a text they construct a text base, reproducing to some extent the meaning intended by the speaker or writer of the text (Section 6.3.1). This process is a constructive one because inferences of various kinds form an integral part of it (Section 6.3.2). At the time of recall further inferential processes may occur, so that the contents of memory are not simply reproduced but rather reconstructed (Section 6.3.3). Where do all these inferences and reconstructions come from? What do we know about the inference rules that play such an important part in language processing? Problem solving and thinking is the topic of the next chapter, but we shall take a look here at those reasoning processes that are most directly involved in the comprehension and recall of texts.

Some simple inference rules have already been discussed. For instance, set inclusion rules of the form *Asparagus is a vegetable; Vegetables are plants; Therefore asparagus is a plant* were investigated in the chapter on semantic memory (Section 5.5.1). Verb frames provide the basis for many other inferences: upon hearing *George hit John* we know that an instrument must have been involved, and since the speaker did not regard it as necessary to specify this instrument, we are prone to conclude that George hit John with his hand (Table 6.4). Fillmore (1968) has described the semantic case structure of verb frames and the further semantic restrictions implied. These were discussed in Section 6.2.4. The verb *hit,* for instance, may take an instrument, but there are only a few objects that usually function in that role, and the class of objects that can be used as the instrument of *hit* is quite restricted. Obviously the knowledge of such verb frames is part of people's semantic memory and a very important part of their language competency.

The notion of a verb frame can easily be generalized. Selz (1922) talked about knowledge schemata, of which verb frames are a particular case. A schema, or frame, is an organized representation of a person's knowledge about some concept, action, or event, or a larger unit of knowledge. The use of words, whether they are verbs or nouns or propositions, is governed by schemata; people have a schema for such stereotyped action sequences as going to school or going to a restaurant, and they operate with such higher order schemata as "The American Revolution," or "cognitive psychology." Selz maintained that schemata are activated in two ways. One or more input items match the elements of a schema and, by a process of pattern completion, activate the whole schema. Thus, the black marks on the paper here match certain orthographic patterns the reader has in his memory and thereby activate not only these orthographic memory traces but the whole word schemata of which they are a part. At a more global level, *George Washington, The siege of Quebec,* and

*1776* will match elements of our "Revolutionary War" schema, and hence activate the whole schema, so that a new word like *tea party* is immediately interpreted within that schema. Thus, schemata are activated from below via pattern matching and pattern completion processes. Schemata can also be activated from above, thereby providing the organism with a powerful inference-making capacity. The scheme for coffee drinking activates the schema for cup—with the effect that an object that might otherwise be identified as a vase or pot will be classified as a cup (see the discussion in Section 5.5.2). Given the knowledge that someone is drinking coffee, numerous inferences can be made through the activation of the appropriate schema: that the coffee was hot, that he used a cup, that he swallowed—*ad infinitum*. For related examples and a more detailed discussion of these problems see Norman (1976).

Schema theory was popularized within psychology primarily by Bartlett (1932). Bartlett was concerned especially with story schemata and the role they play in recall. He maintained that most reconstructions during recall can be explained if one assumes that subjects remember the gist of stories and then use the schemata they have available to reconstruct the rest of it. There have been many objections to Bartlett's notions, usually on the basis of their vagueness, but in recent years schema theory has undergone a remarkable revival. Minsky (1975), who uses the synonymous term frame, applied the theory to both visual perception and language comprehension. One of his examples describes how the "room" frame permits a person to perceive a room. The various objects in a room, walls and ceiling, etc., are assigned their places within that frame, and are therefore continuously perceived as the same, although their perceptual images change dramatically as a person moves around the room. As a basis for organizing really large amounts of data, frames or schemata appear indispensable today, and these concepts are used in one form or another by most present generation artificial intelligence models as well as psychological theories for the representation of knowledge in memory.

Table 6.10 gives an example of what a "Taking the bus to the airport" schema might look like for someone who lives in Boulder, Colorado. First note that the schema is hierarchical in that it is grouped here into five subframes, which in turn consist of several lower order frames. Indeed, many of the terminal nodes in this schema call up other schemata, e.g., airport. This hierarchical organization is very economic: it would be highly inefficient to store the route from home to bus station as part of the bus schema; it is much more economical

**TABLE 6.10.  An Example of a Schema**

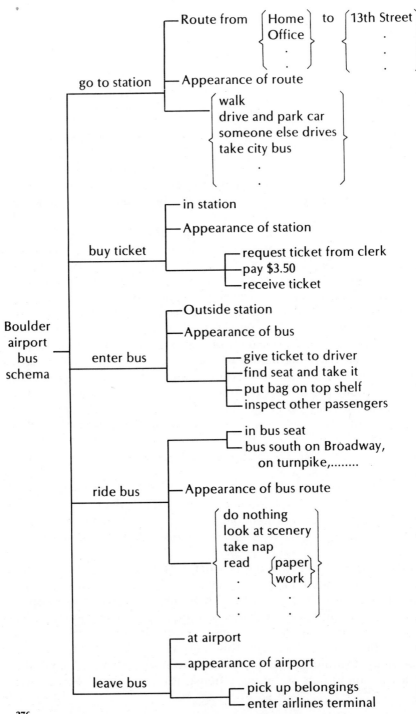

to store such information once, say as part of a "Getting around town" schema, and calling up this information whenever it is needed. Much of Table 6.10 is part of a more general bus schema; other parts of the schema are, however, entirely specific to the experience of someone who is used to taking that particular bus. Furthermore, the Table 6.10 schema clearly is itself a subschema of a more general schema, such as "Taking a plane trip."

How is a schema such as that in Table 6.10 used? Suppose someone is told the following little story: "*Jennifer left here at 10 minutes to nine and walked down to the bus station. She caught the 9 o'clock bus to the airport. She was still tired when she got there.*" Let us consider what it takes to understand this simple text. First of all we need some nonlinguistic context to specify the deictic element *here*. If we know what *here* refers to, the definite article *the* with *bus station* and *airport* makes sense. Without some kind of a context, however, the use of a definite article is meaningless. One cannot talk about *the bus station* unless some particular bus station is actually specified; if this rule is violated, nonsense sentences rather than text is produced, which cannot be understood unless the comprehender is able to provide the appropriate context by himself (Bransford and Johnson, 1972). We also must know who Jennifer is, although it is easy to make some hypothesis about that. What remains unclear in our story now is the relationship between the first two and the last sentences. The presupposition of *still* in the last sentence is that Jennifer was tired not only when she got to the airport, but also before that, presumably when she entered the bus. Why did a 10-minute walk tire Jennifer? Jennifer might be a weak old lady, but the information in our bus schema suggests another reason: the only way to get from *here* to *the bus station* in 10 minutes is by walking very fast and running part of the way. Thus, our knowledge of the route between here and the bus station permits us to make the necessary inference that explains our story.

Suppose now someone recalls this text after a time interval sufficient to interfere with most of the surface memory traces, that is the actual phrases used. He has made the inferences described above, and his recall will probably reflect these, e.g., "*Jennifer ran down to catch the 9 o'clock bus. She got so tired that she was still tired when she arrived at the airport.*"

Our imaginary comprehender could answer all kinds of questions about Jennifer's trip, e.g., "*Did she buy a ticket?*" "*Did the bus take I-285?*" but not "*Did she put her bag on the top shelf*" or "*Did she see any acquaintances in the bus?*" Nothing was said about her having a bag (though we are quite sure she did not have a heavy one), or about meeting someone on the bus.

The point of this example is that text understanding, even of quite trivial texts, is impossible without the help from schemata such as the one in Table 6.10. Charniak (1974) has attempted to classify the kind of knowledge requirements for text understanding. Schank (1975) has actually written a computer program for story understanding based on these principles. Schank's program is called SAM, and SAM operates with a few well-worked out schemata. The most important one is a restaurant schema, that tells SAM's memory exactly what is involved in going to a restaurant, and indeed to different types of restaurants. This knowledge permits SAM to interpret texts about such events and infer, much as a human listener would, the whole sequence of events. What is stored in SAM's memory is not the original input text, but a conceptual representation of that text arrived at by filling out the information provided by the text with that contained in SAM's restaurant schema. Therefore, SAM can recall the text in any desired detail: a lot of detail that is usually not mentioned in stories about going to a restaurant, such as sitting down, reaching for the menu, ordering, leaving a tip, etc. can be reconstructed and included in a "recall" protocol, or it can be deleted if such detail is not required. In other words, SAM produces long or short paraphrases with equal ease. Since SAM's internal representation is not in terms of words but in terms of concepts, it is possible to translate SAM's output into other languages. Thus, SAM might be told a story in English—and return a long Chinese paraphrase of it! In principle at least it is no harder to express SAM's conceptual structures in Chinese than in English.

Not only computer programs, people, too, need to have the right kind of schemata available for understanding. Of particular interest in this respect are the higher order schemata involved in organizing large texts. A person's familiarity with the conventions that regulate the structure of long texts is a very important factor in text comprehension. For instance, if one wants to read a psychological research article, knowledge of the typical format of such an article greatly facilitates comprehension. As indicated by the subheadings, such articles comprise an introduction, a method section (with various subsections), a result section, and a discussion section. The type of material that is supposed to go into each of these sections is strictly circumscribed. Furthermore, certain relationships among the various sections are expected (e.g., the discussion should contain an update of the introduction in view of the new information presented in the results section). A professional psychologist knows where to look for what information; one who does not share this schema finds such articles very difficult to understand. This problem has been explored in more detail in Kintsch (1974).

Another type of text structure that has been studied for some time is the narrative. Narratives have fairly rigid culture-specific structures. For instance, Colby (1975) described the structure of eskimo folk tales. These structures are quite simple and Colby has shown that one needs only a few rules to account for them. Yugoslav folk poets, who compose complex tales in the tradition of the Homeric epos, are similarly governed by a system of generative rules that they handle with great skill. These rules specify the kind of materials that can be used, the way this material can be put together, how variations on standard themes can be obtained, etc. Indeed, these are formulas for composing a tale, but generative formulas that do not stifle originality (Lord, 1965).

Narratives in Western European culture are also constructed according to certain conventions that have been explored by both linguists and psychologists (Rumelhart, 1975; Kintsch and van Dijk, 1975). These narratives consist of a setting that specifies time and place, plus a variable number of episodes. Each episode describes an interesting event involving directly or indirectly the hero of the story. It consists of a complication followed by a resolution. In the simplest type of narrative the events follow each other in time and are related causally; there is only one hero. Such a story is outlined in Table 6.11. The table shows the macrostructure of a story from Boccaccio's *Decameron*. The hero, Landolfo, was an Italian merchant who lost his fortune in a speculation, became rich again as a pirate, was captured and shipwrecked, but accidentally found a new fortune. Each of the three episodes of this story contains a number of propositions, indicated by the *P*'s in Table 6.11. These propositions may be represented as in Table 6.9. What is new here is the macrostructure of the text, that is, the propositions written inside the boxes. Note that this macrostructure is schema-based: the schema provides an outline, and comprehending the story involves filling in this outline with the appropriate information derived from that story.

Kintsch and van Dijk (1975) hypothesized that subjects summarize a story by basing their summaries directly on these macrostructure propositions. Thus, the summaries subjects write after reading a story should indicate the macrostructures that were constructed during reading. If a culture-specific schema is necessary for this process, it should follow that American college students should write better abstracts of *Decameron* stories, which are constructed according to a schema with which they are familiar, than of stories from a foreign culture. Indeed, Kintsch and van Dijk found that subjects agreed reasonably well among each other about what to include in a 60 to 80 word summary when they worked with 1800-word *Decameron* stories,

TABLE 6.11. Outline of a Macrostructure for a Demaceron Story. (after Kintsch & van Dijk, 1975)

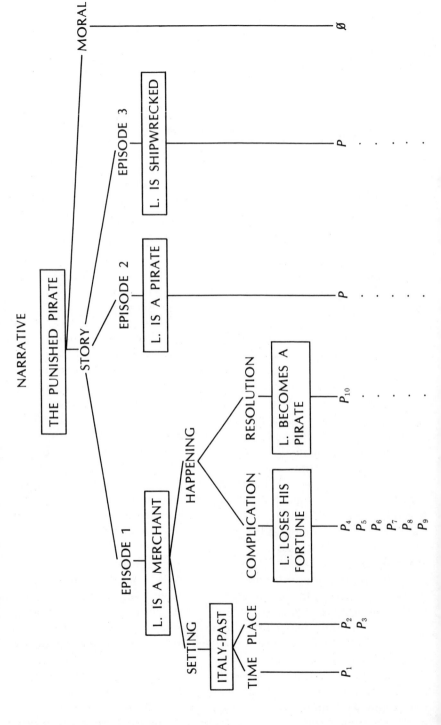

but not when they worked with an Apache Indian folk tale of comparable length. The Apache story was difficult only because of its unfamiliar structure: if one takes sentences out of the story context, the sentences from the Apache story were if anything easier to comprehend and richer in imagery than the sentences from the *Decameron*. However, events in the Indian story were not always causally related, they did not follow the complication-resolution principle, and there was no single hero to give the story continuity. These violations of their expectations confused the readers and made it difficult or impossible for them to organize the story, that is, to construct a macrostructure.

In the same study, readers were also given *Decameron* stories for which the paragraphs had been randomly rearranged. Although it took them longer to read the stories in random order than in their natural order, they had no trouble reorganizing the stories. The story schema is so informative that even though a text is confused, college students can easily put it back into its proper order, and write a perfectly good summary. Indeed, the summaries written after reading randomly ordered stories could not be distinguished by raters from the summaries written after reading normal stories. Reading a disorganized story was a little harder, but the end product apparently was a well-organized memory representation, just as if the story had been read in its proper order.

Although the work of Kintsch and van Dijk (1975) lends some plausibility to the view expressed here that the macrostructure forms an integral part of the memory representation of a story and that this structure is based on a culture-specific schema, many questions remain. How are the macrostructure propositions derived from a text? In Table 6.11 the sentence "*Landolfo was shipwrecked*" is shown as the superordinate for the last episode of the story. Nowhere in the story is this fact directly stated. Instead, there is a rather long account of a storm, a sinking ship, people and debris being tossed about by the waves, etc. which somehow must be compressed into the macrostructure proposition (SHIPWRECKED,LANDOLFO). In fact, most macrostructure propositions are inferences from the text, like the example discussed here. Rumelhart (1975) has written a story grammar that generates the required kind of inferences and that is a first step toward the goal of understanding how people are able to summarize stories.

Most of the work discussed above is, at the time of this writing, less than 5 years old. Clearly, experimental psychologists have barely begun to investigate the important problem of how people understand and remember texts. Much more is left to learn, and our ideas about these processes will undoubtedly change a great deal in the years ahead. But it seems certain that psychology will never again retreat to the nonsense syllable: the experimental techniques and theoretical concepts developed during several decades of work with simpler materials are finally beginning to enable us to study the highly complex processes involved in text processing.

# concept formation and problem solving

In this last chapter we shall review an area of research that is
concerned with the study of thinking. However, unlike in the previous
chapter, we shall concentrate on thinking processes in which the use
of language is secondary. Starting with the topic of concept identification, that is, simple classification learning, we shall proceed to more
complex classifications and then discuss how people learn to use
other rules beyond mere classifications. First the rules involved in
serial pattern learning will be reviewed, then we shall turn to problem
solving, and finally to some questions concerning productive thinking
and creativity. This order is dictated by the state of psychological
research in this area. It would be nice to emphasize topics such as
creative thinking, but psychologists have hardly treated the subject
and have little to say about it; there is no use concerning ourselves
with a glamorous problem if we do not know how to go about studying it. On the other hand, the simple classification problem to be dis-

cussed here represents one of the triumphs of modern cognitive psychology: there is hardly another topic treated in this book that has been researched as well as concept identification and about which we know as much. It is only a slight exaggeration to say that between 1956 and 1970 psychologists have found out practically everything worth knowing about concept identification. The problem of how people learn to categorize simple stimulus materials into artificial, usually binary classes (as distinguished from natural categories—see Section 5.5.2) is primarily one of stimulus encoding, and it could just as well have been described in Chapter 3 of this text, following the discussion of discrimination learning; it is, indeed, a special kind of discrimination learning. However, it also forms the starting point for the investigation of more complex problem solving tasks, and a careful study of the psychological research in this area will permit us to understand better the methods, experimental designs, and theoretical analyses that form the arsenal of the modern cognitive psychologist. Our goal, then, will be to find similarly powerful methods that are suitable for the investigation of more complex problem solving tasks.

## CONCEPT IDENTIFICATION

In a concept identification experiment the subject is confronted with a carefully constructed set of stimuli which are divided into two or more classes by the experimenter. It is the subject's task to identify the experimenter's classification rule. Frequently the experimental stimuli are simple line drawings that vary along such *dimensions* as shape, color, size, numerosity, presence, and position of additional lines or dots. Each dimension may have two or more *values*; for instance, shape may be either square, circle, or triangle, size may be large or small. The concept is arbitrarily defined by the experimenter in terms of some stimulus characteristic. In the simplest case the experimenter chooses one dimension, say size, and assigns items to classes on the basis of their values on this dimension (e.g., all large figures are class A, all small figures are class B). Obviously, more complex concepts can be formed with stimulus materials of this type, but for the most part this section will be concerned with the very simplest kinds of concepts.

It is clear that concept identification is a particularly simple kind of discrimination learning. Thus, what was said about discrimination learning in general applies to concept learning. Most importantly, stimulus coding is central to concept identification: once the subject selects the relevant stimulus dimension, the problem is as good as solved. Therefore, concept identification, especially the identification of very simple concepts, may be considered primarily as a problem of discovering the right stimulus dimension.

One may look at concept learning as a search process: a search is made for the relevant cue that determines the experimenter's classification. Formally this search process seems to be very close to an all-or-none process. That conclusion follows from the fact that it is often possible to describe simple concept identification data with the all-or-none learning model (Suppes and Ginsberg, 1962; 1963). Of course, the model can be interpreted in several ways. As will be remembered, the model comes from stimulus sampling theory where learning is conceptualized as the conditioning of stimulus elements, in this case a single stimulus pattern. However, the model can also be viewed as a special case of the coding theory of discrimination learning which was discussed earlier (Section 3.4). The conditioning probability can be interpreted as the product of two probabilities, the probability that the right coding response will be used times the probability that the stimulus-as-coded will be connected with the right response. Most of the difficulty in concept identification experiments lies in the selection of a proper coding response, and the model primarily reflects this selection process. The conditioning of the stimulus-as-coded to the correct response is almost trivial for adult subjects in the simple tasks considered here. If a subject has just been told that a red stimulus card belongs to class A and he thereupon selects color as his hypothesis, he considers only color hypotheses that are consistent with the information he has just received. Note that this is not necessarily the case when retarded children are used as subjects. The experiments of Zeaman and House described in Section 3.4 have shown that once the proper coding response occurs improvement may be rapid but is by no means immediate.

A third interpretation of the model is in terms of hypothesis testing. Because of the importance and popularity of hypothesis testing theories of concept identification, this approach will be described in more detail before commenting further on the relationship between the all-or-none model and hypothesis testing theories.

Hypothesis testing theories assume that subjects in concept identification experiments make a guess as to the solution of the problem which is consistent with the information available to them. Such a guess is called a hypothesis. As new information is provided to the subject he modifies his initial hypothesis or, if necessary, abandons it and chooses a new one. The subject's overt responses are controlled by his hypotheses. Once he has arrived at a hypothesis that is identical or equivalent to the experimenter's classification rule the problem is solved. Hypothesis theories are reminiscent of coding theories: a hypothesis is like a coding response together with the overt response. If the experimenter presents the subject with a red object and tells him that it belongs to class A, saying that the subject formed the hypothesis "red is A" is equivalent to saying that the subject learned to code the stimulus in terms of color and associated the color red with response A. On the other hand, hypothesis theories go beyond coding theories in stressing the constructive activity of the subject. The subject forms hypotheses, tests them and evaluates them, he doesn't just learn and is reinforced.

Some of the implications that the term hypothesis testing carries with it seem doubtful. "Hypothesis testing" suggests that subjects always have some clearly formulated plan in mind and are testing it purposefully. Some subjects, sometimes, certainly do. However, subjects do not do so all the time, as has been clearly demonstrated in one of the classical studies on concept learning by Hull (1920). Hull studied concepts defined in terms of common elements among Chinese letters. All letters that shared a certain part were assigned to a common response class. Many of Hull's subjects learned this task, in the sense of consistently responding correctly, but were unable to formulate their solution verbally. This observation led Hull to introduce the term "functional concept"; a subject may respond correctly but cannot tell why. Hull's finding was responsible for a methodological revolution in concept learning. While previous experimenters had relied mainly on the introspections of subjects during concept learning, interest shifted to the subject's behavior, and his verbal report was considered to be of secondary importance, or sometimes completely neglected. More recently, psychologists have rediscovered that what the subject says he does may often be quite interesting and informative after all, but certainly one can not disregard the lesson of Hull's experiment that conscious hypotheses and well-formulated rules are by no means necessary for the solution of a concept learning problem. Therefore, most modern investigators do not identify a hypothesis from the subject's introspection, but rather from his response pattern. Suppose that someone is sorting a stack of playing cards into two piles and we want to determine the hypothesis upon which his sorting is based. We could ask him, and he might say, for example, that he is putting all the red cards in one pile and the black ones in the other; or we could observe his behavior—and find out that he is sorting all the black cards into one pile and all the red ones into the other. In this case, both observations would lead us to infer that the subject's hypothesis is based on the color of the cards. Hull's point was that the introspective report alone is not enough, because in more complex cases, introspection does not always agree with the actual behavior, and that in case of such a discrepancy we must go by what a person does, rather than what he says.

The most influential treatment of concept learning as hypothesis testing was published in 1956 by Bruner, Goodnow, and Austin. Their book contains a wealth of descriptive material, but no precise theory of concept learning. They suggested that the subject chooses a hypothesis consistent with the stimulus input and proceeds to test it. Alternatively, the subject may decide to test all possible hypotheses simultaneously, or only a subset of the possible hypotheses. Clearly, the scheme according to which the subject selects hypotheses must be specified more precisely. Once the subject has formed a hypothesis he tests it systematically. Bruner et al. provided some interesting descriptions of different strategies subjects employ for this purpose. Their experimental paradigm for studying these strategies permitted the subject to select stimulus items, rather than presenting items at random. One of the strategies observed by Bruner et al. has been called "conservative focusing." The subject considers all possible hypotheses simultaneously and on each trial asks for a stimulus card that differs from the last in exactly one dimension. Thus he is able to tell whether the dimension tested is or is not relevant. An example will help to clarify how this selection strategy works. Suppose that the subject is told that the first item, a *large, red square*, belongs to class A. The subject now selects as his hypothesis "Large, red square is A" and asks for a *small, red square*. If the small, red square is also on A, he knows that size is an irrelevant dimension, and he can test the other dimensions one by one to see which of them is necessary for the definition of class A. Conservative focusing is obviously an excellent strategy if the solution is of the form "Square is A." It will always result in a correct solution in just as many trials as there are dimensions to test. However, there are obviously other ways to go about learning a concept. Indeed, it is only for simple concepts that are defined by the presence or absence of single attributes that this strategy works well. Obviously some problems require considerably more complex solution strategies. Different subjects, as well as the same subject at different times, use different strategies. Often no particular strategy is identifiable in the behavior of a subject. In any case, the strategy that a subject uses does not explain his behavior, but it in itself needs to be explained. Somehow task variables (such as stimulus complexity, manner of presentation, or time given for solution) and previous experience combine to determine a subject's strategies—but how? In order to answer this question it is necessary to provide a much more specific formulation of the hypothesis testing process.

The first precise formulation of hypothesis testing theory was provided by Restle (1962). Restle's model is much more restricted in scope than that of Bruner et al. Indeed, it is clearly oversimplified. However, it provides us with a solid starting point around which experimental work, as well as further explanatory attempts, can fruitfully be organized.

Restle assumes that a subject takes a sample of hypotheses and tests them. Whenever a hypothesis leads to a correct classification response, or whenever it is consistent with the information feedback provided by the experimenter, the subject retains it; whenever a hypothesis leads to an error or is inconsistent with the experimenter's classification, the hypothesis is rejected.

The class of possible hypotheses can be subdivided into three subsets: correct, wrong, and irrelevant hypotheses. The problem is solved once the subject finds a correct hypothesis and eliminates all irrelevant and wrong hypotheses. Three possible sampling schemes have been considered for this process of hypothesis elimination. First, suppose the subject samples only one hypothesis at a time at random from the total pool of hypotheses. If the hypothesis sampled is correct the problem is solved. If the hypothesis is not correct, it will sooner or later lead to an incorrect response. Whenever an incorrect response occurs the hypothesis upon which this response was based is discarded and the subject resamples. Resampling is again from the total pool of hypotheses, thus disallowing for memory effects. Alternatively, the subject might consider all hypotheses simultaneously and on every trial eliminate those hypotheses that he does not use and which are inconsistent with the information obtained on that trial. As long as the subject uses more than one strategy, the probability that he will make a correct response on any given trial is assumed to equal the proportion of strategies that led to that response. Finally, Restle considered the possibility that subjects sample at random a subset of hypotheses and eliminate wrong and irrelevant hypotheses from it on subsequent trials. If the sample of hypotheses contains a correct hypothesis the problem will eventually be solved. If it does not contain a correct hypothesis, the subject must take a new random sample of hypotheses once all hypotheses of the first sample have been eliminated. Restle's three cases imply rather different psychological processes. The third case seems to be intuitively most appealing. However, Restle (1962) has shown that the three cases are mathematically equivalent. For simple concept learning experiments the three models make exactly identical predictions as far as the probabilities of observable response sequences are concerned. Restle's equivalence theorem is extremely important, because if one is interested in knowing which of the three procedures subjects actually use for hypothesis testing, simple concept experiments can provide no information. Experiments must be especially designed to obtain information concerning this problem.

If Restle's strategy selection model is formulated mathematically it turns out to be a member of the general class of all-or-none learning models.

## 7.1.1    A HYPOTHESIS TESTING MODEL OF CONCEPT LEARNING

An experiment reported by Bower and Trabasso (1964) provides an excellent example of the good fit of the all-or-none model to concept identification data. The stimulus material in this experiment consisted of 5-letter nonsense syllables. In each of the five positions one of two possible letters appeared. The fourth position was designated as the relevant position and the response assignments were made on the basis of the letter in that position: if it was an R, response 1 was reinforced, if it was a Q response 2 was reinforced. Thus an item like JVKRZ belonged to the first response class.

The analysis of the results can be divided into two parts. First, statistics independent of parameter estimates can be considered. Response probabilities before the last error were reasonably stationary, as is shown in Figure 7.1. It is obvious from Figure 7.1 that subjects did not improve on trials before the last error. Statistical tests confirm this impression. The second test concerns the independence of successes and failures on trials before the last error. The model implies that the conditional probability of a success on trials before the last error is the same whether a success or a failure had occurred on the previous trial. This independence prediction was also confirmed by the data.

Before the model can be fitted to other data statistics the parameters of the model must be estimated. The model has two parameters, $q$ the probability of a correct response before learning has occurred, and $c$ the probability of a transition from the initial state to the learning state on a learning trial. An informal but intuitively appealing procedure for estimating $q$ and $c$ was discussed in Section 2.2.1. It was suggested that the observed proportion of successes prior

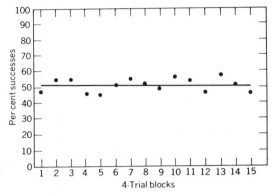

FIGURE 7.1    **Stationarity data: percentage of successes prior to the last error in blocks of four trials. (after Bower and Trabasso, 1964)**

to the last error could be considered an estimate of $q$. In this case $q = .523$. The estimate for the learning rate was obtained by setting the observed mean number of errors equal to the theoretical expression and solving for $c$, using the previous estimate $q$. The expected number of trials before solution equals $1/c$, since $c$ is the probability of learning on any given trial. The probability of an error in the unconditioned state equals $p = 1 - q$, and therefore the expected number of errors equals $p/c$. The subjects in Bower's experiment made on the average 12.16 errors in learning the concept. Hence we obtain the estimate $c = .477/12.16 = .039$. Using these estimates one can calculate predictions for many different statistics. Some of the necessary formulas have been given in Chapter 2: for others the reader must refer to the original sources. Table 7.1 provides a comparison between the predictions of the all-or-none model and the Bower and Trabasso data. Evidently the all-or-none model describes concept identification data just as well as it describes paired-associate results.

One should not make too much of this similarity between paired-associate and concept identification data. The ability of the all-or-none model to describe both sets of data simply means that the learning process is discrete in both cases: paired-associate learning in sufficiently simple situations is all-or-none, and so is concept learning. However, one should not forget the important differences that exist in the unit of analysis in paired-associate learning and concept learning. Single stimulus-response connections are acquired in the former, but a whole set of items is connected with a response in the latter. Thus, although the statistical properties of the learning data require the

TABLE 7.1. **Observed and Predicted Statistics from the Concept Identification Experiment of Bower and Trabasso (1964)**

| Statistic | Observed | Predicted |
|---|---|---|
| Average errors | 12.16 | — |
| Standard deviation | 12.22 | 12.18 |
| Errors before the first success | .92 | .89 |
| Standard deviation | .98 | 1.14 |
| Average trial of last error | 25.70 | 24.50 |
| Standard deviation | 28.90 | 25.00 |
| Probability of an error following an error | .47 | .46 |
| Runs of errors | 6.44 | 6.57 |
| Runs of 1 error | 3.62 | 3.57 |
| 2 errors | 1.32 | 1.63 |
| 3 errors | .64 | .75 |
| 4 errors | .40 | .35 |
| Alternations of success and failure | 12.33 | 12.41 |
| Error-error pairs | | |
| 1 trial apart | 5.76 | 5.45 |
| 2 trials apart | 5.04 | 5.22 |

same formal model for the two cases, the interpretation of the model must be quite different.

What, then, is one to make of the excellent fit of the all-or-none model to the concept identification data in the Bower and Trabasso experiment? Such a fit is not an isolated instance, since an equally good correspondence between data and theory has been obtained in several other studies. Nevertheless, it is not easy to turn these statistical demonstrations into conclusions about the psychological processes involved in concept learning. The problem is that the mathematical model can be formulated in two ways that are formally, but not psychologically equivalent. One may write the model in such a way that learning is possible on all trials, independent of the subject's response, or one may write the model in such a way that learning may occur only when the subject makes an error; correct guesses in the latter case are wasted opportunities, since the subject never learns anything on those trials. Each model is a simple all-or-none model with two parameters, the guessing probability $q$ and the learning probability $c$. However, for each pair $(q,c)$ in one model there exists a parameter pair $(q', c')$ in the other model that yields identical predictions for all data statistics (Atkinson and Crothers, 1964; Greeno and Steiner, 1964). Therefore, there is no chance of deciding between these two models on the basis of goodness of fit to data from standard concept formation experiments. Some new source of information must be found by designing suitable experiments. And, since we have our problem clearly formulated we know what sort of information to look for and what kinds of experiments to design.

Experiments designed to choose between these two alternatives have generally favored the error learning model (Bower and Trabasso, 1964; Trabasso and Bower, 1966; Levine, 1966). The most direct test of this hypothesis (that subjects learn only on error trials in concept identification experiments) was devised by Levine (1966). Levine was not satisfied with inferring the kind of strategies that subjects use indirectly, but wanted to observe strategies directly. The obvious way of asking subjects what their strategies were on each trial was rejected because of the possibility of biasing the subjects through the questioning and because of the well-known observation that subjects may exhibit a strategy in their behavior but be unable to verbalize it correctly. Thus, Levine designed an experiment with special restrictions, so that the experimenter could tell by the subject's responses which hypothesis, if any, a subject was using on each trial. In this way changes in the hypotheses after errors and after successes could be observed directly.

In Levine's experiment subjects had to choose one of two letters on each stimulus card. The letters differed in color (black or white), form (X or T), position (right or left), and size (small or large). The subject thus could choose among eight different hypotheses. More complex hypotheses were excluded by the instructions given to the subject, which emphasized the structure of the stimulus set and the nature of the possible solutions. On the first trial of the experiment the subject was shown a stimulus card and told which of the two choices was correct. The experimenter then forced the subject to show him which of the eight hypotheses he had selected by asking him to respond to four selected stimulus cards without receiving any feedback from the experimenter. The cards were selected in such a way that the experimenter could unambiguously infer from the subject's four responses which of the admissable hypotheses was being used, if any. Figure 7.2 shows an example of four such stimulus cards and the corresponding identifiable response patterns. Since the subject received no feedback during these four choices he would presumably respond on the basis of the same hypothesis on all four trials. If he changed his hypothesis an uninterpretable response pattern resulted. On the fifth trial the

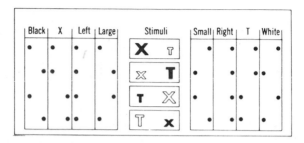

FIGURE 7.2  **Eight patterns of choices corresponding to each of the eight hypotheses when the four stimulus pairs are presented consecutively without outcomes. (after Levine, 1966)**

experimenter could predict the subject's response on the basis of the inferred hypothesis. On this trial the experimenter also told the subject "right" or "wrong" according to a preestablished scheme. Then another four blank trials were given during which the subject's new hypothesis could be inferred, and finally another reinforced trial. This cycle was repeated a third time.

Levine's subjects clearly did use hypotheses: 92.4% of the response patterns on the blank trials were in agreement with one of the eight admissible hypotheses. Furthermore, the hypothesis inferred from a block of four blank trials could be used to predict correctly the subject's response on the fifth trial in 97.5% of all cases.

Of much greater interest is the effect which a reinforced trial has upon the subject's behavior. According to the error learning model, the subject should discard his hypothesis if he is told "wrong" and try a new one, but should retain it after a "right." This is quite what Levine observed: 95% of the time a hypothesis was retained after a "right," and only 2% of the time after a "wrong."

Note that the very low percentage of hypothesis retention after an error means that subjects almost never picked a hypothesis that had just been called wrong. If they were sampling at random from the total pool of eight hypotheses there would be a probability of $\frac{1}{8} = .125$ of getting the same hypothesis again right after an error.

Given that subjects exclude a hypothesis from consideration if they have just been told that it is wrong, one might expect that they can remember at least some of the hypotheses that were excluded earlier in the experiment. A rational subject endowed with memory could surely do better than merely exclude one hypothesis when he makes an error. Suppose a subject was shown a card with a large black X on the left, and a small white T on the right. Further, suppose that his hypothesis on that trial was "choose X" and that he was told wrong.

Clearly, the subject should exclude not only the hypothesis "choose X," but also "choose large," "choose black," and "choose left." Bruner, Goodnow, and Austin (1956) have observed such behavior in their subjects and have named it perfect focusing. Efficient information processing devices employ this strategy. Random sampling with replacement is the opposite of perfect focusing in terms of efficiency: while the latter uses all available information, the former uses very little. Not too surprisingly, Levine's subjects operated somewhere between these extremes. Levine was able to estimate the size of the set of hypotheses from which subjects were making their choices after they were told "wrong" on each of the three reinforced trials. According to the sampling with replacement assumption this size remains at 8 throughout; perfect focusing implies that the subjects reduce their hypotheses set by one half on each trial. Both of these assumptions, along with the actual data points, are shown in Figure 7.3. Although by no means perfect focusers, subjects do manage to reject some hypotheses that should be rejected.

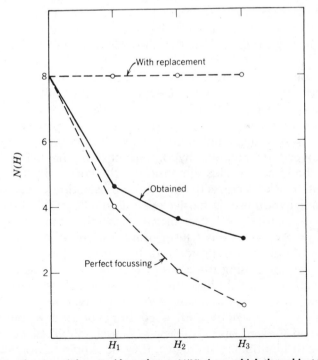

FIGURE 7.3  **The size of the set of hypotheses, N(H), from which the subject is sampling immediately following a "wrong" on trials 1, 2, and 3. (after Levine, 1966)**

While the results summarized in Figure 7.3 show that the model is gravely inadequate in that it does not account for the use of memory in concept identification tasks, another of Levine's results forces us to modify our interpretation of what "learning" means in a concept learning task. If learning means that a subject actually changes his hypothesis and tries a new one, then it is true that learning occurs only on errors, as mentioned before. But there is another kind of learning going on, in the sense that subjects may reduce the set of hypotheses under consideration. Whether an experimenter says "right" or "wrong" he always provides the same amount of information in Levine's experiment. Each reinforcement is worth exactly one bit of information, enabling a perfect focusing device to cut the set of possible hypotheses in half. Suppose that in the example described above the experimenter had said "right." Then the subject could exclude the hypotheses "small," "white," "T," and "right," thus learning something after a success. Of course, this learning would have an observable effect on his responding only after he makes an error on some later trial and selects a new hypothesis. Levine was able to show that subjects actually process information in this manner, again with less than 100% efficiency, but in amounts that cannot be neglected.

In another experiment using a similar procedure Levine investigated the stationarity prediction of the all-or-none model (Levine, Miller, and Steinmeyer, 1967). He found that the probability of a correct response on trials before the last error was stationary at the chance level. Furthermore, Levine's procedure permitted him to determine how often subjects used what was in fact the correct hypothesis on trials before the last error. As expected, such instances were extremely rare. The most interesting finding, however, concerns the subject's use of the complementary hypothesis, that is, the hypothesis that involves the same stimulus dimension as the correct hypothesis (e.g., "white" if "black" is correct). During the presolution period the complementary hypothesis is hardly ever used (.02). Only on the trial immediately before the last error was there a tendency to select the complementary hypothesis (.16). During the presolution period subjects were simply not responding to the correct stimulus dimension, i.e., they were not using the appropriate stimulus coding, rather than choosing among all eight hypotheses at random. Once they found the right coding response, the problem was solved rapidly.

Levine's work provides both a confirmation and a refutation of Restle's and Bower and Trabasso's model. Subjects do respond according to identifiable strategies, they do employ a win-stay, lose-shift policy, and the data are generally in good accord with the model. On the other hand, the no-memory assumption of the model is clearly wrong, and secondly, subjects learn on successes in the sense that they adjust the set of possible hypotheses in accordance with the information provided by the experimenter. Both of these problems which arose in the Levine study have to do with the use of memory in concept learning. Further studies concerned with this issue, as well as some tentative solutions will be considered below.


## CUE SALIENCY

Subjects do not choose randomly among all possible cues. Both a subject's set and the characteristics of the stimulus material affect his choices. Psychologists have long been concerned with the properties of cues that determine their attention value or salience.

One prominent hypothesis holds that saliency is a matter of concreteness: classifications based on concrete cues are easier to learn than those based on abstract cues. This hypothesis was formulated by Gelb and Goldstein (1925) and Goldstein and Scheerer (1941), who showed that brain-damaged patients could not learn to sort simple line drawings according to abstract rules (e.g., *red objects*), while they had no trouble sorting these drawings according to more concrete rules (e.g., *houses*). However, it is not clear whether the difficulties these subjects had with abstract cues can really be attributed to "abstractness," because "abstract" sorts (e.g., *angular* vs. *rounded*) are more complex perceptually: subjects must disregard concrete characteristics in assigning *clocks* to *round* and *roofs* to *angular,* while in a concrete sort they can respond directly to the depicted objects.

Similar comments apply to Heidbreder's suggestion that the saliency of a cue is determined by its "thing character" (e.g., Heidbreder, 1946). In Heidbreder's experiments the stimuli were line drawings and the experimenter selected such dimensions as objects, form, color, or numerosity to define the to be learned classification. Subjects found object classifications easiest to learn, form and color more difficult, and numerosity most difficult. Heidbreder concluded that the thing character of the cues influenced concept acquisition. However, abstractness is again confounded with perceptual complexity: in order to learn a classification based on form the subjects must see *clocks* and *wreaths* as circles, i.e., he must learn to disregard the objects depicted and respond to a cue that is less obvious perceptually. In order to respond to numerosity, which was the hardest classification to learn, subjects must learn to disregard not only the objects depicted, but also their form and color.

It is more appropriate to assume that perceptual complexity is the basic variable in Heidbreder's experiments, rather than the ill-defined thing character. Indeed, it is easy to change the order of difficulty mentioned above, merely by making a cue more salient perceptually. Heidbreder herself had shown that color can be made easier to learn than object if color is made distinct by coloring the whole card, instead of merely the drawing itself. Similarly, one can make a brightness cue distinct and easy to learn by using a black-white contrast, or one can make brightness a very difficult cue by using two shades of grey.

How does the model that was developed in the previous section deal with cue saliency? The model does not include a theory of cue saliency that would allow one to predict that, for a given set of stimuli, a concept identification problem based on a form cue would be learned with some particular learning rate, say $c = .4$, while another problem based on numerosity would be learned with the parameter $c = .2$, for example. All one can do is to estimate the c-values in the two cases from actual data (and then see whether the remaining data statistics are in agreement with the model when these parameter estimates are inserted into the various prediction formulas). The need to estimate these parameters should not be regarded as a weakness of the theory. Similar limitations exist in many other established scientific theories. As an example, take Kepler's laws of planetary motion. Kepler treated the exact values of the planetary orbits as parameters of the process that need not be specified by the theory, which is restricted to the structural aspects of the process.

Though learning rates themselves are not explicable within the theory, the theory has a lot to say about the way in which they combine. To illustrate the nature of the problem, suppose one group of subjects is learning a concept identification problem with Cue 1 relevant and a second group is learning a problem with Cue 2 relevant. We have no means of predicting a priori what the learning rates will be for the two groups of subjects, although we can make some guesses such as that a perceptually striking cue will be picked up faster than a cue which is not easily noticed. However, suppose a third group of subjects learns a problem with both cues relevant. Given that we have estimated the learning rates from the data of the subjects learning with either cue separately, we can now ask how cues combine.

This problem has been thoroughly discussed by Restle (1957). Learning in concept identification tasks is a problem of cue selection. In order to obtain an expression for the probability of selecting any particular cue Restle associated with each cue $i$ a weight $w_i$, and assumed that the probability of selecting cue $i$ is given by the ratio of the weight of cue $i$, $w_i$, to the sum of all cue weights. Or, in general, when there is more than one relevant cue in a problem,

$$(1) \qquad c = \frac{\displaystyle\sum_{\text{all relevant } i \text{ s}} w_i}{\displaystyle\sum_{\text{all } j \text{ s}} w_j}$$

Thus, if a cue is introduced, the change in the learning rate can be calculated by adding the weight of the new cue to both the numerator and denominator, if the new cue is relevant, or by adding its weight to the denominator only, if the new cue is merely a distractor.

Equation (1) is called the additivity of cues assumption. It is actually a very strong and powerful assumption; it is the simplest one that can be made mathematically. Cues could combine in many other ways, and it would be foolish to assume that they always combine according to Eq. (1). Rather, the task is one of investigating under what conditions cues combine additively. Consider the following example for nonadditive combination of cues (after Luce, 1959). Imagine a gourmet making a selection from a menu that offers a choice between hamburger and steak only. Our gourmet may be twice as likely to pick hamburger than steak from such a menu. Now suppose we add a new "cue" to the menu, say lobster thermidor, and let us also make the unrealistic assumption that the gourmet greatly dislikes lobster, and would never consider ordering it. If the new cue combines additively with the two previous items, the preference of hamburger over steak cannot change, because adding a weight of zero to the denominator of Eq. (1) does not affect the equation. However, one could easily imagine how adding lobster thermidor to the menu could have a quite different effect: the gourmet may have chosen hamburger over steak only because he would not trust the restaurant with a steak, but seeing a demanding item like lobster thermidor on the menu might reassure him as to the competence of the kitchen, and he might dare to order the steak. Thus, it is not hard to imagine how cues could combine nonadditively, but only experimental work can show how subjects actually combine cues.

The additivity of cues assumption was first tested by Restle in a maze learning experiment. There has been a long-standing controversy about whether rats learn a T-shaped maze by learning where to go (place learning) or by learning a turning response (right or left). Restle (1957) showed that rats could learn it either way, and then, more importantly, demonstrated that if one knew the weights of the place and response cues from experiments in which only one or the other of these cues were relevant, the additive combination of these weights predicted learning very well in studies where both cues were relevant. The additivity of cues assumption was also successful in predicting learning rates with various cue combinations in a concept identification experiment by Trabasso (1963). The stimulus materials in Trabasso's experiment were flower designs that varied in several ways, such as number and form of leaves, color, and size of the angle between stem and leaf, etc. Trabasso's strategy was to estimate separately the weight of each cue from the performance of subjects who learned the task with only that cue relevant. Once the estimates for the various $w_i$ values were available, he could then predict via Eq. (1) the learning rates (and hence all the data statistics derivable from the model) for various tasks in which more than one cue was relevant, or in which certain irrelevant cues were absent or present. Trabasso's predictions were extremely successful. This, of course, does not imply that cues will always combine additively, but it shows that at least in some tasks Eq. (1) provides an accurate description of the cue selection process.

The attention value of a cue can be changed by emphasizing that cue perceptually. For instance, Hull (1920) showed that emphasis of the common element in the Chinese letters that constituted the stimulus material in his experiment increased the rate of concept acquisition. Hull's method of emphasizing the relevant cue consisted in coloring it, thereby making it stand out from the rather complex stimulus figures. Hull's results have been replicated and extended by Trabasso (1963). It will be remembered that Trabasso's stimulus materials were line drawings of flowers. When the relevant cue was the size of the angle formed by the flower stem and the leaves, subjects found the problem quite hard to learn. Apparently, more salient cues were considered first, such as the shape of the flowers or the shape of the leaves, and the angle cue was investigated only after these more obvious cues failed to lead to a solution. However, by emphasizing the angle cue—either by increasing the angle size or by coloring the angle red—performance could be considerably improved. Coloring the angle green had no emphasis effect: red flower stems attract the subject's attention, but green ones don't.

Another finding of Hull (1920) was that when subjects learned several concept learning problems in succession, learning was facilitated when the problems were presented in simple to complex order rather than in complex to simple order. This observation is closely related to the results on stimulus emphasis. Anything that will induce the subject to use the right kind of coding response will facilitate learning. An impressive demonstration of the importance of this factor has been provided by Zeaman and House (1963) in their report on discrimination learning by retarded children referred to in 3.4. The authors tried to teach a discrimination between line drawings of a red cross and a blue triangle to 15 retarded children. Only four of the children learned this discrimination in 500 trials. However, when actual objects of the same kind were substituted for the line drawings, thus emphasizing the relevant stimulus dimensions, 13 out of another group of 19 children learned the task. More importantly, all those who learned the object discrimination readily transferred to the picture discrimination. The results of this experiment are quite spectacular and have strong implications as to how one should go about teaching discrimination effectively. Figure 7.4 shows the backward learning curve for the few subjects who learned the original picture discrimination, and also includes the data from two groups of subjects who were first trained on a discrimination between real objects before learning to discriminate pictures. The learning curve labeled $O_1 \rightarrow P_1$ shows the transfer behavior from objects to pictures just discussed. The second curve $O_2 \rightarrow P_1$ shows the performance of subjects who first learned a discrimination between objects and then learned the discrimination between drawings, but for whom the actual stimulus values were changed in transfer. Even in that case performance is greatly superior to that of subjects who start out learning to discriminate drawings.

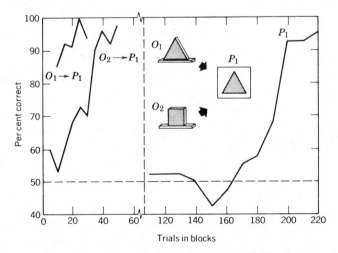

FIGURE 7.4    **Object-to-pattern transfer. Backward learning curve of pattern group (far right) and two object-to-pattern transfer groups (left). (after Zeaman and House, 1963)**

What the particular stimulus values are obviously matters little as long as a subject has learned to attend to the right stimulus dimension.

To teach a discrimination one should emphasize the relevant cue as strongly as possible in order to elicit the appropriate coding response and abbreviate the initial search process. Once the coding response is established, the emphasizer may be withdrawn. This seems to be true of discrimination learning in general, not just of concept identification. Lawrence (1952) has shown that the best way to teach a simultaneous discrimination between two shades of grey to rats is to start out with a very easy discrimination (white versus black) and then gradually shift to the test stimuli. This procedure was superior to one in which the test stimuli were used from the beginning, and it was also better than starting with the easy problem and suddenly introducing the difficult problem. The same principle appears to be behind the method of errorless discrimination learning that Terrace (1963) has used so successfully with pigeons. Indeed, it seems that the maximally inefficient strategy for discrimination learning would be to start with the most difficult version of the problem first.

### 7.1.3    THE NUMBER OF CUES IN THE SUBJECT'S SAMPLE

We have thus far assumed that subjects work with one cue at a time in concept formation experiments. Two comments need to be made concerning this assumption. First, it is certainly not generally valid. The general problem of cue selection in discrimination learning has been described previously. It has been shown that subjects do not always select cues, but may respond to the total stimulus pattern instead. Furthermore, even if cue selection occurs, subjects may very well select more than one cue. Secondly, the reader should remember that there were good theoretical reasons for considering in detail here the case of selecting one cue at a time. Although this is surely an oversimplification Restle (1962) has shown that this case is formally equivalent to other more complex assumptions. In particular, as long as one assumes that subjects are choosing cues or strategies at random from the total pool of strategies, it does not matter whether the subject picks one strategy at a time, all at once, or a subset of strategies.

If the subject considers all strategies at once, Restle assumes that he then starts to eliminate incorrect strategies. When he makes a response, he sets aside all the strategies that he did not use (i.e., strategies that would have predicted the opposite response). In this way, of course, the correct strategy may sometimes be eliminated, too, and the subject will eventually run out of strategies to test. When this happens, he must begin over again with the whole set of strategies. This all-at-once model predicts exactly the same response sequences as the one-at-a-time model. The proof is easy, though not intuitively obvious, and will not be reproduced here. Restle's third case, where the subject is permitted to take a sample of s strategies at a time, is also formally equivalent to the earlier two cases. These models are equivalent, or course, only in so far as sequences of correct and incorrect responses are concerned. If one would design an experiment that goes beyond that, so that one can tell not only how fast a concept is learned, but also which cues were used in learning it, the three models of Restle (1962) make differential predictions.

Before turning to such experiments, Restle's third case should be discussed in some more detail, as it is obviously the most reasonable case psychologically. Suppose the subject picks a random sample of s hypotheses. The proportions of correct, wrong, and irrelevant cues in that sample determine the probability that the response which the subject makes on the basis of the sample will be correct or incorrect. Suppose the response is correct. The subject can now eliminate all strategies from his sample which would have led to the opposite response, that is, all wrong strategies and some proportion of the irrelevant strategies. This process of elimination goes on until either only correct strategies are left in the subject's sample, or until an error occurs. In this case the subject takes a new sample and starts the whole process all over again. Note that this is still a no-memory model. Once the subject has eliminated a strategy he cannot recover it.

Experiments which can discriminate among the three versions of Restle's model employ redundant relevant cues. Suppose in an experiment on concept acquisition using the familiar geometric stimulus material, two redundant cues are used to specify a concept, say shape and color. Through suitable transfer tests after concept learning one can determine whether subjects had learned the problem on the basis of the shape cue, the color cue, or both. If there are subjects who learned both cues the one-strategy-at-a-time model is contraindicated. Whether any of the other versions of the model can fit the data in this case is, of course, an empirical question.

The problem of what the subject learns in concept acquisition experiments with redundant relevant cues has been extensively studied by Trabasso and Bower (1968). One of their studies used geometric figures with five binary attributes as stimulus material. Two of the attributes, shape (circle versus triangle) and dot (above or below figure), were used to define the concept to be learned. For one group of subjects (S + D) both shape and dot were relevant. Group S learned the problem with shape as the relevant cue and dot irrelevant. Group D learned the problem with dot relevant and shape irrelevant. Finally, there were two control groups: S′, which learned the shape problem in the absence of dots, and D′ for which dot was the relevant cue and shape was held constant (all figures were squares). Subjects learned these problems to criterion and were given postcriterion training during which both dot and shape were relevant cues. Finally, subjects were given single-cue tests to determine which of the two cues had been learned.

The results of the learning phase of the experiment were entirely in agreement with the cue selection model. In particular, the additivity-of-cues assumption yielded very accurate predictions when cue weights for shape and dots were estimated from the performance of the S′ and D′ subjects and were then used to predict performance for the S, D, and (S + D) subjects via Eq. (1).

The most important results, however, are those from the single-cue tests which were administered to the subjects learning the two-cue problem $S + D$ after they reached criterion. All subjects were asked how they had solved the problem and on the basis of their responses were subdivided into three groups: subjects who had solved on the basis of shape alone, subjects who had solved on the basis of the dot cue alone, and subjects who had solved on the basis of both cues. Table 7.2 shows the number of subjects in each of these groups, as well as their performance on the single cue tests. First note that the subjects' verbalizations and their performance agreed extremely well: they performed almost perfectly on the cues they said they had worked with and were at chance level on the cues they said they had not noticed. Secondly, note that there were indeed subjects who had learned both cues in this problem, as evidenced both by their verbal

TABLE 7.2. **Solution Types in the Bower and Trabasso (1968) Experiment**

| Number of subjects | Predicted number of subjects ($s = 2$) | Verbal report | Proportion of correct sorts on single cue tests: | |
| --- | --- | --- | --- | --- |
| | | | Shape | Dot |
| 31 | 29 | Shape | 1.00 | .50 |
| 45 | 49 | Dot | .52 | .99 |
| 13 | 11 | Both | .95 | .97 |

report and their performance on the single cue tests. Thus, the one-cue version of Restle's model is clearly inadequate. Trabasso and Bower (1968) have further explored that version of Restle's model which assumes that subjects are working with a sample of $s$ cues. In this model, $s$ is a new parameter, in addition to the learning rate $c$. From everything that has been said before about the equivalence of the various versions of Restle's model, it should be obvious that the parameter $s$ does not enter any of the expressions that have to do with the subject's learning rate. However, $s$ becomes important in the prediction of "solution types," i.e., the number of subjects who solved the problem on the basis of each cue separately or on the basis of both cues. If $s > 1$, learning about both cues occurs with a frequency depending on the size of $s$, as well as the relative weights of the two relevant cues. For any given value of $s$ one can calculate the probability that, if a subject has solved the problem, he has done so on the basis of Cue 1, Cue 2, or both. Trabasso and Bower found that a sample size $s = 2$ gives a fairly accurate account of the solution types in their experiment. The predicted number of subjects solving on the basis of shape, dot, and both cues are also shown in Table 7.2.

The subjects who learned only a single cue were given further training on the two-cue problem after reaching criterion on their original problem. Trabasso and Bower found that this training had absolutely no effect on their subjects in Groups $S$ and $D$: none of the 86 subjects showed any learning when the second cue was made relevant during overtraining. On the other hand, 8% of the subjects in Groups $S'$ and $D'$ learned the newly introduced redundant cue during overtraining. When a cue is newly introduced into a problem that the subject has already solved it arouses an orienting reaction, which apparently led some subjects to resample and thus produced some learning of the redundant cue. However, resampling cannot be simply equated with noticing a cue, because in another study reported in their book Trabasso and Bower made subjects verbalize all cues during overtraining, but still obtained no learning of redundant relevant cues which were present but irrelevant during original learning.

## THE USE OF MEMORY IN CONCEPT IDENTIFICATION

The most significant oversimplification that we have made in our discussion of concept identification concerns the neglect of memory processes. We have concentrated here on the coding aspects of the process, but no satisfactory account of concept identification can be provided that neglects the use of memory in this task. Some data have already been reported that demonstrate the importance of memory processes in concept learning. For instance, Levine's (1966) subjects did not sample their hypotheses with replacement (as a no-memory device would) but they progressively reduced the set of hypotheses from which they made their choices (Figure 7.3). Their memory was imperfect and they did not reduce the hypothesis set as much as would have been possible, but by no means could their behavior be characterized as sampling with replacement. There exists a great deal of other evidence in the literature that clearly indicates that subjects do not turn off their memory when working on concept identification problems; the interesting questions are, of course, *when* memory is used and *how*.

An experimental design inaugurated by Restle and Emmerich (1966) provides some insights into the first question. It involves giving subjects several concept identification problems concurrently. If concept formation is a pure trial-and-error process, concurrent problems should be no more difficult than single problems. On the other hand, if subjects make use of the information that they remember, the interference introduced through concurrent problems should reflect the size of the subject's workable memory. Restle and Emmerich gave subjects either 1, 2, 3 or 6 concept identification problems concurrently. The subjects in the four groups averaged 4, 5, 8, and 7 errors per problem, respectively. Thus, making subjects remember back more than three stimuli significantly retarded performance. In another experiment the authors repeated stimuli after errors in order to obtain an indication of the subject's memory. According to the sampling with replacement assumption, the probability of a correct response when a card is repeated after an error should be strictly ½. With perfect memory for at least one trial this probability should be 1. The authors obtained a value of .95 when subjects were working on only one problem. When subjects were working on six problems concurrently, the probability of a correct response to a repeated stimulus decreased to .72, but was still significantly above chance.

Converging results were obtained through the investigation of response latencies in concept identification experiments (Erickson, Zajkowski, and Ehrmann, 1966). Erickson et al. argued that response latencies should be related to the size of the set of hypotheses from which a subject makes his selection. The more hypotheses to be considered, the more time the sampling process takes. With this additional assumption a number of obvious predictions regarding response latencies can be derived from the Bower and Trabasso model:

1.  Latencies after errors are larger than latencies after successes.
2.  Latencies are constant on trials before the last error.
3.  Latencies after the last error are constant and equal to latencies after successes before the last error.
4.  Error latencies are equal to success latencies.
5.  Latencies after an uninformed error equal latencies after a success.

In an experimental test of these assumptions predictions 1, 4, and 5 were confirmed. However, as Figure 7.5 shows, predictions 2 and 3 were clearly incorrect. The latencies after the last error were not constant, but decreased to a value much lower than success latencies before the last error. This observation may merely reflect an increase in the subject's confidence, however, an aspect of behavior that the model neglects. A trend to decrease latencies was also observed on trials before the last error when long success runs occurred (> 4), which fits in with the explanation that confidence affects latencies in

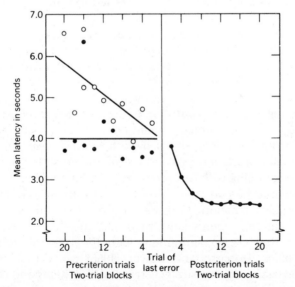

FIGURE 7.5  **Mean latency on trials preceding the last error. The precriterion trials show latencies on trial n following errors (open circles) and following correct responses (closed circles) on trial n-1. (after Erickson et al., 1966)**

addition to whatever other factors that must be considered. The more important result of the Erickson et al. experiment is the failure of Prediction 2: latencies after errors decreased considerably on trials before the last error, although they remained at least as large as latencies after successes. This suggests that subjects were excluding hypotheses, that is, memory effects. Early in the experiment there were many hypotheses from which subjects had to make their selection, and hence latencies were large when subjects resampled after errors. As the experiment progressed the hypothesis pool became smaller because subjects excluded some of the hypotheses they had already tried before, and resampling after errors took less time. The error data in the Erickson et al. experiment were found to be in complete agreement with the Bower and Trabasso model: presolution responses were stationary and independent, and the detailed predictions of the model fit the data reasonably well. The memory effects observed in the response latencies had no noticeable effect on the learning data.

In a follow-up experiment Erickson and Zajkowski (1967) showed that if subjects are given three concurrent concept identification problems no evidence of memory is obtained. The latencies after errors in this case remained constant, indicating that the subject's hypothesis pool did not decrease. Overloading memory led to sampling with replacement.

One can summarize the experimental results on the use of memory in concept identification by saying that the subject's working memory depends on the experimental conditions. Under optimal or near optimal conditions—one problem only, enough time to process information—memory plays a significant role. In this case the sampling with replacement assumption of Restle (1962) and Bower and Trabasso (1964) is wrong. Subjects retain information which enables them to sample from a reduced set of hypotheses. However, under conditions of stress subjects rely less and less on memory, and their behavior approaches sampling with replacement as a limiting case.

There seem to be two major alternatives for theories of memory use in concept identification. One can assume that subjects remember particular stimulus values and their classification and select only hypotheses that are in agreement with the remembered stimulus-response pairs. Trabasso and Bower (1966) call this a consistency-check. They assumed that subjects remember $k$ items and choose only among those hypotheses that pass a $k$-item consistency-check. In this way memory may be introduced into the framework of the Bower and Trabasso (1964) model, which now becomes a special case for $k = 1$.

This leaves the earlier model quite intact; the modification that samples of size *s* are taken rather than one hypothesis at a time can also be incorporated within this model without difficulty.

However, all the data indicate that subject's memory for specific items is quite poor (Coltheart, 1971) and it is by no means sure that memory is really used for making consistency-checks. An alternative conception of the use of memory would be that subjects remember the hypotheses which have been tried before. Levine (1966) suggested such a process, and Chumbley (1969) has formulated a specific model for it. Suppose that a subject samples a set *H* of hypotheses in a concept identification experiment with two response classes *A* and *B*. Call the subset of hypotheses that predict an *A*-response on the next trial $H_A$, and the subset of hypotheses that lead to a *B*-response $H_B$. Suppose the *A*-response is made. If the experimenter calls it correct, the subject keeps the set $H_A$ and discards all hypotheses in $H_B$. On the next trial only the hypotheses in $H_A$ are considered. So far this model is identical with that of Trabasso and Bower (1968) where subjects are assumed to sample *s* hypotheses at once. However, Trabasso and Bower assumed that when a response *A* was made and it was called wrong the subject could not recover the hypotheses in $H_B$ and had to start again with a new random sample. Chumbley proposed instead that subjects can recover the rejected hypotheses in case of an error with some probability *m*. With probability (1 − *m*) the subject forgets the hypotheses that he had not used and starts all over again, as in the Trabasso and Bower model. Thus, the subject works like a perfect focusing device, except that he is occasionally reset to zero because of memory failure. An example will make this argument clearer. Imagine stimulus materials with four binary dimensions, such as Levine's (1966, Figure 7.2). The total set of hypotheses will then consist of eight members if instructions ensure that more complex hypotheses are excluded. Given any particular stimulus item, four of these hypotheses will predict that the item belongs to class *A* and the other four will predict that it belongs to class *B*. If the subject chooses to say *A* and was correct he has now narrowed down the total set of hypotheses from 8 to 4, since only the hypotheses predicting an *A* need to be considered. If the subject said *A*, but was incorrect, we now assume that he can recall the four hypotheses that predicted the opposite response with probability *m*. Since the probability of being correct or incorrect is ½ in this situation, the subject can reduce the number of hypotheses with probability (½ + *m*/2), the probability that he is correct plus the probability that he is wrong but remembers the hypotheses that would have been right. With probability $\frac{1}{2}(1 - m)$ he is wrong and cannot remember the right hypotheses and has to start all over again.

In an experiment patterned after that of Levine (1966) Chumbley (1969) tried to distinguish between the two models for memory in concept learning. Trials without feedback were given in order to permit tracking of the actual hypotheses that the subject was using. The proportion of subjects working with the correct hypotheses was the dependent variable of interest. Without discussing Chumbley's experiment in detail, one can say that the model that assumed memory for hypotheses fared generally better than the consistency-check model. As a minimum modification of the latter, one would have to assume that consistency-checks may sometimes be imperfect, and that giving subjects more time and reducing their memory load increases the probability of a correct check.

Chumbley provided some interesting estimates of the memory parameter $m$ when subjects were learning one concept identification problem and when they were learning three problems concurrently. In the latter case the best estimate of $m$ turned out to be zero, thus confirming earlier results that subjects are essentially sampling with replacement under conditions of memory overload. On the other hand, under more suitable conditions memory estimates as high as .63 were obtained. Chumbley also showed that his model provided a solution to a rather puzzling problem concerning the value of the estimates of the learning rate in many concept identification experiments. The problem is this. When subjects learn an $n$-dimensional concept identification problem, $2n$ simple hypotheses can be formed. If subjects are sampling hypotheses at random from this set, the probability of getting the right one should be about $c = 1/2n$. Some variation around this value would be expected because of differential cue saliency. In general, however, estimates of the learning rate in concept identification experiments have been appreciably higher than $1/2n$. For instance, in the experiment of Erickson and Zajkowski (1967) which was discussed earlier, $c = .25$ for the one-problem condition, and $c = .15$ for the three-problem condition, while $1/2n = .125$. It seems likely that these $c$-estimates are inflated by memory effects. Chumbley estimated $m = .35$ for the one-problem condition of Erikson et al., and $m = .09$ for their three-problem condition. These values agree quite well with those obtained in his own experiment. Results obtained by Clayton, Merryman, and Leonard (1969) also bear on this issue. With six-dimensional stimulus material Clayton had six groups of subjects learning a classification problem, one group for each stimulus dimension. Since for each dimension two hypotheses can be formed $2 \sum_{i=1}^{6} c_i$ should equal 1, and $c_i$ is the estimated learning rate for the $i$-th group. This follows because the summation goes over all possible cues. Instead, Clayton observed a sum of 1.6, which presents quite a puzzle if the $c$-estimates are to be proportions of relevant cues. However, if Chumbley is right, these proportions are artifically high because of memory effects not otherwise accounted for in the model. If unconfounded estimates could be obtained, they would presumably sum to one. Finally, we note that in a series of studies Bower and Trabasso (1964) obtained estimates of learning rates that were quite close to $1/2n$, which means that under their experimental conditions memory played only a minimal role and which also explains why their no-memory model fit their data so extremely well.

Why the differential memory use in these studies? In Chapter 3 the human organism was described as a resource-limited system; depending on how much of these resources must be devoted to other aspects of the concept identification task, the resources remaining for memory will differ. These tasks can be performed with a less than ideal memory use; hence whenever the problem solver runs out of resources memory will suffer, while other, more crucial, components of performance (e.g., selecting and testing hypotheses) remain intact. Thus, with difficult stimulus materials, or under time pressure, or when presented with concurrent problems the resources available for memory use are insufficient, and subjects employ no-memory strategies, while under more favorable conditions they are quite capable of more sophisticated behavior.

The attentive reader who has followed us through half a dozen different models of hypothesis testing in this section, from the simplest random-sampling-on-errors to rather complex schemes of memory involvement, will be excused if he inwardly cries for help at this point: "No more models, modifications, or extensions—just tell me which one is correct!" He will be pleased to hear that the answer is simple: what is correct is the whole set of hypothesis-testing models discussed here—which particular model is applicable in a given situation depends on the task demands, and the abilities and inclinations of the subjects. These models are not mutually exclusive alternatives; instead, they provide quite an accurate account of behavior in concept identification tasks in their totality. Indeed, it is no exaggeration to say that there are few areas in psychology that are understood as well as simple concept identification.

The systematic relations among the models discussed here have been explored and stated with great clarity in a review paper by Millward and Wickens (1974) that better than anything else illustrates the mature development that psychological theory has reached in this field. It all started out with some rather simple notions about attention and the encoding of stimuli, but as Millward and Wickens point out, it does not stop there. If given a chance, subjects do use their memory in these tasks (and there are other ways than the one described above to do so), and, indeed, properly motivated and experienced subjects may exhibit highly sophisticated problem-solving behavior in the same tasks that are approached by others with only some primitive coding strategies.

## 7.2    RULE LEARNING

How people learn rules, and how they operate with them, is one of the most pervasive problems in cognitive psychology. We have already discussed the rules involved in the comprehension and generation of natural language. The previous section was concerned with rules of a particularly simple kind: find the relevant stimulus dimension and base your responses on the values of that dimension. In the present section we shall extend this work in two ways. First we shall discuss work that has been done on concept formation in which two or more dimensions of the stimulus are relevant for category membership. Moreover, the ways in which these dimensions are combined may vary, too. This work is a straightforward extension of the studies on simple concept identification described in the last section, except that the solution to these problems involves the learning of some nontrivial rule, in addition to the stimulus encoding problem. We shall also discuss a quite different type of rule learning, the rules involved in the formation of sequential patterns. Here the basic problem is no longer one of set membership, as in the concept formation work, but of learning generation rules for strings of numbers or letters. Stimulus encoding processes and problem solving strategies interact in complex ways in these problems.

## 7.2.1    MULTIDIMENSIONAL CONCEPTS

With two relevant binary dimensions one can form 16 distinct partitions of the stimulus items. Suppose the first dimension has values $R$ and $\bar{R}$ (which may be red and nonred) and the second dimension has values $S$ and $\bar{S}$ (square and nonsquare, for instance). Thus, all stimulus items can be categorized as $(R,S)$, $(R,\bar{S})$, $(\bar{R},S)$, or $(\bar{R},\bar{S})$, irrespective of the values of irrelevant attributes. In defining a concept on this stimulus set each of the four categories may be called an instance of the concept or not and hence $2^4$ different concepts can be obtained in this way. Two of these concepts are trivial (all items are members of the concept, or none of them is a member) and several more are identical, except that the relevant attributes are interchanged. The 10 remaining distinct concepts are shown in Table 7.3 where they are subdivided into two complementary classes. Each rule defining a concept has a counterpart which is identical with it except that positive and negative instances are interchanged. Thus, only five different concepts must be considered. The assignments of items to positive and negative categories is further illustrated for each of the five basic rules in Table 7.3. The rules differ greatly in complexity. The first rule partitions the stimulus set simply on the basis of the presence or absence of one particular attribute. This is the kind of rule that has been employed in the attribute identification studies discussed in the previous section. The Level II rules take into account the values of both

TABLE 7.3. **Conceptual Rules Describing Partitions of a Population with Two Relevant Attributes (after Haygood and Bourne, 1965)**

| | Basic Rule | | | Complementary Rule | |
| Name | Symbolic Description | Verbal Description | Name | Symbolic Description | Verbal Description |
|---|---|---|---|---|---|
| Affirmation | R | All red items are examples | Negation | $\bar{R}$ | All not red items are examples |
| Conjunction | $R \cap S$ | All red and square items | Alternative denial | $\bar{R} \cup \bar{S}$ | All items either not red or not square |
| Inclusive disjunction | $R \cup S$ | All items red or square or both | Joint denial | $\bar{R} \cap \bar{S}$ | All items neither red nor square |
| Conditional | $R \rightarrow S$ | If the item is red then it must be square | Exclusion | $R \cap \bar{S}$ | All items red and not square |
| Biconditional | $R \leftrightarrow S$ | Red items if and only if they are square | Exclusive disjunction | $R \bar{\cup} S$ | All items which are red or square but not both |

attributes. Conjunction requires positive instances to be both red and square, and corresponds to the set-theoretic operator "intersection." Disjunction corresponds to the operator "union" and classifies all items that are either red or square or both as positive instances. The conditional rule is somewhat less familiar: if an item is red, then it must be square to be classified as a positive instance. This rule assigns positive membership to all nonred items. This is the "material implication" of logic which, as students of introductory logic know very well, is quite at variance with the everyday sense of "implication." All Level II rules involve a 1:3 split of the item categories $(R,S)$, $(R,\bar{S})$, $(\bar{R},S)$, and $(\bar{R},\bar{S})$. The Level III rule, the biconditional, divides the categories into subsets of equal size. Thus, there is more uncertainty in the sense of information theory in this case. One can do better just guessing with a Level II rule than with the biconditional, since ¾ of all items belong to the same class in the former case, while no such frequency bias exists in the latter case.

Of the rules based on logical relationships, as described in Tables 7.3 and 7.4, conjunction and disjunction have been studied most thoroughly. Bruner, Goodnow, and Austin (1956) observed that subjects generally used quite efficient strategies to solve conjunctive problems, but that they had great difficulty with disjunctive concepts. The problem appeared to be that naive subjects used methods that worked very well with conjunctive problems, but not with disjunctive problems. In particular, the positive focusing strategy described earlier, which is quite suitable for learning conjunctive problems, leads to inefficient performance when the concept is defined by a disjunctive rule. Hunt and Hovland (1960) gave subjects a problem that

TABLE 7.4   **The Mappings of the Stimulus Items According to the Five Rules of Table 7.3**

| Partitioning of the Item Set on the Basis of Color and Form | Rules | | | | |
| --- | --- | --- | --- | --- | --- |
| | Level I | Level II | | | Level III |
| | Affirmation | Conjunction | Disjunction | Conditional | Biconditional |
| Red Square | + | + | + | + | + |
| Red Nonsquare | + | − | + | − | − |
| Nonred Square | − | − | + | + | − |
| Nonred Nonsquare | − | − | − | + | + |

could be learned either by a conjunctive or by a disjunctive rule. After reaching criterion subjects were tested to see which rule they had actually acquired. A strong bias in favor of conjunctive rules was found. However, this probably reflects the greater familiarity which subjects have with conjunctive rules. When subjects were trained on a series of disjunctive concepts before they were given a test problem that could be treated either as a conjunction or a disjunction, they were more likely to offer a disjunctive solution (Wells, 1963).

Learning of the rules shown in Table 7.3 has been studied systematically by Neisser and Weene (1962), Haygood and Bourne (1965), and Hunt, Marin, and Stone (1966). As a representative experiment, Experiment I of Haygood and Bourne will be described. Conjunction, disjunction, joint denial, and conditional were the rules studied in this experiment. Three different training conditions were used: Attribute Identification—the rule was described and illustrated with examples before learning began; Rule Learning—subjects were told which attributes were relevant; and Concept Learning—both attribute identification and rule learning were required. Each subject learned five problems in succession, each with the same rule, but with different relevant attributes. The stimulus values were geometric designs with four trinary dimensions (size, color, form, and number). The construction of the items was explained to subjects so that they were familiar with the stimulus dimensions and values. Subjects worked on each problem until they reached a criterion of 16 successive correct responses. Mean trials to solution are shown in Figure 7.6 for the three experimental conditions. Subjects learned the rule-learning and attribute-identification problems significantly faster than the concept-learning problems, which shows that the partial knowledge given to them was indeed used and did facilitate learning. The rules differed significantly in difficulty, at least initially. In the rule-learning condition subjects made almost no errors on conjunctive concepts, indicating that they were familiar with such problems. Disjunction and joint denial were difficult in the beginning, but subjects soon mastered these rules. The conditional rule was most difficult and subjects did not reach a facility with it comparable to that with the other three rules. However, one may suppose that had they been given more conditional problems they would have learned this rule eventually, just as the other rules were learned. In a follow-up experiment, precisely this was demonstrated (Bourne, 1967, Experiment III). Attribute identification always takes longer than rule learning, even after considerable practice. This, of course, lies in the nature of the task. Subjects must be able to observe enough instances of each

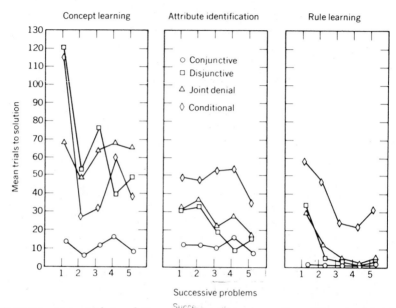

FIGURE 7.6   **Mean trials to solution of problems based upon four different rules. (after Bourne, 1967)**

category before they can decide which attributes are relevant. Haygood and Bourne have shown that subjects operated with almost maximal efficiency on the fifth problem, with exception of the conditional concept, where performance still was relatively inefficient.

The ordering of the various rules in terms of difficulty that was obtained in the Haygood and Bourne (1965) study has been generally confirmed in the other studies mentioned above. When a biconditional rule is included, it is more difficult to learn than any other rule.

The work on rule learning fits quite well into the general framework of our discussion of discrimination learning and concept learning. The subject learns to code the stimulus input in a particular way (here the four contingencies exemplified by Table 7.4) and then learns to connect the stimulus-as-coded with the proper response alternatives. Thus, the learning of logical relationships is closely related to discrimination learning and concept identification, except that both the category-response relationships and the coding process itself are more complex (two attributes and their relationship to each other must be considered in the experiments discussed here). The output of the coding system—the four stimulus categories $(R,S)$, $(\bar{R},S)$, $(R,\bar{S})$, and $(\bar{R},\bar{S})$— is connected with the response alternatives by a paired-associate learning process, although one with complicated and as yet unspecified dependencies among the pairs learned. This is essentially the position of Bourne (1967). Neisser and Weene (1962), who also studied the learning of the various rules in Table 7.3, offered the hypothesis that the higher level rules are more difficult to learn because they presuppose the availability of components which themselves are constructed according to lower order rules. For instance, in order to learn the biconditional rule one must have available the conjunctions $(R,S)$ and $(\bar{R},\bar{S})$. Bourne's interpretation is obviously similar to that, if one takes as the components that must be available the stimulus categories obtained by the two-dimensional classification. Hunt, Marin, and Stone (1966) interpret rule learning somewhat differently. They too work with the fourfold categorizations which are obtained by combining two relevant attributes, as anyone must since the concepts to be learned are defined in terms of these categories. However, they postulate that the subject imposes a hierarchical organization upon the stimulus material. Hunt assumed that logical relationships are learned by establishing decision trees. For Hunt concepts are decision rules which permit one to determine whether the concept name can be applied to a given instance. He gives the example of how one determines whether someone is a legal driver: a legal driver must have passed a driver's test and he must not be a felon. The decision rule involved in applying this concept is therefore

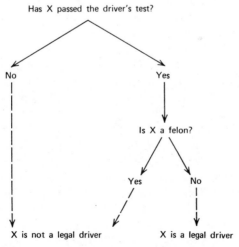

There are two lines of evidence in favor of Hunt's theory. One involves the observation made by a number of investigators that there

are large differences in the difficulty with which different rules are learned, and that these differences are very orderly. Figure 7.6 is quite typical in this respect. Hunt et al. have shown that this order of difficulty is highly correlated with the complexity of the decision tree that underlies each concept. This correlation supports the notion that subjects learn decision trees in concept formation experiments, but the evidence is weak. There are a number of exceptions to the general relationship between the difficulty of acquiring a concept and the complexity of the corresponding decision tree, which make it quite clear that the complexity of the decision tree cannot be the only factor that determines learning difficulty. For instance, conditional rules are much harder to learn than disjunctions, though the decision trees are alike in complexity in the two cases.

Much stronger evidence comes from a chronometric study by Trabasso, Rollins, and Shaughnessy (1971). Trabasso et al. argue that each step in a sequential decision tree takes a certain amount of time. If one gives subjects an item to be classified by means of a decision tree, the time it takes to make this decision can be expressed as the sum of the elementary decision times that are part of the process. This model is applied to conjunctive and disjunctive concepts in Figure 7.7. In each case, the first operation is to store in memory the two relevant attributes, A1 and A2. The concepts are then defined by means of a series of questions about these two attributes, as shown in the figure. The final operation is to make the decision whether or not the item is a member of the category in question. Trabasso et al. assume that the time to store the attributes and decide the truth of a concept is a constant, $K$. The time it takes to answer a question "yes" is a constant $Y$, and the time it takes to answer a question "no" is a constant $N$. Tracing down the branches in Figure 7.7, we can derive predictions for the decision times for various types of concept instances. For a conjunctive concept, for instance, if the truth values of the two attributes are $(T, T)$, a yes-answer is given to both questions, and the total time becomes $K + 2Y$. When both attribute values are different $(F, F)$, the predicted total time is $K + N$, because the process is self-terminating as soon as it detects one missing attribute. The situation is more complex when one attribute is present and one absent. According to Figure 7.7, the total time becomes $K + Y + N$ if the answer to the first question is "no" and the answer to the second question is "yes"; on the other hand, if the sequence of the questions is reversed, the total time is only $K + N$. Since it is quite arbitrary which attribute we call A1 and which A2, Trabasso et al. assume that subjects start once with one attribute and once with another, so that the predicted total time

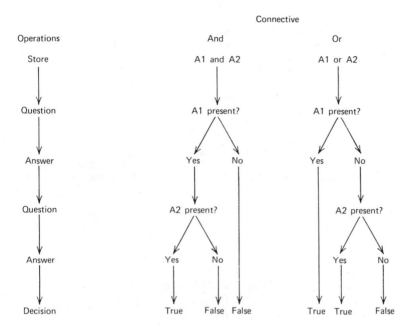

FIGURE 7.7   **Decision trees for processing conjunctive and inclusive disjunctive concepts. (after Trabasso et al., 1971).**

would be the average of the two values, i.e., $\frac{1}{2}(K + Y + N) + \frac{1}{2}(K + N)$ $= K + \frac{1}{2}(Y + 2N)$. These values are shown in Table 7.5, which also contains predictions for disjunctive concepts, as well as a set of empirical data. If the parameters $K$, $Y$, and $N$ are estimated by standard statistical methods, numerical predictions can be generated and compared with the actual data. For the set of parameter estimates shown in the table, the model fits the data quite well. Indeed, by adding a few embellishments to the model, Trabasso et al. could make it fit the data extremely well.

An important observation about the parameter estimates in Table 7.5 is that it takes more than twice as long to answer a question "no" than "yes." It is a fact of wide generality that negation always takes extra time, which has been observed in language comprehension as well as in reasoning tasks (see Section 6.2.1).

Trabasso's demonstration that verification times can be predicted from decision tree models is strong evidence in favor of such models. The paper by Trabasso et al. goes considerably beyond the examples discussed here (they present a series of 10 experiments), and permits

TABLE 7.5. **Predictions of Reaction Times from the Serial, Self-Terminating Decision Model Shown in Figure 7.7, together with Observed Values (after Trabasso et al., 1971)**

|  |  | Predictions | Data |
|---|---|---|---|
| *AND* | | | |
| | (T,T) | $K + 2Y$ | 639 msec |
| | (T,F) | $K + \frac{1}{2}(2N + Y)$ | 749 msec |
| | (F,T) | | 799 msec |
| | (F,F) | $K + N$ | 691 msec |
| *OR* | | | |
| | (T,T) | $K + Y$ | 527 msec |
| | (T,F) | $K + \frac{1}{2}(N + 2Y)$ | 762 msec |
| | (F,T) | | 766 msec |
| | (F,F) | $K + 2N$ | 926 msec |

Parameter estimates:
$K = 472$ msec
$Y = 106$ msec
$N = 242$ msec

one to fill in several details in the model. All in all, it appears that the decision tree analysis, suggested by Hunt in 1962 and later elaborated by Trabasso and others, can provide a satisfactory model of how subjects process hypotheses in multidimensional concept formation experiments.

## 7.2.2 SERIAL PATTERNS

Of the many different types of rules that have been studied in the psychological laboratory in recent years, other than the rules defined as functions of attribute sets just discussed, the structures of serial patterns are of particular interest. The problem for the psychologist is twofold. First, we need to inquire, given a serial pattern such as a letter series, what its structure is and how we can represent this structure. Secondly, we must ask ourselves how subjects acquire such patterns, and how psychological factors (immediate memory, ability to encode the stimulus sequence and to reason analogically) affect this acquisition process. It is crucial in this endeavor to find a suitable language for the representation of the pattern, for the hypotheses about the structure of a problem influence our hypotheses about what the subject does and learns when he operates upon this structure.

As a part of many intelligence tests subjects are often given a letter series completion task. They are shown brief series of letters such as *atbataatbat-* and are asked to continue the series. Simon and Kotovsky (1963) have presented an interesting investigation of the behavior involved in this task. In order to solve such tasks, subjects must be able to abstract from the given series a rule that specifies how to generate the series, and furthermore they must be able to use this rule to continue the series. It is not necessary for subjects to be able to state these rules and operations explicitly but they must have a functional knowledge of that sort. Clearly, before one can ask how subjects induce and use the necessary rules, one must specify exactly what rules are involved. This means that one must select some kind of "language" (i.e., some kind of formalism) for the description of the rules. Simon and Kotovsky have chosen an information processing language for this task. This language has two advantages: it is very well suited to the description of the rules in question and it has been employed successfully in other studies of problem solving (Newell and Simon, 1962). It assumes that subjects come to the task outfitted with some basic knowledge. In this case, subjects must know the alphabet, forward and backward, the two relations *equal* and *next*, and the concept *cycle*. These primitive terms suffice to describe the rules involved in letter series completions. Several examples are shown in Table 7.6. In every case the rule description specifies a cycle of the corresponding series. For instance, in series (i) a cycle consists of an *a*, followed by a *t*, followed by either an *a* or a *b*. For the description of rule (ii) the concept of a variable is needed; variables are designated here by the letter *M*. The rule description is in two parts: the first part says that there is a variable *M1*, which is the alphabet starting with the letter *a*. The second part specifies the cycle: produce three times the letter specified by the variable *M1*, and then go to the next value of the variable and recycle. Series (iii) is a little more complex, because it is necessary to keep track of two variables, one starting with *w* and the other with *a*. The rule is read as follows: produce the letter specified by the variable *M1*, go to the next letter of *M1*, produce it, produce the letter specified by *M2*, go to the next letter of *M2*, and recycle.

The basic assumption Simon and Kotovsky make is that to obtain a letter series concept implies generating and fixating a rule description. Once this much has been specified one can ask how the subject learns

TABLE 7.6   **Letter series completion problems and their rule descriptions from Simon and Kotovsky (1963).**

| Test Sequence | Rule Description |
|---|---|
| (i)   *atbataatbat-* | $[a,t,(b,a)]$ |
| (ii)   *aaabbbcccdd-* | Initialization: $[M1 = \text{Alphabet}; a]$<br>Sequence iteration: $[M1,M1,M1,\text{Next}(M1)]$ |
| (iii)   *wxaxybyzczadab-* | Initialization: $[M1 = \text{Alphabet};w.M2 = \text{Alphabet};a]$<br>Sequence iteration:<br>$[M1,\text{Next}(M1),M1,M2,\text{Next}(M2)]$ |
| (iv)   *urtustuttu-* | Initialization: $[M1 = \text{Alphabet}; r]$<br>Sequence iteration: $[u,M1, \text{Next}(M1), t]$ |

these rules. Simon and Kotovsky suggest a simple procedure: first the subject looks for cycles in the series, i.e., for a repeated letter, alphabetical progressions, or for interruptions of a regular pattern (as in series (*i*)). Once a cycle has been identified the relationships among the letters within the cycle are determined in terms of *equal* and *next*. If the subject is successful the result is expressed in the form of a rule description as shown in Table 7.6. The next question is how series are generated once the rule is known. In order to generate the corresponding series subjects must have available in memory a program capable of interpreting and executing rule descriptions. That is, the subject must be able to perform a few basic operations, as for instance those that are involved in the production of series (iv):

1.   *Hold* the letter *r* on the list named *alphabet* in *immediate memory.*
2.   *Produce u.*
3.   *Produce* the letter that is in *immediate memory.*
4.   *Put the next* letter on the list *alphabet* into *immediate memory.*
5.   *Produce t.*
6.   *Return* to step 2 and repeat the cycle as often as desired.

The reader should compare this program for the production of a series with the rule description of the series. The program is simply a step-by-step translation of the rule description into operational terms, such as *hold in immediate memory, produce, put the next letter on the list into immediate memory,* and the like.

Note how specific this theory of rule learning and rule utilization is to the rules for completing letter series, or more precisely, to the formalism that Simon and Kotovsky have chosen to express these rules. It is very important to keep this task-specific component of rule learning in mind. In the same way, the work reported in the previous section of the learning of various classifications was task specific. However, the same task-independent psychological factors enter into the learning of various types of rules, such as the capacity of immediate memory.

Simon and Kotovsky have stated their theory as a computer program and they have evaluated it by comparing the performance of real subjects on series-completion tasks with the performance of their program. There was considerable correspondence between the two in that the difficulty which subjects had with various series tended to be correlated with the performance of the simulation program. Perhaps more interesting than that, the theory made it possible to locate precisely where subjects have difficulties with letter series of this type. The length of the rule description correlated with the difficulty of a series, but this correlation was only apparent. Underlying it was the factor of immediate memory: those rules that made the heaviest demands on immediate memory were the hardest to learn!

Since Simon and Kotovsky's (1963) pioneering work, a number of different types of serial patterns have been studied. The importance of short-term memory capacity as a performance-limiting factor has been confirmed by this later work. Kotovsky and Simon (1973), for instance, have given subjects series of the form 37159-. In order to solve such problems, subjects must compare pairs of elements and note their analogous relationships: $3:7$, $7:1$, $1:5$, $5:9$. Thus, a sufficiently large number of pairs must be retained and compared in short-term memory at one time. It makes no difference whether the numbers of the series are presented to the subject one by one sequentially, requiring the subject to hold them in memory, or whether these items are all presented simultaneously, permitting the subject to scan the whole sequence: in order to solve the problem, the whole series must be kept in working memory anyway.

Complex patterns, which require several rules for their formation, are learned in parts, each rule being learned in an all-or-none fashion, but at differing rates (Bjork, 1968; Suppes, 1966). Patterns differ quite strongly in their saliency, and the learning rates reflect these saliency differences. One factor that determines how salient a relationship appears to subjects is simply the physical distance between two related items in a series: relationships among adjacent items are easier to detect than relationships among distant items. For instance, Restle and Brown (1970) used hierarchically structured sequences in their experiments and observed that these structures were usually learned from bottom to top; subjects first worked out the lower order relationships among the adjacent items before noticing the superordinate structures involving whole item clusters.

Theoretical work concerning serial pattern learning has consisted mostly of information-processing models like that of Simon and Kotovsky discussed above. These models are highly specific to one particular type of serial pattern: they specify algorithms used by subjects to solve certain classes of series problems. A general theory of sequential pattern induction requires hypotheses at two levels of complexity: in general, a subject must first find out what type of problem he is faced with, and only after he has determined the general nature of the problem can he begin to work out the particular structure of the problem, using a solution strategy that is specific to the problem class encountered.

Up to now we have been concerned mainly with the question how people induce descriptions of a sequential rule from a given pattern. There is, of course, a second, equally interesting problem and that is how people use that rule, once they have found it. Greeno and Simon (1974) have obtained some important theoretical results concerning this problem.

Suppose a subject has found the rule underlying the series 56564545. This is a hierarchical sequence of the type used by Restle and Brown (1970), and it can be described by giving the initial element and a sequence of operators. There are just two operators we need to be concerned with, the $R$ operator, which simply repeats whatever input it receives, and a transpose operator $T$, which either adds or subtracts a number $(\pm i)$ from its input. The series is generated as follows. First we start our series $S$ with the initial value 5:

(1)                           $S \rightarrow (5)$

Then we apply the operator $T_{\pm 1}$ to that initial value, producing a new element by adding 1 to the old one:

(2)                           $T_{+1}(5) \rightarrow (56)$

Next we use the repeat operator to double this sequence:

(3)                           $R(56) \rightarrow (5656)$

and finally we subtract 1 from it by means of the $T_{-1}$ operator and add the result to what we already have:

(4)                                $T_{-1}(5656) \rightarrow (56564545)$.

A more compact way of writing this sequence of operations would be

(5)                                $T_{-1}(R(T_{+1}(5)))$.

Note that in producing this sequence we have used at each step as an input to the operator the whole string so far produced. This is what makes the series hierarchical, which can be best seen by making the hierarchy of operations explicit as in Figure 7.8. This figure is a graphical representation of Eqs. (1) to (4), or equivalently, Eq. (5).

The question Greeno and Simon investigated was how people interpret rule descriptions such as those given above. How do they generate an actual string of elements by means of such formal rules? Two points need to be made. First, note that the interpretive process must hold in short-term memory information about previous inputs. For instance, if we arrive at step (3) in the example above we need as an input the sequence (5656) in order to perform the specified operation. But at the same time, we also need to know where we are in our production, that is, we need housekeeping procedures to keep track of the operators that must be applied in sequence. Greeno and Simon point out that there are several different ways to do this, involving a trade-off between memory load and the amount of computation that must be done. For instance, suppose that a subject has arrived at the fifth element in Figure 7.8 and needs to generate the next one in the series. There are two rather different ways to do this. Given the 4 he can produce the 5 merely by applying one operator, $T_{+1}$—but in order

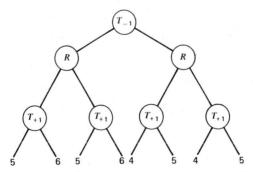

FIGURE 7.8    **Hierarchical representation of a serial pattern. (after Greeno and Simon, 1974)**

to do so he must know exactly his place in the hierarchy. Thus, the computation involved is very simple, but the memory load is large, because the subject needs to know what he has already done and where he is in his production. Alternatively, the sequence in Figure 7.8 could be produced by starting the production of each element always from the initial one. Thus the load on memory is minimized because intermediate productions need not be remembered, and the number of housekeeping operations needed to keep track of where in a series one is becomes smaller. However, the computations involved are more complex, because instead of one single operator, now a whole series of operators must be applied at each step in the process. Greeno and Simon have made exact calculations of the computations and memory loads involved in each process. Both seem a *priori* feasible for people to perform, but what people really do when they apply such rules is still an open empirical question. What Greeno and Simon have done is to make it clear that it is not sufficient to investigate what rule people learn; quite separate from that problem is the question of how they use this rule, because very different processing models are possible, making very different demands on the human processor.

## 7.3    PROBLEM SOLVING

One talks about a "problem" whenever there is something that one wants to do or achieve, but it is not immediately clear how to go about doing it. The reasons why the solution to a problem may not be obvious are manifold. Specifically, we should distinguish between well-defined problems and ill-specified problems. For a well-defined problem, we know that a solution exists and we can tell when we have found the solution; that is, a test exists to determine what is a solution to the problem and what is not. For instance, we know when we have solved a puzzle or proven a theorem. Ill-specified problems, on the other hand, lack such tests. Even if, by some stroke of luck, we have found the best possible method for diagnosing schizophrenia, it might be hard for us to realize our luck, because there are no well-defined criteria for what counts as schizophrenia and what does not, and different experts will evaluate our solution in different ways. Psychologists have as yet made very little progress in understanding the thinking processes involved in the solution of ill-defined problems, and therefore we shall first discuss the simpler case, dealing with well-defined problems.

Two strong influences are apparent in modern work on problem solving. The first derives from the work of the Gestalt theorists and investigators influenced by them during the 1930s and 1940s. The second is the work of a group of researchers at Carnegie-Mellon University, headed by Newell and Simon, who have profoundly shaped the manner in which contemporary psychologists talk and think about problem solving (Newell, Shaw, and Simon, 1960; Newell and Simon, 1962, 1972). We shall start out by describing some of their main ideas, because they provide a convenient framework around which the discussion in this section may be organized.

A problem-solving task is characterized by its *state space,* which consists of all possible courses of action that can be undertaken in trying to solve the problem. However, for any given problem solver at any given time, the whole state space may not be available: the problem solver operates only within a certain restricted *problem space,* that may not correspond fully to all logically possible actions. In addition, a person's problem space contains not only possible solution paths, but also false starts, illegal moves, misunderstandings—anything that characterizes that person's knowledge about the problem situation.

The subset of possible solution attempts that will actually produce a solution, is called the *goal set.* The difficulty of problem solving arises because the problem space of most tasks is very large, while solutions are rare and dispersed throughout the problem space. Thus, the strategy of simply trying out all possible solutions until one of them works is usually impossible: The cost of generating all possible actions and then testing their adequacy is prohibitive. For example, the method of opening a safe by trying out all possible combinations until one works is impractical, simply because the number of possibilities to be tested is huge, even though each test is easy to make (the safe opens or does not). On the other hand, sometimes it is not the number of possible moves that is troublesome, but the difficulty of testing the adequacy of each move. This would be the case in playing a card in a bridge game, where the player has to consider only 16 cards, but where it is hard to figure out which of these would make the best play. Therefore, problem solving by trying out all possibilities is generally not feasible, except for the most trivial problems. Even computers, with processing capabilities that are greatly superior to those of humans, fail at such tasks.

Successful problem solving is governed by two general principles. Problem solving must be *hierarchical,* that is, complex problems must be decomposed into subproblems, until each subproblem becomes simple enough to be solved. Although your ultimate goal in playing chess is to checkmate your partner, this goal must be decomposed into a whole sequence of subgoals. For instance, a player's first subgoal must be to establish a good field position. This subgoal must in turn be decomposed into further subgoals, perhaps to attack a particular pawn, or to occupy a certain square, down to the level of an actual move.

Secondly, solution attempts cannot be blind but must be goal directed. The search through the problem space must be guided by *heuristic principles* that concentrate the search on promising regions of the problem space and avoid getting lost in an endless exploration of blind alleys. To illustrate what is at issue here, consider a familiar problem-solving task, the concept identification paradigm of Section 7.1. A blind solution procedure might be the following one: make a sequential list of all logically possible solutions; try each one in sequence; keep the first one that works. What subjects do, is different from such a strategy (partly because they cannot keep in memory a list of the required length and work through it systematically): they try a hypothesis, disregard it if it is falsified, and resample another one. Frequently, indeed, the selection of hypotheses is guided by some primitive heuristics: Instead of selecting hypotheses at random, those based on perceptually salient stimulus characteristics are tried first, or information stored in long-term memory about likely candidates is used in choosing among hypotheses. Most of the experimental tasks described in Section 7.1 were carefully controlled to minimize the involvement of real-world knowledge, but in realistic problem-solving situations hypothesis selection is even more strongly guided by heuristic principles and goal directed. These heuristics may take the form of a means-ends analysis: Given the present problem state and the desired goal, apply only those operations that reduce the difference between the actual and desired state. Other heuristics are based on simplifying the problem; e.g., by noticing a similarity between the given problem and another, simpler one for which a solution is known, and then trying to generate this solution. The specific heuristics that are used depend, of course, on the nature of the problem to be solved. Newell and Simon (1972) have explored these processes in chess playing, theorem proving, and in solving cryptarithmetic problems. In the next section we shall see how the notions of problem space, heuristic search, and problem structure have been employed in some experimental investigations of problem solving.

## PROBLEMS WITH WELL-DEFINED SOLUTIONS

In a recent review of inductive problem solving Egan and Greeno (1974) distinguished three types of problem-solving strategies: past-, present-, and future-oriented. In the first case, the problem solver has learned, through previous experience with the same problem type, certain ways to approach the problem, and he relies mostly on this knowledge in solving new problems. A present-oriented solution strategy may be compared to paired-associate learning: a certain problem configuration is associated with a particular solution response. Finally, in a future-oriented strategy, problem solving is governed by the goal that is to be reached: Neither past history, nor knowledge of the present situation determines what the problem solver will do, but the goal of an action directs the action. In most problem-solving situations these three types of strategies overlap in various combinations, but rather clear instances of each type have been analyzed experimentally.

The classic study of past-oriented problem solving was reported by Luchins in 1942. Luchins gave his subjects several problems of the same type in succession, and showed that these subjects learned a certain sequence of actions to solve these problems, afterwards relying on this strategy rather blindly, even when the strategy was no longer useful. Some of his subjects were given the following water-jar problem: "If you had three empty jars that hold 21, 127, and 3 quarts, respectively, tell how you might measure 100 quarts of water." The subject, of course, responded that he would fill the largest jar, and then take out the required amount with the help of the other two jars. The subject was given six problems of this type. The seventh problem was "Given three jars that hold, respectively, 23, 49, and 3 quarts, tell how to get 20 quarts." To solve this problem 81% of his subjects employed the involved method using all three jars! These subjects had learned a certain solution strategy and were blindly applying this strategy to the new problem; their behavior was governed by a set acquired from working with the earlier problems, and they failed to respond to the change in the nature of the problem. Luchins, of course, also had control subjects who solved the last problem without such a set and, naturally, not one of these control subjects used the involved method to solve this problem. Everyone solved it in a single step. Luchins went on to show that these set effects were extremely powerful. For instance, he told his subjects "not to act foolishly," but even with this warning over half of them failed to notice the obvious solution to the problem. Indeed, when Luchins gave subjects the problem, "Given three jars that hold, respectively, 28, 78, and 3 quarts, get 25 quarts," which cannot be solved with the involved method, between 66 and 87% of his subjects failed to solve this problem within the 2½ minutes of time allowed. In other experiments, high-school students in a competitive, repeated test atmosphere were asked to get 3 quarts, given jars of 3, 64, and 23 quarts—with a failure rate between 52 and 85%.

Luchins' almost unbelievable results are no isolated curiosity. Essentially identical observations have been made within the familiar concept identification paradigm by Levine (1971). He too showed how easy it is to trap the problem solver within his own past experience. Levine used a trivial experimental task: he showed subjects cards with an A and a B printed on it in either the right or left position. The subject had to pick one or the other of the letters on each trial, and was then told "correct" or "wrong." The rule that was to be learned was actually very simple: always pick the A. Usually, if college students are given this task, they learn it in two or three trials. However, Levine first gave his subjects six problems in which the correct solution was a position sequence. For instance, a rather simple position sequence might be "first choose right, then left, then right twice, then left twice, then repeat." Once the subject has learned six problems in a row in which the solution consisted of a position sequence, he restricts his problem space (in this case, the set of hypotheses he will consider) to position sequences. If the experimenter now changes the rules of the game without telling him, and gives him the trivial "always A" problem, he will continue to test various position hypotheses, but since the number of such hypotheses is essentially infinite—one can always try an even longer and more complex sequence—he will never exhaust this hypothesis set, and simply fail to notice that a much simpler hypothesis would solve his problem immediately. In Levine's experiment, 80% of his college-student subjects failed to solve this trivial problem within 100 trials. Note that this means that the experimenter told the subjects 100 times that A was "correct" and B was "wrong," but they never noticed this simple contingency. They kept saying A 50% of the time and tried out ever more complicated position hypotheses. Indeed, many of the subjects even failed to recognize the correct solution when they were shown it among a set of alternatives!

Luchins' and Levine's results demonstrate how extremely strong the effects of past experience can be in problem-solving situations. In most situations, of course, the effects are beneficial: We solve problems easily the way we have done it before. If the problem type does not change, subjects' problem-solving efficiency improves with experience. Some well-known experimental demonstrations of this improvement were discussed in Section 3.4.3: the phenomenon of learning-to-learn discrimination problems. We have seen there that monkeys can become extremely efficient solvers of simple discrimination problems with repeated exposure. Such learning was described there as the acquisition of an appropriate coding response. While one could think of this coding response as essentially perceptual in nature (attending to the right cues), the problem spaces in Luchins' and Levine's experiments are somewhat more abstract and conceptual. Nevertheless, there is a clear parallel between learning to encode a perceptual stimulus, selecting the right hypothesis from a hypothesis set, or restructuring a problem space. Indeed, very strong learning-to-learn effects have been demonstrated in concept identification tasks (Wickens and Millward, 1971). But past experience can be a trap, as Luchins and Levine have shown so dramatically, when the problem changes and the old solution methods continue to be applied to it.

An interesting example of a paired-associate like problem-solving strategy comes from chess. In his extensive studies of chess playing, de Groot investigated many different types of behavior that might differentiate between master players and average chess players, such as the number of positions examined at each move or the number of moves planned ahead (e.g., de Groot, 1966). Most of these statistics failed to separate weak from strong players, except one: the ability to reproduce chess positions from memory after a brief inspection. After looking at a chess board for 5 seconds someone who does not play chess at all, or who is very weak, can place about six or seven pieces correctly (which is just what one would expect on the basis of the memory literature which puts the capacity of short-term memory at about seven chunks). The stronger the player, the better is his ability to reproduce the board, up to master and grandmaster players, who can reproduce chess positions almost without error. However, this striking ability of the expert chess player is restricted to actual, meaningful chess positions: If the pieces are put on the board at random, the expert's memory is reduced to the normal six or seven pieces, just the same as the rank beginner.

De Groot's results suggest that the master chess player has developed a special coding system for chess positions that allows him to recognize and label, not necessarily verbally, chess positions at a glance. Presumably he has stored in his memory, associated with these chess positions, information about how to respond to these positions. Therefore, a master player can often make his move in a paired-associate fashion, merely in response to the present configuration on the board, without having to consider either the history of this configuration or future developments. Of course, such a paired-associate strategy is merely one of many available to the expert player. At other times, as in some opening games, a whole sequence of moves may be learned, just as Luchins' subjects had learned a sequence of moves in the water-jar problem. In addition, future-oriented, goal-directed strategies are indispensable. In chess playing as well as in the most other problem-solving tasks, the ability to plan behavior with respect to some goal is surely the most significant one and the most interesting one.

Newell and Simon (1972) have investigated goal-directed problem-solving behavior mostly by the method of protocol analysis. Subjects were asked to "think aloud" while they were solving a problem. Their reports were carefully analyzed, and the problem-solving processes of the subjects were then reconstructed from such protocols. This method of protocol analysis has been very productive; the whole conceptual framework introduced by Newell and Simon is derived from it. However, the method's greatest use is in helping us generate hypotheses about problem solving; it is hard to confirm hypotheses that way. Indeed, there is no good substitute for the traditional method of confirming or disconfirming hypotheses by experiment. Recently, there has been an upsurge of interest in the experimental analysis of problem solving using the framework that Newell and Simon derived from protocol analysis. Some studies by Greeno and his associates exemplify this trend.

Thomas (1974) and Greeno (1974) studied problem-solving strategies with the missionary-and-cannibal problem: Three missionaries and three cannibals must be transported across a river with a boat that holds only two people; the complication is that the cannibals may not be trusted and one can never let the cannibals outnumber the missionaries or they will eat them. This problem has also been investigated by Newell, Shaw, and Simon (1960), who have in fact written a computer program, the General Problem Solver, that simulates human problem solving in this task. The program employs a means-end analysis to decide the next move at each step, always trying such moves that reduce the difference between the present state and the goal state. The missionary-and-cannibal problem (or hobbits-and-orcs problem, as Thomas and Greeno call it) is actually quite simple, because most of the time the correct move is quite obvious, but there are two choices that tend to give subjects trouble, especially at the point where all the cannibals are on one side and one has to go back with the boat for the missionaries. Thomas and Greeno observed how subjects learned to solve this problem when they were given multiple trials with it. One of their main findings was that although the problem requires 11 external moves, there were indications that psychologically there were only three or four cognitive acts. That is, subjects were looking ahead several moves at a time, planning whole sets of moves rather than single moves. Thomas (1974) based this conclusion on an analysis of solution times, as well as on subjects' protocols, while Greeno (1974) reached the same conclusion from transfer studies in which subjects first learned a part of the problem and were then shifted to the whole task. The looking-ahead capacity that was identified in these studies is rather important theoretically, because it shows that the psychological units of behavior do not necessarily correspond to those determined from an external task analysis.

Greeno (1974) was able to make further observations about how such problems are learned. First of all he showed that the effective learning event did not occur on trials when subjects made an error, but when they were given information about the correct response (in contrast to concept identification tasks where error trials are most effective). Secondly, Greeno demonstrated that the learning of single moves occurs in an all-or-none manner. This latter observation lends considerable generality to the finding that the components of learning are simple all-or-none processes, not only in verbal learning (Chapter 2), but also in concept identification (Section 7.1), serial pattern learning (Section 7.2), as well as in sequential problem solving.

A somewhat different set of problems was investigated by Egan and Greeno (1974). The question raised in their study concerns *what* is being learned as the result of training with a particular kind of problem. More specifically, do subjects acquire a representation of the problem that corresponds to the goal-tree representation of that problem, as postulated by a theoretical analysis of the task? The problem, and the corresponding theoretical problem structure that Egan used, are shown in Figures 7.9 and 7.10, respectively. The problem is the well-known Tower of Hanoi puzzle. Four disks, graduated in size, are to be transferred from one peg to another. The rules are simple: move only one disk at a time and only from the top of a stack; never place a larger disk on top of a smaller one; and complete the transfer from A to C in the smallest number of moves possible. Figure 7.9 shows the initial problem state; the goal state is reached when all four disks are stacked on C in the proper order. Crucial in this puzzle is the decomposition of the total task into subtasks. The first subgoal of a

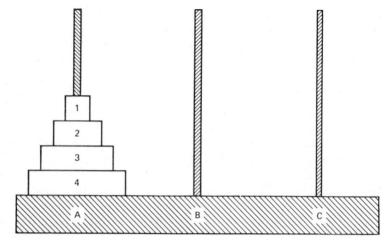

FIGURE 7.9  **Initial state in the four-disk Tower of Hanoi problem. (after Egan and Greeno, 1974)**

rational problem solver should certainly be to get the largest disk (4) into position C. In order to do so, he must get the three smaller disks into a stack on position B. Thus, the first subgoal constitutes itself a complex problem that must be decomposed into subgoals. This decomposition is shown in Figure 7.10. Note that the problem structure is hierarchical. Each task can only be executed when all subordinated tasks have been completed.

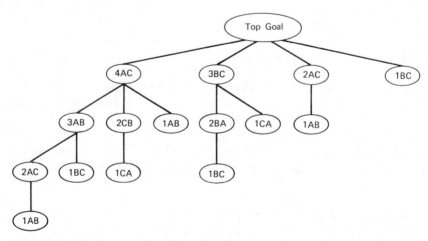

FIGURE 7.10  **Goal structure for the Tower of Hanoi problem. 4AC means "move disk 4 from peg A to peg C". (after Egan and Greeno, 1974)**

Given this theoretical analysis of the problem, the question for the psychologist becomes whether what subjects actually do in solving such a problem corresponds to the hypothesized processes and whether the representation that they have of the problem corresponds to the hierarchical goal tree of Figure 7.10. Egan and Greeno (1974) reported a number of analyses that indicate that the answer to this important question is probably "yeṣ."

First of all, these authors reasoned that if the analysis provided in Figure 7.10 is correct, then the difficulty of solving each subtask should depend on how far down in the goal structure this task was. Subjects should have little trouble with the top-level goals, but those subtasks for which a greater amount of planning must be performed because they are deeply embedded in the goal structure ought to be harder to learn. Thus, one may predict that the number of errors made for moves generated at each level of the goal tree during learning the Tower of Hanoi problem should increase as a function of level. Figure 7.11 shows that this is actually the case. The data here are from

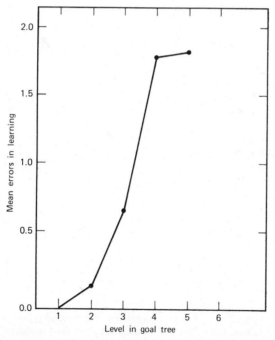

FIGURE 7.11 **Errors in learning moves in the Tower of Hanoi puzzle as a function of the level of the move in the goal tree. The data are for naive subjects. (after Egan and Greeno, 1974)**

a six-disk transfer puzzle, and the predicted increase in difficulty as a function of level is quite dramatic. Thus, the difficulty of making a move is directly related to the amount of planning necessary for this move. An exception occurs at the lowest level, which should be the most difficult move, where subjects apparently change to a paired-associate strategy: it is the first move in the puzzle and subjects simply learn this move by rote.

The idea that in learning to solve the Tower of Hanoi problem subjects acquire a goal tree as shown in Figure 7.10, and then process this goal tree from the top down when solving the puzzle, leads to some further predictions that have been explored by Egan and Greeno, e.g., that the amount of goal processing that occurs just prior to a move should be related to the number of errors made. This prediction, too, was strikingly confirmed by their results. Furthermore, Egan and Greeno also gave their subjects a recognition test, where they asked

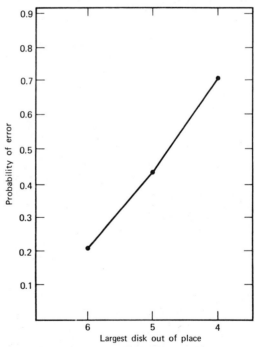

FIGURE 7.12 **Probability of falsely recognizing disk configurations in the Tower of Hanoi puzzle as a function of the discrepancy between the configuration and the goal structure, as indicated by the size of the largest disk which is out of place. (after Egan and Greeno, 1974)**

them whether they had seen a certain arrangement of disks before or not. The results clearly showed that subjects were basing their recognition responses not on familiarity judgments, as they do when recognizing a list of unrelated words (see Chapter 1), but that they were remembering or generating the problem's goal structure and using that information to answer questions about the problem. Specifically, they tended to give "yes" responses when the arrangement of disks was such that it could have occurred during the solution of the problem, and "no" responses to arrangements that differed from those specified by the goal tree. The greater the discrepancy between a state and the goal tree, the less difficulty subjects had in detecting that discrepancy. For instance, Figure 7.12 shows that subjects made very few errors when there was a large discrepancy (Disk 6 out of place), but as the discrepancies became more subtle (Disks 5 and 4 were the largest ones shown out of place) subjects had more difficulty. Thus, subjects in this situation behaved very much like those of Bransford and Franks (1971) or Barclay (1973), in that they "recognized" what was meaningful and should have occurred, rather than what actually had occurred (see Section 6.2.3). Similarly, Winograd's program (Winograd, 1972—see Section 6.2.4) remembers the goal structure and uses that information to answer questions, except, of course, that the computer has a perfect memory, while people become confused when the goal structures are complex, as we have just seen.

## PRODUCTIVE THINKING

The problem-solving situations that were discussed in the previous section were characterized by a well-defined problem space. It was clear what needed to be done, the problem was merely to find the best, or at least a feasible way of doing it. In many other types of problem-solving situations this is not the case. Problems may be only vaguely formulated, and it is not at all clear how to go about solving them. The first step in the solution of these problems must consist in the formulation of the problem itself. Indeed, quite frequently, once a clear formulation of the problem has been achieved, the actual search for the solution may be trivial. Such is the case in most of the experimental problems to be discussed below, though in more serious cases a problem may be far from solved even after the first, crucial step of specifying it clearly. A scientist may be in the latter situation, for instance, who has finally found the right question to ask, i.e., who has found an appropriate formulation for the problem, but who still may need a great deal of nontrivial problem solving before he has the answers to his questions.

The process of finding the right questions to ask for an ill-defined problem has been characterized by theorists in different ways. Gestalt theorists (Köhler, 1925; Duncker, 1945; Wertheimer, 1945) have mostly relied on perceptual metaphors, such as recentering or restructuring of the problem. Problem formulation is here likened to the restructuring of a perceptual field; suddenly, the problem is seen in a new way, its relevant aspects spring into focus, an insight occurs that clarifies the hitherto hidden problem structure. Either some initial knowledge or the problem-solving situation itself become reorganized, transforming the problem from a vague, amorphous one to a well-defined one. Selz (1922) has tried to make these notions more precise by introducing the concept of problem-solving schemata. Each problem is characterized by its own solution schema, and the first task is always to determine the appropriate schema. Once this has been found, goal-directed search methods such as those described in the previous section can be used to solve the problem. Selz's schema appear to be closely related to the problem space of Newell and Simon (1972). Both serve to characterize the relevant apsects of a problem and are preconditions for the actual search for a solution. A problem is well-defined when we have a schema for it, or when we understand its problem space. How this understanding is achieved has been the target of some of the most ingenious studies of problem solving yet reported.

The reorganization of the problem-solving situation that is central to successful problem solving has been explored in a number of studies. Wertheimer (1945) discussed the problem of finding the area of a parallelogram. One way of solving this problem is to encode the parallelogram in terms of its base and its height, as shown in Figure 7.13a. This is a dumb solution, because very likely it will get us into trouble with part b of the figure, and it certainly fails with part c. A better solution requires that the problem be reformulated in terms of rectangles and triangles, as shown in Figure 7.13d. This solution is good, because it easily generalizes to the other cases. Note that what is involved here is truly a perceptual restructuring of the field; triangles and rectangles, not height or base are seen as the elements upon which the solution process must operate.

Wertheimer gives an even more fundamental example of this process of restructuring with his story of the two boys playing badminton. The problem was that the older of the two was very much better than the younger one, who had no chance of beating the older

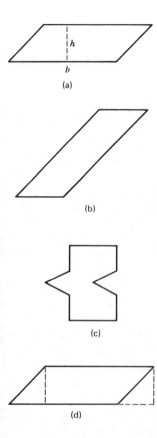

(a)

(b)

(c)

(d)

FIGURE 7.13  **The parallelogram problem. (after Wertheimer, 1959)**

boy, and after a while refused to go on playing. Since the older boy wanted to continue playing very much, he had a problem on his hands. The reader may think of several ways to solve this problem, such as appealing to the weak player's sense of honor, or giving him a handicap. The boy found a much more original solution than this and he achieved it by radically restructuring the situation. He suggested that they should not play against each other, but cooperate in keeping the ball in the air as long as possible—which turned out to be a highly successful proposal. The critical feature of this situation is that the boy did not continue to look for a situation within the old schema of competitive play, but he found one by transforming the situation into a fresh one that was more amenable to solution than the old one. This ability to see the problem in a new light is probably central to all productive thinking.

Maier (1931) performed a series of experiments that provided further evidence for this thesis. In one study, for instance, subjects were asked to tie together two strings hanging from the ceiling too far apart to reach one while holding the other. There were several solutions to this problem, e.g., anchoring one string to a chair and then going to get the other, but subjects were asked to continue finding new solutions until they hit on the one the experimenter was interested in: to set one string into a swinging motion by tying something heavy (e.g., pliers) to it, and catching it while holding on to the other string. Again, the trick was to perceive the string hanging from the ceiling as a potential pendulum, that is, to restructure a situation characterized by the hanging-string schema into one that is organized by means of the pendulum schema. Maier observed that one of the factors that made this task difficult was a strong tendency on the part of the subjects to think about variations of previous solutions, instead of restructuring the situation as required. Especially the poorer subjects could not rid themselves of thinking of the problem in a certain way. Maier also observed that his subjects engaged in a good deal of trial-and-error behavior during problem solving. Subjects tended to think of one thing, try it out, think of something else, realize that it would not work, etc. Maier points out, however, that it would be false to conclude that problem solving is a trial-and-error process, because the subjects' solution attempts were by no means random. Even the ineffective attempts were goal directed. Maier's subjects tried out various schemata, as well as dead alleys within a given problem space, in a trial-and-error manner—but that is a very different process from blind trial-and-error behavior.

There has been quite a controversy within psychology about whether problem solving is basically a random trial-and error-process, guided by reinforcement, or whether it is insightful and goal directed. The opposing positions are best characterized by the work of Thorndike (1911) and Köhler (1925), respectively. Köhler put his chimpanzee into a cage, with a banana and a stick outside. The banana was out of reach, but the chimp could grasp the stick and with it rake in the banana. The chimp's behavior showed all the characteristics of a sudden insight; after trying in vain to reach the banana with hands and feet, chewing on the stick or playing with it, the chimp suddenly saw the stick as an instrument to rake in the banana and started to do so. The "raking-in" schema was applied to the situation, and the chimp got his banana. Similar terms apply to the chimps' behavior in other situations that Köhler investigated, especially when his star performer, Sultan, was given two hollow sticks, each too short to reach the banana, and inserted one into the other to produce a stick long enough for his purpose.

Thorndike, on the other hand, put his cat into a puzzle box full of strings and levers, one of which, if pulled, opened a door and let the animal out. The cat frantically tried all of them, until she hit the right one, and then rushed out of the box. On the next trial, the cat needed a little less time to push the correct lever and after a large number of trials she opened the door as soon as she was put into the box. Thorndike maintained that the cat's behavior at first was random trial and error, but that the response of pushing the correct lever was strengthened through reinforcement (escaping the box, and there was also a piece of fish outside), so that during the course of learning it came to be the dominant response. Nothing in this process of trial-and-error learning smacked of insight.

For a long time psychologists either took Thorndike's or Köhler's side in this controversy—usually Thorndike's in America—and did not realize that there really was no contradiction at all between these two sets of data. A problem solver, especially a human problem solver, will use goal directed methods if he is given the slightest chance to do so. Köhler's chimps were given such a chance; Thorndike's cats were not. Even a Gestalt psychologist would have to use blind trial and error to get out of one of Thorndike's puzzle boxes. None of the knowledge schemata that a person has acquired apply in this situation. The problem space of the puzzle box consists simply of all possible responses, and there is no way of ordering these responses in terms of their likelihood of success without trying them all out. Thus, the problem is not whether behavior is insightful or trial-and-error, but to determine under which conditions it is one or the other.

Both trial and error and insight are descriptive terms rather than explanations. When subjects in a problem-solving experiment try out various solutions, the psychologist must explain why these particular solutions were attempted and how. On the other hand, an appeal to insight constitutes no explanation either. In fact, the role of consciousness in problem solving is a very complex one. Hull (1920) has shown that subjects often are able to perform correctly in concept identification problems without being aware of the correct solution (see Section 7.1), and Maier (1931) and others have pointed out that even when subjects are conscious of a solution, when they have the experience of an insight, they are not aware of how this insight was obtained. Maier states that once an idea is conscious, the fundamental processes of problem solving are over. Phenomenologically, we experience an original idea in much the same way as an idea that returns to consciousness from memory. Proust, who was a meticulous observer of such phenomena, describes "reminiscences that contain not sensations of the past, but a new truth, a precious image, which I tried to discover in the way one tries to remember something, just as if our most beautiful ideas were melodies that we remember without ever having heard them."* The restructuring, the productive processing that led up to the original idea are not themselves phenomenal facts; but it is precisely these processes that lead up to the phenomenal end product, be it of thinking or memory, which are the concern of the psychologist.

Hard data that would illuminate these processes are as yet rare. There are some intriguing suggestions in the literature about how people use their knowledge in solving problems. It appears that a distinction needs to be made between knowledge that people have available and knowledge that they are actually able to use in solving a problem. The distinction is one between reproducibility and functionally operative knowledge. Duncker's "13" problem provides a good illustration (Duncker, 1945). Duncker experimented with the following problem: why are all six-place numbers of the form 276,276, 591,591, 112,112 divisible by 13? His data were thinking-aloud protocols, but he also studied systematically the effectiveness of certain types of hints. Duncker reported that all hints that merely provided the subject with the general solution principle (e.g., "If a divisor of a number is divisible by $p$, then the number itself is divisible by $p$") were of no help. The only hint that was useful was drawing the subject's attention to the number 1001, either by saying "The numbers are divisible by 1001," or merely by hinting "1001 is divisible by 13." Once subjects were given this concrete hint they often realized that numbers of the form $abc,abc$ can always be factored into $abc \times 1001$, and that 1001 is divisible by 13. Indeed, the problem was significantly facilitated even when the allusion to the critical number 1001 was quite indirect. When Duncker changed the examples given in the problem statement from those given above to "276,276, 277,277, 278,278," the likelihood that subjects would find a solution jumped from about .08 to .75! The neighbor relation of the illustrative numbers apparently functioned here as a hint: It led the subjects to discover the critical number 1001, and thus permitted them to solve the problem.

Szekely (1945) made some rather similar observations. One of the problems he used is illustrated in Figure 7.14. The wagon was to be balanced as shown; the problem was that the block tied to it was too heavy and would pull the wagon over the edge, unless it was sup-

* M. Proust, *A la recherche du temps perdu*, VII, *Le temps retrouvé*. Paris:Gallimard, 1927. P. 284.

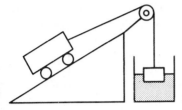

FIGURE 7.14 **The problem is to balance the wagon as shown by letting the block rest on water. (after Szekely, 1945).**

ported by the water. All subjects solved this problem when the block was made out of wood; few solved it when the block was metal. Furthermore, many of the subjects who could not solve the problem could reproduce the hydrostatic principle, and many of the subjects who did solve the problem could not remember the principle! Knowledge of the hydrostatic principle—that floating and sinking are governed by the same law—was apparently quite unrelated to problem solution, though at the same time the subjects' naive knowledge of physics (wood floats, metal sinks) was functionally operative in this situation. Why is it that both Duncker's and Szekely's subjects could not use certain kinds of knowledge (e.g., general principles), but did use other kinds (e.g., naive empirical knowledge about wood and metal)? Apparently, characteristics of the problem-solving situation itself will determine what will be the functionally operative initial knowledge in the situation (e.g., metal versus wood, a 1001-difference between the numbers in the illustration set). In addition, Szekely went ahead to show that the initial knowledge depends on the nature of the learning process that preceded the problem situation. Productive application of knowledge depends on the manner in which the material was mentally processed during learning. Principles learned by rote are hard to use in later problem solving; only principles that the subject has learned to use in other situations will be readily available in a new problem-solving situation.

A related research problem, first formulated by Duncker (1945) concerns the functional fixedness of objects in the problem-solving situation. Many problems are difficult to solve because the subject does not use an available object in the solution of the problem, perceiving this object as having a different, fixed function from the one required. For instance, Duncker asked his subjects to fix a candle to a screen, given candles, matches, and tacks, all in separate boxes. Only about 40% of the subjects solved the task (fasten the candle to the box with wax, then tack the box to the screen). The problem was that subjects failed to realize that the boxes could be part of the solution: the function of the boxes was to hold the tacks, matches, and candles, and subjects were often unable to restructure the situation so that the function of the box became holding the candle. When the same problem was given to the subjects in such a way that the candles, matches, and tacks were not inside the boxes (that is, no fixed function was assigned to the boxes), twice as many subjects managed to solve the problem.

Clearly, the question of how knowledge is used in problem solving is far from answered, though psychologists are becoming interested in this question, once again (e.g., Greeno, 1973). The issue is probably central for an understanding of creative thinking. As yet psychologists know woefully little about creativity. There are numerous testimonials provided by artists and scientists about their thinking processes (e.g., Ghiselin, 1952), but although these protocols may be stimulating and interesting to study, their usefulness for the psychologist is limited. We must find ways and means to go beyond introspection, if we want to find an answer to the age-old question of productive thinking that was succinctly stated by Plato over 2000 years ago: "And how will you enquire into that which you do not know? What will you put forth as the subject of enquiry? And if you find what you want, how will you ever know that this is what you did not know?"*

---

* Meno. In the *Dialogues of Plato,* translated by B. Jowett, Vol. 1, Oxford: Clarendon Press, 1875. P. 281.

# eferences

Aaronson, D. and Scarborough H. S. (1976), Performance theories for sentence coding: Some quantitative evidence, *Journal of Experimental Psychology: Human Perception and Performance*, 2, 56–70.

Ach, N. (1910), *Über den Willensakt und das Temperament*, Quelle und Meyer, Leipzig.

Adams, J. A. and Dijkstra, S. (1966), Short-term memory for motor responses, *Journal of Experimental Psychology*, 71, 314–318.

Allen, M. M. (1969), Cueing and retrieval in free recall, *Journal of Experimental Psychology*, 81, 29–35.

Anderson, J. R. (1974), Verbatim and propositional representation of sentences in immediate and long-term memory, *Journal of Verbal Learning and Verbal Behavior*, 13, 149–162.

Anderson, J. R. and Bower, G. H. (1972), Recognition and retrieval processes in free recall, *Psychological Review*, 79, 97–123.

Anderson, J. R. and Bower G. H. (1973), *Human associative memory*, Washington D.C., Winston.

Anderson, R. C. and Biddle, W. B. (1976), On asking people questions about what they are reading. In G. H. Bower (Ed.), *The psychology of learning and motivation*, Vol. 9, New York, Academic Press.

Anderson, R. C. and Ortony, A. (1975), On putting apples into bottles, *Cognitive Psychology*, 7, 167–180.

Anisfeld, M. and Knapp, M. (1968), Association, synonymity, and directionality in false recognition, *Journal of Experimental Psychology*, 77, 171–179.

Archer, E. J. (1960), A re-evaluation of the meaningfulness of all possible CVC trigrams, *Psychological Monographs*, 74, Whole No. 497.

Asch, S. and Ebenholtz, S. M. (1962), The principle of associative symmetry, *Proceedings of the American Philosophical Society*, 106, 135–163.

Atkinson, R. C. (1962), Choice behavior and monetary payoff: Strong and weak conditioning. In J. H. Criswell, H. Solomon, and P. Suppes (Eds.),

*Mathematical methods in small group processes,* Stanford, Stanford University Press.

Atkinson, R. C. (1975), Mnemotechnics in second-language learning, *American Psychologist,* 30, 821–828.

Atkinson, R. C. and Estes, W. K. (1963), Stimulus sampling theory. In R. D. Luce, R. R. Bush, and E. Galanter (Eds.), *Handbook of mathematical psychology,* Vol. 2, New York, Wiley, pp. 121–168.

Atkinson, R. C. and Juola, J. F. (1974), Search and decision processes in recognition memory. In D. H. Krantz, R. C. Atkinson, R. D. Luce, and P. Suppes (Eds.), *Contemporary developments in mathematical psychology,* Vol. 1, San Francisco, Freeman, pp. 242–293.

Atkinson, R. C. and Shiffrin, R. M. (1968), Human memory: A proposed system and its control processes. In K. W. Spence and J. T. Spence (Eds.), *The psychology of learning and motivation: Advances in research and theory,* Vol. II, New York, Academic Press, pp. 89–195.

Atkinson, R. C. and Shiffrin, R. M. (1971), The control of short-term memory. *Scientific American,* 225, 82–90.

Atwood, G. (1971), An experimental study of visual imagination and memory, *Cognitive Psychology,* 2, 290–297.

Averbach, E. and Sperling, G. (1961), Short-term storage of information in vision. In C. Cherry (Ed.), *Information Theory,* London, Butterworth, pp. 196–211.

Baggett, P. (1975), Memory for explicit and implicit information in picture stories. *Journal of Verbal Learning and Verbal Behavior,* 14, 538–548.

Bahrick, H. P. (1970), Two-phase model for prompted recall, *Psychological Review,* 77, 215–222.

Barclay, J. R. (1973), The role of comprehension in remembering sentences, *Cognitive Psychology,* 4, 229–254.

Barclay, J. R., Bransford J. D., Franks, J. J., McCarrell, N. S., Nitsch, K. (1974), Comprehension and semantic flexibility, *Journal of Verbal Learning and Verbal Behavior,* 13, 471–481.

Barnes, J. M. and Underwood, B. J. (1959), "Fate" of first-list associations in transfer-theory, *Journal of Experimental Psychology,* 58, 97–105.

Bartlett, F. C. (1932), *Remembering,* Cambridge, Cambridge University Press.

Battig, W. F. and Montague, W. E. (1969), Category norms for verbal items in 56 categories: A replication and extension of the Connecticut norms, *Journal of Experimental Psychology,* 80, Part 2, 1–46.

Battig, W. F. and Young, R. K. (1969), Simultaneous serial recall of two serial orders of the same list, *Journal of Verbal Learning and Verbal Behavior,* 8, 393–402.

Begg, I. (1971), Recognition memory for sentence meaning and wording. *Journal of Verbal Learning and Verbal Behavior,* 10, 176–181.

Begg, I., and Wickelgren, W. A. (1974), Retention functions for syntactic and lexical versus semantic information in recognition memory. *Memory and Cognition,* 2, 353–359.

Bernbach, H. A. (1967), Stimulus learning and recognition in paired-associate learning, *Journal of Experimental Psychology,* 75, 513–519.

Bever, T. G. (1970), The cognitive basis for linguistic structures. In J. R. Hayes (Ed.), *Cognition and the development of language,* New York, Wiley.

Bewley, W. L. (1972), The functional stimulus in serial learning. In R. F. Thompson and J. F. Voss (Eds.), *Topics in learning and performance.* New York, Academic Press, pp. 187–214.

Bierwisch, M. (1967), Some semantic universals of German adjectivals, *Foundations of Language,* 3, 1–36.

Bilodeau, I. McD. and Schlosberg, H. (1951), Similarity in stimulating conditions as a variable in retroactive inhibition, *Journal of Experimental Psychology,* 41, 199–204.

Bjork, R. A. (1968), All-or-none subprocesses in the learning of complete sequences. *Journal of Mathematical Psychology,* 5, 182–195.

Bjork, R. A. (1972), Theoretical implications of directed forgetting. In A. W. Melton and E. Martin (Eds.), *Coding processes in human memory.* Washington, D.C., Winston, pp. 217–236.

Bjork, R. A. and Whitten, W. B. (1974), Recency-sensitive retrieval processes in long-term free recall, *Cognitive Psychology,* 6, 173–189.

Bobrow, D. G. and Collins, A. (Eds.) (1975), *Representation and understanding,* New York, Academic Press.

Bourne, L. E., Jr. (1967), Learning and utilization of conceptual rules. In B. Kleinmuntz (Ed.), *Concepts and the structure of memory,* New York, Wiley, pp. 1–32.

Bousfield, W. A. (1953), The occurrence of clustering in the recall of randomly arranged associates, *Journal of General Psychology,* 49, 229–240.

Bousfield, W. A. and Cohen, B. H. (1953), The effects of reinforcement on the occurrence of clustering in the recall of randomly arranged associates, *Journal of Psychology,* 36, 67–81.

Bousfield, W. A., Cohen, B. H., and Whitmarsh, G. A. (1958), Associative clustering in the recall of words of different taxonomic frequencies of occurrence, *Psychological Reports,* 4, 39–44.

Bower, G. H. (1961), Applications of a model to paired-associate learning, *Psychometrika,* 26, 255–180.

Bower, G. H. (1962), A model of response and training variables in paired-associate learning, *Psychological Review,* 69, 34–53.

Bower, G. H. (1967), A multicomponent theory of the memory trace. In K. W. Spence and J. T. Spence (Eds.), *The psychology of learning and motivation: Advances in research and theory,* Vol. I., New York, Academic Press, pp. 299–325.

Bower, G. H. (1970), Imagery as a relational organizer in associative learning, *Journal of Verbal Learning and Verbal Behavior,* 9, 529–533.

Bower, G. H. and Clark, M. C. (1969), Narrative stories as mediators for serial learning, *Psychonomic Science,* 14, 181–182.

Bower, G. H., Clark, M. C., Lesgold, A. M., and Winzenz, D. (1969), Hierarchical retrieval schemes in recall of categorized word lists, *Journal of Verbal Learning and Verbal Behavior, 8,* 323–343.

Bower, G. H., Lesgold, A. M., and Tieman, D. (1969), Grouping operations in free recall, *Journal of Verbal Learning and Verbal Behavior, 8,* 481–493.

Bower, G. H. and Springston, F. (1970), Pauses as recoding points in letter series, *Journal of Experimental Psychology, 83,* 421–436.

Bower, G. H. and Trabasso, T. R. (1964), Concept identification. In R. C. Atkinson (Ed.), *Studies in mathematical psychology,* Stanford, Stanford University Press, pp. 32–94.

Bradley, R. A. and Terry, M. E. (1952), Rank analysis of incomplete block designs, I. The method of paired comparisons, *Biometrika, 39,* 324–345.

Bransford, J. D., Barclay, J. R., and Franks, J. J. (1972), Sentence memory: A constructive versus interpretive approach, *Cognitive Psychology, 3,* 193–209.

Bransford, J. D. and Franks, J. J. (1971), The abstraction of linguistic ideas. *Cognitive Psychology, 2,* 331–350.

Bransford, J. D. and Johnson, M. K., (1972), Contextual prerequisites for understanding: Some investigations of comprehension and recall, *Journal of Verbal Learning and Verbal Behavior, 11,* 717–720.

Bray, N. W. and Batchelder, W. H. (1972), Effects of instructions and retention interval on memory of presentation mode, *Journal of Verbal Learning and Verbal Behavior, 11,* 367–374.

Brewer, W. F. (1974), There is no convincing evidence for operant or classical conditioning in adult humans. In W. B. Weimer and D. S. Palermo (Eds.), *Cognition and the symbolic process.* Hillsdale, N.J., Erlbaum, pp. 1–42.

Brewer, W. F. and Harris, R. J. (1974), Memory for deictic elements in sentences, *Journal of Verbal Learning and Verbal Behavior, 15,* 321–327.

Brewer, W. F. and Lichtenstein, E. H. (1974), Memory for marked semantic features versus memory for meaning, *Journal of Verbal Learning and Verbal Behavior, 13,* 172–180.

Broadbent, D. E. (1958), *Perception and communication,* New York, Pergamon Press.

Broadbent, D. E. (1963), Flow of information within the organism, *Journal of Verbal Learning and Verbal Behavior, 2,* 34–39.

Broadbent, D. E. (1971), *Decision and stress,* New York, Academic Press.

Brockway, J., Chmielewski, D., and Cofer, C. N. (1974), Remembering prose: Productivity and accuracy constraints in recognition memory, *Journal of Verbal Learning and Verbal Behavior, 13,* 194–208.

Brooks, L. R. (1968), Spatial and verbal components in the act of recall, *Canadian Journal of Psychology, 22,* 349–368.

Brown, J. A. (1958), Some tests of the decay theory of immediate memory, *Quarterly Journal of Experimental Psychology, 10,* 12–21.

Brown, R. and McNeill, D. (1966), The "tip of the tongue" phenomenon, *Journal of Verbal Learning and Verbal Behavior, 5,* 325–337.

Bruner, J. S., Goodnow, J. J., and Austin, G. A. (1956), *A study of thinking,* New York, Wiley.

Bugelski, B. R., (1962), Presentation time, total time, and mediation in paired-associate learning, *Journal of Experimental Psychology*, 63, 409–412.

Bugelski, B. R. and Cadwallader, T. C. (1956), A reappraisal of the transfer and retroaction surface, *Journal of Experimental Psychology*, 52, 320–365.

Bühler, K. (1908), Tatsachen and Probleme zu einer Psychologie der Denkvorgänge, *Archiv für die gesamte Psychologie*, 12, 1–123.

Buschke, H. (1968), Input-output short-term storage, *Journal of Verbal Learning and Verbal Behavior*, 7, 900–903.

Buschke, H. (1973), Selective reminding for analysis of memory and learning, *Journal of Verbal Learning and Verbal Behavior*, 12, 543–550.

Bush, R. R. and Mosteller, F. (1955), *Stochastic models for learning*, New York, Wiley.

Buss, A. H. (1953), Rigidity as a function of reversal and nonreversal shifts in the learning of successive discriminations, *Journal of Experimental Psychology*, 45, 75–81.

Caird, W. K. (1964), Reverberating activity and memory disorder, *Nature*, 201, 1150.

Carey, S. T. and Lockhart, R. S. (1973), Encoding differences in recognition and recall, *Memory and Cognition*, 1, 297–300.

Carmicheal, L., Hogan, H. P., and Walter, A. A. (1932), An experimental study of the effect of language on the reproduction of visually perceived forms, *Journal of Experimental Psychology*, 15, 73–86.

Carnap, R. (1952), Meaning postulates, *Philosophical Studies*, 3, 65–73.

Carpenter, P. A. (1974), On the comprehension, storage, and retrieval of comparative sentences, *Journal of Verbal Learning and Verbal Behavior*, 13, 401–411.

Carpenter, P. A. and Just, M. A. (1975), Sentence comprehension: A psycholinguistic processing model of verification, *Psychological Review*, 82, 45–73.

Cattell, J. McK. (1885), Über die Zeit der Erkennung und Benennung von Schriftzeichen, Bildern und Farben, *Philosophische Studien*, 2, 635–650.

Cavanagh, J. P. (1973), Relation between the immediate memory span and the memory search rate, *Psychological Review*, 79, 525–530.

Charniak, E. (1974), "He will make you take it back": A study in the pragmatics of language, Working papers, Fondazione della Molle, Castagnola, Switzerland.

Chomsky, N. (1957), *Syntactic structures*. The Hague, Mouton.

Chomsky, N. (1965), *Aspects of the theory of syntax*, Cambridge, MIT Press.

Chumbley, J. (1969), Hypothesis memory in concept learning, *Journal of Mathematical Psychology*, 6, 528–540.

Cieutat, V. J., Stockwell, F. E., and Noble, C. E. (1958), The interaction of ability and amount of practice with stimulus and response meaningfulness (*m,m'*) in paired-associate learning, *Journal of Experimental Psychology*, 56, 193–202.

Clark, E. V. (1971), On the acquisition of the meaning of *before* and *after*, *Journal of Verbal Learning and Verbal Behavior*, 10, 266–275.

Clark, H. H. (1969), Linguistic processes in deductive reasoning, *Psychological Review,* 76, 387–404.

Clark, H. H. and Chase, W. G. (1972), On the process of comparing sentences against pictures, *Cognitive Psychology,* 3, 472–517.

Clark, H. H. and Lucy, P. (1975), Understanding what is meant from what is said: A study of conversationally conveyed postulates, *Journal of Verbal Learning and Verbal Behavior,* 14, 56–72.

Clayton, K. N., Merryman, C. T. and Leonard, T. B. (1969), Rate of concept identification and the noticeability of the relevant dimension, *Psychonomic Science,* 15, 109–110.

Clifton, C., Jr. and Odom, P. (1966), Similarity relations among certain English sentence constructions, *Psychological Monographs,* 80, Whole No. 613.

Cofer, C. N. (1973), Constructive processes in memory, *American Scientist,* 61, 537–543.

Cofer, C. N., Bruce, D. R., and Reicher, G. M. (1966), Clustering in free recall as a function of certain methodological variations, *Journal of Experimental Psychology,* 71, 858–866.

Cohen, B. H. (1966), Some-or-none characteristics of coding behavior, *Journal of Verbal Learning and Verbal Behavior,* 5, 182–187.

Coleman, E. B. (1963), Approximations to English, *American Journal of Psychology,* 76, 239–247.

Collins, A. M. and Quillian, M. R. (1969), Retrieval from semantic memory, *Journal of Verbal Learning and Verbal Behavior,* 8, 240–247.

Coltheart, V. (1971), Memory for stimuli and memory for hypotheses in concept identification, *Journal of Experimental Psychology,* 89, 102–108.

Conrad, C. (1972), Cognitive economy in semantic memory, *Journal of Experimental Psychology,* 92, 149–154.

Coombs, C. H., Dawes, R. M., and Tversky, A. (1970), *Mathematical psychology: An elementary introduction,* Englewood Cliffs, N.J., Prentice-Hall.

Cooper, L. A. and Shepard, R. N. (1973), Chronometric studies of the rotation of mental images. In W. G. Chase (Ed.), *Visual information processing,* New York, Academic Press.

Corballis, M. C., Kirby, J. and Miller, A. (1972), Access to elements of a memorized list, *Journal of Experimental Psychology,* 94, 185–190.

Craik, F. I. M. (1970), The fate of primary memory items in free recall, *Journal of Verbal Learning and Verbal Behavior,* 9, 143–148.

Craik, F. I. M. and Lockhart, R. S. (1972), Levels of processing: A framework for memory research, *Journal of Verbal Learning and Verbal Behavior,* 11, 671–684.

Craik, F. I. M. and Tulving, E. (1975), Depth of processing and the retention of words in episodic memory, *Journal of Experimental Psychology: General,* 104, 268–294.

Craik, F. I. M. and Watkins, M. J. (1973), The role of rehearsal in short-term memory, *Journal of Verbal Learning and Verbal Behavior,* 12, 599–607.

Crowder, R. G. (1974), Inferential problems in echoic memory. In P. M. A. Rabbitt and S. Dornic (Eds.), *Attention and performance,* Vol. V., London, Academic Press.

Crowder, R. G. and Morton, J. (1969), Precategorical acoustic storage (PAS), *Perception and Psychophysics,* 5, 365–373.

Dallett, K. M. (1962), The transfer surface re-examined, *Journal of Verbal Learning and Verbal Behavior,* 1, 91–94.

Darwin, C. J., Turvey, M. T., and Crowder, R. G. (1972), An auditory analogue of the Sperling partial report procedure: Evidence for brief auditory storage, *Cognitive Psychology,* 3, 255–267.

Deese, J. (1957), Serial organization in the recall of disconnected items, *Psychological Reports,* 3, 577–582.

Deese, J. (1959), On the prediction of occurrence of particular verbal intrusions in immediate recall, *Journal of Experimental Psychology,* 58, 17–22.

Deese, J. (1961), From the isolated verbal unit to connected discourse. In C. N. Cofer (Ed.), *Verbal learning and verbal behavior,* New York, McGraw-Hill, pp. 11–31.

Deese, J. (1962), On the structure of associative meaning, *Psychological Review,* 69, 161–175.

Deese, J. (1965), *The structure of associations in language and thought,* Baltimore, The John Hopkins Press.

Derks, P. L. (1974), The length-difficulty relation in immediate serial recall, *Journal of Verbal Learning and Verbal Behavior,* 13, 335–354.

Deutsch, J. A. and Deutsch, D. (1963), Attention: Some theoretical considerations, *Psychological Review,* 70, 80–90.

Donders, F. C. (1969), Over de snelheid van psychische processen, *Ondersoekingen gedaan in het Psysiologisch Laboratium der Utrechtsche Hoogeschool,* 1868–1869, 2, 92–120. Translated by W. G. Koster, *Acta Psychologica,* 30, 412–431.

Dufort, R. H., Guttman, N., and Kimble, G. A. (1954), One trial discrimination reversal in the white rat, *Journal of Comparative and Physiological Psychology,* 47, 248–249.

Duncker, K. (1945), On problem solving, *Psychological Monographs,* 58 (Whole No. 270).

Ebbinghaus, H. (1885), *Über das Gedächtnis,* Leipzig, Duncker. Translation by H. Ruyer and C. E. Bussenius, *Memory,* New York, Teachers College, Columbia University, 1913.

Ebbinhaus, H. (1902), *Grundzüge der Psychologie,* Leipzig, Viet & Co.

Egan, D. E. and Greeno, J. G. (1974), Theory of rule induction: Knowledge acquired in concept learning, serial pattern learning, and problem solving. In L. W. Gregg (Ed.), *Knowledge and cognition.* Potomac, Md., Lawrence Erlbaum Associates, pp. 43–104.

Egan, J. P. (1958), Recognition memory and the operating characteristic, Technical Note AFCRC-TN-58-51, Indiana University Hearing and Communication Laboratory.

Egan, J. P., Schulman, A. I., and Greenberg, G. Z. (1959), Operating characteristics determined by binary decisions and by ratings, *Journal of the Acoustical Society of America,* 31, 768–773.

Ehri, L. C. and Muzio, I. M. (1974), The influence of verb meanings on memory for adjectives, *Journal of Verbal Learning and Verbal Behavior,* 13, 265–271.

Ekstrand, B. R., Wallace, W. P. and Underwood, B. J. (1966), A frequency theory of verbal discrimination learning, *Psychological Review,* 73, 566–578.

Elliott, P. B. (1964), Tables of *d'*. In J. A. Swets (Ed.), *Signal detection and recognition by human observers,* New York, Wiley, pp. 651–684.

Engen, T., Kuisma, J. E. and Eimas, P. D. (1973), Short-term memory of odors, *Journal of Experimental Psychology,* 99, 222–225.

Erdelyi, M. H. (1974), A new look at the New Look: Perceptual defense and vigilance, *Psychological Review,* 81, 1–25.

Erdmann, B. and Dodge, R. (1898), *Psychologische Untersuchungen über das Lesen,* Halle, M. Niemeyer.

Erickson, J. R. and Zajkowski, M. M. (1967), Learning several concept-identification problems concurrently: A test of the sampling-with-replacement assumption, *Journal of Experimental Psychology,* 74, 212–218.

Erickson, J. R., Zajkowski, M. M., and Ehrmann, E. D. (1966), All-or-none assumptions in concept identification: Analysis of latency data, *Journal of Experimental Psychology,* 72, 690–697.

Estes, W. K. (1950), Toward a statistical theory of learning, *Psychological Review,* 57, 94–107.

Estes, W. K. (1959), The statistical approach to learning theory. In S. Koch (Ed.), *Psychology: A study of a science,* Vol. II, New York, McGraw-Hill, pp. 380–491.

Estes, W. K. (1962), Theoretical treatment of differential reward in multiple-choice learning and two-person interactions. In J. H. Criswell, H. Solomon, and P. Suppes (Eds.), *Mathematical methods in small group processes,* Stanford, Stanford University Press, pp. 133–149.

Estes, W. K. (1964), Probability learning. In A. W. Melton (Ed.), *Categories of human learning,* New York, Academic Press, pp. 90–128.

Estes, W. K. (1965), A technique for assessing variability of perceptual span, *Proceedings of the National Academy of Sciences,* 54, 403–407.

Estes, W. K. (1967), *Reinforcement in human learning,* Technical Report No. 125, Institute for Mathematical Studies in the Social Sciences, Stanford, Calif.

Estes, W. K. (1972), An associative basis for coding and organization in memory. In A. W. Melton and E. Martin (Eds.), *Coding processes in human memory,* Washington, D.C., Winston, pp. 161–190.

Estes, W. K. (1973), Phonetic coding and rehearsal in short-term memory for letter strings. *Journal of Verbal Learning and Verbal Behavior,* 12, 360–372.

Estes, W. K. (1975), Memory, perception, and decision in letter identification. In R. L. Solso (Ed.), *Information processing and cognition,* Hillsdale, N. J., Erlbaum.

Estes, W. K. and Burke, C. J. (1953), A theory of stimulus variability in learning, *Psychological Review*, 60, 276–286.

Estes, W. K. and DaPolito, F. (1967), Independent variation of information storage and retrieval processes in paired-associate learning, *Journal of Experimental Psychology*, 75, 18–26.

Estes, W. K. and Straughan, J. H. (1954), Analysis of a verbal conditioning situation in terms of statistical learning theory, *Journal of Experimental Psychology*, 47, 225–234.

Estes, W. K. and Suppes, P. (1959), Foundations of linear models. In R. R. Bush and W. K. Estes (Eds.), *Studies in mathematical learning theory*, Stanford, Stanford University Press, pp. 137–179.

Estes, W. K. and Taylor, H. A. (1966), visual detection in relation to display size and redundancy of critical elements, *Perception and Psychophysics*, 1, 9–16.

Fillmore, C. J. (1968), The case for case. In E. Bach and R. T. Harms (Eds.), *Universals in linguistic theory*. New York, Holt, Rinehart & Winston.

Fodor, J. A. and Bever, T. G. (1965), The psychological reality of linguistic segments, *Journal of Verbal Learning and Verbal Behavior*, 4, 414–420.

Fodor, J. A., Bever, T. G., and Garrett, M. F. (1974), *The psychology of language*, New York, McGraw-Hill.

Fodor, J. A. and Garrett, M. F.(1967), Some syntactic determinants of sentential complexity, *Perception and Psychophysics*, 2, 289–296.

Foss, D. J. and Harwood, D. A. (1975), Memory for sentences: Implications for human associative memory, *Journal of Verbal Learning and Verbal Behavior*, 14, 1–16.

Frase, L. (1976), Prose processing. In G. H. Bower (Ed.), *Psychology of learning and motivation*, Vol. 9, New York, Academic Press.

Frederiksen, C. H. (1975), Acquisition of semantic information from discourse: Effects of repeated exposures, *Journal of Verbal Learning and Verbal Behavior*, 14, 158–169.

Frege, G. (1952), On sense and reference. In P. Geach and M. Black (Eds.), *Philosophical writings of Gottlob Frege*. London, Blackwell and Mott.

Friedman, M. P., Burke, C. J., Cole, M., Estes, W. K., Keller, L., and Millward, R. B. (1963), Two-choice behavior under extended training with shifting probabilities of reinforcement. In R. C. Atkinson (Ed.), *Studies in mathematical psychology*, Stanford, Stanford University Press, pp. 250–291.

Friedman, M. P., Carterette, E. C. and Anderson, N. H. (1968), Long-term probability learning with a random schedule of reinforcement, *Journal of Experimental Psychology*, 78, 442–455.

Frost, N. (1972), Encoding and retrieval in visual memory tasks, *Journal of Experimental Psychology*, 95, 317–326.

Garner, W. R. (1962), *Uncertainty and structure as psychological concepts*, New York, Wiley.

Garner, W. R. (1974), *The processing of information and structure*, Potomac, Md., L. Erlbaum Associates.

Garrett, M. F., Bever, T., and Fodor, J. A. (1966), The active use of grammar in speech perception, *Perception and Psychophysics,* 1, 30–32.

Garrod, S., and Trabasso, T. (1973), A dual-memory information processing interpretation of sentence comprehension, *Journal of Verbal Learning and Verbal Behavior,* 12, 155–167.

Gartman, L. M. and Johnson, N. F. (1972), Massed versus distributed repetitions of homographs: A test of the differential encoding hypothesis, *Journal of Verbal Learning and Verbal Behavior,* 11, 800–808.

Gazzaniga, M. S. (1970), *The bisected brain,* New York, Appleton.

Gelb, A. and Goldstein, K. (1925), Psychologische Analysen hirnpathologischer Fälle. X. Über Farbenamnesie, *Psychologische Forschung,* 6, 127–199.

Gentner, D. (1975), Evidence for the psychological reality of semantic components: The verbs of possession. In D. A. Norman and D. E. Rumelhart (Eds.), *Explorations in cognition,* San Francisco, Freeman.

Ghiselin, B. (1952), *The creative process,* New York, New American Library.

Gibson, E. J. (1940), A systematic application of the concepts of generalization and differentiation to verbal learning, *Psychological Review,* 47, 196–229.

Gibson, E. J. (1942), Intralist generalization as a factor in verbal learning, *Journal of Experimental Psychology,* 30, 185–200.

Gibson, E. J. (1965), Learning to read, *Science,* 148, 1066–1072.

Gibson, E. J., Bishop, C. H., Schiff, W., and Smith, J. (1964), Comparison of meaningfulness and pronounceability as grouping principles in the perception and retention of verbal material, *Journal of Experimental Psychology,* 67, 173–182.

Gibson, E. J., Shurcliff, A., and Yonas, A. (1970), Utilization of spelling patterns by deaf and hearing subjects. In H. Levin and J. P. Williams (Eds.), *Basic studies on reading,* New York, Basic Books.

Glanzer, M. (1976), Intonation grouping and related words in free recall, *Journal of Verbal Learning and Verbal Behavior,* 15, 85–92.

Glanzer, M. and Cunitz, A. R. (1966), Two storage mechanisms in free recall, *Journal of Verbal Learning and Verbal Behavior,* 5, 351–360.

Glanzer, M., Koppenaal, L., and Nelson, R. (1972), Effects of relations between words on short-term storage and long-term storage, *Journal of Verbal Learning and Verbal Behavior,* 11, 403–416.

Glanzer, M. and Razel, M. (1974), The size of the unit in short-term storage, *Journal of Verbal Learning and Verbal Behavior,* 13, 114–131.

Glaze, J. A. (1928), The association value of nonsense syllables, *Journal of Genetic Psychology,* 35, 255–269.

Glucksberg, S. and Cowan, G. N. (1970), Memory for nonattended auditory material, *Cognitive Psychology,* 1, 149–156.

Goggin, J. and Wickens, D. D. (1971), Proactive interference and language change in short-term memory, *Journal of Verbal Learning and Verbal Behavior,* 10, 453–458.

K. and Scheerer, M. (1941), Abstract and concrete behavior: An study with special tests, *Psychological Monographs,* 53, Whole

Gomulicki, B. G. (1956), Recall as an abstractive process, *Acta Psychologica,* 12, 77–94.

Gordon, D. and Lakoff, G. (1971), Conversational postulates, *Papers from the seventh regional meeting, Chicago Linguistics Society,* 7, 63–84.

Grant, D. A., Hake, H. W., and Hornseth, J. P. (1951), Acquisition and extinction of a verbal conditioned response with different percentages of reinforcement, *Journal of Experimental Psychology,* 42, 1–5.

Green, D. M. and Swets, J. A. (1966), *Signal detection theory and psychophysics,* New York, Wiley.

Greeno, J. G. (1964), Paired-associate learning with massed and distributed repetitions of items, *Journal of Experimental Psychology,* 67, 286–295.

Greeno, J. G. (1968), *Elementary theoretical psychology,* Reading, Mass., Addison-Wesley.

Greeno, J. G. (1970), How associations are memorized. In D. A. Norman (Ed.), *Models of human memory,* New York, Academic Press, pp. 257–284.

Greeno, J. G. (1973), The structure of memory and the process of solving problems. In R. L. Solso (Ed.), *Contemporary issues in cognitive psychology: The Loyola Symposium.* Washington, D.C., Winston, pp. 103–134.

Greeno, J. G. (1974), Hobbits and orcs: Acquistion of a sequential concept, *Cognitive Psychology,* 6, 270–292.

Greeno, J. G., James, C. T., and DaPolito, F. J. (1971), A cognitive interpretation of negative transfer and forgetting of paired associates, *Journal of Verbal Learning and Verbal Behavior,* 10, 331–345.

Greeno, J. G. and Simon, H. A. (1974), Processes for sequence production, *Psychological Review,* 81, 187–198.

Greeno, J. G. and Steiner, T. E. (1964), Markovian processes with identifiable states: General considerations and application to all-or-none learning, *Psychometrika,* 29, 309–333.

Grice, H. P. (1967), The logic of conversation, William James Lectures, Harvard University.

de Groot, A. D. (1966), Perception and memory versus thought: Some ideas and recent findings. In B. Kleinmuntz (Ed.), *Problem solving: Research, method, and theory.* New York, Wiley.

Guilford, J. P. (1967), *The nature of human intelligence,* New York, McGraw-Hill.

Guthrie, E. R. (1935), *The psychology of learning,* New York, Harper.

Guthrie, E. R. (1959), Association by contiguity. In S. Koch (Ed.), *Psychology: A study of a science,* Vol. II, New York, McGraw-Hill, pp. 158–195.

Haber, R. N. and Erdelyi, M. H. (1967), Emergence and recovery of initially unavailable perceptual material, *Journal of Verbal Learning and Verbal Behavior,* 6, 618–628.

Hakes, D. T. (1972), Effects of reducing complement constructions on sentence comprehension, *Journal of Verbal Learning and Verbal Behavior,* 11, 278–286.

Hakes, D. T. and Cairns, H. S. (1970), Sentence comprehension and relative pronouns, *Perception and Psychophysics,* 8, 5–8.

Hall, J. F. (1954), Learning as a function of word frequency, *American Journal of Psychology*, 67, 138–140.

Hanawalt, N. G. and Demarest, I. H. (1939), The effect of verbal suggestion in the recall period upon the reproduction of visually perceived forms, *Journal of Experimental Psychology*, 25, 159–174.

Harlow, H. F. (1949), The formation of learning sets, *Psychological Review*, 56, 51–65.

Harris, C. S. and Haber, R. N. (1963), Selective attention and encoding in visual perception, *Journal of Experimental Psychology*, 65, 328–333.

Harris, R. J. and Brewer, W. F. (1973), Deixis in memory for verb tense, *Journal of Verbal Learning and Verbal Behavior*, 12, 590–597.

Havilland, S. E. and Clark, H. H. (1974), What's new? Acquiring new information as a process in comprehension, *Journal of Verbal Learning and Verbal Behavior*, 13, 515–521.

Haygood, R. C. and Bourne, L. E., Jr. (1965), Attribute- and rule-learning aspects of conceptual behavior, *Psychological Review*, 72, 175–195.

Healy, A. F. (1974), Separating item from order information in short-term memory, *Journal of Verbal Learning and Verbal Behavior*, 13, 644–655.

Hebb, D. O. (1949), *The organization of behavior*, New York, Wiley.

Hebb, D. O. (1961), Distinctive features of learning in the higher animal. In J. F. Delafresnaye (Ed.), *Brain mechanisms and learning*, London, Oxford University Press.

Heidbreder, E. (1946), The attainment of concepts: I. Terminology and methodology, *Journal of General Psychology*, 35, 173–189.

Herrnstein, R. J. and Loveland, D. H. (1964), Complex visual concept in the pigeon, *Science*, 146, 549–551.

Hintzman, D. L., Block, R. A. and Inskeep, N. R. (1972), Memory for mode of input, *Journal of Verbal Learning and Verbal Behavior*, 11, 741–749.

Höffding, H. (1891), *Outlines of psychology*, London, Macmillan.

Hogan, R. M. and Kintsch, W. (1971), Differential effects of study and test trials on long-term recognition and recall, *Journal of Verbal Learning and Verbal Behavior*, 10, 562–567.

Holyoak, K. J. and Walker, J. H. (1976), Representation of subjective magnitude information in semantic orderings, *Journal of Verbal Learning and Verbal Behavior*, 15, 287–300.

Honeck, R. P. (1973), Interpretive vs. structural effects on semantic memory, *Journal of Verbal Learning and Verbal Behavior*, 12, 448–455.

Hornby, P. A. (1974), Surface structure and presupposition, *Journal of Verbal Learning and Verbal Behavior*, 13, 530–538.

Horowitz, L. M. (1961), Free recall and ordering of trigrams, *Journal of Experimental Psychology*, 62, 51–57.

Horowitz, L. M. and Prytulak, L. S. (1969), Redintegrative memory, *Psychological Review*, 76, 519–531.

ᴿ. I. and Kurtz, K. N. (1952), Experimental studies in rote learning
    ᴇ-learning syllable familiarization and the length-difficulty rela-
    ᴊrnal of Experimental Psychology*, 44, 31–39.

Hubel, D. H. and Wiesel, T. N. (1962), Receptive fields, binocular interaction, and functional architecture in the cat's visual cortex, *Journal of Physiology*, 160, 106–154.

Hull, C. L. (1920), Quantitative aspects of the evolution of concepts, *Psychological Monographs*, 28, Whole No. 123.

Hull, C. L. (1943), *Principles of behavior*, New York, Appleton-Century-Crofts.

Humphreys, L. G. (1939), Acquisition and extinction of verbal expectations in a situation analogous to conditioning, *Journal of Experimental Psychology*, 25, 294–301.

Hunt, E. B. (1962), *Concept learning: An information processing problem*, New York, Wiley.

Hunt, E. B. and Hovland, C. I. (1960), Order of consideration of different types of concepts, *Journal of Experimental Psychology*, 59, 220–225.

Hunt, E. B. and Love, T. (1972), How good can memory be? In A. W. Melton and E. Martin (Eds.), *Coding processes in human memory*, Washington, D.C., Winston, pp. 237–260.

Hunt, E. B., Marin, J., and Stone, P. J. (1966), *Experiments in induction*, New York, Academic Press.

Hyde, T. S. and Jenkins, J. J. (1969), Differential effects of incidental tasks on the organization of a list of highly associated words, *Journal of Experimental Psychology*, 82, 472–481.

Hyde, T. S. and Jenkins, J. J. (1973), Recall of words as a function of semantic, graphic, and syntactic orienting tasks, *Journal of Verbal Learning and Verbal Behavior*, 12, 471–480.

Jacoby, L. L. (1974), The role of mental contiguity in memory: Registration and retrieval effects, *Journal of Verbal Learning and Verbal Behavior*, 13, 483–496.

Jacoby, L. L. (1975), Physical features vs. meaning: A difference in decay, *Memory and Cognition*, 3, 247–251.

Jacoby, L. L. and Bantz, W. H. (1972), Rehearsal and transfer to LTM, *Journal of Verbal Learning and Verbal Behavior*, 11, 561–565.

James, C. T., Thompson, J. G., and Baldwin, J. M. (1973), The reconstructive process in sentence memory, *Journal of Verbal Learning and Verbal Behavior*, 12, 51–63.

James, W. (1890), *Principles of psychology*, New York, Holt.

Jarvella, R. J. (1971), Syntactic processing of connected speech, *Journal of Verbal Learning and Verbal Behavior*, 10, 409–416.

Jarvik, M. E. (1951), Probability learning and a negative recency effect in the serial anticipation of alternative symbols, *Journal of Experimental Psychology*, 41, 291–297.

Jenkins, J. G. and Dallenbach, K. M. (1924), Obliviscence during sleep and waking, *American Journal of Psychology*, 35, 605–612.

Jenkins, J. J. (1974), Remember that old theory of memory? Well, forget it! *American Psychologist*, 29, 785–795.

Jenkins, J. J., Mink, W. D., and Russel, W. A. (1958), Associative clustering as a function of verbal association strength, *Psychological Reports*, 4, 127–136.

Jenkins, J. J. and Russell, W. A. (1952), Associative clustering during recall, *Journal of Abnormal and Social Psychology*, 47, 818–821.

Jensen, A. R. (1962), An empirical theory of the serial position effect, *Journal of Psychology*, 53, 127–152.

Johnson, N. F. (1965), The psychological reality of phrase-structure rules, *Journal of Verbal Learning and Verbal Behavior*, 4, 469–475.

Johnson, N. F. (1975), On the function of letters in word identification: Some data and a preliminary model, *Journal of Verbal Learning and Verbal Behavior*, 14, 17–29.

Johnson, P. J. (1967), Nature of mediational responses in concept identification problems, *Journal of Experimental Psychology*, 73, 391–393.

Jost, A. (1897), Die Assoziationsfestigkeit in ihrer Abhängigkeit von der Verteilung der Wiederholungen, *Zeitschrift für Psychologie*, 14, 436–472.

Katz, J. J. (1966), *The philosophy of language*, New York, Harper and Row.

Katz, J. J. and Fodor, J. A. (1963), The structure of semantic theory, *Language*, 39, 170–210.

Keenan, J. M. and Kintsch, W. (1974), The identification of explicitly and implicitly presented information. In W. Kintsch, *The representation of meaning in memory*, Hillsdale, N.J., Erlbaum.

Kelleher, R. T. (1956), Discrimination learning as a function of reversal and nonreversal shifts, *Journal of Experimental Psychology*, 51, 379–384.

Kendler, H. H. and Kendler, T. S. (1962), Vertical and horizontal processes in problem solving, *Psychological Review*, 69, 1–16.

Kendler, T. S. and Kendler, H. H. (1959), Reversal and nonreversal shifts in kindergarten children, *Journal of Experimental Psychology*, 58, 56–60.

Kendler, T. S., Kendler, H. H., and Wells, D. (1960), Reversal and nonreversal shifts in nursery school children, *Journal of Comparative and Physiological Psychology*, 53, 83–88.

Kent, G. H. and Rosanoff, A. J. (1910), A study of association in insanity, *American Journal of Insanity*, 67, 37–96.

Kimble, G. A. (1961), *Conditioning and learning*, New York, Appleton-Century-Crofts.

Kimera, D. (1973), The asymmetry of the human brain, *Scientific American*, 228, 70–78.

King, D. R. W. and Greeno, J. G. (1974), Invariance of inference times when information was presented in different linguistic formats, *Memory and Cognition*, 2, 233–235.

Kintsch, W. (1963), All-or-none learning and the role of repetition in paired-associate learning, *Science*, 140, 310–312.

Kintsch, W. (1965), Habituation of the GSR component of the orienting reflex during paired-associate learning before and after learning has taken place, *Journal of Mathematical Psychology*, 2, 330–341.

Kintsch, W. (1966), Recognition learning as a function of the length of the interval and changes in the retention interval, *Journal of Psychology*, 3, 412–433.

Kintsch, W. (1968a), An experimental comparison of single-stimulus tests and multiple-choice tests of recognition memory, *Journal of Experimental Psychology,* 76, 1–6.

Kintsch, W. (1968b), Recognition and free recall of organized lists, *Journal of Experimental Psychology,* 78, 481–487.

Kintsch, W. (1970), Models for free recall and recognition. In D. A. Norman (Ed.), *Models of human memory,* New York, Academic Press.

Kintsch, W. (1974), *The representation of meaning in memory,* Hillsdale, N.J., Erlbaum.

Kintsch, W. (1975), Memory representations of text. In R. L. Solso (Ed.), *Information processing and cognition,* Hillsdale, N.J., Erlbaum.

Kintsch, W. and Buschke, H. (1969), Homophones and synonyms in short-term memory, *Journal of Experimental Psychology,* 80, 403–407.

Kintsch, W., Crothers, E. J., and Jorgensen, C. C. (1971), On the role of semantic processing in short-term retention, *Journal of Experimental Psychology,* 90, 96–101.

Kintsch, W. and van Dijk, T. A. (1975), Comment on se rappelle et on résume des histoires, *Langages,* 40, 98–116.

Kintsch, W. and Glass, G. (1974), Effects of propositional structure upon sentence recall. In W. Kintsch, *The representation of meaning in memory,* Hillsdale, N.J., Erlbaum.

Kintsch, W. and Keenan, J. M. (1973), Reading rate and retention as a function of the number of propositions in the base structure of sentences, *Cognitive Psychology,* 5, 257–274.

Kintsch, W., Kozminsky, E., Streby, W. J., McKoon, G., and Keenan, J. M. (1975), Comprehension and recall of text as a function of content variables, *Journal of Verbal Learning and Verbal Behavior,* 14, 196–214.

Kintsch, W. and Monk, D. (1972), Storage of complex information in memory: Some implications of the speed with which inferences can be made, *Journal of Experimental Psychology,* 94, 25–32.

Koffka, K. (1935), *Principles of Gestalt psychology,* New York, Harcourt, Brace.

Koh, S. D., Kayton, L., and Berry, R. (1973), Mnemonic organization in young nonpsychotic schizophrenics. *Journal of Abnormal Psychology,* 81, 229–310.

Koh, S. D., Kayton, L., and Peterson, R. A. (1976), Affective encoding and consequent remembering in schizophrenic adults. *Journal of Abnormal Psychology,* 85, 156–166.

Köhler, W. (1925), *The mentality of apes,* London, Routledge and Kegan.

Köhler, W. (1941), On the nature of associations, *Proceedings of the American Philosophical Society,* 84, 489–502.

Kolers, P. A. (1966), Interlingual facilitation of short-term memory, *Journal of Verbal Learning and Verbal Behavior,* 5, 314–319.

Kolers, P. A. and Ostry, D. J. (1974), Time course of loss of information regarding pattern analyzing operations, *Journal of Verbal Learning and Verbal Behavior,* 13, 599–612.

Koppenaal, R. J. (1963), Time changes in the strength of A-B, A-C lists; spontaneous recovery? *Journal of Verbal Learning and Verbal Behavior,* 2, 310–319.

Kotovsky, K. and Simon, H. A. (1973), Empirical tests of a theory of human acquisition of concepts for sequential events, *Cognitive Psychology,* 4, 399–424.

Krechevksy, I. (1932), Antagonistic visual discrimination habits in the white rat, *Journal of Comparative Psychology,* 14, 263–277.

Labov, W. (1973), The boundaries of words and their meaning. In C. N. Bailey and R. W. Shuy (Eds.), *New ways of analyzing variation in English.* Washington, D.C., Georgetown University Press, pp. 340–373.

Ladefoged, P. and Broadbent, D. E. (1960), Perception of sequences in auditory events, *Quarterly Journal of Experimental Psychology,* 12, 162–170.

Lakoff, G. (1973), Hedges: A study in meaning criteria and the logic of fuzzy concepts. *Papers from the Eighth Regional Meeting, Chicago Linguistic Society,* Chicago, University of Chicago Linguistics Department.

Lashley, K. S. and Wade, M. (1946), The Pavlovian theory of generalization, *Psychological Review,* 53, 72–87.

Lawrence, D. H. (1949), Acquired distinctiveness of cues: I. Transfer between discriminations on the basis of familiarity with the stimulus, *Journal of Experimental Psychology,* 39, 770–784.

Lawrence, D. H. (1952), The transfer of a discrimination along a continuum, *Journal of Comparative and Psychological Psychology,* 45, 511–518.

Lawrence, D. H. and DeRivera, J. (1954), Evidence for relational discrimination, *Journal of Comparative and Physiological Psychology,* 47, 465–471.

Lettvin, J. Y., Maturana, H. R., McCulloch, W. S., and Pitts, W. H. (1959), What the frog's eye tells the frog's brain, *Proceedings of the Institute of Radio Engineers,* 47, 1940–1951.

Levine, M. (1966), Hypothesis behavior by humans during discrimination learning, *Journal of Experimental Psychology,* 71, 331–338.

Levine, M. (1971), Hypothesis theory and nonlearning despite ideal S-R reinforcement contingencies, *Psychological Review,* 78, 130–140.

Levine, M., Miller, P. I., and Steinmeyer, H. (1967), The none-to-all theorem of human discrimination learning, *Journal of Experimental Psychology,* 73, 568–573.

Lewin, K. (1917), Die psychologische Tätigkeit bei der Hemmung von Willensvorgängen und das Grundgesetz der Association, *Zeitschrift für Psychologie,* 77, 212–247.

Liberman, B. (1962), Experimental studies of conflict in two-person and three-person games. In J. H. Criswell, H. Solomon, and P. Suppes (Eds.), *Mathematical methods in small group processes,* Stanford, Stanford University Press, pp. 203–220.

Light, L. L. and Carter-Sobell, L. (1970), Effects of changed semantic context on ˜ˆognition memory, *Journal of Verbal Learning and Verbal Behavior,* 9,

d Palmer, J. C. (1974), Reconstruction of automobile destruc-
ᴉmple of the interaction between language and memory, *Journal
ᴉarning and Verbal Behavior,* 13, 585–589.

Loftus, E. F. and Suppes, P. (1972), Structural variables that determine the speed of retrieving words from long-term memory, *Journal of Verbal Learning and Verbal Behavior*, 11, 770–777.

Loftus, G. R. and Patterson, K. K. (1975), Components of short-term proactive interference, *Journal of Verbal Learning and Verbal Behavior*, 14, 105–121.

Lorente de Nó, R. (1938), Analysis of the activity of the chains of internuncial neurons, *Journal of Neurophysiology*, 1, 207–244.

Lovejoy, E. (1968), *Attention in discrimination learning: A point of view and a theory*, San Francisco, Holden-Day.

Lovelace, E. A. and Snodgrass, R. D. (1971), Decision times for alphabetic orders of letter pairs, *Journal of Experimental Psychology*, 88, 258–264.

Luce, R. D. (1959), *Individual choice behavior: A theoretical analysis*, New York, Wiley.

Luchins, A. S. (1942), Mechanization in problem solving: The effect of Einstellung, *Psychological Monographs*, 54, Whole No. 248.

Luria, A. R. (1968), *The mind of a mnemonist*, New York, Basic Books.

Mackintosh, N. J. (1965), Selective attention in animal discrimination learning, *Psychological Bulletin*, 64, 124–140.

Maier, N. R. F. (1931), Reasoning in humans. II. The solution of a problem and its appearance in consciousness, *Journal of Comparative Psychology*, 12, 181–194.

Mandler, G. (1962), From association to structure, *Psychological Review*, 69, 415–427.

Mandler, G. (1967a), Verbal learning. In G. Mandler and P. Mussen (Eds.), *New directions in psychology*, Vol. *III*, New York, Holt, Rinehart & Winston, pp. 1–50.

Mandler, G. (1967b), Organization and memory. In K. W. Spence and J. T. Spence (Eds.), *The psychology of learning and motivation: Advances in research and theory*, Vol. I, New York, Academic Press, pp. 328–372.

Mandler, G. (1972), Organization and recognition. In E. Tulving and W. Donaldson (Eds.), *Organization of memory*, New York, Academic Press.

Mandler, G. and Boeck, W. J. (1974), Retrieval processes in recognition, *Memory and Cognition*, 2, 613–615.

Mandler, G. and Pearlstone, Z. (1966), Free and constrained concept learning and subsequent recall, *Journal of Verbal Learning and Verbal Behavior*, 5, 126–131.

Manelis, L. and Yekovich, F. R. (1976), Repetition of propositional arguments in sentences, *Journal of Verbal Learning and Verbal Behavior*, 15, 301–312.

Marks, L. E. and Miller, G. A. (1964), The role of semantic and syntactic constraints in the memorization of English sentences, *Journal of Verbal Learning and Verbal Behavior*, 3, 1–5.

Marks, M. R. and Jack, O. (1952), Verbal context and memory span for meaningful material, *American Journal of Psychology*, 65, 298–300.

Martin, E. (1965), Transfer of verbal paired associates, *Psychological Review*, 72, 327–343.

Martin, E. (1967), Stimulus recognition in aural paired-associate learning, *Journal of Verbal Learning and Verbal Behavior*, 6, 272–276.

Martin, E. (1968), Stimulus meaningfulness and paired-associate transfer: An encoding variability hypothesis, *Psychological Review,* 75, 421–441.

Martin, E. (1971), Verbal learning theory and independent retrieval phenomena, *Psychological Review,* 78, 314–332.

Martin, E. (1972), Stimulus encoding in learning and transfer. In A. W. Melton and E. Martin (Eds.), *Coding processes in human memory,* Washington, D.C., Winston.

Martin, E. and Noreen, D. L. (1974), Serial learning: Identification of subjective subsequences, *Cognitive Psychology,* 6, 421–435.

Massaro, D. W. (1970), Preperceptual auditory images, *Journal of Experimental Psychology,* 85, 411–417.

McCormack, P. D. (1972), Recognition memory: How complex a retrieval system? *Canadian Journal of Psychology,* 26, 19–41.

McCrary, J. W. and Hunter, W. S. (1953), Serial position curves in verbal learning, *Science,* 117, 131–134.

McGeoch, J. A. (1929), The influence of degree of learning upon retroactive inhibition, *American Journal of Psychology,* 41, 252–262.

McGeoch, J. A. (1930), The influence of associative value upon the difficulty of nonsense syllable lists, *Journal of Genetic Psychology,* 37, 421–426.

McGeoch, J. A. (1932), Forgetting and the law of disuse, *Psychological Review,* 39, 352–370.

McGeoch, J. A. (1942), *The psychology of human learning,* New York, Longmans.

McGovern, J. B. (1964), Extinction of associations in four transfer paradigms, *Psychological Monographs,* 78, Whole No. 593.

McKoon, G. and Keenan, J. M. (1974), Response latencies to explicit and implicit statements as a function of the delay between reading and test. In W. Kintsch, *The representation of meaning in memory.* Hillsdale, N.J., Erlbaum.

McLean, R. S. and Gregg, L. W. (1967), Effects of induced chunking on temporal aspects of serial recitation, *Journal of Experimental Psychology,* 74, 455–459.

Melton, A. W. (1963), Implications of short-term memory for a general theory of memory, *Journal of Verbal Learning and Verbal Behavior,* 2, 1–21.

Melton, A. W. (1970), The situation with respect to the spacing of repetitions in memory, *Journal of Verbal Learning and Verbal Behavior,* 9, 546–606.

Melton, A. W. and Irwin, J. M. (1940), The influence of degree of interpolated learning on retroactive inhibition and the overt transfer of specific responses, *American Journal of Psychology,* 53, 173–203.

Melton, A. W. and Martin, E. (1972), (Eds.), *Coding processes in human memory,* Washington, D.C., Winston.

Merikle, P. M. and Battig, W. F. (1963), Transfer of training as a function of experimental paradigm and meaningfulness, *Journal of Verbal Learning and Verbal Behavior,* 2, 485–488.

Meyer, B. (1975), *The organization of prose and its effect upon memory,* Amsterdam, North Holland Publishing Co.

Meyer, D. E. and Schvaneveldt, R. W. (1971), Facilitation in recognizing pairs of words: Evidence of a dependence between retrieval operations, *Journal of Experimental Psychology*, 90, 227–234.

Miller, G. A. (1956), The magical number seven, plus or minus two: Some limits on our capacity for processing information, *Psychological Review*, 63, 81–97.

Miller, G. A. (1958), Free recall of redundant strings of letters, *Journal of Experimental Psychology*, 56, 485–491.

Miller, G. A. and Isard, S. (1963), Some perceptual consequences of linguistic rules, *Journal of Verbal Learning and Verbal Behavior*, 2, 217–228.

Miller, G. A. and McKean, K. O. (1964), A chronometric study of some relations between sentences, *Quarterly Journal of Experimental Psychology*, 16, 297–308.

Miller, G. A. and Nicely, P. E. (1955), An analysis of perceptual confusion among some English consonants, *Journal of the Acoustical Society of America*, 27, 338–352.

Miller, G. A. and Selfridge, J. A. (1950), Verbal context and the recall of meaningful material, *American Journal of Psychology*, 63, 176–185.

Millward, R. B. (1964), Latency in a modified paired-associate learning experiment, *Journal of Verbal Learning and Verbal Behavior*, 3, 309–316.

Millward, R. B. and Wickens, T. D. (1974), Concept identification models. In D. H. Krantz, R. C. Atkinson, R. D. Luce, and P. Suppes (Eds.), *Contemporary developments in mathematical psychology*, Vol. 1, San Francisco, Freeman, pp. 45–100.

Milner, B. (1967), Amnesia following operation on the temporal lobes. In O. L. Zangwill and C. M. W. Whitty (Eds.), *Amnesia*, London, Butterworth.

Minsky, M. (1975), A framework for representing knowledge. In P. Winston (Ed.), *The psychology of computer vision*, New York, McGraw-Hill.

Mistler-Lachman, J. L. (1974), Depth of comprehension and sentence memory, *Journal of Verbal Learning and Verbal Behavior*, 13, 98–106.

Moray, N. (1958), Attention in dichotic listening: Attentive cues and the influence of instructions, *Quarterly Journal of Experimental Psychology*, 11, 56–60.

Moray, N. (1970), *Attention: Selective processes in vision and hearing*, New York, Academic Press.

Morton, J. (1970), A functional model for memory, In D. A. Norman (Ed.), *Models of human memory*, New York, Academic Press, pp. 203–254.

Moyer, R. S. (1973), Comparing objects in memory: Evidence suggesting an internal psychophysics, *Perception and Psychophysics*, 13, 180–184.

Moyer, R. S. and Landauer, T. K. (1967), Time required for judgments of numerical inequality, *Nature*, 215, 1519–1520.

Müller, G. E. (1913), Zur Analyse der Gedächtnistätigkeit und des Vorstellungsverlaufes, III. Teil. *Zeitschrift für Psychologie*, Ergänzungsband 8.

Müller, G. E. and Pilzecker, A. (1900), Experimentelle Beiträge zur Lehre vom Gedächtnis, *Zeitschrift für Psychologie*, Ergänzungsband 1.

Müller, G. E. and Schumann, F. (1894), Experimentelle Beiträge zur Untersuchung des Gedächtnisses, *Zeitschrift für Psychologie,* 6, 81–190, 257–339.

Murdock, B. B., Jr. (1960), The distinctiveness of stimuli, *Psychological Review,* 67, 16–31.

Murdock, B. B., Jr. (1961), The retention of individual items, *Journal of Experimental Psychology,* 62, 618–625.

Murdock, B. B., Jr. (1962), The serial position effect in free recall, *Journal of Experimental Psychology,* 64, 482–488.

Murdock, B. B., Jr. (1963a), Short-term memory and paired-associate learning, *Journal of Verbal Learning and Verbal Behavior,* 2, 320–328.

Murdock, B. B., Jr. (1963b), An analysis of the recognition process. In C. N. Cofer and B. S. Musgrave (Eds.), *Verbal behavior and learning,* New York, McGraw-Hill, pp. 10–22.

Murdock, B. B., Jr. (1963c), Interpolated recall in short-term memory, *Journal of Experimental Psychology,* 66, 525–532.

Murdock, B. B., Jr. (1964), Proactive inhibition in short-term memory, *Journal of Experimental Psychology,* 68, 184–189.

Murdock, B. B., Jr. (1965a), Effects of a subsidiary task on short-term memory, *British Journal of Psychology,* 56, 413–419.

Murdock, B. B., Jr. (1965b), Signal detection theory and short-term memory, *Journal of Experimental Psychology,* 70, 453–447.

Murdock, B.B., Jr. (1967), Recent developments in short-term memory, *British Journal of Psychology,* 58, 421–433.

Murdock, B. B., Jr. (1971), A parallel processing model for scanning, *Perception and Psychophysics,* 10, 289–291.

Murdock, B. B., Jr. (1974), *Human memory: Theory and data,* Hillsdale, N.J., Erlbaum.

Murdock, B. B., Jr. and Duffy, P. O. (1972), Strength theory and recognition memory, *Journal of Experimental Psychology,* 94, 284–290.

Neimark, E. D. and Estes, W. K. (1967), *Stimulus sampling theory,* San Francisco, Holden-Day.

Neimark, E. D., Greenhouse, P., Laws, S., and Weinheimer, S. (1965), The effect of rehearsal preventing tasks upon retention of CVC syllables, *Journal of Verbal Learning and Verbal Behavior,* 4, 280–285.

Neisser, U. (1967), *Cognitive psychology,* New York, Appleton-Century-Crofts.

Neisser, U. and Weene, P. (1962), Hierarchies in concept attainment, *Journal of Experimental Psychology,* 64, 640–645.

Newell, A., Shaw, J. C., and Simon, H. A. (1960), A variety of intelligent learning in a general problem solver. In M. C. Yovitz and S. Cameron (Eds.), *Self-organizing systems.* New York, Pergamon Press.

Newell, A. and Simon, H. A. (1962), Computer simulation of human thinking, *Science,* 134, 2011–2017.

Newell, A. and Simon, H. A. (1972), *Human problem solving,* Englewood Cliffs, N.J., Prentice-Hall.

Noble, C. E. (1952), An analysis of meaning, *Psychological Review,* 59, 421–430.

Norman, D. A. (1966), Acquisition and retention in short-term memory, *Journal of Experimental Psychology*, 72, 369–381.

Norman, D. A. (1970), (Ed.), *Models of human memory*, New York, Academic Press.

Norman, D. A. (1973), Memory, knowledge, and the answering of questions. In R. L. Solso (Ed.), *Contemporary issues in cognitive psychology*, Washington, D.C., Winston.

Norman, D. A. and Bobrow, D. G. (1975), On data limited and resource limited processes, *Cognitive Psychology*, 7, 44–64.

Norman, D. A. and Rumelhart, D. E. (1975), *Explorations in cognition*, San Francisco, Freeman.

Offir, C. E. (1973), Recognition memory for presuppositions of relative clause sentences. *Journal of Verbal Learning and Verbal Behavior*, 12, 636–643.

Osgood, C. E. (1949), The similarity paradox in human learning: A resolution, *Psychological Review*, 56, 132–143.

Paivio, A. (1971), *Imagery and verbal processes*, New York, Holt, Rinehart & Winston.

Paivio, A. (1975a), Imagery and long-term memory. In A. Kennedy and A. Wilkes (Eds.), *Studies in long-term memory*. London, Wiley, pp. 57–88.

Paivio, A., (1975b), Perceptual comparisons through the mind's eye, *Memory and Cognition*, 3, 635–647.

Paivio, A. and Csapo, K. (1973), Picture superiority in free recall: Imagery or dual coding? *Cognitive Psychology*, 5, 176–206.

Parks, T. E. (1966), Signal-detectability theory of recognition-memory performance, *Psychological Review*, 73, 44–58.

Pavlov, I. P. (1927), *Conditioned reflexes: An investigation of the physiological activity of the cerebral cortex*, London, Oxford University Press.

Pavlov, I. P. (1928), *Lectures on conditioned reflexes*. Translated by W. H. Gantt, New York, International Publishers.

Peterson, L. R. and Peterson, M. J. (1959), Short-term retention of individual items, *Journal of Experimental Psychology*, 58, 193–198.

Peterson, L. R., Wampler, R., Kirkpatrick, M., and Saltzman, D. (1963), Effects of spacing presentations on retention of paired-associates over short intervals, *Journal of Experimental Psychology*, 66, 206–209.

Pick, A. D. (1965), Improvement of visual and tactual form discrimination, *Journal of Experimental Psychology*, 69, 331–339.

Pillsbury, W. B. and Sylvester, A. (1940), Retroactive and proactive inhibition in immediate memory, *Journal of Experimental Psychology*, 27, 532–545.

Pollack, I. (1953), The assimilation of sequentially encoded information, *American Journal of Psychology*, 66, 421–435.

Pollack, I., and Decker, L. R. (1958), Confidence ratings, message reception, and the receiver operating characteristic, *Journal of the Acoustical Society of America*, 30, 286–292.

Pollio, H. R. (1966), Oppositional serial structures and paired-associate learning, *Psychological Reports*, 79, 643–647.

Polson, M. C., Restle, F., and Polson, P. G. (1965), Association and discrimination in paired-associate learning, *Journal of Experimental Psychology,* 69, 47–55.

Posnansky, C. J., Battig, W. F. and Voss, J. F. (1972), A new probe technique for the identification of serial learning processes, *Behavior Research Methodology and Instrumentation,* 4, 129–132.

Posner, M. I. and Boies, S. J. (1971), Components of attention, *Psychological Review,* 78, 391–408.

Posner, M. I. and Konick, A. F. (1966), Short-term retention of visual and kinesthetic information, *Organizational Behavior and Human Performance,* 1, 71–86.

Posner, M. I. and Rossman, E. (1965), Effect of size and location of information transforms upon short-term retention, *Journal of Experimental Psychology,* 70, 496–505.

Postman, L. (1950), Choice behavior and the process of recognition, *American Journal of Psychology,* 63, 576–583.

Postman, L. (1961), The present status of interference theory. In C. N. Cofer (Ed.), *Verbal learning and verbal behavior,* New York, McGraw-Hill, pp. 152–178.

Postman, L. (1963), One-trial learning. In C. N. Cofer and B. S. Musgrave (Eds.), *Verbal behavior and learning: Problems and processes,* New York, McGraw-Hill, pp. 295–321.

Postman, L. (1964), Short-term memory and incidental learning. In A. W. Melton (Ed.), *Categories of human learning,* New York, Academic Press, pp. 146–201.

Postman, L. (1972), A pragmatic view of organization theory. In E. Tulving and W. Donaldson (Eds.), *Organization of memory,* New York, Academic Press, pp. 4–50.

Postman, L. and Goggin, J. (1966), Whole versus part learning of paired associate lists. *Journal of Experimental Psychology,* 71, 867–877.

Postman, L. and Phillips, L. W. (1965), Short-term temporal changes in free recall, *Quarterly Journal of Experimental Psychology.* 17, 132–138.

Postman, L. and Postman, D. L. (1948), Changes in set as a determinant of retroactive inhibition, *American Journal of Psychology,* 61, 236–242.

Postman, L. and Riley, D. A. (1959), Degree of learning and interserial interference in retention, *University of California Publications in Psychology,* 8, 271–346.

Postman, L. and Schwartz, M. (1964), Studies of learning to learn: I. Transfer as a function of method of practice and class of verbal materials, *Journal of Verbal Learning and Verbal Behavior,* 3, 37–49.

Postman, L. and Stark, K. (1969), The role of response availability in transfer and interference, *Journal of Experimental Psychology,* 79, 168–177.

Postman, L., Stark, K., and Fraser, J. (1968), Temporal changes in interference. *Journal of Verbal Learning and Verbal Behavior,* 7, 672–694.

Postman, L. and Underwood, B. J. (1973), Critical issues in interference theory, *Memory and Cognition*, 1, 19–40.

Potts, G. R. (1972), Information processing strategies used in encoding linear orderings. *Journal of Verbal Learning and Verbal Behavior*, 11, 727–740.

Premack, D. (1965), Reinforcement theory. In M. R. Jones (Ed.), *Nebraska symposium on motivation*, Lincoln, University of Nebraska Press, pp. 123–188.

Pylyshyn, Z. W. (1973), What the mind's eye tells the mind's brain: A critique of mental imagery, *Psychological Bulletin*, 80, 1–4.

Quine, W. O. (1961), *From a logical point of view*, New York, Harper.

Raffel, G. (1936), Two determinants of the effects of primacy, *American Journal of Psychology*, 48, 654–657.

Raser, G. A. (1972), Recoding of semantic and acoustic information in short-term memory, *Journal of Verbal Learning and Verbal Behavior*, 11, 692–697.

Reder, L. M., Anderson, J. R., and Bjork, R. A. (1974), A semantic interpretation of encoding specificity, *Journal of Experimental Psychology*, 102, 648–656.

Reicher, G. M. (1969), Perceptual recognition as a function of the meaningfulness of the material, *Journal of Experimental Psychology*, 81, 275–280.

Reitman, J. S. (1974), Without surreptitious rehearsal, information in short-term memory decays, *Journal of Verbal Learning and Verbal Behavior*, 13, 365–377.

Restle, F. (1957), Discrimination of cues in mazes: A resolution of the "place versus response" question, *Psychological Review*, 64, 217–228.

Restle, F. (1962), The selection of strategies in cue learning, *Psychological Review*, 69, 329–343.

Restle, F. (1965), Significance of all-or-none learning, *Psychological Bulletin*, 64, 313–325.

Restel, F. and Brown, E. (1970), Organization of serial pattern learning. In G. H. Bower (Ed.), *The psychology of learning and motivation: Advances in research and theory*, Vol. 4, New York, Academic Press.

Restle, F. and Emmerich, D. (1966), Memory in concept attainment: Effect of giving several problems concurrently, *Journal of Experimental Psychology*, 71, 794–799.

Restle, F. and Greeno, J. G. (1970), *Introduction to mathematical psychology*, Reading, Mass., Addison-Wesley.

Riley, D. A. (1962), Memory for form. In L. Postman (Ed.), *Psychology in the making*, New York, Knopf, pp. 402–465.

Rips, L. J., Shoben, E. J. and Smith, E. E. (1973), Semantic distance and the verification of semantic relations. *Journal of Verbal Learning and Verbal Behavior*, 12, 1–20.

Rock, I. (1957), The role of repetition in associative learning, *American Journal of Psychology*, 70, 186–193.

Rosch, E. H. (1973), Natural categories, *Cognitive Psychology*, 4, 328–350.

Rosenberg, S. (1968), Association and phrase structure in sentence recall, *Journal of Verbal Learning and Verbal Behavior*, 7, 1077–1081.

Rosenberg, S. and Jarvella, R. J. (1970), Semantic integration and sentence perception, *Journal of Verbal Learning and Verbal Behavior*, 9, 548–553.

Rosenblatt, F. (1958), The perceptron: A probabalistic model for information storage and organization in the brain, *Psychological Review*, 65, 386–401.

Rothkopf, E. Z. (1971), Incidental memory for location of information in text, *Journal of Verbal Learning and Verbal Behavior*, 10, 608–613.

Rothkopf, E. Z. (1972), Structural text features and the control of processes in learning from written materials. In J. Carroll and R. Freedle (Eds.), *Language comprehension and the acquisition of knowledge*, Washington, D.C., Winston.

Rothkopf, E. Z. and Coke, E. U. (1961), The prediction of free recall from word association measures, *Journal of Experimental Psychology*, 62, 433–438.

Rowe, E. J. and Paivio, A. (1971), Imagery and repetition instructions in verbal discrimination and incidental paired-associate learning, *Journal of Verbal Learning and Verbal Behavior*, 10, 668–672.

Rumelhart, D. E. (1975), Notes on a schema for stories. In D. G. Bobrow and A. Collins (Eds.), *Representation and understanding*, New York, Academic Press.

Rundus, D. (1971), Analysis of rehearsal processes in free recall, *Journal of Experimental Psychology*, 89, 63–77.

Rundus, D. and Atkinson, R. C. (1970), Rehearsal processes in free recall: A procedure for direct observation, *Journal of Verbal Learning and Verbal Behavior*, 9, 99–105.

Sachs, J. D. S. (1967), Recognition memory for syntactic and semantic aspects of connected discourse, *Perception and Psychophysics*, 2, 437–442.

Santa, J. L., Ruskin, A. B., Snuttjer, D. and Baker, L. (1975), Retrieval in cued recall, *Memory and Cognition*, 3, 341–348.

Savin, H. B. and Bever, T. G. (1970), The nonperceptual reality of the phoneme. *Journal of Verbal Learning and Verbal Behavior*, 9, 295–302.

Savin, H. B. and Perchonock, E. (1965), Grammatical structure and the immediate recall of English sentences, *Journal of Verbal Learning and Verbal Behavior*, 4, 348–353.

Schaeffer, B. and Wallace, R. (1969), Semantic similarity and the comparison of word meanings, *Journal of Experimental Psychology*, 82, 343–346.

Schank, R. C. (1972), Conceptual dependency: A theory of natural language understanding, *Cognitive Psychology*, 3, 552–631.

Schank, R. C. (1975), SAM—A story understander, Technical Report No. 43, Department of Computer Science, Yale University.

Schank, R. C. and Colby, K. M. (1973), *Computer models of thought and language*, San Francisco, Freeman.

Searle, J. R. (1969), *Speech acts*, Cambridge, England, University Press.

Seitz, M. R. and Weber, B. A. (1974), Effects of response requirements on the location of clicks superimposed on sentences, *Memory and Cognition*, 2, 43–46.

Selz, O. (1922), *Zur Psychologie des produktiven Denkens und Irrtums*, Bonn, Cohen.

Shannon, C. E. (1948), A mathematical theory of communication, *Bell Systems Technical Journal, 27*, 379–423; 623–656.

Shephard, R. N. (1967), Recognition memory for words, sentences, and pictures, *Journal of Verbal Learning and Verbal Behavior, 6*, 156–163.

Shephard, R. N. and Metzler, J. (1971), Mental rotation of three-dimensional objects, *Science, 171*, 701–703.

Shephard, R. N. and Teghtsoonian, M. (1961), Retention of information under conditions approaching a steady state, *Journal of Experimental Psychology, 62*, 302–309.

Sherman, M. A. (1976), Adjectival negation and the comprehension of multiply negated sentences, *Journal of Verbal Learning and Verbal Behavior, 15*, 15, 143–156.

Shiffrin, R. M. and Gardner, G. T. (1972), Visual processing capacity and attentional controls, *Journal of Experimental Psychology, 93*, 72–82.

Shiffrin, R. M. and Geisler, W. S. (1973), Visual recognition in a theory of information processing. In R. L. Solso (Ed.), *Contemporary issues in cognitive psychology*, Washington, D.C., Winston.

Shulman, H. G. (1972), Semantic comparison errors in short-term memory, *Journal of Verbal Learning and Verbal Behavior, 11*, 221–227.

Siegel, S. (1961), Decision making and learning under varying conditions of reinforcement, *Annals of the New York Academy of Science, 89*, 715–896.

Siegel, S. and Goldstein, D. A. (1959), Decision making behavior in a two-choice uncertain outcome situation, *Journal of Experimental Psychology, 57*, 37–42.

Simon, H. A. and Kotovsky, K. (1963), Human acquisition of concepts for sequential patterns, *Psychological Review, 70*, 543–546.

Skinner, B. F. (1938), *The behavior of organisms*, New York, Appleton-Century-Crofts.

Skinner, B. F. (1957), *Verbal behavior*, New York, Appleton.

Slamecka, N. J. (1966), Differentiation versus unlearning of verbal associations, *Journal of Experimental Psychology, 71*, 822–828.

Slamecka, N. J. (1968), An examination of trace storage in free recall, *Journal of Experimental Psychology, 76*, 504–513.

Small, D. W. (1975), The abstraction of arbitrary categories, *Memory and Cognition, 3*, 581–585.

Smith, E. E., Shoben, E. J., and Rips, L. J. (1974), Structure and process in semantic memory: A feature model for semantic decision, *Psychological Review, 81*, 214–241.

Sokolov, E. N. (1963), *Perception and the conditioned reflex*, New York, Pergamon.

Spence, K. W. (1937), The differential response in animals to stimuli varying within a single dimension, *Psychological Review, 44*, 430–444.

Spence, K. W. (1942), The basis of solution by chimpanzees of the intermediate size problem, *Journal of Experimental Psychology, 31*, 257–271.

Sperling, G. (1963), A model for visual memory tasks, *Human Factors, 5*, 19–30.

Stern, W. (1938), *General psychology from the personalistic standpoint,* New York, Macmillan.

Sternberg, S. (1966), High-speed scanning in human memory, *Science,* 153, 652–654.

Sternberg, S. (1969), The discovery of processing stages: Extensions of Donder's method, *Acta Psychologica,* 30, 276–315.

Sternberg, S. (1975), Memory scanning: New findings and current controversies, *Quarterly Journal of Experimental Psychology,* 27, 1–32.

Sulin, R. A. and Dooling, D. J. (1974), Intrusion of a thematic idea in retention of prose, *Journal of Experimental Psychology,* 103, 255–262.

Sullivan, E. V. and Turvey, M. T. (1974), On short term retention of serial, tactile stimuli, *Memory and Cognition,* 2, 601–606.

Sumby, W. H. (1963), Word frequency and the serial position effect, *Journal of Verbal Learning and Verbal Behavior,* 1, 443–450.

Suppes, P. (1966), Mathematical concept formation in children, *American Psychologist,* 21, 139–150.

Suppes, P. and Ginsberg, R. A. (1962), Application of a stimulus-sampling model to children's concept formation with and without correction of responses, *Journal of Experimental Psychology,* 63, 330–336.

Suppes, P. and Ginsberg, R. (1963), A fundamental property of all-or-none models, binomial distribution of responses prior to conditioning, with application to concept formation in children, *Psychological Review,* 70, 139–161.

Suppes, P., Groen, G., and Schlag-Rey, M. (1966), A model for response latency in paired-associate learning, *Journal of Mathematical Psychology,* 3, 99–128.

Sutherland, N. S. (1959), Stimulus analyzing mechanisms. In *Proceedings of a Symposium for the Mechanization of Thought Processes,* Vol. II, London, H. M. Stationary Office, pp. 575–609.

Szekely, L. (1945), Zur Psychologie des geistigen Schaffens, *Schweizerische Zeitschrift für Psychologie und ihre Anwendungen,* 4, 110–124.

Terrace, H. S. (1963), Errorless transfer of a discrimination across two continua, *Journal of the Experimental Analysis of Behavior,* 6, 223–232.

Theios, J. (1973) Reaction time measurements in the study of memory processes: Theory and data. In G. H. Bower, (Ed.), *The psychology of learning and motivation,* Vol. 7, New York, Academic Press, pp. 43–85.

Thomas, J. C., Jr. (1974), An analysis of behavior in the Hobbits-Orcs problem, *Cognitive Psychology,* 6, 257–269.

Thomson, D. M. (1972), Context effects in recognition memory, *Journal of Verbal Learning and Verbal Behavior,* 11, 497–511.

Thorndike, E. L. (1911), *Animal intelligence,* New York, Macmillan.

Thorndike, E. L. (1931), *Human learning,* New York, Appleton-Century-Crofts.

Thorndike, E. L. and Lorge, I. (1944), *The teacher's word book of 30,000 words,* New York, Columbia University Press.

Tinbergen, N. (1951), *The study of instinct,* Oxford, Oxford University Press.

Tolman, E. C. (1932), *Purposive behavior in animals and men,* New York, Century.

Trabasso, T. R. (1963), Stimulus emphasis and all-or-none learning in concept identification, *Journal of Experimental Psychology,* 65, 398–406.

Trabasso, T. R. and Bower, G. H. (1966), Presolution dimensional shifts in concept identification: A test of the sampling with replacement axiom in all-or-none models, *Journal of Mathematical Psychology,* 3, 163–173.

Trabasso, T. R. and Bower, G. H. (1968), *Attention in learning: Theory and research,* New York, Wiley.

Trabasso, T. R., Rollins, H., and Shaughnessy, E. (1971), Storage and verification stages in processing concepts, *Cognitive Psychology,* 2, 239–289.

Treisman, A. (1964), Selective attention in man, *British Medical Bulletin,* 20, 12–16.

Treisman, A. and Tuxworth, J. (1974), Immediate and delayed recall of sentences after perceptual processing at different levels, *Journal of Verbal Learning and Verbal Behavior,* 13, 38–44.

Tulving, E. (1962), Subjective organization in free recall of unrelated words, *Psychological Review,* 69, 344–354.

Tulving, E. (1964), Intratrial and intertrial retention: Notes toward a theory of free-recall verbal learning, *Psychological Review,* 71, 219–237.

Tulving, E. (1972), Episodic and semantic memory. In E. Tulving and W. Donaldson (Eds.), *Organization of memory,* New York, Academic Press, pp. 382–404.

Tulving, E. and Arbuckel, T. Y. (1963), Sources of intertrial interference in immediate recall of paired-associates, *Journal of Verbal Learning and Verbal Behavior,* 1, 321–324.

Tulving, E. and Donaldson, W. (1972), (Eds.), *Organization of memory,* New York, Academic Press.

Tulving, E. and Osler, S. (1968), Effectiveness of retrieval cues in memory for words, *Journal of Experimental Psychology,* 77, 593–601.

Tulving, E. and Pearlstone, Z. (1966), Availability versus accessibility of information in memory for words, *Journal of Verbal Learning and Verbal Behavior,* 5, 381–391.

Tulving, E. and Psotka, J. (1971), Retroactive inhibition in free recall: Inaccessability of information available in the memory store, *Journal of Experimental Psychology,* 87, 1–8.

Tulving, E. and Thomson, D. M. (1973), Encoding specificity and retrieval processes in episodic memory, *Psychological Review,* 80, 352–373.

Tulving, E. and Watkins, M. T. (1975), Structure of memory traces, *Psychological Review,* 82, 261–276.

Tulving, E. and Wiseman, S. (1975), Relation between recognition and recognition failure of recallable words, *Bulletin of the Psychonomic Society,* 6, 78–82.

Underwood, B. J. (1948), "Spontaneous recovery" of verbal associations, *Journal of Experimental Psychology,* 38, 429–439.

Underwood, B. J. (1953), Studies of distributed practice: VIII. Learning and retention of paired nonsense syllables as a function of intralist similarity, *Journal of Experimental Psychology*, 45, 133–142.

Underwood, B. J. (1957), Interference and forgetting, *Psychological Review*, 64, 49–60.

Underwood, B. J. (1961), An evaluation of the Gibson theory of verbal learning. In C. N. Cofer (Ed.), *Verbal learning and verbal behavior*, New York, McGraw-Hill, pp. 197–216.

Underwood, B. J. (1963), Stimulus selection in verbal learning. In C. N. Cofer and B. S. Musgrave (Eds.), *Verbal behavior and learning: Problems and processes*, New York, McGraw-Hill, pp. 33–48.

Underwood, B. J. (1969), Attributes of memory, *Psychological Review*, 76, 559–573.

Underwood, B. J. and Ekstrand, B. R. (1966), An analysis of some shortcomings in the interference theory of forgetting, *Psychological Review*, 73, 540–549.

Underwood, B. J. and Freund, J. S. (1968a), Errors in recognition learning and retention, *Journal of Experimental Psychology*, 78, 55–63.

Underwood, B. J. and Freund, J. S. (1968b), Two tests of a theory of verbal discrimination learning, *Canadian Journal of Psychology*, 22, 96–104.

Underwood, B. J. and Postman, L. (1960), Extraexperimental sources of interference in forgetting, *Psychological Review*, 67, 73–95.

Underwood, B. J., Runquist, W. N., and Schultz, R. W. (1959), Response learning in paired-associate lists as a function of intralist similarity, *Journal of Experimental Psychology*, 58, 70–78.

Underwood, B. J. and Schultz, R. W. (1960), *Meaningfulness and verbal learning*, Philadelphia, Lippincot.

Walsh, D. A. and Jenkins, J. J. (1973), Effects of orienting tasks on free recall in incidental learning: "Difficulty", "Effort", and "Process" explanations. *Journal of Verbal Learning and Verbal Behavior*, 12, 481–488.

Wanner, E. (1974), *On remembering, forgetting and understanding sentences*, The Hague, Mouton.

Watkins, M. J. and Tulving E. (1975), Episodic memory: When recognition fails, *Journal of Experimental Psychology: General*, 104, 5–20.

Waugh, N. C. and Norman, D. A. (1965), Primary memory, *Psychological Review*, 72, 89–104.

Waugh, N. C. and Norman, D. A. (1968), The measure of interference in primary memory, *Journal of Verbal Learning and Verbal Behavior*, 7, 617–626.

Weist, R. M. (1972), The role of rehearsal: Recopy or reconstruct, *Journal of Verbal Learning and Verbal Behavior*, 11, 440–450.

Wells, H. (1963), Effects of transfer and problem structure in disjunctive concept formation, *Journal of Experimental Psychology*, 65, 63–69.

Wells, J. E. (1974), Strength theory and judgments of recency and frequency, *Journal of Verbal Learning and Verbal Behavior*, 13, 378–392.

Wertheimer, M. (1945), *Productive thinking*, New York, Harper (2nd edition, 1959).

Wescourt, K. T. and Atkinson, R. C. (1976), Fact retrieval processes in human memory. In W. K. Estes (Ed.), *Handbook of learning and cognitive processes,* Vol. 4, Hillsdale, N.J., Erlbaum.

Whitman, J. R. and Garner, W. R. (1962), Free recall learning of visual figures as a function of form of internal structure, *Journal of Experimental Psychology,* 64, 558–564.

Wickelgren, W. A. (1965), Acoustic similarity and intrusion errors in short-term memory, *Journal of Experimental Psychology,* 70, 102–108.

Wickelgren, W. A. (1966), Distinctive features and errors in short-term memory for English consonants, *Journal of the Acoustical Society of America,* 39, 388–398.

Wickens, D. D. (1972), Characteristics of word encoding. In A. W. Melton and E. Martin (Eds.), *Coding processes in human memory,* Washington, D.C., Winston.

Wickens, D. D., Born, D. G., and Allen, C. K. (1963), Proactive inhibition and item similarity in short-term memory, *Journal of Verbal Learning and Verbal Behavior,* 2, 440–445.

Wickens, T. D. and Millward, R. B. (1971), Attribute elimination strategies for concept identification with practiced subjects, *Journal of Mathematical Psychology,* 8, 453–480.

Wicker, F. W. (1970), On the locus of picture-word differences in paired-associate learning, *Journal of Verbal Learning and Verbal Behavior,* 9, 52–57.

Wilkins, A. T. (1971), Conjoint frequency, category size, and categorization time, *Journal of Verbal Learning and Verbal Behavior,* 10, 382–385.

Wimer, R. (1964), Osgood's transfer surface: Extension and test, *Journal of Verbal Learning and Verbal Behavior,* 3, 274–279.

Winograd, T. (1972), Understanding natural language, *Cognitive Psychology,* 3, 1–191.

Wittgenstein, L. (1953), *Philosophical investigations.* Translated by G. E. M. Anscombe, New York, Macmillan.

Wollen, K. A. (1968), Effects of maximizing availability and minimizing rehearsal upon associative symmetry in two modalities, *Journal of Experimental Psychology.* 77, 626–630.

Wollen, K. A., Weber, A., and Lowry, D. H. (1972), Bizarreness versus interaction of mental image as determinants of learning, *Cognitive Psychology,* 3, 518–523.

Wood, G. (1969), Retrieval cues and the accessability of higher-order memory units in multi-trial free recall, *Journal of Verbal Learning and Verbal Behavior,* 8, 782–789.

Woodward, A. E., Jr., Bjork, R. A. and Jongeward, R. H., Jr. (1973), Recall and recognition as a function of primary rehearsal, *Journal of Verbal Learning and Verbal Behavior,* 12, 608–617.

Woodworth, R. S. (1938), *Experimental psychology,* New York, Holt.

Wulff, F., (1922), Über die Veränderung von Vorstellungen, *Psychologische Forschung,* 1, 333–373.

Wundt, W. (1880) (2nd Edition), *Grundzüge der physiologischen Psychologie*, Leipzig, Engelmann.

Wundt, W. (1905), *Grundriss der Psychologie*, Leipzig, Engelmann.

Yates, F. A. (1966), *The art of memory*, Chicago, University of Chicago Press.

Young, J. L. (1971), Reinforcement-test intervals in paired-associate learning, *Journal of Mathematical Psychology*, 8, 58–81.

Zadeh, L. A., Fu, K., Tanaka, K., and Shimura, M. (1975), *Fuzzy sets and their applications to cognitive and decision processes*, New York, Academic Press.

Zangwill, O. L. (1972), Remembering revisited, *Quarterly Journal of Experimental Psychology*, 24, 123–138.

Zeaman, D. and House, B. J. (1963), The role of attention in retardate discrimination learning. In N. R. Ellis (Ed.), *Handbook of mental deficiency*, New York, McGraw-Hill, pp. 159–223.

# author index

**475**

# subject index and glossary

*§This glossary does not provide definitions of terms, but attempts to give useful hints to the user of this book.

**483**